AMERICAN COUNTRY COLLECTIBLES

The Official®
Identification and Price Guide
to

AMERICAN COUNTRY COLLECTIBLES

DAWN E. RENO

FIRST EDITION

House of Collectibles • New York

Important Notice. All of the information, including valuations, in this book has been compiled from the most reliable sources, and every effort has been made to eliminate errors and questionable data. Nevertheless, the possibility of error, in a work of such immense scope, always exists. The publisher will not be held responsible for losses which may occur in the purchase, sale, or other transaction of items because of information contained herein. Readers who feel they have discovered errors are invited to *write* and inform us, so they may be corrected in subsequent editions. Those seeking further information on the topics covered in this book are advised to refer to the complete line of *Official Price Guides* published by the House of Collectibles.

Items appearing in cover photo are courtesy of Staten Island Historical Society, Richmondtown Restoration.

Published by: House of Collectibles
201 East 50th Street
New York, New York 10022

Distributed by Ballantine Books, a division of Random House, Inc., New York, and simultaneously in Canada by Random House of Canada Limited, Toronto.

Manufactured in the United States of America

ISBN: 0-876-37796-7

First Edition: November 1990

10 9 8 7 6 5 4 3 2 1

For my country husband, Bobby,
my partner in both marriage and the pursuit of antiques

Table of Contents

Acknowledgments

THERE ARE MANY PEOPLE one should thank when putting together a book of this size and magnitude. First, my editor, Dottie Harris, for the hours spent on the phone, the support and ideas she offered, and for sharing my excitement for the subject.

Second, my photographer, Donald Vogt, for his patience during all types of adversity, for his sense of humor, for his suggestions and advice, and for his excellent photographs.

Third, this book, and all books of this type, would never come to fruition without the support and contributions of collectors, dealers, auctioneers, and museums throughout the United States. To them, I extend a hearty "thank you" and the hope that you will enjoy reading what I have compiled as much as I enjoyed putting it all together.

And last, but not in the least bit "least": When my photographer, Donald Vogt, and I travelled to photograph collections and gather research, the folks who took us into their homes and shops became the backbone of the book—for they are truly the country people about whom I have written. To those collectors and dealers who welcomed us during our trip throughout the Midwest, especially to those who were hospitable enough to open the doors of their homes, a simple thank you does not suffice. Therefore, I dedicate this book to them, my real country friends, and to all those like them across the United States.

Introduction

WHEN I FIRST BEGAN doing the research for this book, I thought I knew a fair amount about country collectibles. What I have unearthed is much more than I ever could have imagined existed. In fact, this book could have been twice as long as it is and still not cover every country collectible available. As a result, I have been selective in what I have chosen for inclusion here. I hope you will find what you collect in these pages.

The field of country collectibles is constantly shifting and changing shape. Ten years ago, when I started collecting items for a future time when I would have a country home, primitive furniture was easy to find and affordable. No one else wanted it. Now, if you can find it, it's extraordinarily expensive. Today we are seeing a resurgence of interest in Native American items, and some magazines are touting the Southwestern/Spanish-American look or the combination of Victorian frills and lace with country items. Whatever the case may be, country appears here to stay.

The History of "Country"

In the early part of the twentieth century, a movement dedicated to shifting some of the population back to the country was inspired in part by a "back-to-the-land" desire. The people involved in this movement believed they could solve the problems of rural-to-urban migration by persuading people to move to areas where they could experience the joys of country living centered around a small working farm. They believed that the existing number of farms would not be able to sufficiently feed the American population; they were worried about overpopulation in the cities, with large numbers of immigrants crowding in; and they had become disenchanted with the crowded and hectic conditions associated with urban living.

Times had changed from when the American way of life traditionally stressed the family-owned farm. By the turn of the century, absentee landlords and tenant farming were the norm. Americans had become more mobile and less attached to the land.

With the return movement came the need for education in how to farm the land and utilize its resources. Farmers pressed for better education systems in small towns, the agricultural colleges were upgraded, health conditions in rural communities were improved, and a myriad of government agencies and associations were formed. The Sears, Roebuck catalogs allowed the country family the ease of ordering by mail instead of enduring the long trip to a nearby city, and the railroad brought farm equipment and other supplies almost to the farmer's door.

Many changes took place during this era, and it is important for country collectors to understand the historical background of this movement. With that understanding, one is better able to see items such as the Hoosier cabinet as an outgrowth of that need to bring the farmer into the twentieth century and to make life in the country more palatable to "city folks" willing to take a chance on an agrarian life-style.

Both the "new" farmers (those who moved to the country after the turn of the century) and the earlier settlers who had forged trails through the wilderness left their mark and their stories for future generations to study. As a result, our knowledge of America's past comes from a variety of sources. Writings, paintings, folk art, samplers, early photographs, wall decorations, even eating utensils—all give us concrete examples of what country life was like back then.

These reiterations of what artists and artisans saw before them will tell us many things—for instance, what people wore; what was hung at their windows; what their plates, pots, and pans looked like; and how their houses were built. We can accurately date toys when we see them depicted in portraits of children. It is important, when applying oneself to the study of our American heritage and to the quest for good country collectibles, to pay attention to the details, the little things that give us clues about the age of the items we collect.

We can even see how the country and its people felt about politics by studying the many forms of country art, where nationalism and patriotism predominated. Navajo weavers copied the flag motif for blankets and other weavings; paintings done during the mid- to late 1700s reflected the American spirit; figures carved for ships' prows or cigar stores were draped in red, white, and blue; quilts reproduced the country's colors, and even weather vanes atop country barns waved the flag of freedom.

Not only was the flag reproduced time and time again but other symbols as well. Furniture makers carved the bald eagle onto headboards for beds, itinerant carvers used the bird to decorate boxes or tramp art pieces, potters decorated jugs with the eagle's outstretched wings. Miss Liberty held the flag in paintings, etchings, advertising, magazine ads, and on signs for many years before she came to us in gigantic form to grace New York Harbor. And Uncle Sam's image was reproduced in wood, paint, and metal from the mid-1800s to the present day. They are all symbols of the freedom Americans treasure.

It has always been the *people* who have made this country so special, and it is the country people I want to highlight in this book. We can appreciate the hard work of a rancher when we see a well-worn saddle; we can feel the calluses on a farmwoman's hand when we touch a calico dress so worn that the pattern is faded; we can hear the ocean's roar when we place a sailor's valentine on our mantel; we hear the soft clicks and slaps of a weaver's loom when we touch a Navajo blanket; and we can see the somber dress of the Amish when we lay a dark-edged quilt across our bed.

I have delved into diaries and journals written by those early settlers who paved the way across windswept prairies and through snowswept mountain passes. They had loves, fights with their families, worries about money or about whether their garden would produce a satisfactory crop. They wrote of the beauty of a sunset or of the price of flour, the birth of a baby or the death of a parent. Whether those country people were black, red, white, or yellow, they all contributed to the life we enjoy today and are ancestors to *all* of us.

What was different about country folk a hundred or two hundred years ago was that they lived off the land without any modern-day conveniences to help them. In today's society, most people don't even know the first name of the person who lives next door, nor do they know anything about planting a garden or reaping its harvest. Country people not only knew the names of all of the people who lived in their community, but they could count on those neighbors to help out in times of crisis—whether that meant putting out a barn fire and raising a new one or helping in the birth of a baby.

Country news was spread by word of mouth, and gossip was predominant (*Little House on the Prairie*'s depiction of the store owner's wife was probably more accurate than one would think). Country living was embroidered by visits to or from neighbors, the center of a farm family's social life.

Today, we can simply turn on the television or radio or pick up a newspaper or magazine and learn all about local, national, and world news. In the past, if a farmer or other country resident wished to let people know his horse had been stolen, or if a politician wanted to spread his views over valleys and dirt roads without following each one of them individually, broadsides were printed up to be distributed throughout the countryside.

The ads or news bulletins were pinned to the walls beside country store doors or to trees on a well-traveled road in an effort to make local citizens aware of news, announcements, discoveries, or inventions. Poems, psalms, and hymns were printed for distribution, as well as proclamations and military announcements.

Most broadsides were printed and distributed during the period from 1750 to 1850. During the War of 1812, they were used to tell citizens about the outcome of battles or to entice young men to enlist. Politicians used this vehicle of advertising more widely than anyone else. By the mid-nineteenth century, however, their use declined due to the rapid growth of newspaper production. Today broadsides are so valuable that their only known copies are held by historical societies and museums.

Life was simpler then, but it was also a hard life, one in which people depended on what they could produce. Perhaps that is what collectors celebrate when they pick up a sampler, a hand-made chair, or a piece of decorated pottery—the fact that it was made by someone else's *hands*, not a machine.

The Future of Country Collectibles

American Country by Mary Emmerling, published in 1980, includes a photo in the "Country Collections" chapter that shows a grouping of collectibles. Each has a price printed over its image; for example, a stoneware jug that appears to be rather large and handsomely decorated is priced at $38; a large splint basket with handle is marked $30, and so on.

Today there is no way we could buy the objects pictured for anywhere near those prices. Granted, we still come across bargains occasionally at lawn or barn sales (or an auction where no one else shows up), but any dealer or auctioneer worthy of the title would not be likely to sell a patchwork quilt for $25 or a wool Navajo blanket for $12.

Prices have rapidly increased for country collectibles in the past decade, and I don't see a decrease in interest or prices for such items anytime in the near future. Now that we're coming into a new decade and the end of a century, there are, however, some things you should keep an eye on.

I always feel as though I should wear a turban around my head and put both hands on a crystal ball when people ask me what I think will be "hot" in the future. However, I'll take a stab at it, in the hope that none of you reading my words will take your money out of CDs and put it into country collectibles. Antiques *are* a good investment, if you can afford to invest your money for a long period of time or if you know that what you're buying was sold to you at a good price. However, unless you're well versed in the area, a quick turnover profit is just not something you should expect.

From my study of hundreds of auction catalogs, newspapers, and magazines and from speaking with collectors, auctioneers, and dealers across the country, I believe that country collectibles are showing no sign of decline in their popularity, although certain items are no longer as "hot" as they were five or ten years ago. For instance, Hoosier cabinets, which were reasonably priced by dealers at shows I attended five to seven years ago, have gone up considerably. Now even the poorest example of a Hoosier is priced from $500 to $700. I don't believe they will go any higher; in fact, some of my dealer friends who have priced their Hoosiers in that range have been holding onto them much longer than they would have been a couple of years ago—a sure sign that interest has peaked and is on a decline. Why? Probably because of the influx of cabinets imported from Europe and because of the affordability of newly-made-to-look-old cupboards that are surfacing in every department store. Most Americans don't want to have to hunt for something they can find in a visit to the mall.

American Indian collectibles (also termed Native American or Amerind throughout the book) are enjoying a swell in popularity. The American public has shown an interest in Amerind items every twenty years or so. What I would suggest for those of you anxious to add some Native American pieces to your country collection is, first, to learn more about the Indian culture, then attend auctions or shows, ask lots of questions of auctioneers or dealers, and *listen*. I personally have an affinity for the new Kachinas being carved by such artists as Cecil Calnimptewa, the miniature pottery done by Joseph Lonewolf, and the cedar boxes carved and painted by Jamie Tawodi Reason. However, keep an eye on pottery made in the storyteller form, parfleches made by the Plains tribes, and any decorated clothing that is in good condition.

Amish quilts have been popular for years, and the soft cloth toys made by quiltmakers for their children are still priced below $50 in most shops. They are not easy to find unless you live in Amish country (Pennsylvania, Ohio, Indiana, Illinois, and southern Michigan), but they are a welcome addition to a child's toy collection. I'm not talking about dolls but the animals made out of quilt pieces (horses, dogs, etc.).

Fishing collectibles have surfaced as good country items that can be had for under $50. In fact, I know several people who have creel collections that they have amassed for next to nothing. Little has been written about the subject, but you can find old articles in the antiques tradepapers or magazines, and books on fishing as a sport help you to identify lures, rods, and creels.

Adirondack furniture (sometimes called "twig furniture") has long been ignored because people considered it ugly. Made for hunting or summer camps in the Adirondack Mountains, the furniture was constructed from oddly shaped limbs and trunks of the trees available in the area. Some pieces feature animal skins, heads, claws, antlers, and hooves. There are a few dealers in the country who have begun to specialize in this field, and they are paving the way for those brave people who want to add a few unusual pieces to their country home. The prices are rapidly increasing, so if you want to get on the bandwagon, do it now.

Other items to watch: Southern folk pottery, anything western (e.g., cowboy memorabilia), chintz quilts, southwestern/Spanish items (e.g., carved figures of saints), anything made during the turn of the century.

I wish you all the best of luck in collecting your country treasures. Perhaps we'll meet at an auction or show someday and share our stories. In the meantime, let me tell you a little more about country places, people, homes, and barns.

COUNTRY PLACES

THE PEOPLE who lived in different country places around the United States were as different as the areas they inhabited. The Amish and Mennonite chose the rolling meadows and farmland of Pennsylvania, Ohio, Indiana, Illinois, and other midwestern states. The Shakers settled mostly in the Northeast, though there were some in Kentucky. Native Americans, here long before a white man set foot on our shores, were all over the country; and African-Americans were forced to leave their homeland to settle on steamy plantations throughout the South.

The land on which each group settled strongly influenced what they produced. The deserts in the Southwest offered clay to Amerinds, who fashioned it into pottery, while the tribes that lived on the Plains were more likely to decorate their clothing with porcupine quills or beadwork. Adirondack craftspeople used the wood they had at hand to make their unusual furniture, while the basketmakers of the South wove reeds or woods found in their backyards into attractive, useful baskets.

Each of the groups who settled the country places I describe in this chapter was intrinsically important to the way America grew. Each offered its artistic talents in varying forms: the Amish with their somber, abstract-design quilts; the Shakers and their perfectly proportioned baskets; African-Americans with their strong influence on, and input into, the tobacco, iron, and pottery industries; and Native Americans, who excelled in all of the decorative arts, such as pottery, rugs, baskets, and paintings.

Some of the groups described fall into two or more categories (such as American Indians). And you may recognize that some peoples have not been mentioned. I have purposely included only those who made items that have come to be considered collectible as country items. Even after making that decision, I had to put parameters on how much I wanted to say about each group.

For instance, places by the seashore are often forgotten in the country vernacular. Yet those weathered shingles on the houses of Nantucket Island or along the sandswept beaches of Cape Cod reflect just as strong a country attitude as do the sod houses that once dotted the Great Plains. Anyone who has lived in such an area or spent a summer there will agree that the old whaling communities of New England have contributed just as much to the flavor of our country as have the white, sprawling farmhouses of the Midwest.

It is from seaside country places that we got whale oil lamps, nautical weather vanes, and sailors' valentines, as well as many other objects that grace the walls, floors, and cupboards in country houses. It was through those weathered doors that items from the Orient passed, and it was from the men who sailed the oceans surrounding the New World that we learned new ways of making furniture, pottery, and glassware.

We also have incorporated into the "country scheme of things" formal country items, such as country Chippendale pieces or hunt boards from Virginia; English country pine pieces (in fact, the cabbage rose print fabrics were more often found in English country cottages than in any other); French country furniture and lace curtains have become popular, as well as the pottery pieces made in that area of the world, but this book is focused on American country collectibles and it is those antiques upon which we will concentrate.

Therefore, it is to *all* country groups in all areas of the United States that this chapter is dedicated—and to those modern country folk who have yet to make their own niche in this nation's legacy.

Amish Country

Amish Life

THE AMISH have chosen a quiet life of dew-filled mornings and lantern-lit nights, where neighbors work together to build a barn or extinguish a fire and where family is never more than a carriage ride away. Bread is baked fresh on Tuesdays and Thursdays, and a large garden grows to fruition and is harvested in August to be canned and stored to feed the family throughout a chilly winter. It is a life of hand-washed clothes, homemade quilts, and the smell of new-mown hay, an old-fashioned way of living. The Amish are hard workers. It goes without saying that any group that lives in the country, off the land, puts in long, hard days. But what better feeling than to drop into a warm bed at night and to be able to fall directly to sleep?

Without telephones or electricity, their news is passed from person to person, often using the same kind of "grapevine telegraph" that Paul Revere used to warn fellow Bostonians of the arrival of the British. One man will ride from house to house to relay important news. Without television or radio, the important contact with other people is established face-to-face.

These people of the earth regard themselves not as landowners but as land guardians, and they occupy themselves with the responsibility of keeping the land in healthy condition for future generations. It is that attitude toward nature that unifies country people, and those of us who revere American country collectibles show respect for the natural world when we take such an item into our homes.

History

When dissenting groups broke away from the Roman Catholic church—Martin Luther and the Protestant Reformation—many different religious sects were formed. From these came the Mennonites and Amish.

The Amish followed Jakob Ammann in 1697 when he broke away from the Swiss Brethren Mennonites. It was at that time that the Amish became known as *Haftlers* (hook-and-eyers) and the Mennonites as *Knopflers* (buttoners), terms that related strictly to the way the two sects dressed.

The Amish stayed in Germany until William Penn fled England and the rule of King Charles II to settle in Philadelphia, Pennsylvania. Francis Daniel Pastorius of the Frankfort Land Company of Germany followed Penn and wrote to his friends and relatives regarding the new home he had found in America.

The first Amish immigrants left Switzerland and Germany in 1727, settling near what is now Reading, Pennsylvania. England looked down on these new, competent farming people and tried to Anglicize them. But the Amish, determined to hold onto their religion, considered the English (*Englischer* came to mean "worldly people") a threat to all they held sacred.

After a while, the Amish settlement spread throughout Pennsylvania and into Ohio, the state that now boasts of having the largest Amish population in the country. Settlements are also located in Indiana, Illinois, Iowa, Arkansas, Minnesota, Missouri, Kansas, Oklahoma, and Wisconsin, and there is a fairly new (15–20 years old) burgeoning settlement in upstate New York. The earlier mideastern settlements were established in the 1950s. There appears to have been a movement to other settlements during the period from the mid-1960s to the mid-1970s; some of the newer communities have expanded rapidly since 1970. It should be noted that Old Order and Beachy Amish are the ones most commonly found in the Midwest.

There is no accurate count of the Amish in the United States because they shy away from giving church membership figures. We do know, however, that there are only about twelve family names among the Amish of Lancaster, and some estimate the total Amish population as exceeding 75,000.

Lancaster County, Pennsylvania, is a tourist area where throngs of people flock each year to view the Amish people in their natural environment. Visitors to the area gaze at the horse-drawn black buggies, the somberly dressed people, and the immaculate farms. Tourism in Lancaster County began with a house and farm opened for the local people to show how the Amish lived. Then plays were published, magazine and newspaper articles generated, and Lancaster County felt the impact of city people's curiosity.

The Amish resent the intrusion on their privacy. They particularly do not want their photographs taken and are constantly on guard against zoom lenses angled toward them from car windows, for the Bible says: "Thou shalt not make unto thee any graven image" (Exodus 20:4).

Clothing and Distinguishing Features

The Amish are able to tell their sects apart by subtle differences in the way they dress or what they drive. For instance, Amish men of the "Old School" wear no suspenders. Their trousers are brown and laced in the rear. The women wear black kerchiefs (bonnets are taboo). They drive buggies with white tops. "Byler" Amish ("Beansoupers") wear a single suspender on their trousers and drive buggies with yellow tops.

The "Zook" Amish men have two suspenders on their trousers as well as zippers on their jackets, and they wear their hair short. This sect is much more liberal than the others; they own cars and have electricity in their homes and meetinghouses.

In most Amish and Mennonite sects a woman's head is covered because the Bible says there should be no "outward adorning of plaiting the hair" (1 Peter 3:3, 4, as well as 1 Corinthians 11:3–15). Certain colors, such as pink, red, and yellow and patterned fabrics are forbidden, as are buttons and safety pins. The triangular shawl (*Holsz duuch*) worn by women is pinned in front and back to the apron. The tab at the waistline of the dress is called the *Lepli.*

A white cap is worn by women at all times after marriage, and their hair is never cut, curled, or allowed to hang loose. All unmarried girls over the age of twelve wear a black cap for Sunday preaching services. Small differences in the width of the front of a cap, the length of the ties, the seam style, and the pleats in the cap are what signify the difference between church districts.

On Sundays the men wear long black frock coats (*Mutze*) with split tails and hook-and-eye closings but no collars or lapels. Trousers have no fly but a wide front flap like sailors' pants. There are no creases in the pants, nor are they worn with a belt (suspenders are used). A *Wamus*, or black sack coat, is worn on days other then preaching days.

Amish men wear no neckties, stripes, or prints. Buttoned sweaters are sometimes permitted as long as the buttons have no military or decorative significance.

In the winter, black felt hats are worn; in the summer, straw hats. Hats are significant in that one with a crease at the top of the crown signifies a newly married man; a bishop's hat is high with a rounded crown and the broadest brim. The width of the brim signifies the Amish man's status and degree of orthodoxy. The broader the brim, the more conservative the man's religious beliefs. Young boys may wear their brims a little short of the suggested width; however, if they go too far, they will not be baptized.

Though Amish men have beards, mustaches are not permitted. The upper lip of the face is the only part that is shaved.

Courtships and Weddings

Rumspringa (or "running around") is the common term for the dating season of the young Amish. Boys usually begin dating around age sixteen, girls between fourteen and sixteen. Such activity is kept under wraps by the couple because they will be teased by their families should the secret get out. In fact, a boy with a steady girlfriend will often visit her after her parents are in bed, letting her know of his arrival by shining a flashlight through her bedroom window.

The buggies used by dating boys are topless and are called "courting" or "bachelor" buggies. The brake used in such buggies is prescribed by *Ordnung;* different types are allowed by different secs. *Ordnung* rules also decide whether the buggy will have a dashboard, whipsocket, or other variations. It is said that the clip-clop of horses' hooves in the early hours of morning reveals those boys who are heading home after long visits with their girlfriends.

Bei-schlof ("with sleep") is the old word used for the term "bundling," which refers to a way of visiting in which the dating couple would lie on a bed while fully clad. The custom is an old one, often practiced in Europe, especially in large unheated houses. In more recent times, the practice has been vehemently condemned by most Amish leaders.

The average age at which an Amish woman gets married is twenty-two. For men, it is twenty-three or older. The Amish married couple is often closer in age than other American couples, and, knowing the Amish community, one imagines the average married couple has known each other for most of their lives.

Marriages usually take place after the crops are harvested, and the ceremony involves a two-day period of preparation and festivity. The wedding ceremony is an all-day affair held on Tuesday or Thursday, usually in November. Pennsylvania Amish marriages are concentrated in the months of November and December, while the Indiana Amish appear to prefer January, February, and March and the Ohio Amish favor March, April, and May. The bride wears the color of her choice (blue, lavender, or green with a white organdy cap and apron) for her wedding, but once married, she wears the traditional black cap and apron. Presents are not given to the wedding couple until the guests visit them in their new home. Useful items make up the bulk of their gifts. Marriages are taken seriously, and there is no such thing as divorce or separation.

First-cousin marriages are taboo, and second-cousin marriages are discouraged. In fact, in Lancaster County, it is forbidden to marry a "Swartz" cousin (the child of a first cousin). The Amish have to be married within their sect or else they are placed under *Meidung* and shunned for life.

There are several major differences between most of today's couples and the Amish. Among Amish couples the husband is considered to be the head of the family; however, the wife is independent and answerable only to God. She shares in the decision-making process at home but has only a silent vote at church. Though she is her husband's helper, she is not his equal.

The birth rate among Amish couples is much higher than that of other Americans, the average being seven children in a family. Of the Amish communities in the United States, the Pennsylvania and Indiana Amish have the highest number of live births, while the Ohio Amish have the least. Since Ohio Amish women get married later, these figures make sense.

The wife's responsibilities include all of the housekeeping chores, child rearing, making clothes, and gardening. The women also help with harvesting and are responsible for the upkeep of landscaping around the house. As a result, it appears that the women may assist the men in their work, but the reverse is not often the case. The husband is responsible for managing and overseeing the farm and livestock, and he will make purchases without consulting his mate.

Children are taught at a very young age to help around the family farm, and they are expected to keep up with daily chores. The younger members of an Amish family are brought up with love and discipline, which prepares them well for adulthood within the community. If a child misbehaves, obedience is taught by giving the youngster a sound thrashing.

The Church

The rules of the church, called *Ordnung*, govern every detail of Amish life. If *Ordnung* is not firmly adhered to, the offender is shunned, a procedure called *Meidung*. The *Ordnung* determines how an Amish person will act under different circumstances, whether the Plain People may have cars or electricity, how the women wear their hair, whether there should be buttons or zippers on clothing, and even whether or not a dating buggy has a certain kind of brake.

The Bible is often the only book found in an Amish household and is referred to constantly by the family. The mother may use a passage to explain growing up to a young girl; the father may quote a chapter when delivering his opinion on a subject.

Church is a large meetinghouse with straight rows of benches, where the singing is done in unison. The *Vorsanger* (preacher/leader) sings the first note, then the congregation follows. Some historians think that the Amish style of singing came from Gregorian chants of the Middle Ages. The *Ausbund,* the oldest Protestant hymnal, is the one used in Amish church services. The tunes of the hymns are passed by ear from generation to generation.

Amish sermons are sometimes given in a mixture of three languages—High German, Pennsylvania Dutch, and English. It is not hard to realize why Amish children are often bi- or trilingual upon entering school.

When the service is over, the benches are moved, and food that was made earlier by the women is served. (A cookbook of Amish and Mennonite recipes includes such dishes as Crunchy Hot Chicken Casserole, Dairyland Casserole, Snitz and Knepp—ham, dried applies, and brown sugar—Potato Puffs, Cold Bread Soup, and Plum Kuchen.) The social groups that form at such gatherings are divided by age and set and stay together all afternoon.

There are three kinds of ministers in the Amish church. Men nominated for the position of deacon are chosen in a democratic fashion: they put a slip of paper in a Bible, and whoever picks up that Bible is declared deacon. A bishop holds the office above a deacon, and the deacon usually replaces the bishop after he dies.

During an Amish baptism, the people make vows that they will keep forever, like renouncing the devil, confirming their belief in Jesus Christ, and promising to be faithful to *Ordnung.* Amish families also follow the tradition of fasting on the day before Communion Sunday, when they have bread and wine and a foot-washing ceremony, as did Jesus with his disciples.

Most of the holidays celebrated by other religions are also celebrated by the Amish. Sundays are always considered non-working holidays. Christmas is celebrated with a special meal and a simple gift; there are no decorations or a Santa character. Good Friday is celebrated, as is Easter, when the children dye and sometimes hide eggs. Thanksgiving and New Year are also observed. Ascension Day and Pentecost are Amish holidays celebrated by participating in outdoor recreation such as fishing or playing ball.

The religious beliefs of the Amish declare them to be pacifists. They refuse to bear arms, though they have been drafted into alternative service during a national emergency. If confronted with hostility, the Plain People will just move rather than defend themselves.

When attending to their dead, the Amish show very little prejudice. Their funerals are uniform; every Amish person is buried wearing white clothing in the same type of coffin. There are no flowers on Amish graves. There is little outward emotion shown by the Amish at the loss of a loved one. They believe strongly in the resurrection and soothe their grief with that thought.

The Farm

Farming is the Amish community's main occupation, though they will work in other trades when necessary. There are some Amish blacksmiths in certain communities, and there are others who do carpentry work or other such jobs.

Amish farmers raise such crops as tobacco, corn, and black walnuts; others raise dairy cows, producing cheese products. Tobacco is raised because it's a good cash crop, though some Amish are now considering the health aspects of tobacco and its byproducts.

Farms are small, the largest being fifty or sixty acres. It is necessary for farms to remain this size because the farmers do their work by hand or horsepower. If they had any more acreage to contend with, the job would become impossible, even for a large family.

Mealtime

The seating pattern at an Amish dinner table puts the father at the head of the table, his sons (youngest to oldest) on his right, and his wife to his left, with the girls seated on the wife's side of the table.

Because the family works hard, they eat heartily, and their diet normally consists of foods rich in fats and carbohydrates. Though the bulk of the food out of Amish kitchens is traditional, contemporary foods like meat loaf and pizza have been added to their diet. Desserts are numerous, as are fresh vegetables from the garden. The women preserve whatever vegetables are not eaten in the course of a normal growing season, and the family will subsist on those canned goods throughout the winter.

The School

As I have mentioned, most Amish know more than one language by the time they are ready for school; some even know three: High German, Pennsylvania Dutch, and English. Children attend school through their fourteenth birthday or the eighth grade. There they learn how to work together, not in competition with each other.

The schoolroom is housed in a one-room schoolhouse where old books or readers are used because modern ones are too worldly. Math is the most important subject because farmers must use it on a regular basis. The rest of the knowledge they need to survive on a farm is taught through practice alongside their elders. Singing is part of the daily school curriculum as well.

The teachers, as well as all other adults, are called by their first names. They may be either male or female and are often not college-educated. In 1972, the Supreme Court ruled that the Amish were exempt from compulsory education laws.

The Amish and "the World"

Amish often deal with outsiders when they are selling their farm goods, ice cream, rugs, quilts, china, and handicrafts, but the community would prefer to keep to itself.

They pay whatever taxes are necessary to keep their land and abide by the rules of the county, district, or town where they live. If they come by extra money, they quickly invest it in more land or livestock.

The community takes care of its own elderly, seldom accepting social security benefits or Medicare. The old are kept with their family and given much respect, and they are often active members of society until the day they die.

No insurance of any kind is used by the Amish. Should one or more of their community experience a disaster such as flood or fire, the expenses are paid by the Amish Aid Society. In some districts, a fund of money may also be put aside for unexpected hospitalization expenses. Though they do use doctors and hospitals, they depend greatly on home remedies when fighting illnesses.

Both the Amish and Mennonite communities object to all wars. This position has often brought severe persecution by the countries in which they live. They believe in nonresistance and look to the Bible to support their beliefs.

Amish homes are simple in decor and are heated by gas, oil, coal, or propane space heaters. Beds are kept warm with quilts and comforters, and the people dress mostly in natural fibers, with long woolen underwear a must in cold winter months.

The Amish are changing their view of art, though it remains, as do their homes, modest. This new attitude is mostly evident in needlecraft, penmanship, and family records. Sometimes they sell antiques or combine colored china with family china displayed in cupboards or on open shelves.

Items Made by the Amish Community

The name "Plain People" fits the Amish because the objects made by them are not decorated, as are the Pennsylvania Dutch hex signs you see throughout that state. The Amish made their items for everyday use, shunning fanciful items.

Quilts

Amish quilts were not popular or known in the antiques world and few were owned by museums until the late 1960s. Interest grew by leaps and bounds after the 1971 show at the Whitney Museum in New York, when the exhibit of the Holstein quilt collection was held. Dealers began going after the quilts, buying them straight from Amish families, and the auction prices of such quilts shot up dramatically.

After the quilt revival of the 1970s, collectors began to see quilts as folk art instead of just as bedcoverings. It is a phenomenon fairly new to the history of antiques and is totally responsible for the skyrocketing prices.

Through studies of the quilts, experts have discovered that some designs thought to be Amish were originally made by other groups (such as the Pennsylvania Dutch), and those patterns were simply shared with Amish quiltmakers. One such pattern is the Rainbow pattern.

When one studies Amish history, it appears that quiltmaking is not a craft native to the sect but one they adopted shortly after their arrival in America. Very few Amish quilts appear to have been made before the 1870s, a time when American quiltmaking was at its peak.

Amish quilts are considered antique if they date before World War II. Prior to that time, all natural fabrics were used in rich, vibrant colors, and old cotton or blanket-type fillings were the norm. The major differences between an antique and a modern Amish quilt is the use of the fabric and type of filling. Today's Amish women may quilt with synthetic fabrics and polyester batting, a combination that gives the quilts a totally different look.

Quilts have traditionally been made from leftover scraps of materials used to make clothing; therefore, the traditional colors that Amish people wear are reflected in their quilts. The projects are usually worked on during the winter and are put up for sale during the summer. Though Amish people don't care for too many tourists, the families have realized it is a way to make money. The women make quilts and comforters for each child in the family during cold winter months. All quilts are used during their lifetime, and usually two or three are made for each child.

Amish quilts are generally identified by the area from which their maker hails. For example, Lancaster County quilts are the most conservative both in pattern and in color. Colors of quilts made in this county range from dark reds to dark greens, with many of the patterns requiring larger sections of fabric (e.g., Center Diamond and Bars patterns).

The Amish of Mifflin County, Pennsylvania, are more imaginative and daring, both in the colors they choose and the patterns they design. Garish hues, even bright yellows, were often used by these quiltmakers, and they also use a much wider range of other colors than do quilters from Lancaster County. It is said that Mifflin County Amish women had more interaction with non-Amish neighbors, giving them an opportunity to trade patterns more often than women of other Amish groups were able to.

No matter what the differences among various Amish groups, one fact remains constant with regard to the quilts they made—only solid-color fabrics were used and they were generally pieced against a solid, dark background.

Amish women quilt pieces generously, with straight lines, flowing designs, flowers, hearts, and vines flowing through the body of the quilt, as well as along the border. Often quilted with dark thread against a dark background, these designs are nonetheless artistic, and Amish needlecrafters are well known for their tiny and precise stitches.

In Pennsylvania, the Amish use a variety of patterns (e.g., 9-Patch Block, Sawtooth, Crazy) and have shared them with their neighbors. However, their quilts are distinctive in the colors used and in designs that are uniquely their own, like Diamond and Bars.

The larger, central pieces of their quilts are sewed together on treadle sewing machines. It is thought that their designs are large because the more intricate, smaller piecework may have smacked of worldly vanity and pride (some Midwest sect leaders forbade piecing for that very reason). That also may be the reason why there is usually no appliqué work on Amish quilts. The quilting, done by hand, is where the Amish excel. Their intricate designs are superb, the stitching is fine, and the motifs interesting and well planned.

Though most American quilts are made of cotton and stuffed with cotton, the Amish examples of the art follow the earlier practice, being made of wool and stuffed with wool. This tradition was carried well into the twentieth century. During the 1920s,

Amish women began using synthetics to make their quilts, often combining the use of that material with their traditional wool—a striking contrast.

There are distinct differences between midwestern Amish quilts and Pennsylvania Amish quilts, the first of which is that the Midwest uses black as a basic color, sometimes combining it with lighter or brighter colors not used by the Pennsylvania Amish. The Midwest quilters also use a cotton sateen material that is not as highly reflective as wool. Wool tends to handle a great deal of light without washing out, thus giving the quilt a richer, deeper hue. The designs of the two groups differ in that the Pennsylvanians' are more unusual and the Midwest patterns are more of a general conglomeration of American patterns of the day.

When thinking of what inspires certain patterns for Amish quilts, one has only to envision their pastoral farm life to understand designs such as Bars and Rail Fence or Log Cabin, or the Star patterns, taken from the heavenly bodies visible in the country nighttime sky.

The Center in Diamond Square design is one of the oldest Amish patterns and is made almost exclusively in Lancaster County, Pennsylvania. As few as two or as many as five colors may be used. Though quilting is often elaborate on a plain design such as this, there have been examples found that were not quilted, obviously designed by the maker to be strictly utilitarian.

Another variation on this design is the Sawtooth Diamond in Square. It is decorated in the same fashion and uses the same number of colors; however, the diamond and the square surrounding it have jagged (sawtooth) edges.

Patch quilts can be as simple as a One-Patch or as complicated as Blockwork. Each patch is made separately, designed to match its neighbor and set within the framework of a larger block. This particular design has been copied by non-Amish quilters and is extremely popular among quilt collectors.

The Bars pattern, indicative of rows of corn or wheat ready to be harvested, is a simple Amish pattern favored by the Pennsylvania groups. Two to five colors are used for this striking design, and its simplicity lends itself well to plain quilting stitches that follow the straight lines of the pattern. Variations on the bars theme are many.

Also indicative of Lancaster County is the Sunshine and Shadow pattern. The center of this design is made up of tiny multicolored pieces shaped into a large diamond pattern. The pieces are grouped by color, leading the eye into the center of the diamond. The border of this quilt is wide, allowing room for the intricate quilting for which Amish women are famous.

The Midwest Amish are known for their Basket design. Usually trimmed in black, the baskets can be made of a combination of striking colors, or all may be of the same color. Again, there are many variations on the theme. Such popular designs as Ocean Waves, Roman Stripe, Bear Paw, and Railroad Crossing also were favored.

In March 1989, an auction held in Lancaster County utilized the services of twenty-five auctioneers to sell more than four hundred Amish quilts, as well as a variety of other items. The previous year, the auction had an attendance of more than seven thousand people. This is just one example of the popularity of Amish-made items.

Crib Quilts

Full-size quilts are easy to recognize and categorize, but crib-size quilts are harder to group by pattern. There were fewer crib-size quilts made; thus fewer have survived the passing of time.

Crib quilts were made to be used, often passed down from child to child, and they went through a good deal of abuse. Therefore, quilters apparently did not spend as much time working on these smaller bed coverings.

Doll Quilts

Made for practice and play, these miniature imitations of full-size quilts were often made from leftover scraps, providing a young girl with the opportunity to practice her needlework while giving her a goal. Once they were played with and worn out, they were discarded; thus, fewer doll quilts survive than their slightly larger counterparts, crib quilts.

The same colors and materials as were used in full-size quilts are found in these smaller versions. Often the doll quilts were made from leftover pieces used by the young girl's mother, grandmother, or aunt.

Beginning with small projects such as doll quilts and clothes, Amish girls are trained to fit into the clearly defined male/female roles of their community. Their chores will be the domestic ones, and they are taught from a young age how to sew and cook, while their male counterparts learn how to farm and take care of the animals.

Some doll quilts follow the same traditional patterns as larger ones, but most are haphazard arrangements; doll quilts that show fine creative talent are rare.

Dolls

Amish dolls are distinctive because of one particularly noticeable feature—they have no faces. The reason for this is that the Amish follow the Bible dictate that states: "Thou shalt not make unto thee any graven image." That edict resulted in the Amish ban on photography (in 1856), as well as determining how the Amish wear their hair and why dolls have no faces. The dolls, usually made of cottons or feed sacks, were as heartily loved by their owners as their fancier counterparts.

As with quilts, dolls made by the Amish reflect the beliefs of their particular communities. For example, the Ohio Swartzentruber Amish made dolls that were merely a head and trunk. The dresses had sleeves that hung limply by their sides. Occasionally, an adventuresome child drew a face on a doll or crudely embroidered features, but for the most part, Amish children were satisfied with their faceless babes.

Lancaster County dolls are often a bit more detailed, with hands sporting thumbs and the fingers occasionally stitched separately.

Though Amish dolls were usually made by a female member of the family, there are some makers who became a bit more notable outside the clan. One such dollmaker is Lizzie Lapp, a Lancaster County Amish woman who lived from 1860 to 1932. Lapp suffered from a speech impediment that caused her to speak only in single words or use simple gestures.

A single woman, Lizzie spent her days making dolls consisting of three basic parts—the head, trunk, and arms were made of two like pieces of fabric stitched together, then stuffed with rags; then the legs were made and attached so that the doll was able to sit; finally, hands were attached to the arms.

She used denim almost exclusively as the chosen fabric for her dolls' hands, and a stick was buried within the rag stuffing in the dolls' bodies so that their heads were kept upright. The doll's body was made of feed sack, but its face was white and the back of its head was made of dark fabric. Unlike other Amish dolls, Lapp's "children" wore no bonnets, though their clothing was Amish-style.

Store-bought dolls were considered a luxury by the Amish; thus, rag dolls were not made simply to save money but to follow their belief in simplicity and humility. The dolls given to or made for Amish children were well loved and often lasted for the life of the child, its clothing or vital parts replaced as they wore out.

Other Playthings

Most Amish toys are handmade by the adults of the family for the children, but because children didn't have much free time to play, toys and other types of playthings are rare in that culture. Tending to farm chores and animals keeps Amish families, including children, occupied from dawn to dusk. We also note that Amish families are generally large, so the children do not lack for playmates.

Of the toys that are made, the ones that have found their way into collections are often reflective of farm life (i.e., stuffed horses and other farm animals, wooden stilts, paper boats, and animals made of dry corncobs).

Wooden toys are made by fathers or grandfathers out of scraps left over from their latest projects. Imitations of farm animals would be carved from these scraps and sometimes hand-painted to simulate Holstein cows or brightly colored roosters. Blocks were used to build tiny cities or barns, and cradles or beds were made for the dolls that belonged to the girls of the family.

Bikes are frowned on in the Amish community because they are speedy and may be used to transport children across town, where they could get into "worldly" trouble. However, scooters and wagons have been used by the children, and some communities now allow the use of tricycles for smaller children.

Live animals are often adopted as pets and playthings. Children will dress dogs, chickens, or cats in clothing and attempt to rock them in a cradle or give them a ride in their wagon. Sometimes ponies are used to pull smaller versions of adult carriages, a good way for the young children to emulate the adults in the family.

Samplers and Frakturs

Long passed up by dealers in their search for Amish quilts, samplers and frakturs are sure to gain strength in the collector's eye, especially since the publication of Daniel and Kathryn McCauley's book on the subject, *Decorative Arts of the Amish of Lancaster County.* The McCauleys have noted that these forms did not become popular with the Amish until between 1870 and 1910, though frakturs and samplers were popular with the Pennsylvania German people almost one hundred years earlier.

Items that were once purchased for $5 to $25 at farm sales now bring well over $1,000. For example, at a sale in June 1988, an Amish song book *(Ausbund)* with fraktur bookplate made by Barbara Ebersol, an Amish dwarf who decorated bookplates from approximately 1860 to 1918, was sold for $2,725. Another book with bookplate sold for $1,200 at a farm sale in 1989.

The Amish style of making samplers and frakturs, though slow to come to the forefront, has achieved recognition. These items will soon be as collectible as the more eye-catching quilts.

Weather Vanes

Since the Amish communities are largely made up of farmhouses and barns, it makes sense that they would produce weather vanes for the tops of their buildings. What surprises most collectors, however, is just how fanciful those vanes are. Amish "designers" use the traditional farm animals (horses, pigs, cows, roosters, etc.) to make vanes, but there have also been airplanes, fish, glassblowers, trains, and other unusual objects fashioned into vanes.

One collector of this type of craft notes that the Amish may comb newspapers to get new ideas for their work.

Mennonite Country

MENNONITES, named after Menno Simons, a Dutch priest who was a member of the radical religious reform group called the Anabaptists, believe, as the Amish do, in separation of religion and the world. Though they came from the same type of religious background, Mennonites differ from the Amish in that they do not follow the strict rules of Amish dress, they own and use modern conveniences like cars and electricity, and they are strong advocates of higher education. But the biggest difference between the two is that Mennonites do not withdraw from the world; instead they witness to people about their religion, proselytizing to outsiders, in an effort to expand their ranks. They also perform certain services for others and may work for those who they consider "of the world."

Like the Amish, the Mennonite are simple people. They hold their public meetings in meetinghouses and are very involved in church life (i.e., Sunday school, Bible school, and missions). Unlike the Amish, they hold world conferences every five years, not to make binding decisions but to study, inspire each other, and form fellowships.

The estimated total Mennonite population in the United States is 260,000, scattered throughout many of the same areas in which Amish communities are located. Even today Mennonites continue to migrate from places like Russia to North and South America, and their missionaries are constantly developing new communities in Africa, India, Asia, and Latin America.

Unlike the Amish, Mennonite weddings follow traditional Christian practices, with the men wearing tuxedos and the bride and her maids wearing matching bridal dresses. However, women usually wear caps at all times and are expected to dress somberly and to act decorously.

In the United States, most Mennonites still work with the land in some form, though fewer are farmers (unlike the Amish, of whom 95 percent farm the land). They are occupied in other trades, after becoming an integral part of their communities and assimilating into the area. Mennonites enter the helping professions, and several have gone into politics. It is evident that their beliefs and concerns over social issues such as race, poverty, and war contribute to their becoming more involved with the world around them.

They, like the Amish, pay their taxes and most Mennonite workers pay social security taxes. They also have a Mennonite Mutual Aid Fund that covers hospitalization, as well as funds for fire and automobile insurance.

History

After their persecution in Europe ended, Mennonites began to move into the center of Dutch life, becoming prominent in shipbuilding, herring fisheries, and whaling. Eventually, they gained control of the linen and silk industries and became wealthy, influential individuals. Because those who were businesspeople aimed toward becoming ministers of higher learning or patrons of the arts, they transferred their wealth to higher culture.

The persecutions in Switzerland during the late seventeenth and early eighteenth centuries drove Mennonites to other parts of Europe and, beginning in 1663, to the United States. They wanted to preserve the faith of their fathers, find better economic opportunities, and escape the militarism they had found in Europe.

In 1688, at a meeting in Germantown, Pennsylvania, three Mennonites signed a petition against slavery. Twenty-five years earlier, "25 Mennonist families" from Amsterdam had rejected human bondage in their colony on the Delaware. One of their points was that if one bought slaves, one was buying stolen goods.

By 1717, among the members of one large Mennonite settlement in Lancaster County, one could find members engaging in a variety of occupations—bricklayers, millers, weavers, physicians—though the bulk of Mennonite communities were farmers.

They addressed a statement to the Pennsylvania Assembly in 1775, which stated that their principles included the responsibility to feed the hungry and to help people in all ways but that they could not find any freedom in "giving, or doing, or assisting in anything by which men's lives are destroyed or hurt." The Mennonite communities held to their belief even though the Lancaster County group was accused of treason in 1783 because they fed destitute British soldiers. They continued to follow the same beliefs throughout the Civil War, refusing to fight. Some hired substitutes or paid an exemption fee. Those who did what their country told them to do—fighting in the armed forces—were excommunicated from their church.

Most Mennonites continued to engage in farming and lived in rural communities until the late nineteenth century. They maintained their German language as an insulation against their environment.

After the two world wars, many things changed throughout the United States. Cars were owned by almost everyone, the Mennonites were working at other occupations besides farming, and tourism was being developed throughout Lancaster County, Pennsylvania. The Mennonites viewed Pennsylvania tourism as a chance to expand their missionary activities to include tourists. In 1958, they opened the Mennonite Information Center and produced a 22-minute documentary called "The Mennonite Story." That film has been shown to many thousands of visitors to the center every year since then.

Today there are Mennonite communities throughout the same areas where the Amish have settled, as well as in many other parts of the country. They work on farms and in schools, act as missionaries and hospital workers, and still make every effort to maintain their separateness through their religion.

Arts and Crafts

When I was at the Renninger's Antique Market in Kutztown, Pennsylvania, a few years ago, I had the opportunity to shop the area and was determined to come home with a few Amish quilts. We had been through Lancaster County before the show and were disappointed at the commercialism we found there. My heart went out to the simple people who were just trying to live their lives as they believed they should, and I found it hard to believe that they had become a tourist attraction.

Some ten years ago I lived on a farm in upstate New York near a small Amish community. They were my neighbors and the people from whom I bought baked goods on a Saturday morning in a local supermarket parking lot. Quiet and unassuming, they were the first ones I would turn to to get a special piece of wood or advice on gardening. Their farms were neat and tidy; the houses always painted white. When we would pass one of their black buggies on the road, a hand or two always waved from inside. Occasionally, a family would bring a quilt or a few hand-sewn items to a town fair, but I would never have thought of going to their doors to disturb them.

In Kutztown, I recognized a few of the same neat farms, the white houses, the bedclothes airing on the line, and felt at home. One such house had a sign out front announcing that the family had quilts for sale. My partner and I drove apprehensively into the dooryard, where we were greeted by a bearded man in a black hat who was working in the barn. He indicated that we needed to go into the house, and as we turned around, a woman in a white bonnet welcomed us quietly.

We spent at least two hours in that unassuming white house as our Mennonite hostess pulled out quilt after quilt, which had been stored in huge drawers in a small room built specifically for the purpose of storing her goods. Her whole community worked on the quilts, she explained patiently, as she probably had to many other customers before us. Each woman was busy making different types of quilts, and they were all given to Mabel because she was the one responsible for selling them.

Some of the quilts were hand-sewn, some were sewn on a treadle machine, and some on an electric sewing machine. However, all of the quilting was hand-stitched, some finer than others. The women of that Mennonite community had discovered that people going through the area wanted Amish quilts in the dark, somber colors of that people, but there just weren't enough to go around.

"The Amish," Mabel told us in a serious, quiet voice, "just make quilts for themselves, so they often don't meet modern needs."

Mabel and her Mennonite sisters had filled that gap. She showed us queen- and king-size quilts in traditional patterns, crib quilts, quilts done in the Amish colors, quilts done with old fabrics. The women realized that a good portion of quilts bought by collectors were being hung on walls, so they made a smaller version, complete with a sleeve in the back through which a rod could be slipped for hanging the quilt.

I bought two of the hanging quilts in Amish colors and one appliquéd version; a little girl in a bonnet, which my daughter still has on her bedroom wall. Time and time again I've thought of going back and buying more, but my travels have not taken me back to Pennsylvania for some years now. Someday, though, I will go again, to sit and listen to the quiet woman's lilting voice and to have the delicious pleasure of trying to choose a quilt from the mountains of choices she provides.

The Mennonites are also serving the antique world by producing various types of miniature furniture made in the old way, with old wood. One might also find toys, pillows, hooked rugs, and tools made by the Mennonite community. The best way to know whether or not something is handmade by the Mennonites is to buy directly from them. Some will even sign their pieces for you so that you will be able to date them and assign them to a maker (my daughter's quilt has a little note attached to it with a safety pin that tells who made it, when, and where).

The humble musical instrument used by the Mennonite community is called the zitter (or zither) and is a hollow box approximately 2¾" to 3½" wide and approximately 31½" long. The construction and playing of the instrument is like that of the dulcimer, a stringed instrument made and used in the Southern Appalachians.

Zithers can be as described above or trapezodial in shape, and they are usually made of one piece of wood. They are used by the Mennonites to accompany themselves when singing hymns in church or when welcoming a bride at a wedding.

Shaker Country

*A Shaker Hymn**

'Tis a gift to be simple, 'tis a gift to be free,
'Tis a gift to come down where we ought to be,
And when we find ourselves in the place just right,
We'll be in the valley of love and delight.

When true simplicity is gained,
To bow and to bend we'll not be ashamed;
To turn, turn will be our delight,
Till by turning, turning, we come round right.

LIKE OTHER COUNTRY GROUPS before them, the Shakers established communities far from what they called "the great and wicked cities." An industrious people, the Shakers flourished in communities spread from Maine to Kentucky during the late 1700s through the late 1800s.

Though their religious beliefs caused them to keep apart from "the world" as the Amish do, the Shakers were an enterprising people who produced everything from simple, useful furniture to finely woven baskets. Few things were bought from the "world" by the Shaker communities—only items like glass, chinaware, and sheets of tin, items the Shakers could not produce themselves.

Their self-sufficiency and diligence enabled the Shakers to become a financial success. Some of the items that communities, such as the village at Canterbury, New Hampshire, or the one in Sabbathday Lake, Maine, produced for sale to the outside world included patent medicines, seeds, bricks, even a water-powered mechanical washing machine.

*Brewer, Priscilla J.: *Shaker Communities, Shaker Lives.* University Press of New England, Hanover and London, 1986.

Unlike other country groups, such as the Amish or the Mennonites, the Shakers embraced new inventions and were often the first in their area to use electricity or telephones. In fact, the Sabbathday Lake Shakers today have three computers in their village, and it has been noted that one eldress was fascinated by the automatic windows in her new car.

Today Shaker items are bought with fervor by such collectors as actor Bill Cosby at auctions held throughout the country. In fact, a few years ago I attended one held on the Mount Lebanon, Pennsylvania, site (now a school), where a record $80,000 was paid for a high revolving chair. The items sold at that auction were simple in style yet beautifully made, and I would love to have gone home with one or more of the cupboards, which were reasonably priced. I think it safe to say that we will see more records set in the next couple of years by auctioneers and that Shaker items have yet to hit their peak in the antiques world.

However, it must be noted that Shaker items are not as plentiful as one is led to believe—thus, be *sure* of the origin of your item before you make a purchase.

History

The Shaker way of life began in the 1750s, when a young woman named Ann Lee founded a new faith, called Shakerism, with a group of former Quakers in Manchester, England.

Mother Ann, as Ann Lee came to be known, was soon recognized as the spiritual center of the small group, and she led them out of England in 1744. They sailed the Atlantic Ocean and settled in New York State later that year. Then they began to concentrate on obtaining new members because their ranks could not swell by means of new births. The members neither married nor had children though they preferred to live communally, with the sexes kept separated.

Their first years in their new country were not easy ones. They were often accused of being British spies, since their arrival in America coincided with the Revolutionary period and Mother Ann was accused of being a witch. By the mid-1780s, however, there were over a thousand new converts to Shakerism, yet when

Mother Ann died in 1784, she had not seen the community at its peak or a Shaker village established.

By the early 1800s, eleven Shaker communities had been established, and members were pressing west to eventually found two villages in Kentucky, four in Ohio, and one in Indiana. In the second half of the nineteenth century, one of several African-American Shakers, Mother Rebecca Johnson, led a small troup of her followers in Philadelphia.

Today only the communities at Canterbury and Sabbathday Lake still exist, and fewer than a dozen Shakers occupy the buildings there. Other communities have been restored and are active now as museums which pass on the history of the Shaker religion.

The Church

The Shaker way of worship dismayed some of the earliest observers of the faith because of the whirling dances and seemingly uncontrollable shaking of the believers during a church service. To people of the late eighteenth and early nineteenth centuries, such actions appeared devilish and frightening. If those same observers had had a chance to watch the Shaker Brothers in their straw hats and the Sisters in somber clothing, bonnets shading their faces, hard at work making hand-turned wall pegs or hoeing a neat row in one of their abundant gardens, perhaps they would have had a different opinion of this hardworking, peaceful group of people.

By the twentieth century, the Shaker religion had gone through some changes and had passed its peak (which is noted by scholars to have occurred from approximately 1840 to 1850). No longer was dancing a part of their church service, though members were encouraged to speak out if the spirit moved them to do so. But they retained their spirit of worship and their beliefs in sharing their property, their work, and their ideas.

The Shaker motto "Hands to Work, Hearts to God" most eloquently and simply describes the common belief held by all involved in the faith. They also held tight to the belief that their celibacy released them from limits on their ability to love; instead of just bestowing those gentle feelings on a small family group, the Shakers were able to share their love with the whole community. That shared feeling of love is evident when one studies photos of Shaker members. Often the women are touching each other's shoulders or holding hands as family members do.

Their celibacy was enforced, yet they had ways to make the division easier for themselves. For instance, in some Shaker buildings twin entrances were made—one for the men and one for the women—so that they need never cross paths.

Each member of the community, regardless of sex, age, or color, was treated as an equal. No one was put above any other; talents were community, not individual, talents. In fact, the Shaker religious doctrine even points out that:

> No one should write or print his name on any article of manufacture, that others may hereafter know the work of his hand.
>
> The names of individuals may not be put upon the outside of the covers of books, of any kind.*

Other such rules were written into the *Millenial Laws,* a set of regulations thought to have been divinely received by a member in 1821. This set of laws revealed how the Shakers were to carry out their lives, and everything practical and spiritual was covered.

As pacifists, the Shakers fought slavery with words and prayer, and they sought to be granted the equivalent status of conscientious objectors when the draft was instituted during the Civil War. Because of an appeal by Elder Frederick Evans of Mount Lebanon, Pennsylvania, to President Lincoln, the exemption status was granted, and Shakers no longer were required to undergo the demeaning physical examinations required of draftees nor were they required to break their all-important rules of pacifism.

Marriage

The Shakers did not believe in marriage, as stated earlier, yet they did not impose their beliefs on others, even to the point of un-

*Brewer, Priscilla J.: *Shaker Communities, Shaker Lives.* University Press of New England, Hanover and London, 1986.

derstanding if a young couple left the faith to marry. It was understood that members had the freedom to come and go as they pleased. In fact, belief in freedom was the one on which all of the others were based. The Shakers strongly adhered to their freedoms—from sin, sickness, jealousy, bad habits, or filth, the freedom to be celibate, and, most important, the freedom to follow their chosen religion.

Some have wondered how Shaker children entered the community, and the answer is quite simple. Some Shakers took in orphaned children or those who came from broken homes. Though cared for by their new "families" throughout childhood and often into early adulthood, most of these children left the Shaker villages before signing the covenant. That fact saddened the elders and probably contributed to the gradual decline of the community.

Buildings

The Millenial Laws of 1854 decreed which colors certain buildings in the Shaker community would be painted. Cream or yellow was used for workshops, the meetinghouse was white, barns and other service buildings were deep red or brown.

When the new villages were designed, maps were drawn up indicating the buildings (in full architectural detail) as well as the areas were planting was to be done or animals allowed to graze. Most buildings in Shaker compounds are more than one story tall; some have three or more stories. Each is a neat, Federal-type design, the larger ones with two brick chimneys, the smaller with just one. However, at the Hancock village in New Hampshire, there was a round barn built in 1826 that could house more than fifty head of dairy cattle. Quite a different design from the buildings found in other villages!

Shaker Country Items

Shakers prided themselves on the work they did. Nothing but perfection was tolerated, which is one of the reasons Shaker pieces are held in such high regard and bring such incredible prices in today's market. The articles they made did not have to be highly decorated or fancifully carved—they just had to be perfect.

Their work was hard and their days were long, but the satisfaction of living in an agrarian society was what they strived for, and the fact that the items they made still exist causes me to believe they would be happy with their long-lived success.

Shaker daily life was a ritual that continued from week to week, uninterrupted unless some great issue brought itself forward and interrupted the heavenward progress of the society. Their concerns were with gardening, livestock, and what to cook for dinner, rather than the political and social influences that grasped the attention of outside families. It was a simple life that kept its members free of decision making and unencumbered by the pressures of daily life outside the community.

They said to new members: "Salvation is to be happy here, and when you are happy you are in heaven" (letter of Frederick W. Evans to George H. Evans, June 11, 1830).*

The Shaker people have the distinction of being one of the first country groups to support themselves through what we would now call "cottage industries."

One of the first items to be packaged and sold by Shakers were seeds. At first, the seeds were marketed by traveling peddlers, who loaded their carts with seeds, as well as other Shaker products, and brought the goods from door to door.

The New York Shakers were one of the first Shaker communities to market their products in larger cities such as Albany, New York City, and Brooklyn. The New Hampshire Shakers used Boston as their distribution center.

Once the seeds were marketed, there was a natural progression to selling herbs, often used for medicinal purposes. Soon large herb houses were built in the New England Shaker communities in order to keep up with the demand.

Growing and selling fruits and vegetables resulted from the Shakers' natural ability to cultivate the land. Dairy products and

*Shaker documentation code: WRHS IV A 36).

raising livestock soon followed, making the Shaker community almost totally self-sufficient.

Another early Shaker industry was broom making. They popularized the flat broom as we know it today; prior to that time, most brooms had been round.

Each new problem the Shakers encountered resulted in an invention that eased or eliminated the problem. They are responsible for such items as built-in cabinets, the needle with the eye in the middle, the washing machine, the first circular saw, the first one-horse buggy, a mowing machine, the revolving harrow, the automatic spring, and Babbit Metal.

Though there is not enough room in this chapter to describe them all, we will discuss a number of Shaker items that are high on the list of valuable American country collectibles.

Baskets

The Shakers made baskets in an infinite variety of sizes and shapes. Like other country/farm people, they used baskets to gather their vegetables, fruits, and eggs, to gather and/or store seeds, and for storing medicines, weaving, laundry, sewing implements, and other items.

The materials used for early baskets were poplar, split black ash, and palm leaf, which was imported from Cuba. It is thought that Indian women who lived near the early Shaker settlements taught the Sisters how to make their first baskets.

As in other cultures, basketmaking was done primarily by the women of the community. It was a Shaker industry that did not healthily survive the Civil War, except for the woven poplar boxes and baskets that the Sisters made and sold in their shops from 1850 on.

The wood used for the baskets was cut when the trees were still frozen, chopped into 2-foot lengths, and put through a plane specifically designed by the Shakers. The plane took off very thin strips of poplar, which were then hand-shredded into even finer strips. (An electrically powered machine invented by Brother Irving Greenwood later took up the shredding task.) The Sisters wove the strips on hand looms and then pasted a sheet of paper to the reverse side of the straw cloth to make the basket firmer and less likely to break. This straw cloth was woven into many fine baskets; some of the sewing baskets were lined with satin and decorated with edging tape.

The Shakers followed molded forms when weaving their baskets, which is one reason their woven masterpices were so evenly made. There were approximately eight styles of Shaker baskets, some of which are instantly recognizable (like the quatrefoil design or a bottom woven on a Watervliet mold) while others were of a size and shape commonly known to many New England basketmakers. The baskets made at the Hancock Shaker Village were woven from black ash splints, as that tree was commonly found on or near the Hancock Village.

The Algonquin Indians lived near Shaker villages, and the two groups quickly became friends. That group of Native Americans shared some of their basketmaking techniques with the Shakers who, in turn, perfected the style and took it to a new height.

One cannot say enough about the perfectly clean way a Shaker basket is woven. It almost appears as though each space, each splint, each handle was measured to make sure they were precisely the right size. The weaving is tight, with no sloppiness around the edges or in the wrapping of a rim. Each splint edge is so neatly woven into the basket's overall design that there is no sign of the ends. The Shakers made nothing of low quality, and baskets were certainly no exception.

Master basketmaker John McGuire, a contributor to this book, has spent many years at the Shaker community in Hancock. His knowledge of their weaving styles and their history is shared through his book on the subject, a must for anyone interested in Shaker basketry.

In a catalog published for a sale held by well-known New York dealer David Schorsch earlier this year, several fine examples of Shaker baskets were represented, including a rectangular gathering basket with carved bail handle from Alfred of Sabbathday Lake. Made in the mid-1800s, the basket is of ash splint and still retains an original, rare coat of blue paint. It is a beauty of a basket, measuring 11½″ long, 8½″ deep, and 6½″ wide and is an example that shows the superior workmanship of the Shaker Sisters.

In the same catalog there is a shallow drying basket with carved side handles that was probably made at the Mount Lebanon, Pennsylvania, community in the mid-nineteenth century. It is 18″ by 18″ by 9″, and made of woodsplint. Other baskets sold in the Schorsch sale included a rare oval gathering basket with carved bail handle, a tall storage basket with a classical pottery shape, a hexagonally woven drying basket with wrapped side handles, and a cutlery basket with carved open handle.

Brooms and Brushes

As we've already mentioned, the Shakers are responsible for making the first flat-sided broom, a feat I'm sure thousands of women have thanked them for day after long cleaning day.

It was written in the Millenial Laws that no rubbish or scraps were to be allowed to accumulate anywhere on Shaker community land, and all were expected to do their part in keeping the grounds and buildings as immaculate as possible. Perhaps that urge to keep things clean is what caused the Shakers to furnish their homes and other buildings with *only* what they needed and nothing more. We all know that the more you have, the more there is to clean. I should have thought of that when I filled my house with dusty antiques . . .

The Shaker broom, invented by Theodore Bates, was sold to the American public as early as 1798. Broom corn, grown specifically for the production of brooms and brushes, was thought to have been first grown by the New England and New York Shakers.

With the advent of the flat broom, a more efficient way of cleaning took place in American households. Now those who wielded the broom could reach into corners and under low furniture and could get into nooks and crannies that were once left to gather dust.

Different types of brooms and brushes were made, including long, wide ones used to clean ceilings, whisk brooms in various sizes, shoe brushes, scrubbing brushes, and clothes brushes.

As with other Shaker industries, the broom and brush business prospered until the Civil War, then went into a decline following the reduction in the Shaker population.

Clothing

Clothes in the plain Shaker style were originally made for their own use but later became available to the general public. The community at Mount Lebanon, Pennsylvania, shows records of clothing being sold to outsiders as early as 1789. Its tailoring shop, managed by David Slosson, made coats, breeches, trousers, suit coats, shirts, and drawers to order for their customers.

All fabrics were woven by the Sisters in accordance with projected needs, and the width, weave, and color of the textile was determined by the eventual use of the material.

The sewing rooms used by Shaker Sisters were designed with order and efficiency in mind, with special furniture for cutting and sewing designed by these inventive people. Minimal bending was required over the long and wide cutting tables (a boon for those who worked at them all day), and drawers were built into the tables so that the worker did not have to leave the table to obtain the equipment necessary to complete the task. Some of the sewing desks could be used by more than one person at a time because there were drawers positioned at both ends, again, for convenience.

Sisters were allowed a certain number of articles of clothing on which their initials could be hand-embroidered. Though the Millenial Law gave strict rules for the wardrobe a person might have, there were ample pieces to assure that no one would go without and that all would be able to follow the law, which stated that "no one should wear very ragged clothes, even about their own work, if it can consistently be avoided."

No new fashions were made by the Shaker sects. The women wore pleated skirts, collarless blouses, and triangular scarves over their bodices (as a means hiding the bosom). The silk capelets worn over the women's dresses are called "berthas." Berthas were originally made of black silk, but later, white lawn or linen was the material used. In the Victorian days, they might have been trimmed with a bit of black or gray lace around the collar, middle, and bottom. Even as late in the twentieth century as the 1960s, the Sisters still wore severely drawn-back hairdos and bonnets, yet their dress length had risen to midcalf.

Knitted pieces of clothing were also made by Shaker tailoring-shops (i.e., gloves and socks), by the young girls and elderly sisters who could not do more strenuous work. Wood stretchers were made for blocking knitted gloves and were folded in half for easy storage when not being used (another Shaker invention).

Uniformity in clothing was dictated by Shaker law in order to reinforce their separation from the world. However, colors and small details in style were often evident from family to family. To this day, "Shaker" is synonymous with a style of slipover, hand-knit sweater sold by most larger clothing stores.

The eighteenth-century version of bonnets worn by Shaker women was made of braided straw, covered and lined with black silk. Its crown was covered with inch-deep plaited silk, and ribbons were attached there, then brought down over the brim to tie at the back of the neck.

After the turn of the nineteenth century, the bonnet style changed, and Shaker hats resembled Quaker hats made during the same period, being of pasteboard covered in light-colored silk. Bonnets made of palm leaf straw and trimmed with a short cape and ribbons, tied under the chin, were made by 1827 and continued to be worn throughout the nineteenth century.

Another popular item—originally Shaker, then sold to the public—was the roomy, warm "Dorothy" cloak worn in the last quarter of the nineteenth century. Shaker Eldress Dorothy Durgin (Canterbury, New Hampshire) was credited with originating this cloak, which was made in a variety of colors and sizes from infant to adult. The commercial version of this cloak was made of French broadcloth, while its original was made of blue or gray handwoven Shaker wool. Shaker cloaks were so popular that even Mrs. Grover Cleveland ordered one to wear at her husband's second inaugural in 1893. The patent for the cloak's design was applied for in 1901 by Eldress Emma Neale and was used until the business terminated in 1929.

Furniture

Anyone who has seen a photograph of Shaker furniture or who has had occasion to see in person or to buy a piece will agree that the straight and simple lines make the piece extremely graceful, yet extraordinarily plain and beautiful. If any of the old-time Shaker furniture makers were alive today, I am sure they would be astonished at the skyrocketing prices these utilitarian pieces bring in today's market. Their furniture was made to order to fit their homes and the furniture's function, not for use by the rest of the world.

All consideration was given to the fact that furniture in Shaker homes had to be moved so that the dwelling could be kept clean. With that in mind, wall pegs were designed so that chairs could be hung up out of the way, beds were made with wheels, chests were given longer legs so that a broom could easily sweep under them, and children's furniture was made in a smaller size so that younger Shakers would not experience any discomfort. Each piece of furniture had its own purpose, which explains why some Shaker pieces are highly distinctive and unusual.

It is obvious that the Sisters had a say in the size or height of a table, how many drawers filled a sewing desk, or how a spool chest or cupboard was constructed because so many of the items were specifically tailored for their owners. In fact, high stools were designed to be paired with ironing tables so that the women could sit down during this arduous task. Because the men did not perform these duties, the Sisters must have had ample opportunity to explain to the men, the furniture makers, what they needed to make life easier for them. (When seeing Shakers in this context, one is able to realize fully the extent of their ability to communicate and to realize how much of a partnership they had even though that partnership did not include a sexual relationship.)

All pieces were extremely useful and/or unique, yet no ornamentation was used above and beyond plain wooden pulls, latches, and simple escutcheons.

Chairs

One of the most recognizable items made by the Shaker communities is the three-slatted chair with ribbon-webbed seat. We are most familiar with this industry because it was one of the last to exist in the twentieth century. Spare and delicate, Shaker chairs and rockers were probably the first to be commercially manufactured in the United States. Every community was engaged in chair making at one time or another.

Armchairs were also made for commercial distribution, as well as other, individually shaped chairs for special purposes (e.g., low-backed dining room chairs that were pushed under the tables when not being used). Children's chairs were made, as well as a revolving high chair (one example was sold at a Willis Henry auction in 1987 for a record price of $80,000).

The business of selling Shaker chairs was often assigned to one or two members of the community. Those members were responsible for taking the merchandise to town as well as for buying the goods other members needed.

After 1852, chair manufacture became a major industry in the Shaker community, and a patent was applied for by George O'Donnell (New Lebanon, New Hampshire) for a new type of chair that featured a ball-and-socket device in the rear feet. The device allowed the chair to tip back without damaging the floor or the chair itself. Because O'Donnell did not remain in the Shaker community, we do not know the total number of chairs produced.

The exclusive rights to chair making were given to the South Family at Mount Lebanon, Pennsylvania, in 1863, and they continued making chairs for Shaker use until 1867. There were companies known to distribute Shaker-made chairs in New York City; Providence, RI; Boston; Troy, NY; Albany, NY; Philadelphia; Racine, WI; and Chicago.

The first catalogs containing Shaker chairs show and describe the various models, giving them identifying numbers; for example, "No. 5. This size is well adapted for dining or office use, when an armchair is desirable" and "No. 1. This is a small chair, calculated to suit small persons or grown-up children. We make this chair with arms and with or without rockers." The most expensive chair (the No. 0) was $8.25 with a web seat, and all are stated to have "a Gold Transfer Trade Mark attached to them, and none others are Shakers' Chairs." Also sold in these catalogs were chair cushions, foot benches, and floor rugs.

The Mount Lebanon, Pennsylvania, chair-making industry largely grew from the hard work of Robert Wagan and his successor, Elder William Anderson. After Anderson, the person responsible for the business was Eldress Sarah Collins, who continued in her post until 1933. The business terminated in 1947 under her direction.

Other communities produced chairs, though not as prolifically as Mount Lebanon, and most of what was made by others was strictly for Shaker use. Some other makers (such as Ohio and Kentucky Shakers) were influenced by "worldly" designs and used some details that were considered more decorative than functional.

Of the chairs produced for the Shakers' private use, some were painted yellow and red, and the woven seats were made in a variety of color combinations. The woods used in making early Shaker chairs included maple (for the frames) and later birch, cherry, or butternut for the slats. The gracefully tapered finials were often of various shapes, and, as mentioned before, the tilting device was used under the back legs.

Though the early styles are distinctive, in the latter part of the nineteenth century the Shakers were influenced by such worldly styles as the bentwood chair, made of wood that was steamed and bent.

As with everything else, the Shakers would not tolerate shoddy workmanship nor inferior materials; thus, furniture made by these people is among the best produced in America's history.

Oval Boxes

Oval boxes were made by the Shakers to be used as enclosures or receptacles. They were pieces of beauty and simplicity made without error.

Maple was the primary wood used. A thin band of the wood would be cut into "fingers" with the help of a template. The wood was then steamed, wrapped around an oval mold, and the fingers secured by copper or wrought-iron rivets. Pine disks were fitted into the base and cover.

These oval boxes were first made in the latter part of the eighteenth century and continued to be manufactured at the last-surviving Shaker settlements. They were often made in graduated sizes or "nests" and were equipped with handles or "carriers."

Seed and Herb Industry

One of the first Shaker collectibles to be recognized by aficionados of American country were seed boxes. These colorful packages and wooden display units are the remnants of one of the most profitable of all Shaker industries. The industry began around 1789 in Watervliet, New York, and New Lebanon, New Hampshire, and it declined, as did many other seed industries, after the Civil War.

At the height of the seed industry, yearly sales of the product were reported to reach $1,000 and more. Each community participated in the distribution and selling of seeds; thus, territories often overlapped. Still, those in the various communities involved in sales had no problem selling all that they had on hand.

Between 1836 and 1840, the New Lebanon Community alone printed almost a million seed bags. The packages, printed in bright colors, proclaimed that the seeds were packed by the Shakers and identified community as well. Also distributed with the seed packets were posters and banners that were used to promote the sale of Shaker seeds. This early advertising material was usually printed by an outside (worldly) printing company, as were the seed boxes and labels.

The Shakers, astute in business as they were, soon realized that other printed material, such as gardening manuals, helped to promote their seed industry. Leaflets were written and printed that told the buyer how to cultivate "some of the most useful culinary vegetables," and the booklets sold for approximately 6 cents.

Again the Shakers invented machines to make more efficient use of their work time. A machine for filling seed bags was invented in the Watervliet community, as well as other machines such as a threshing machine and a fertilizing machine.

The herb and medicine industry was a by-product of the Shaker seed business and probably brought the Shaker way of life more into the worldly family. The Shakers were concerned with their members' health, and certain members of the family were assigned to be responsible for the health of the others. They did not believe in using worldly doctors unless absolutely necessary, and at that point the final decision was to be made by the Ministry or Elders.

Because of their beliefs, the Shakers learned at an early age which herbs would be used, for example, to cure a cold or an upset stomach. Certain flowerbeds were put together for this specific purpose, and rows of foxglove, bloodroot, and lobelia were cultivated to be specifically used as medicine. The Shaker "Botanic Medicines" were mixed, packaged, and labeled within the community and sold to the public as early as 1809.

The women were responsible for gathering, drying, and preparing the plants, giving them a pretty extensive knowledge of the botanical elements in their area as well as a strong folk medicine understanding.

The business of packaging and shipping herbs became international when orders started coming in from a London botanist named Charles Whitlaw. By 1836, the Shaker herb industry was, for the most part, supplied by the gardens grown in each community. However, a number of herbs still had to be ordered from other sources.

By the mid-1800s, the Shaker medicine industry had earned the group a worldwide reputation for developing the "soothing syrup," a cure for asthma. They also produced other well-known medicines. Even opium, made from poppies grown by the Shakers, was supplied to druggists and chemists.

Separate buildings were set aside for the preparation and packaging of medicines, and the business became almost as profitable as the seed industry. Almanacs were printed to advertise Shaker medicines during the late 1800s, and the industry continued in a profitable manner until the Food and Drug Act of 1906 began to put stipulations on their business.

Miscellaneous

We have just touched on the most highly collected items the Shakers made, and it must be noted here that there is an incredible array of other types of Shaker items in which the collector may be interested, such as lighting devices, wooden objects, textiles, sieves, clocks, art, copper items, and many more.

There are a number of very interesting books on the market today that specialize in Shaker items, and there are some auctioneers, such as Willis Henry of Massachusetts, whose specialized sales of Shaker collectibles are enough to tickle the fancies of even the most knowledgeable of collectors.

Native American Country

MOST AMERICANS have a limited knowledge of the contributions Native Americans have made to our culture, and most history books barely touch on any part of Indian history besides the wars between white men and Amerinds.

I hope the newly kindled interest in American Indian collectibles and the emphasis that the marketplace is putting on Native American crafts will encourage people to learn more about the culture of the "first Americans." Most country collectors have been exposed to Indian rugs, baskets, or pottery. Those who haven't should become so in the next year or two because most of the decorating magazines I've peeked through lately have had some Amerind items decorating walls, floors, or tables.

I encourage collectors to learn as much as possible about what they are planning to buy before making any antique purchases; however, I emphasize that point even more strongly when a collector turns to Native American art. The reason I make this point is that there were more than 150 American tribes at one point, and it is important for collectors to know who made what. It is also necessary to note here that there have been reproductions or new Oriental versions made of some Indian collectibles, and the collector certainly doesn't want to plunk down any hard-earned money when the piece for sale isn't authentic. Keeping all of this advice in mind, I would urge you to read as much as possible if your inclinations draw you to this collecting field.

History

Though the Native American's knowledge of the wheel and its uses was limited when the Pilgrims landed on the northeastern coast of the United States, they taught the new settlers much about living off the land. In fact, more than half of the agricultural products known in the United States today were ones grown and developed by this country's native peoples.

We all know that corn (maize) was originally an American Indian vegetable, but how many of us know that tomatoes, peppers, squash, potatoes, and beans were unknown in any other parts of the world when Columbus landed on our shores? Cotton and tobacco, two of early America's major crops, were also known to natives long before Virginia plantation owners started growing them.

Those early days of cooperation and an active interchange of ideas ended shortly after Native Americans realized that the white intruder was usurping land the Europeans appeared to believe was free for the taking. The freedom of hunting and fishing to provide food and other living materials began to disappear. Confusion and miscommunication interfered with the lives of many Native Americans, and before long, illnesses and wars were rampant, wiping out some of the Indian nations even before this country was declared free from England's control.

When settlers moved into the northernmost regions of New England in the eighteenth century, they discovered that the Abenaki tribe had been there long before them. Large villages were discovered, and with those discoveries came the realization that these people followed annual cycles adapted to what the land provided for them. They hunted, fished, farmed, and gathered food. They used their natural resources to make clothing, baskets, snowshoes, and traps and traded these items with the white settlers. For instance, a basket made by a member of the tribe for a white family often earned the Native American some hay for his horse.

Maple sugaring secrets were shared by the Indian tribes in the Northeast (see the Barn chapter); they also shared knowledge of farming and berry gathering, helped the settlers with trapping techniques, and taught them about medicinal herbs. In turn, the white settler traded cloth, weapons, and other kinds of food not grown by the Amerind.

By the beginning of the 1800s, the Abenaki had been pushed farther north and into the woods—pushed away from their homeland by the encroachment of the white settlers and their new homes. Some Abenaki married into American or French Canadian families; others simply died, no longer able to live off the land they had had to themselves for centuries.

The Abenaki wasn't the only Indian tribe to disappear. In fact, the scenario seems to have replayed itself time and time again in Amerind history. Most of the tribes in the northeast and southeast had dwindled seriously in number by the nineteenth century.

By the beginning of the 1800s, the settlers had ventured forth in a general western direction. The Plains tribes (Sioux, Cherokee, Arapaho, etc.) were affected by the advent of the white man, some negatively, some positively. Red trade cloth found its way into Indian garments or was unraveled to be rewoven into rugs or blankets. Trade beads were used by the white man to trade for the furs and skins the Amerind owned. The beads later showed up as decoration on tribal clothing.

The southwestern desert tribes (Apache, Zuni, Hopi, Navajo, and others) continued to produce the pottery that had become a necessity for them long before the settlers arrived. They too, however, were moved to reservations, unable to travel elsewhere if the land proved too harsh for them to stay.

In the years just prior to and immediately after the turn of the century, tourists began taking home to the East some of the American Indian treasures they had collected on their trips. Artists like George Catlin traveled throughout the West painting lifelike images of Native American tribes they had encountered along the way. It appeared, for a while, that the American public was trying to educate itself. But they went just so far and stopped. Thankfully, today we are experiencing renewed interest in collecting contemporary crafts by Native Americans and in supporting Amerind arts.

In a recent *National Geographic* article, it was stated that certain burial grounds had been upset and that the tribes were dismayed by the general public's apparent lack of respect. What is in the ground should be offered to the tribe first, no matter what. If you happen to find something that has significant value to Native Americans, please show them the respect of giving it back to them.

If you buy something that has an interesting Amerind history, write it down. Keep the names of the artists from whom you buy your pottery, jewelry, Kachinas, or whatever. Have them sign anything you buy and date it. Most art does not appreciate if it's not signed; also, there is too little known about the Native American artists in this country. Whatever contribution you, as a collector, can make to keeping information about artists accurate will be beneficial—not only to you, but for historical preservation.

But, most important, if you buy only items that are in excellent or good condition and only what you like, I am sure you will enjoy collecting some of the most interesting country items available.

Native American Country Items

Art

Unfortunately, much of what the Amerind has made throughout the past century has been for the tourist trade, not as a celebration of their own heritage. Yet their work was influenced by outside forces (e.g., Victorian styles, American patriotism) as much as Indian designs and life-styles made their influence on white Americans (e.g., the shape and form of snowshoes or the planting and harvesting of corn and other vegetables).

Because the items they made were not for themselves, the styles changed according to what the buyer wanted. Many Native Americans have said that if they didn't have to make these items to sell, their style would be totally different. It's sad that cultures are forced into such a position and their originality thwarted.

The legacy given to us by Native Americans has been treasured by some. Indeed, there are those who have learned their craft from Native Americans and have passed that knowledge to a younger member of their family. We applaud that knowledge of heritage and fervently hope that it continues.

Most Indian patterns and designs have some significance. For example, Abenaki Indians of the Northeast used the symbol sketched on the next page as a popular pattern when decorating items. The symbol signifies the power of the plant world.

Growing plants and herbs supplied Native Americans with medicine and represented spiritual and life-giving properties.

In *The Official® Identification and Price Guide to American Indian Collectibles*, there are examples of other symbols used in Indian art that are often repeated in sand paintings, pottery, and clothing decoration. Some are simple, such as a bolt of lightning, which denotes swiftness. Others are more abstract—for instance, bear tracks are a good omen.

The Plains Indians painted their horses. Though it is not the type of art one is able to collect, they did use certain symbols and colors when decorating the animals. Thick circles with red centers meant that a battle had been fought from behind logs or rocks and that enemies had been killed. Coup marks were shown by three or four short straight lines, and arrowheads on a horse's hooves denoted his quick-footedness.

In the Southwest, the Navajos used the art of sand painting, the art taught to them by "the Holy Ones." It was a medicine man's way of maintaining the world's delicate balance and was used when someone "caused" a disease or illness. The medicine man would come to the offender's lodge and design a sand painting on the hogan floor. An opening that faced east would be incorporated into the painting, making it difficult for evil to enter. Once the painting was completed, the patient was brought into the center, the medicine man finished the ceremony, and the sand painting was swept into a blanket. After the sun set, the blanket was taken outside and the sand flipped into the wind, to be returned to Mother Earth so that the evil forces trapped within could not escape.

More recently, sand paintings have been reproduced, and you are now likely to see contemporary sand paintings by Amerind artists. They have been sold in fairs throughout the Southwest, and certain artists have become well known for this type of art.

•

Some well-known Indian artists include Harrison Begay, Archie Blackowl, Acee Blue Eagle, Woody Crumbo, Bill Rabbit, Jamie Tawodi Reason, Robert Redbird, and Monroe Tsatoke.

Basketry

Amerind baskets were made for a variety of purposes. Some were strictly for storage, some were used in fishing, some were made to hold babies, and others had ceremonial purposes.

Most of the Indian tribes across the United States made some type of basket at one time or another. The majority of the basketmakers have remained anonymous, though collectors are familiar with Pomo basketmaker Mary Benson and Dat-So-La-Lee from the Great Basin. Myths and legends surround the art of basketry. The Navajo, Pueblo, and Hopi tribes all tell different stories about the process.

Basketmakers use the materials available in their area and practice the weaving styles of their ancestors. Different colors and symbols are used by various tribes and make it a little easier to discover the origin of the basket you might collect.

For instance, the Cahuilla tribe in California used only yellow, white, black, and brown, while the Hopi use aniline dyes on much of their modern basketry. Colors specified different things to the Native American. The Cherokees believe that red means triumph/success, blue denotes defeat or trouble, black signifies death, and white stands for peace and happiness. Red is generally considered a sacred color by all.

Some of the tribes that have made baskets are the Aleut, Apache, California Mission tribes, Hopi, Haida, Navajo, and Pomo. The major differences in tribal basketmaking are found in the weave. For example, Hopi basketmakers use the coiling effect when making baskets and are known for their wedding basketry. The Apache make a burden basket out of willow and decorate it with strips of buckskin tipped with tin cones, which make a musical sound when the basket moves. Papago and Pima tribes make miniature horsehair baskets.

When handling any Indian basket bigger than the palm of your hand, scoop both hands under the base of the basket. Do not pick it up by its edges because that weakens the fibers holding the basket together and may cause rim damage.

Blankets and Rugs

One of the nicest experiences I have had was the moment I was allowed to touch the incredibly soft chief's blanket owned by one of the contributors to my American Indian book. I had always imagined the blankets to be coarse, rough material, scratchy to the touch. When I put my hand across the rosy pink blanket, I was unable to withhold a deep sigh. I immediately became cognizant of the fact that the blanket I was touching was made more than two hundred years ago and had been worn by a leader of a group of Amerinds. And I realized that the blanket had become so soft from years of wear and touch, from being beaten against a rock on washday, from soaking up the oils that seep from human skin. I've never felt so personally close to an antique before. It was a unique experience I will never forget.

Navajo blankets, made mostly by the women of the tribe, have been recognized as pieces of art in today's antiques world. They are hung on the walls of country homes or thrown over the back of a couch or a favorite rocking chair. They pair well with the rustic furniture from the Adirondacks or with the milk-based colors of early New England cupboards. They are extremely at home in a country decor.

The early Navajo blankets date from 1800 and were simple coverings. They were made in natural wool colors like brown and white. The chiefs' blankets, made later, used bold colors and strong designs. Geometrics such as boxes and diamonds were used, and the colors most often woven into these blankets were red and blue. Other blankets/rugs, called "eye dazzlers," were made much later and are highly collectible.

Though the Navajo are the best-known rug/blanket makers of the continental U.S. tribes, the Chilkat tribe of the Northwest also made blankets. Their versions were woven from goat hair and are often decorated with animals, geometrics, and deep fringe on three sides.

Used in tribal ceremonies, the blankets were worn by tribe

aristocrats. The animal (whale, eagle, raven, salmon, etc.) used as the main design on the blanket was considered a "crest."

Unlike the Navajo, the Chilkat men made the designs on the blankets worn by tribe members. No deviation was made from the traditional design. However, women wove the fabric onto which the design was woven.

Pottery

Many different types of pottery were made by the tribes in the Southwest, where clay was conveniently found. Nowhere else in the United States was pottery made in such abundance.

Different tribes used different colors of clay or painted their pots with unusual designs. The process of making the pot, firing it, and decorating it has differed even within the tribes, with people such as Maria attempting new artistic ways of making traditional pottery. Still, there are identifying features when collecting Amerind pottery, and certain tribes are well known for the types of pottery they make.

The Pueblo potters, for instance, are responsible for making "Storytellers," seated figures that are accompanied by smaller figures. The first Storyteller was made by a Cochiti potter, Helen Cordero, in the 1950s. Her pottery figure, depicting a seated Indian man with his head raised to the sky, eyes closed, and mouth open, telling a story to the swarming children all around him, has been copied by many other potters. But no one does it quite like Helen. She is now passing along her knowledge to others in the family, and they are quite talented. It is a collectible to keep an interested eye on.

The black-on-black decorated dishes and bowls that bring top dollar at American Indian auctions usually are the creation of Maria Montoya Martinez of the San Ildefonso pueblo or of one of her family. Maria first worked with her husband, Julian, but was later known to have worked with her son, Popovi Da, and her daughter-in-law, Santana. As with most other Indian arts, the secrets are passed down from generation to generation, and I hope that it continues to be that way.

Tribes that made pottery include Hopi (often decorated with Kachinas), San Ildefonso (usually black-on-black or utilizing the rainbird design), and Santa Clara (where some of the best known miniature potters, such as Joseph Lonewolf, do their work). A brief sampling of well-known Amerind potters might include those already mentioned, as well as the Naranjo family, Lucy Lewis, Nampeyo, and Margaret Quintana.

African-American Country

MANY COUNTRY HOMES or collections include one or more items made by or in the character of black Americans. Most pieces are offensive and degrading, yet we add them to our collections almost as a reminder that what happened then will never happen again.

I have had the eye-opening experience of working almost four years researching my first book on antiques and collectibles (*Collecting Black Americana*) and have written many articles on various aspects of the subject since. What I discovered was that there simply wasn't enough documentation available in those areas where African-Americans influenced the arts and the society that we now term American.

Like other country folk, African-Americans worked with their hands, producing whatever was needed for their homes in their free time. Because there are so many areas of black collectibles that country collectors might pursue, I have focused this chapter on items made *by* African-Americans rather than the images made by others. You may find that type of information in other chapters of this book (e.g., "The Kitchen" in The Country Home chapter).

I would give every collector of black memorabilia the same advice I offered to those who wish to collect American Indian items: find out the history of your piece and the name of its maker, then write it down and save it. If you can't find the name of the maker, find out *where* it was made and research the industries in that area—for example, pottery was one of the industries where African-Americans did quite a bit of work but seldom got credit. Know what you are collecting, not only to enhance your own appreciation, but to pass on the history of the piece to future generations.

Prices for some items of black memorabilia appear to have reached a plateau, while others continue to rise. Folk art is always a good investment, as is original art; however, I would be cautious when buying iron items such as banks or doorstops, as they have been reproduced for quite a while now and it is easy to be fooled.

There are now several books on black collectibles, and a bimonthly newsletter, "Black Ethnic Collectibles," is distributed by Jeannette Carson of Hyattsville, Maryland. Shows are held throughout the country strictly for people who wish to collect this type of item, and a collector's society (based in Silver Springs, Maryland) also has been formed.

History

The first black slaves from Africa were brought to our shores in 1619, reaching Virginia almost by chance, and they were brought by a Dutch ship, not an English one. The process of shipping African-Americans to this country to be forced into slavery got off to a slow start. In Virginia, in 1681, there were two thousand black slaves as opposed to six thousand indentured European servants.

However, slavery took root in the colonies when the tobacco industry started to thrive, and by 1714 there were approximately 59,000 black slaves working the fields. After that, the figures kept rising: 263,000 by 1754 and 4,441,830 by the advent of the Civil War in 1860. Figures show that there were far more black people who crossed the seas to be enslaved in this country than there were European or English colonists.

Though slavery had existed almost since the beginning of time, nowhere else in the world had slaves been subjected to the prejudice and discrimination that they endured in the United States. In every slave culture, the child retained the mother's status. It didn't matter what the father's color or position was; if the mother was a slave, so was her child. And no matter how much or how little black ancestry a person had, they were still considered to be "on the other side of the color line." Yet, in other cultures, slaves had worked for certain periods, then received their freedom. With black American slaves, there was no freedom until the end of the Civil War, and some would even question whether they had freedom then.

There was a definite status level in slave society: household servants were at the top, those slaves involved in various trades made up the middle class, and the largest group, those working the plantations, were at the bottom. Each of these distinct levels of society produced something that served to shape the culture in which we live today. Perhaps the household servants learned quilting and were responsible for some of the slave quilts that are held today in museums. The slaves working in the trades were responsible for most of the ironwork that came out of the South, as well as for pottery, and they even went on to open their own businesses, as did Thomas Day, a furniture maker of high regard in South Carolina. The plantation workers did not have much time or energy left over after working the fields, but the songs they sang while working and the hymns that rang out in church are the basis of what we know as gospel, blues, and jazz.

Antislavery forces were spreading in the late 1700s, with groups like the Quakers, Shakers, Amish, and Mennonites voicing their opinions, and emancipation was had after a long and bloody Civil War. Some slaves fled the South at the beginning of the war, 156,000 of them joining with Northern forces or forming their own military units. Twenty-two of those soldiers and sailors received the Congressional Medal of Honor at the end of the war. After the Emancipation Proclamation, the Bureau of Colored Troops was initiated by the War Department.

Even after freedom was declared, the African-American was not granted the same rights as other Americans. The fight for those civil rights did not come to full fruition until the Reverend Martin Luther King led nonviolent protests in the late 1950s and early 1960s. It was his urging and contact with his people that encouraged them to cast their votes for President John F. Kennedy, the first time the black vote had been instrumental in getting anyone elected.

Art

As I have already mentioned, black Americans have contributed quite a bit to our culture. Their art and folk art are unequaled, in my opinion. Henry Ossawa Tanner and Joshua Johnson are at the top of my list of well-loved artists, and their works have made auction history several times. Slave quilts have finally been recognized and documented. In fact, an exhibition of thirty of them have been out on view at Renwick Gallery in Washington, DC. Pottery, such as grotesque jugs, was made by slaves working in the pottery industry, and we are now learning some of their names by studying the records kept by each company. But let me dally no longer and instead begin introducing you to some of the people who made the items about which I've spoken.

Most of the art produced by African-Americans during the early years of our country was that of unschooled artists. Even if a black artist showed a great deal of talent, the likelihood of his or her master fostering that talent was practically nil. Those artists who did produce works that were eventually sold or awarded prizes at exhibitions like the Philadelphia Centennial Exposition in 1876 worked in much the same manner as other artists of that time. There was no way you could tell whether the art you were viewing had been done by a black, white, red, or yellow person.

The art world was no easier on the African-American than on any other trade, and those who felt they needed to follow the calling often went to Europe. One such artist was Henry O. Tanner (1859–1937), whose religious paintings were a result of strong influence by European styles and artists. Tanner painted scenes of black American life (e.g., "The Banjo Lesson" and "Old Couple Looking at Portrait of Lincoln"), but they weren't appreciated in his own country until closer to the end of his life. Once settled in Europe, he refused to come back to America to start a school of black art because he never forgot the prejudice he encountered here.

Edmonia Lewis was born of a Chippewa Indian mother and a free black father in Albany, New York, in 1845. She was the first black woman sculptor in the United States and produced works such as "Old Indian Arrow Maker and Daughter," as well as busts of some of the best-known people of her time. She, like Tanner, found more acceptance in Europe, and she studied the neoclassical style in Rome until she died, in obscurity, in 1890.

The art produced in the 1920s and 1930s was a movement of black culture that has become known as the Harlem Renaissance. Artists, writers, musicians, and others were involved with this movement, which produced some of the finest works in this country's history. Artists working during this period included William Scott, Edwin A. Harleston, and many others. The Great Depression caused the disintegration of the group working together during the Renaissance, and black art began to take a different direction.

By the 1950s and 1960s, museums and art galleries that specialized in African-American art began springing up all over the country. Major shows were held later in the century, such as the Smithsonian's 1985 show entitled "Sharing Traditions: Five Black Artists in 19th Century America." Yet the prejudice continues, and only a few years ago there was a protest held in Boston because a major showing at the Museum of Fine Arts there neglected to include any works by black Americans.

For more in-depth biographies and information on black American artists, see *Collecting Black Americana* or any of the bibliographies of African-American artists available in your library's reference section.

Folk Art

Black folk artists make up more than half the number of known folk artists, though few are as recognized as they should be. It is only in recent history that portraits done by such artists as Joshua Johnson and William Matthew Prior have demanded high prices in the art market.

I define folk art as artistic work done by an untrained hand. In other words, folk art can be a painting done by an artist who has not gone to school to learn his or her craft, or it can be a quilt that defies normal quilting patterns or a piece of pottery made in freehand fashion to resemble something recognizable.

Family records, journals, and stories handed down through the ages have proved that the mistress of the house often taught her household slaves how to quilt. Such documented quilts are treasured by their owners, as they should be. Few of these examples were signed by the African-American women who made them until after the Emancipation Proclamation.

One would expect to see more black folk art with an African influence, but I think we don't because much of what was done early in our history was probably destroyed either by the slave's owner or during the pillage of the Civil War. Yet the quilts that have been unearthed and studied have shown Ashanti influences in the colors and patterns used, and the deep-rooted African belief in witchcraft and religion can be seen as an influence on some carvings and on grotesque pottery jugs from the South. Canes, carved by slaves as well as by free blacks, are said to have been an African craft, and gravestones embellished with animal figures were thought to drive away evil spirits.

Some important black American folk artists include Ulysses Davis (woodcarver), William Edmondson (limestone carver), Sister Gertrude Morgan (artist), Harriet Powers (quilter), and the ones I've already mentioned.

Ironwork

The black craftsperson monopolized all skilled trades and crafts until after 1830, especially in the South. The architectural ironwork that graces the buildings in New Orleans plantation homes, Georgia's elegant houses, and many others was the result of African-American workmanship.

Those workers were trained by white owners who may have come from Spain, Portugal, or France, and that influence shows in the lacy grilles, lunettes, and balconies that were made for their buildings.

Ironworkers often had early backgrounds as blacksmiths on southern plantations, where their main objective was to make tools, horseshoes, and iron necessities for the home. If such a blacksmith was sent to New Orleans or some other large southern city to work in the iron industry, his wages were sent back to his owner. Sometimes the slave ironworker was able to buy his freedom for a sum of approximately $500, which he could obtain by putting in overtime.

By the mid-1800s the ironwork done in the United States was secondary only to that made in England. The slaves who produced the work had found a way to release their artistic abilities by making attractive lawn furniture, railings for porches and balconies, doorstops, stoves, hitching posts, andirons, and matchsafes.

Kitchen Collectibles

(See "The Country Home" chapter)

Adirondack, Appalachian, and Ozark Country

CERTAIN CRAFTS came from the mountainous regions located on or near the eastern seaboard in the early years of our country. It wasn't until this century, though, that antiques collectors enjoyed the fruits of such work. Perhaps it was because the craftspeople who created the baskets, furniture, and folk art we treasure today really didn't consider their wares worthwhile. More likely it was because the items made in these regions just weren't used anywhere else.

In other sections of this book, I talk about other groups of country people who were responsible for giving us certain types of pottery or distinctive quilting. Yet we need to keep in mind that certain areas of the country were more active and produced more collectibles than others, which is the reason for this section.

Adirondack Country

The type of rustic, woodsy furniture and accessories that is labeled "Adirondack style" was not a hot collectible until the past five years or so. When country collectors decided the knobby, knotty chairs and tables looked comfortable in a log home parlor or on a Connecticut porch and that the furniture was reasonably priced as well as extremely durable, the rush was on. Certain dealers climbed on the bandwagon, specializing in the style, decorating magazines began showing it on their covers, and even clothing designers used the rustic furniture in their ads.

The furniture was the type of odd homemade stool, table, or chair that got chucked into the trash when you were cleaning out Aunt Harriet's cabin on the lake. But recently, the Museum of Our National Heritage in Lexington, Massachusetts, put together an exhibit entitled "Rustic Furniture" that explores the various types found all over the United States. Adirondack style had officially "arrived."

Misconceptions abound regarding Adirondack furniture simply because of the lack of written material on the subject. The slatted chair touted as "Adirondack" was never known to be made in that region—only the Westport chair, made by Henry C. Bunnell during the period from 1905–1925, was made in the Adirondacks.

The Westport chair does not resemble either the slatted furniture or the rustic twig furniture called "Adirondack." Instead, it is made of hemlock in large, tonguelike pieces, the back of the chair being only a little wider than the arms.

Though the rustic furniture we call Adirondack was not *made* in that area, it was, however, used quite extensively to decorate the camps and summer homes of the mountains and lakes in New York, as well as throughout the whole Appalachian chain.

The furniture made with mosaic twig decoration or of curved, knotty roots and branches is said to be in the Adirondack style and has brought upward of six figures at auctions in recent years. Certain dealers, such as Ralph Kylloe of Massachusetts, have earned reputations as specialists and experts in the area—a field that dealers would have scoffed at or laughed about thirty or forty years ago.

It is a style that reminds one of the nonconformist form that abounds in nature: the curved, knobby branches of trees, the natural woodsy colors, the feel and look of peeling bark—all contribute to making Adirondack furniture individualistic and unique. That is probably the reason the American public is having a love affair with the style: not one piece is exactly like another.

History

The area called Adirondack Country is located in the state of New York, stretching from the Vermont border in the east to Plattsburgh, New York, in the north to the center of New York State in the west (from Star Lake in the north almost to Utica in the south) and south almost to Sarasota Springs. A number of lakes are included in the region, such as Lake George, Indian Lake, Lower St. Regis, Tupper, Cranberry, and the Fulton Chain lakes. Once a favorite vacation area for New Yorkers, the Adirondacks are now home to quite a few lonely towns and empty guest cottages, but our history of this region goes back much farther than its heyday during the mid-twentieth century.

Originally settled by Indians and discovered by Samuel de Champlain, the Adirondacks were not explored in any great detail until the 1830s; in fact, they were not named until 1837. Once thoroughly explored, the area quickly developed between 1840 and 1880. Soon newly built hotels covered the once quiet mountains, its woods were hunted or stripped for timber, and the natural beauty of the range was ruined.

The Indians who originally inhabited the area were of several tribes—Iroquois, Mohawk, Algonquins, all members of the Five Nations. They were the first to use the trees native to the region to build canoes and dwellings, the first to hunt and fish the land in order to live, and the first to wage a battle on the land to keep it for their own use. Little did they realize they had set the trend for years to come. Even the word "Adirondack" is derivative of a term the Indians used for the mountains, a term that meant "They of the Great Rocks."

Today, a country collector may find objects such as snowshoes, canoes, arrowheads, and hunting tools made by these early tribes and reminiscent of the days before the white people used the wilderness for vacations.

In the mid- to late 1800s, prints of Adirondack country scenes were made in abundance by the now famous lithographing team of Currier & Ives. Prints drawn by such artists as Arthur Fitzwilliam Tait ("Sunrise on Lake Saranac," "Brook Trout Fishing") were first offered to the public for a dollar and now sell for several hundred.

The serenity of being close to nature drew poets such as Ralph Waldo Emerson, the French writer Viscount Chateaubriand, and Louis Agassiz in the late 1700s through the mid-1800s. A variety of works about the Adirondacks were published throughout the world as a result of their and other writers' visits.

Because the major businesses of the area were recreation-oriented or paper mills, a good deal of timber was removed from the Adirondack forests. Some of this timber found its way into vacation homes and hotels as furniture. Those pieces, dubbed "Adirondack furniture," are enjoying a revival of sorts today as country collectors add them to the primitive pieces that decorate their homes.

Baskets, also a by-product of those huge fallen trees, were made for personal use or for the tourist trade and are considered highly collectible in today's market.

Style

The rustic style had its origins in England, where twiggy garden furniture enjoyed popularity during the first half of the nineteenth century. The English stole the idea for rustic furniture from the Chinese, who were enamored of twiggy furniture for many hundreds of years.

Chairs, lounges, tables, gazebos, and lawn furniture were soon produced for England's summerhouses, and books (e.g., *Book of the Garden* by Charles McIntosh, 1853, and *On Planting and Rural Ornament* by William Marshall, 1786) touted the furniture made directly from trees and following the natural shape of boughs and branches.

Those carpenters who made the early examples of rustic furniture are not ones who were recognized for their talent; thus, there is little written information about them. The knack it took to design rustic furniture had little to do with the craftsperson, relying instead on the bend of a branch or a curious overgrowth on the trunk of a tree.

Twisted laurel and rhododendron were used by southern resorts in North Carolina and Virginia that featured rustic furniture. Those makers also used willow and hickory when creating a piece. One must remember that furniture makers, especially ones who worked with unfinished materials like these, worked with whatever woods were common to the region in which they lived.

Mosaic twig work, the type of construction that required split rods formed into patterns, first became popular during the early 1830s, when gardening magazines showed outdoor shelters covered in that fashion. This was the area in which Adirondack craftspeople excelled.

The garden was the spot where early rustic furniture first appeared, giving strollers a place to sit and get shelter from rain, wind, or sun. Public parks also were advocates of the designs, offering benches and gazebos as decorative accents that blended well with bucolic surroundings.

In the Adirondacks, vacation camps and lodges that utilized the basic rustic premise were springing up. The Hornby Lodge (constructed in 1837–38) above the Genessee River in New York was an octagonal building designed to surround a giant oak tree that poked through the center of its roof. The tree's branches and boughs were left to wander through the rooms, which were filled with furniture made from branches.

Wealthy vacationers filled their summer Adirondack homes with such furniture, almost as a whim, to bring the splendor of the mountains and forest as close as possible.

More and more Americans began to filter into remote areas after the Civil War. They needed an escape, a retreat from the world where they could spend summer vacations among the pines, listening to the lapping lake water against the shore. The Adirondacks became "the place to be."

In the late 1800s, state and national parks were established, and rustic furniture enjoyed a resurgence of popularity. Hickory wood was widely used for this purpose, because of both its strength and its odd, crooked shapes. Well-known public figures such as Jon Burroughs, Natale Curtis, and William S. Wicks did much to encourage interest in Adirondack cottages, log cabins, and the relaxing country life.

Though hickory furniture was made by a few shops in Indiana and sold through mail-order catalogs, the best rustic furniture was still made by men who had little formal training. Most pieces were one of a kind, which is the reason why some dealers term the furniture "folk art."

The interiors of log cabins, shanties, or guest camps scattered throughout the Adirondacks had basically the same features: deer racks, snowshoes, fishing gear, and rifles lined the walls; furniture made of tree trunks and branches served as places to sit, eat, and sleep; and the most colorful accents were fresh wildflowers, rather than paintings or photographs. Surprisingly, these rustic settings attracted intellectuals, members of the wealthy society set and people with an artistic bent.

People and Craftspeople

Some of the people remembered as being responsible for opening the area to tourists and building hotels or lodges which would accommodate them included the following:

William West Durant, son of Dr. Thomas Clark Durant, who was a major force in building the American West's railroads, built some of the great camps of the Adirondacks. His empire was constructed during the late 1800s and attracted wealthy buyers when he decided to sell his lodges one by one before the turn of the century. His camps on Raquette Lake were furnished with more rustic furniture than the other camps elsewhere in the Adirondacks and were photographed by the well-known artist/photographer Edward Bierstadt during the late 1880s.

William L. Coulter was responsible for introducing peeled-pole furniture in his camps during the late 1890s. Coulter, an architect, was hired by Alfred G. Vanderbilt to design a recreation building to be added to the building he had bought from William West Durant. Coulter's architectural firm, founded at Saranac Lake, lasted even after his death in 1907 and is credited with designing compounds for a number of wealthy New Yorkers.

Robert H. Robertson's talents as an architect were supplemented by his skill as a watercolorist. He designed Nahasane and Santanoni, two well-known and architecturally impressive Adirondack lodges. Robertson used timbered ceilings, massive stone fireplaces, and ceilings covered in birch bark in his lodges, making them memorable and unique, to say the least.

Through the efforts of these and other inventive architects, the rustic style evolved into a more exotic state, which soon included walls covered with animal skins, stuffed animals, and more intricately designed accoutrements, though the style retained its rustic flavor.

The Adirondack Museum showcases the best designs made during the Adirondack heyday, though many unique pieces are available through dealers and auctions for the country collector's pleasure.

The most amazing thing about Adirondack furniture is that it was never designed to be aesthetically pleasing but to be useful, to suit a purpose. Items were made because they *needed* to be made, and they were *used,* not just hung on a wall or stuck in a corner for decorative purposes.

Yellow birch was the wood favored by most makers of camp furniture because of its iridescence, silky feel, strength, and the fact that the bark adhered to the branch indefinitely. Other types of wood, such as hickory and white birch, also were used—hickory by the Indiana furniture makers and white birch less often because it had a tendency to get soft.

Makers of Adirondack furniture who have memorable styles and are identifiable include Ernest Stowe, who made furniture in Upper Saranac Lake, New York, during the period from 1900 to approximately 1911. Stowe's Adirondack dining room table and twelve chairs sold at a December 1986 auction for $45,000. He used yellow birch and often applied white birch bark to the piece as a decorative finish.

In the Keene Valley of New York, rustic cedar settees and chairs were made by Perry Sleeper, Albert Jaques, and Warren Webb during the early 1900s. The Rustique Work Manufacturing Company in Niagara Falls, New York, also used cedar to produce chairs, tables, boxes, and planters. At this point, it should be noted that, though there were Adirondack builders producing furniture, the workers could not keep up with the demand, so companies in other parts of the country began to take up the slack.

Roots and burls from yellow birch and maples were used for tabletops (one of the largest was made for Kamp Kill Kare at Lake Kora) and made some of the most interesting pieces of furniture to come from the Adirondacks. Table bases were often made from interesting tree roots. The roots were cut by putting the stump into a sap basin full of water and cutting the roots at the waterline.

Less rustic furniture was made from peeled poles and

branches, which were stained and waxed, producing a more formal effect and furniture that was less likely to catch dust. William West Durant, owner of Camp Uncas, Camp Pine Knot (on Raquette Lake), and Sagamore Lodge was one of the first to use this type of Adirondack furniture at his camps. His stain was a secret formula of which only he and Cottier & Co. in New York knew the ingredients.

Other camp owners followed Durant's lead, bringing a whole new look to the Adirondack style. The camps' woodsy look were often broken up by bright splashes of color on the walls (Indian artifacts) and floors (Oriental, American Indian, and fur rugs). This style continued to be used from the early teens through the early 1940s.

Applied-bark pieces were made by Ernest Stowe, D. Savage of Saranac Lake, and Joseph Bryere of Raquette Lake from the late 1890s to the early 1900s. Spruce bark was most commonly used because yellow birch split and curled as it dried. Frames were among the items most often decorated with applied bark, and some of them were additionally festooned with branches or cedar trim.

Mosaic twig work (or what collectors have referred to as tramp art) was the most ambitious kind of decorative accent for Adirondack furniture. Made during the late 1880s and 1890s, furniture of this type called for regular, straight twigs to be nailed to the flat surface of the wood in elaborate geometric patterns. Because the worker had to group twigs by size and color, no two pieces of this type of furniture are exactly alike.

Adirondack chairs, the classic lawn chair with slanted, slatted back and seat and flat wide arms, has never been proved to have come from the Adirondacks. The design appears to have come from the Westport chair designed by Thomas Lee around 1900, which continued in popularity from the 1920s through World War II.

Harry Bunnell of Westport bought the design for the chair from Lee, filed a patent for the chair on April 4, 1904, and continued to make new and different versions from then through the 1920s. To this day, there are companies producing versions of the chair.

Appalachian Country

The Appalachian Highlands are the general descriptive term for the regions of the Appalachian Plateau, Ridge and Valley, Blue Ridge, and Piedmont. The mountains themselves stretch from the Gaspé Peninsula in Quebec 1,200 miles south to central Alabama. Appalachia's boundaries cover 55,000 square miles, and more than 8.6 million people currently live in the area.

Almost all Appalachians were born and raised there, as were their parents and grandparents before them. Most (93%) are white, 6 percent are black, and 1 percent are Native American. The majority of the minorities in the area live in industrial cities and towns.

The coal industry is what occupies most of these people. Seventy-four percent of the residents have received some kind of federal aid during the last decade, and the average income for over 90 percent of Appalachia's residents is below $10,000 per year.

The first to settle in the Appalachians were hearty German and Scotch-Irish immigrants who came to the area through Pennsylvania. Passage to the west was afforded these first settlers through the many spacious water gaps through the central Appalachians. In fact, Daniel Boone was responsible for forging the route through the Cumberland Gap, and other routes led through central Appalachia during the period of the French and Indian War (1756–1763). Despite these traveling routes, some parts of Appalachia remained fairly isolated, and the people who lived there developed a distinguishing culture with handicrafts, music, and folklore that are intrinsically their own.

The Appalachian region has produced quality artisans and crafts that are highly desirable in today's country home. Knowing the people who live in this mountainous region helps us to better understand the items they have produced.

Religion is of extreme importance to the people of Appalachia, as we have seen with other country groups. For years, barns in that region sported signs like "Get Right with God," and the majority of the folks who live and work in the area are Baptists or

Methodists—Protestants with a distinct idea of what God expects from them.

The men in the family worked their spare plots of land with sturdy horses, often animals that had been rejected from the U.S. Army. The women did the gardening, milking, cooking, cleaning, canning, and mending. They were also responsible for "getting religion" for the children by reading the Bible to them on a nightly basis.

There are legends about mountain violence and "hard-drinkin' men" who dipped into the illegal stores of moonshine more often than they should have. As a people, the Appalachian folk are stereotyped, and, as we all know, stereotypes are never fair nor true. But stories passed down through families tell of folk medicine, faith healers, and feuding that give rise to larger-than-life characters.

The land is full of contrasts, as are the people. The mountains are bored through with hundreds of coal mines, yet crystal-clear springs run rampant through green valleys. Folk medicine works next to computer science, illiterate people are closely related to those with doctorate degrees, religious men sit next to snake handlers, and basketmakers have surgeons as devoted customers. The final result of these contrasts is a closely knit group of people who are more likely to defend their self-worth and to demand respect for themselves and their values than many other country groups we have already met.

The old ways are important to this strong segment of American people, and they keep them alive by passing many tales down through the generations. Stories of how a man stripped an elm tree so that his wife could make baskets are as important as the reports of how an herb doctor made special mixtures of sassafras, slippery elm, and bitters.

Arts and Crafts

Baskets are made by the women of the region and have been sold at makeshift roadside stands since before the Depression. They were typically farm or storage baskets, more thoroughly described in The Country Market chapter.

The most interesting item indigenous to the area is the dulcimer. A stringed instrument whose strings are beaten with small hammers instead of strummed like a guitar, the dulcimer was introduced to Europe from Persia in about the fifteenth century. The American dulcimer, or mountain zither, has three or four strings running over a fretted fingerboard, while the European version had two or more. (More information about the dulcimer/zither is offered in other parts of this book.)

Ozark Country

The Ozark Mountains stretch in a general southwesterly direction from St. Louis, Missouri, to the Arkansas River, occupying an area of approximately 50,000 square miles. The majority of that area is within Missouri and Arkansas, with the remainder in southern Illinois and southeastern Kansas. They are the only mountainous region between the Appalachians and the Rockies.

In the novel *The Shepherd of the Hills* (1907), Harold Bell Wright romanticized the Missouri Ozarks, telling of their streams and springs, the people who lived there, and the life they had. Today tourism is the region's chief industry.

The Ozarks were originally home to such Indian tribes as the Quapaw, Osage, Caddo, Cherokee, Choctaw, and Missouri. This diverse group left their mounds and other marks of civilization throughout the area when statehood caused Arkansas to withdraw the tribes' land titles. States in this mountainous area were slave states until the Kansas-Nebraska Act of 1854 set slave states and free states at each other's throats.

The region is rich in natural resources such as minerals, hydroelectric power, timber, and farming. Manufacturing and agriculture are the most common resources, with tourism coming a close third.

Arkansas's folk arts are a matter of state pride, and some of the country's richest contributions have come from this area. The Mountain View area of the state is considered a major folk art center with artisans in fields such as ceramics, wood carving, rug hooking, and basketry coming to display and sell their works.

Missouri also encourages their folk artists, treasuring the folk traditions, tales, and ballads that abound in the area. The crafts once practiced by natives out of necessity are now flourishing because collectors have recognized the merit of such objects. The Missouri Federation of Arts and Crafts encourages the development of such Ozark crafts as weaving, basketmaking, and pottery. (Check other sections of this book for more information on these subjects.)

Southwest Country

IT WASN'T UNTIL RECENTLY that the "Spanish-Southwest look" was incorporated into the country designs that Americans have been so fond of for the past ten to twelve years. Perhaps it is because the work done in that part of the United States was largely religious, and the furniture had a rough-hewn, dark look that didn't fit in with colonial blues and reds. However, the bright oranges, yellows, and reds used by the Spanish carvers of painted figures and religious scenes and repeated in weavings done by these peoples look wonderful against a whitewashed wall.

History

The Spanish settlements were among the first permanent ones in that part of the United States now called Texas, New Mexico, and Arizona. However, you will find that most items date from 1700 to the present, with the most interesting pieces of folk art being made during the early 1800s (Mexico became independent from Spain in 1821, isolating New Mexico).

Religious paintings, altars, and vestments were often brought in by wagon from Mexico City. Other than those items, the new Spanish settlers were pretty self-sufficient.

Arts and Crafts

As is evident from studying the items they produced, the style of the craftspeople and primitive artists of the Southwest was very similar to that of their Spanish ancestors. Even the names they used for their artistic works are the same: *santos,* images of saints;

retablos, paintings on board made with earth and vegetable pigments; *bultos*, round carvings of saints.

Most *santos* were made prior to 1850 because reforms in 1851 forbade the images from being included in church decoration; they were said to be pagan. The majority are signed and undated.

The Spanish, like the Indians with whom they shared the Southwest, traded with easterners, who brought such things as cloth, mirrors, ribbons, and religious chromolithographs. After the railroad was built in the 1880s, items such as the ones mentioned were in abundance, and new settlers also flooded the area. Little did the Yankee settlers realize that both the land and its people were extremely poor. Homes and churches were adobe, buildings made of clay that, though cool, were relatively unattractive and not lined with gold artifacts as were their Spanish counterparts.

Today, many of those early New Mexico adobe missions are disintegrating from lack of care and an overabundance of rain—adobe is mud, hard as a rock when dry but regaining its soft, muddy texture when it becomes too wet. Historical societies and one Catholic priest are attempting to save these antique churches, but it is not likely that they will be able to do so without help from citizens who care about retaining our American heritage.

Furniture and Household Goods

Furniture was made from every kind of wood available, cottonwood and pine being the most abundant. The carvings on chests, bureaus, tables, and chairs were fanciful flowers, geometric designs, stars, and suns. Decorative accents most commonly used included items made from leather, one of the few materials available to poor rancheros.

The most important piece of furniture was the *trastero*, which was a large, heavy cupboard. A box on legs was used to store grain off the floor, away from hungry mice. A chest for clothes and a hanging shelf would complete the furniture in most New Mexican households. Beds were not used until after the Civil War.

New Mexican cupboards are very similar to those made in Mexico or Spain in that they often have raised-panel doors and sides, two long doors instead of two on top and two on bottom (as with New England cupboards), and European-style hinges.

Pie safes, with screened doors, were commonly used throughout Texas and the Southwest. Some safes had punched-tin doors, while others used cheesecloth on the door panels (these were called milk safes because they were used to store pans of fresh milk while the cream separated).They are not as recognizable as their midwestern cousins, but they are collectible and sometimes cheaper.

Texan pie safes were used to store meat and baked goods. They were normally placed in the kitchen or on the back porch and were made of pine, though a few made of walnut are known.

Because wood was readily available, it was used to make spoons, bowls, shovels, spinning wheels, candlestands, and many other utensils used around the home. Early in the nineteenth century, after the Santa Fe trail was established, the colonists started using tin, making chandeliers, candelabra, religious crosses, mirror frames, and many more items.

As in other country homes, family life revolved around a fireplace or outdoor oven, where simple meals, usually consisting of grains, beans, and breads, were cooked. The women would also use that area to do their spinning and weaving, producing blankets and homespun for bedcovers and clothing.

One of the types of blankets made was the Rio Grande, a lightweight, loosely woven blanket with soft, pleasing colors. They were not the same as the ones the Amerinds wove during the same period. One major difference between Spanish-American blankets and Amerind designs is that the Southwestern Spanish used a serape style, with an opening in the center of the blanket so that its user could slip it over his or her head.

The colors used could be broad and narrow bands of brown, cream, and indigo blue. Colors like yellow, green, and bayeta red were used sparingly, whereas the Native Americans used red quite frequently.

The settlers stopped doing this type of weaving in the late 1800s, though there was a rival in the mid-1900s.

Like most country cultures, the objects made by Southwestern colonists were used every day and were often worn out in the process. However, the collector who wants to add a few pieces of Southwestern artifacts to his or her home would be well satisfied with a trip to that part of the United States, both for the ease in buying once there and for the education one might get.

Homes

Sod houses were common throughout the Plains states and the Southwest when those areas were first settled. Their construction was simple, yet the houses were warm in winter and cool in summer. Made out of the materials at hand (long grasses and mud), their walls were up to seven feet deep. Windows were few because it was difficult to prepare the space needed for them.

If there *were* windows in a sod house, they were deeply set one-sash windows whose sills were large enough to hold several house plants. The lintels, casings, and sills were cut from saplings, which were often at a premium in that arid, windswept area of the country. Curtains might be made of newspapers or grocery wrapping paper.

Roof were either grass and sod or a woven layer of willows, prairie hay, and corn stalks. Occasionally, a family was wealthy enough to afford a roof made of store-bought lumber and tar paper, but that was the exception to the rule.

Sometimes the interior walls were plastered with a mixture of native clay and sand. The walls were when whitewashed, making for a cleaner, less somber interior.

The best thing about a sod house was that it lasted as long as the family wanted it to, and there was no mortgage to pay.

The adobe homes that inhabit the arid, brown stretches of New Mexico and Arizona are likely to be whitewashed inside, giving the collector the perfect background for country antiques. A typical Southwesterner's home may be the showcase for an antique weaving loom from the Española region of New Mexico.

Or the mantel above the fireplace (*kiva*) in the living room may be filled with pottery figures or storyteller figurines made by Native Americans (more information about them appears in the Native American section of this chapter). Handwoven woolen carpets (*jergas*) may share floor space with Navajo rugs, and antique Spanish-American architectural pieces may vie for wall attention with sand paintings done by contemporary Amerind artists.

Hutterite and Quaker Country

Hutterite Country Arts and History

SKILLED IN MANY ARTS AND CRAFTS, the Hutterians were known for their knife-making capabilities, the fine quality of bindings on their books, and for being wool weavers of the highest regard. Also within their talents was the making of pottery, and their wares were often compared to those of Italian and Dutch potters.

A young female child might have been taught tole painting, spinning, and various types of needlework. Hutterite samplers are well done and artistically rendered.

Boys might have been brought into the furniture-making profession by their father, grandfather, or uncle. Gifts, like beautifully carved spinning wheels or rolling pins with the name of a mother or sister inlaid in the wood, have been passed down from generation to generation.

Like other country religious sects, the Hutterites are almost immune to worldly influences and carry on their artistic heritage by following the traditions of generations before them. Their works are designed to be useful, pride being considered an expression of vanity.

In the Hutterite communal home, women stocked the kitchen with vegetables and fruits grown in their gardens. Unlike the Amish, Hutterians use electric stoves, mixers, and the like. The women are also responsible for making all of the clothes for the family, spinning the wool, and knitting socks and sweaters.

Hutterites, or the Hutterian brethren, originated in Central Europe during the period known as the Reformation. They were part of the sixteenth-century movement of the evangelical Anabaptists until they separated into a group led by Jacob Huter in 1533. This group was responsible for developing the type of communal living that came to be called "Christian communism." Their communal style of living remained constant for 425 years, a true phenomenon unique in religious, social, and political history.

The Hutterites came to the United States during the 1870s and settled in the Dakota Territory. Because of the persecution they experienced in Europe, they had wandered around quite a bit; and by the time they reached North America, they numbered only a few hundred.

Once the Hutterite colonies were fully established in the Dakotas, Montana, and other states in the Dakota Territory, it became clear that their self-sufficient way of life and economy made them an asset to their communities. They cooperated with the government, paid their taxes on time, cooperated with schools and teachers, and were considered honorable businesspeople.

By the mid-twentieth century, it was estimated there were approximately ten thousand Hutterian people in North America, mostly located in Northwestern states and Canada in Hutterite Bruderhofe.

Studies of the Hutterite civilization have attempted to discern how their communities exist, to understand the deep Christian foundation on which their religion is based and from which it has grown. Those studies have revealed the fact that Hutterites are a simple peasant people who are entirely unsympathetic to civilization as it developed since the Reformation and Renaissance periods.

They adopted a radical Biblicist outlook in which they compared the world as described in the Bible to the "outside world" or civilization as a whole. The writings of early as well as modern Hutterites describe how they obey the Holy Scriptures to the letter, without any deviations, as they understand them. Prominent in their beliefs are brotherly love, following God's rules, and obedience to the Commandments.

Now there are more than a hundred cluster-type colonies (Bruderhofe) in North America, and the Brethren number approximately fifteen thousand.

Like other groups we've spoken about in this section, Hutterites are conscientious objectors to war, retain their old ways of dress and living, and have kept their Tyrolean dialect alive, although they also use English and German frequently. In fact, they have had close ties with the Mennonites, having spent thirty years with them in Russia, learning from them the agricultural skills that helped them to survive on the American prairies and even intermarrying with some Mennonite families.

Quaker Country Arts and History

We have been the recipients of the pleasure Quaker arts and crafts offer to the world through their writers, artists, and artisans for hundreds of years. Because they are so highly educated and take pride in their schooling, most Quakers are very articulate human beings.

Quaker authors include William Penn *(Some Fruits of Solitude,* 1693) and George Fox *(The Great Mistery of the Great Whore,* 1659), as well as many others. Journals were written by such leaders as John Woolman and John Wesley, John Rowntree, Rufus Jones (the most prolific of Quaker writers), Hannah Whitall Smith (the first Quaker to write devotional literature for the general public), Thomas R. Kelly (the outstanding twentieth-century devotional writer), Douglas V. Steere of Haverford College, and John Greenleaf Whitter, the poet. Others, such as Walt Whitman, were strongly influenced by Quakerism, which comes through in the imagery and language used in their writing.

All music was unacceptable to the Quakers, especially "fiddling," which was considered the worst because it was associated with dancing. For almost two hundred years, this practice was continued, though nowadays it has changed, and the majority of Quakers (Members of the Society of Friends) have musical instruments in their places of worship as well as at home.

Quakers did not sing, play musical instruments, dress in any bright colors, have pictures in their homes, or use fancy language. Their lives were simple and plain, enlivened only by books, words, and thoughts of spirituality.

Art was not as strictly regulated as music in the Quaker culture. Thus, there are some extremely well known artists who have come from within the Society of Friends.

Benjamin West (1738–1820), who was born in Pennsylvania, spent most of his life in England and was buried there. He is famous for the painting entitled "Penn's Treaty with the Indians."

Edward Hicks, a primitive artist whose style resembles that of Grandma Moses, is one of the painters whom most country collectors instantly recognize. His paintings have graced wall calendars, greeting cards, and stationery; a collection of his works hangs in the Abby Aldrich Rockefeller Collection in Williamsburg, Virginia.

Quakerism has passed through four distinct periods: the heroic or apostolic period (1650–1700), the period of cultural creativeness (1700–1800), the period of conflict and decline (1800–1900), and the period of modernism (1900–present).

The first period was marked by a strong spiritual inwardness, as well as a zeal to spread their beliefs. Both of these motives met with strong opposition by church and state, making it difficult for the Quaker people to live as they believed they should.

It was difficult for Quakers to get to America because some shipmasters were given strict penalties if they brought Quakers across the ocean. Because of this, a group of eleven Friends sailed their own small vessel to the New World.

This period in history was an active time that produced a great deal of printed material to support and spread Quakerism.

The next period in the history of the Society of Friends (the period of cultural creativeness and mystical inwardness) is referred to by historians as the period of Quietism, when the initial fervor had become subdued and it became time for the religion to enter the home as well as the public square.

During this time, the Quakers governed three American colonies and were politically active in two others. Though the Friends had weathered a number of storms, they still had to endure the trial brought about by the Toleration Act of 1689 in England. Quite a few of their leaders died, some in prison, and a new generation of spiritual leaders was coming forth, a quieter, more pragmatic group of people, whose main interest was in setting up their society in their new world, America.

Between 1700 and 1740, the Golden Age of Quakerism was felt in America. The Friends were at home in Philadelphia, building a strong community and becoming involved in community affairs. Their communities always revolved around the meeting hall and included a library and a school. They looked after their poor, dealt with issues of morality, performed their own marriages and baptisms.

The Book of Extracts was their charter of community life and was used to record changing moral insights. The emphasis of Quakerism was on life in the home, meeting, and community.

During those turbulent years (and for some time after), the Quakers diligently worked to preserve and/or defend the rights of American Indians and Negroes. Quaker homes were often a refuge for escaping slaves who were on their way through the Underground Railroad, and in this respect, as well as many others, Quakers used their religious strength to work to abolish slavery.

In the Society itself, there were many changes during the latter 1700s. Some members, concerned about those who had become wealthy, voiced their thoughts about maintaining simplicity within the Society. By the beginning of the nineteenth century, the Quakers were at their maximum number.

During the period of conflict between mysticism and evangelicalism, a rift arose, and the result was that the elders held onto the traditions of keeping "plainness in dress, speech and behavior."

The conflict between the regular members of the Society and the elders came into play when the elders tried to become guardians of theological opinions. Those who were opposed to such dictatorial actions were inclined to believe in the mystical side of Quakerism. The split began in Philadelphia in 1827 and resulted in separation of the city and country factions of the religion.

By the second half of the nineteenth century, there were three kinds of Quakers: the Hicksites were mystical, liberal, and non-creedal; the Gurneyites were more evangelical, authoritative, and conservative; and the Wilburites were a little bit of each.

Today, the modern Quakers have, for the most part, given up revivalism; most of the Quaker leaders are college-educated, and many have dealt with other aspects of Quakerism. There has been a growth in rationalism and humanitarianism, causing the Friends to be concerned with improving world living conditions. The Quakers strive to combine their mystical, evangelical, nationalist, and humanitarian aspects in order to continue to be of service to others.

Prices

If an item is not indicated as being specifically Shaker, Indian, Amish, etc., then it should be considered strictly a "country" piece. For items specifically made by the country groups spoken of in the first section of this book, consult that chapter.

ADIRONDACK

Rocking chair, made of willow branches in curvilinear design, comb back. *$280–$380*

Rocking chair, made of deer antlers, seat of velvet, mid-19th century. *$3,500–$4,000*

Twig plant stand, painted top. *$190–$230*

Courtesy of Marjorie Staufer; photo by Donald Vogt.

AMISH

Children's large doll, Kentucky, green and brown smock/dress. *$150–$250*

Small doll, Indiana, blue apron and dress. *$150–$250*

Child's chair, early New England, ca. 1790, traces of old paint. *$225–$275*

Courtesy of Eileen Russell, Worthington, Ohio; photo by Donald Vogt.

Children's clothing, handmade wool stocking with initials (left), black with red, yellow, orange, blue ribbing. *$110–$125*

(Middle) *stockings,* tan, factory-made, children's size 6½. *$$8–$10*

(Right) *Amish stockings* with feet cut out to make leggings. *$98–$110*

Courtesy of Mary-Lee Muntz, Bonneyville Knoll Antiques, Middlebury, Indiana:, photo by Donald Vogt.

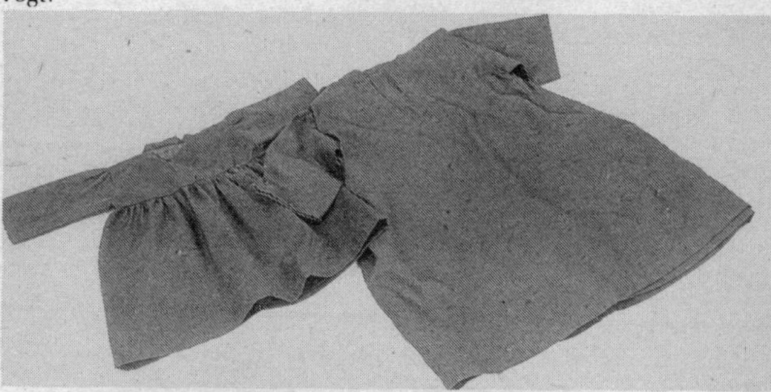

Clothing, dresses and aprons, ca. early 1900s:

Dress, navy blue cotton. *$20–$22*

Medium two-piece with matching apron. *$30–$35*

Crib quilt, 1920, hand-quilted, blues, lavender, green, fans are on black with mauve and pink borders; blue binding; blue backing, made by Mary Beachy (1893–1977) for first son, Abraham (she had 7 children), shell, clamshell, leaf, straight-line quilting, 10 stitches/inch, feather stitching around fans, 44″ × 54″.
$2,600–$3,000

Crib quilt, 9-Patch design. *$1,100–$1,400*

Courtesy of Mary-Lee Muntz, Bonneyville Knoll Antiques, Middlebury, Indiana; photo by Donald Vogt.

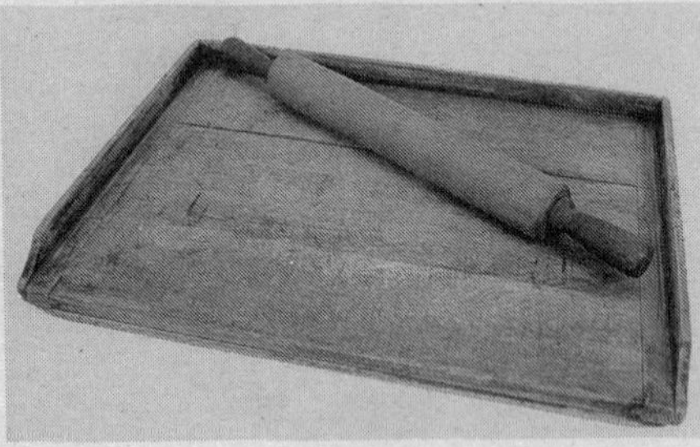

Dough board, pine, gallery on 3 sides, front lip, ca. 1870.
$45–$55

Rolling pin, for heavy dough and pastry, maple with walnut handles, ca. 1880. *$18–$20*

Courtesy of Mary-Lee Muntz, Bonneyville Knoll Antiques, Middlebury, Indiana; photo by Donald Vogt.

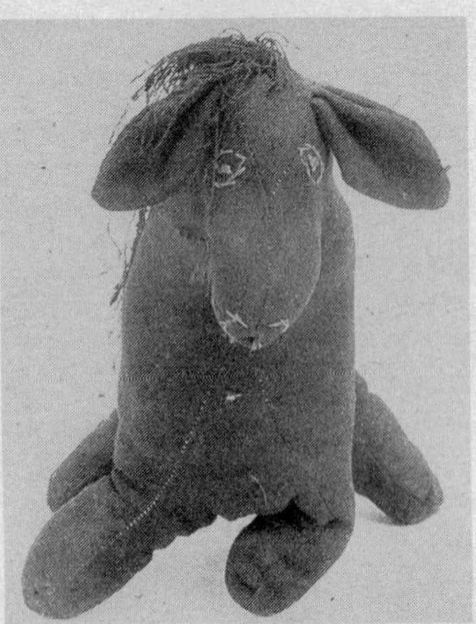

Horse, stuffed, of black wool with embroidered eyes, ca. 1900. ***$35–$45***

Quilt, early 1900s, hand-pieced and hand-quilted, blues/black/lavenders/green, Crown of Thorns pattern, made in Portland, Indiana, by Anna Gingrich (died in 1920), vining leaf and acorn, rope, tulips, square quilting, 9 stitches/inch; 67″ × 80″, blue backing. ***$1,575–$1,650***

Quilt, six-pointed star, Ohio, 20th century, light and dark blue on black ground, 66″ × 74″. ***$3,500–$4,000***

Quilt, variation of 9-Patch, bought in central Ohio, black, red, blue, green, and brown, one stain, excellent condition, 1880–1990s, 80″ × 78″. ***$350–$400***

Quilt, blue, lavender, pink, faded single size, ca. 1900, Bow Tie pattern. ***$150–$175***

Woman's black wool cape with scalloped capelet and matching bonnet, ca. late 1800s. ***$55–$85***

Black

Bank, "Jolly Nigger" cast iron, repainted, bottom plate missing, ca. 19th century. ***$165–$200***

Embroidery, framed, depicting a black family drinking champagne, 20″ × 20″, some staining, late 19th/early 20th centuries. ***$500–$600***

Courtesy of the Keeping Room, Camby, Indiana; photo by Donald Vogt.

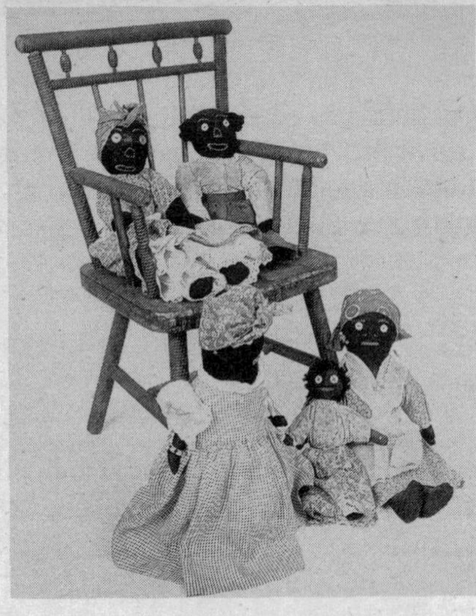

Group of black rag dolls on spool child's chair.

Late 1800s, sock dolls, man and wife. *$250–$300*

Child's chair, spool. *$75–$110*

Little doll (by leg of chair). *$60–$80*

Woman with red kerchief. *$85–$100*

Bottle doll (left) with red gingham dress. *$125–$150*

Group of black dolls, ca. 1900–30.

Doorstop doll. *$65–$90*

Toaster doll with painted face. *$65–$95*

Hand-stitched toaster doll, light tan. *$95–$125*

Doll with hand-stitched body and legs. *$75–$100*

Bell doll. *$35–$55*

Hitching posts, paid of cast-iron jockeys, two black boys in green vests, white shirts, and brown pants with matching hats standing on pedestals, paint 80%, 38″ high, 19th century. *$1,200–$1,500*

Minstrel show poster, rare, hand-painted, executed by Earle Pierce, 1911, 24″ × 14″, early 20th century. *$200–$250*

Painting, Pedro Tovookan Parris, tree, done in watercolor on paper, ca. 1855–60. *$1,100–$1,250*

Portrait, Pedro Tovookan Parris with Billie Barnes, slaves, 6th-plate ambrotype in metal mount, paper seals intact, picturing Pedro (right) and Billie Barnes, who was with Pedro on the slave ship when it was taken into custody, Billie was given into employment of the U.S. marshall of Massachusetts, named Barnes, and was given his name (copies of documentations accompany image). *$1,150–$1,250*

Portrait, Pedro the Slave holding a large chopping ax, dressed in shirt, jacket, overcoat, 6th-plate ambrotype in original metal mount, the paper seals untouched and intact (accompanied by history, documentations). *$1,150–$1,250*

Rag doll, reversible, painted faces and colorful red print and yellow calico dress, one face black, one face white, 16″ high. *$215–$300*

Rag doll, gentleman with striped leggings and jacket, carved wooden head and jaunty hat. *$1,200–$1,500*

Indian

Basket, California Chumash, treasure, 12″ diameter, finely woven in natural and dyed black rush over a golden sumac ground. *$14,000–$15,000*

Basket, Hopi, Oraibi wicker tray, 13″ wide, woven in multicolor design typical of the Third Mesa, along with smaller tray 7¼″ wide. *$50–$75*

Basketry, bowl, California Mission, globular form woven in juncus grasses in a variegated finish, forming a design of three 8-pointed stars set with 3 quatrefoils, 6″ diameter, very good condition. *$220–$275*

Beaded cloth shoulder bag, Seminole. *$44,000–$45,000*

Beaded cuffs, Cheyenne, 19th century, rawhide with green (worn) trade fabric edging, entire surface covered with geometric-design beadwork, white background, triangles, chevrons, and squares in orange, dark and cobalt blues, pale green, and dusty pink, sinew and thread stitching, no bead loss. *$145–$200*

Blanket, Navajo Germantown, woven on bright red ground with natural white, teal green, and lavender gray Germantown yarns in a pattern of zigzag chevrons in counterpoint, 30″ × 50″, tightly woven, fine condition. *$1,650–$2,000*

Blanket, Rio Grande wedding or utility, ca. 1885, tightly woven in single-ply hand-spun Rambouillet-Merino fleece wool on a 4-ply cotton warp in two widths seamed at the center, forming a traditional pattern of broad and narrow stripes in deep indigo blue, natural undyed white, and a yellow ochre (gold) from rabbit-brush dyes, striped pattern overembroidered with wool yarn geometrics, giving an overall design disguising the stripes, 86″ long, 45½″ wide, very good condition. *$600–$800*

Blanket, Navajo, Third Phase Chief's design, ca. 1880, unusual for dazzle-design borders. *$16,000–$18,000*

Bowl, Cochita, ca. 1900, white slip and black paint in form of clouds, lightning, and rain depicted with geometric forms, some pitting and wear. *$55–$75*

Bowl, Hopi, bundle coil, woven in brown, mahogany, and natural grass tones, 6½″ diameter, 4″ high, worked in a geometric pattern overall. *$50–$75*

Bowl, Zia, polychrome, red clay with tan slip, rust and black decoration, ca. 1900–30, 5″ diameter, 2½″ high, fine condition. *$70–$120*

Bowl, Zuni, polychrome, natural clay with white slip, black and rust red decoration, blackish smudged spot that could be a fire-cloud or thumbprint signature, 4″ diameter, 3¾″ high. *$40–$70*

Bowl, Northwest Coast, wood, early and rare, with otter-type figure as its model, otter lying on back, all four paws show on sides of bowl (which is otter's upturned belly). *$111,000–$115,000*

Card Pouch, Sioux, beaded, ration, hide fringe, flap pocket in hide with sinew stitching, a U.S. Indian Service brass button closure, front surface panel completely covered in small seed beads in deep red, brown, yellow geometric Cross and Diamond pattern, very good condition. *$275–$325*

Doll, Navajo, female figure, sewn dress, velour skirt, bead necklace, painted rag face, body, tin metal concho belt, 8″ high, no head bandanna, ca. 1900, also 3 modern hand-sewn Seminole fabric dolls. ***$35–$50***

Herb basket, made by Michigan Indians. ***$250–$300***

Lithograph, hand-colored, Indian print by "Lehman and Duval" (published by Key & Biddle, Philadelphia, 1836), "Waa-Pa-Shaw, Sioux Chief," minor stains, foxing and type stains from facing page, framed, 15″ × 21″. ***$130–$160***

Lithograph, Indian print by "L.T. Bowen," (published by F. W. Greenwood, Philadelphia, 1836), "Le Soldat du Chene, an Osage Chief," minor stains, 15¼″ × 21¼″. ***$135–$170***

Mic Mac covered splint, blue and orange, 12″ × 9″, 8″ high. ***$100–$200***

Pottery, Olla, Acoma, ca. 1870. ***$6,750–$8,000***

Pouch, Plateau, floral, beaded, fringed, with flap top opening, 4 drawstring thongs and beaded top pull handle, floral-design beadwork on front, looped beadwork on perimeter, probably 19th century. ***$45–$60***

Rug, Germantown Eyedazzler, ca. 1890, 89½″ long. ***$8,700–$10,000***

Rug, Navajo Yei, large, woven with 100% wool yarns in multicolors on a mottled gray background, the border in a rich brown with elaborate serrated pattern in black, teal blue, and white, 5 Yei figures predominate the design, two at ends wearing headpieces with 3 feathers, in contrast to the central 3 with 4 feathers and different pendants; 7′ × 4′ × 3′ in very good condition. ***$1,900–$2,400***

Rug, Navajo, Old Granado, woven on a wool warp with 100% handspun wools in a natural white, gray, extended terraced diamonds in deep red with dark brown, black border around white centers containing Navajo crosses in black with red tips, 38″ × 70″, generally good condition throughout, ca. 1910–20. ***$275–$325***

Rug, Navajo, by Maggie Ashley, 3′4″ × 5′. ***$150–$250***

Sand picture, framed, landscape with figures, 14″ × 17″, 19th century. *$150–$250*

Splint wall basket, painted green, 4 pockets. *$3,520–$4,000*

Woman's wedding outfit, Osage. *$14,000–$16,000*

MENNONITE

Cupboard, walnut (painted white), 2 doors over 3 drawers and 2 doors on bottom, from Sonnenberg Community, an early-19th-century Swiss Mennonite settlement. *$7,700–$10,000*

Quilt, 1870–80, dusty pink/orange on sheer black wool, hand-appliquéd and hand-quilted, original design, Scherenschnitte cutting and swirling flowers, brown backing turned to front (typical of Pennsylvania), quilted in shell quilting, 8 stitches/inch, 72″ × 82″ unwashed, made in Myersdale, PA, by two sisters: Mary Fuller, other's name not remembered. It was given to their great-nephew, James Johnson, as payment for work he did for them. Mary died in 1920. James Johnson owned and prized the quilt for 60 years. When he served in WWII, he stored the quilt in a lard can and told his family to guard it. Later he sold the quilt to his niece, from whom it was purchased. *$4,500–$5,000*

Quilt, late 1800s, hand-quilted, light blue calico/watermelon pink calico/yellow calico/red and white shirting, Bars quilt with watermelon pink and yellow calico bars backing, made in Pennsylvania, diamond quilting, 7–8 stitches/inch, 75″ × 75″ unwashed, chalk marks. *$600–$700*

Quilt, fan design, Pennsylvania origin. *$165–$250*

Wardrobe, double-door, walnut, from Sonnenberg Community, an early-19th-century Swiss Mennonite settlement. *$1,900–$2,200*

Wardrobe, single-door, cherry, from Sonnenberg Community, an early-19th-century Swiss Mennonite settlement. *$3,675–$4,000*

MISCELLANEOUS

Fraktur, printed and hand-colored, Pennsylvania German, by "F. Krebs" (Friedrich Krebs), "Geburts and Taufschein" recording

1809 birth in Northampton County, 3-heart format with stylized floral detail in black, red, and yellow, laid paper has edge damage and creases, 12¼″ × 15¼″ framed, 16½″ × 19½″. *$390–$490*

Pennsylvania Dutch cupboard, softwood, 4 drawers in top case and raised-panel doors below, only 46″ wide, ca. 1830, refinished. *$3,900–$4,400*

Pennsylvania Dutch cupboard, cherry, ca. 1830–50, 64″ wide. *$8,500–$10,000*

Pennsylvania Dutch cupboard, from Soap Hollow, Somerset County, PA, original red and black paint with silver and gold stenciled designs, "manufactured by Jeremiah H. Stahl," turned quarter columns in upper and lower cases, original bracket base with shaped apron, ca. 1850, about 60″ wide, 87″ tall. *$48,400–$50,000*

Theorem, on velvet, fruit in a ribbed compote, signed "HRD," with original frame, 9″ × 11½″. *$600–$900*

SHAKER

Courtesy of Pumpkin Vine Line Antiques, Buddy and Atha Wallin, Fairfield, Ohio; photo by Donald Vogt.

Basket, egg, with handle, Ohio origin (Whitewater), ca. 1850–80. *$700–$800*

Boxes, 3 oval, with finger construction: (A) 3 fingers on base and 1 on lid, iron tacks and worn original bluish gray paint, 7⅝″ long; (B) 3 fingers on base and 1 on lid, iron tacks, and worn original orangish red paint, 9⅞″ long; (C) 1 finger on base and lid, copper tacks, original varnish finish, bottom is loose, 4¾″ long. *$2,280–$2,850*

Brushes, lot of 3: a horse brush, a long-handled brush with painted back, and a barber brush. *$80–$100*

Candlestand, finely proportioned, unsigned, no markings, thought to have been made by Samuel Turner at New Lebanon, NY. *$83,000–$86,000*

Candlestand, stamped with names of two Shaker eldresses and dated 1837, thought to have been made by Samuel Turner at New Lebanon, NY. *$154,000–$160,000*

Carrier, delicate design, beautifully shaped handle and rare form (square with flaring sides). *$4,400–$4,600*

Chairs, assembled set of 6 made in Enfield, NH, tilters with 17″-high seats. *$27,720–$29,000*

Cupboard, grain-painted and case of drawers, 82″ high, 36″ wide, possibly Harvard or Hancock. *$22,000–$25,000*

Dry sink, Canterbury, refinished. *$7,970–$8,200*

Drying rack, blue painted surface, simple 3-layer form. *$7,700–$8,000*

Courtesy of Pumpkin Vine Line Antiques, Buddy and Atha Wallin, Fairfield, Ohio; photo by Donald Vogt.

Herb basket, excellent condition, ca. 1850–80. *$350–$400*

Homespun, Mt. Lebanon Shaker Community, natural linen and dark blue wool, handwoven, very good condition, ca. 1850, 80″ × 72″. *$650–$750*

Courtesy of Grandad's Attic; photo by Donald Vogt.

Lavender bucket. *$225–$300*
Two-finger pantry box in old red. *$250–$300*
Berry bucket. *$225–$275*
Mustard bucket. *$250–$300*
Glove stretchers. *$75–$95*

Oval box, 5-finger, original finish, made in Mt. Lebanon, 13″ long. *$4,180–$4,800*

Oval box, made and signed by Delmer Wilson, the last elder and boxmaker, made as Christmas gift early in 20th century. *$9,350–$9,500*

Rocking chair, signed "Mt. Lebanon," 35″ tall, found in attic in Milford, OH. *$875–$975*

Seed box, Enfield, NH, original red stain and stenciling, intact interior label dated 1875, locking mechanism. *$2,750–$3,000*

Seed box. *$1,100–$1,300*

Seed box. *$1,485–$2,000*

Courtesy of Grandad's Attic; photo by Donald Vogt.

Stack of 9 oval boxes, some brides', some Shaker; measuring from 19" to 2¾", all from Pennsylvania. *$65–$365*

Stand, 2-drawer cherry with tiger maple drawer fronts. *$1,400–$1,800*

Storage chest, 12-drawer. *$1,870–$2,000*

Table, cherry, 98" long, 37¼" wide. *$21,000–$24,000*

Water barrel, old green paint, spigot not original, finial on top, height 25" to top. *$295–$325*

Courtesy of Pumpkin Vine Line Antiques, Buddy and Atha Wallin, Fairfield, Ohio; photo by Donald Vogt.

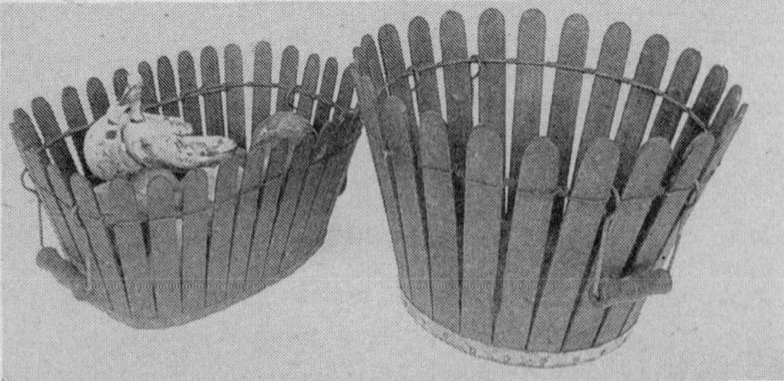

Wool baskets, factory-made *for* Shakers, had been stored in warehouse near Bardstown, round type is 10" tall, rectangular one is 7¼" tall. *$225–$300*

SOUTHWEST

Cowboy boots, white leather, ca. 1950. *$500–$600*

Fiesta skirts (2), Chimayo handbags. *$150–$200*

Holster, Dodge City–made, very old, leather, for a Colt S.A. with 7½″ barrel, the front stamped with maker's name "S.C. Gallup & Co., Dodge City, Ks.," active there around 1878, the back belt loop scratched with marking: "Texas Ranger 1885" by unknown hand. *$185–$225*

Holster, hand-tooled, old, leather, with elaborate hand-tooled figural design for a .45 Colt single-action 7½″ barrel, in good condition, ca. 1870s. *$175–$215*

Roy Rogers and Dale Evans lunch box. *$60–$80*

COUNTRY PEOPLE

As I write this introduction, the temperature has finally risen above freezing (for the first time in three weeks), but it's raining, the roads are slushy, and the wind is threatening to tear my young maple trees right out of the ground. Before the end of the day, we'll probably lose our telephone service and maybe the electrical power to the house. And this is 1990! What would it have been like for people living in the 1700s before house insulation had been invented and when fireplaces were their main source of heat and light?

I've often thought of those country folk who owned the items hanging on the wall in my house, about the woman who made the quilt that warms me at night or the man who made the 9-foot harvest table on which we eat dinner. What were their lives like and who were they?

While doing the research necessary for this chapter, I was privy to many of these people's lives through their diaries, journals, letters, and autobiographies. I read about women who had ten or twelve children, though only five or six lived. I heard about men who lost fingers or toes to frostbite, arms to an ax, legs in the Civil War. I learned how they built their houses, farmed their land, harnessed the power of the wind or water. And through the reading, writing, and imagining I've done, I've made friends with some people long dead.

I'd like to share some of that information and some of those friendships. And, in introducing these people to you, I expect you will be able to put another piece of the country puzzle in place.

Country Children

IT WAS NOT UNTIL the eighteenth century that children had books published strictly for them or had manufactured items to play with that they didn't have to share with adults. Toys were just commodities then, with no real relationship to children, and were lumped into the category that also included jewelry, hairpins, baubles, and buckles. Before this time, everything was made at home—and toys were as simple as the children themselves.

As difficult as it may be to realize, infant and child mortality rates were so high in the seventeenth century that there was little left behind for historians to document. Babies were often taken from their mothers' arms very early in their lives and given to a wet nurse whose care was not always thoughtful or knowledgeable, resulting in the death of many a child.

Beating a child was common and accepted. Schoolmasters used the whip on a regular basis, punishments were often cruel or brutal, and many children brought up in the New World were automatically christened with the guilt of "original sin" to bear along with everything else.

Is it any wonder that this period has been referred to as the "no toy" culture? That culture gradually changed in the late seventeenth and early eighteenth centuries. Though most toys were played with outside, colonists were beginning to realize that children were individuals too and started recognizing the fact that play was an important factor for children's growth. People still did not realize that, through play, children could learn from each other, but things were heading in the right direction.

Educational games were some of the first "toys" used. Acceptable games were those that did not waste the children's time—in other words, games that served a dual purpose: to teach through play.

A country child usually was rewarded with toys only on special occasions like Christmas or birthdays. Though most country toys are of the homemade variety, occasionally a parent would be able to buy a little boy a Star Tool Chest or would get the toddler of the family a set of lithographed picture blocks. A girl might find delight in a complicated picture puzzle or a miniature replica of a kitchen, complete with a stove, pots and pans, and other utensils.

What mattered most was that the child learned something while playing. Often the most obvious thing they learned was what role they would fill in life. The tools little Johnny carried in his carpentry tool chest taught him he was to be the builder, carpenter, plumber, or homeowner. Susie learned to quietly make the pieces of a puzzle fit or to put a needle through fabric, and she understood that her role was to be the organizer, the cook, and housekeeper in the home Johnny built.

Even Bible education was passed on through toys. Though some consider "Noah's Ark" carvings to be folk art, they were originally designed as toys for children—"Sunday toys," suitable to be played with on the Sabbath.

A country family's time was too valuable, the hours not at work too few, for them to allow their children to while away their days playing games. There were everyday chores to be accomplished and a household to be run. Every extra hand was necessary in order for the country family to survive.

Those children who were extremely lucky found a hobbyhorse under the Christmas tree or at their birthday table. Folk artists have included the rocking horse in portraits of children around the mid-nineteenth century, proof that the toy was one of the more popular ones of the century.

Not surprisingly, horse figures can be traced back to the early days of our world's history and linked with children. The Egyptians made toy clay horses; the Oriental culture produced toy horses even earlier than the time of the Pharaohs. When colonial America was ready to join the trend thousands of years later, horses were made out of all types of materials and in all shapes and sizes.

Because country folk were often poor, the children's play items were fashioned from whatever material was available. That could include rocks or shells used by children in counting games, flowers and blossoms (hollyhock dolls were made and milkweed pods were used for tiny cradles), animal bones, willow branches, and acorns.

In Appalachia, the American Indian culture, and most rural areas of the United States, many children had only one toy. For some, toys and games lived only in their imaginations—but what imaginations they were! Who could tell the tallest tale, the biggest lie, the scariest story? Who could take a handkerchief and make it become anything from a ghost to a fairy princess? A child's active imagination could.

Many of the games, toys, and sports we know today, such as lacrosse, skiing, snowshoeing, dice, hoop and pole, football, and cards, were played by the North American Indians long before the white men came. It is the Amerind who is responsible for those long weekends spent in front of the television, and it was also the Amerind who practically perfected the tall tale.

But since we cannot put a price on those games invented one day long ago by a little girl with pigtails that reached to her elbows or on stories that lived in the fantasy world of a red-haired boy in tattered overalls, or by one of the tribes who lived in communities across this nation, we'll talk about *real* toys that can live on in your country collections.

Balls

Sacks of flour could be unwound and the end of the thread wrapped around a small rock—round and round and round that rock until you had a thread ball. Hours of fun could be had by boys and girls who took turns batting the ball with a stick or piece of wood.

Books

The Bible was often the only book a country family owned. Perhaps that is why some of the toys termed "folk toys" by those who sell them are derived from Bible stories. For example: a long strip of leather and a leather pouch makes a wonderful sling strong enough to hurl a smooth, round pebble with speed and accuracy, like the one David hurled against Goliath.

Carriages

Joel A. H. Ellis was an American dollmaker who patented the doll carriage in 1856. He set up the company of Ellis, Britain and Eaton to sell the pram, which was made of maple, bass, and oak.

Carved Figures and Animals

If a child was lucky, a family member was adept at whittling and might make carved figures or animals for birthday or Christmas presents. Toys like these were special to their owners because they were made especially for them, and they are prized by today's collectors because they weren't manufactured by the thousands.

Handmade or whittled toys are considered by most to be folk art because of the artistic skill needed to make them and because no other exactly like them exists.

Cornhusk Dolls

Made by women for their little girls, cornhusk dolls are another example of how country folk utilized all of their leftover material in one way or another. Brooms were made during harvesting season out of broomcorn or corn husks, twine, and wooden handles. Any pieces of cornhusks that were left over might be used to fashion dolls for the little girls of the family. These dolls were well loved, but the materials used to make them did not withstand the test of time; therefore, there are few on the market today.

If the women making the doll was imaginative and had the time, these dolls might be dressed in dyed shuck dresses or in pants (to indicate the doll was male). The silks of the corn were used as hair and were held on by a bonnet. Last, a face was drawn on with a pencil or whatever would make marks on the cornhusk.

Dollhouses

Dollhouses are found in country homes because collectors often mix children's toys in with more primitive objects. In fact, a special friend of mine in Texas has filled her dollhouses and cupboards with children's toys of all shapes and sizes, making her home one of my favorite places to stay. However, the only dollhouses I consider "country" are those that were made by hand (though I will add some information about others for those of you who might never find a handmade one).

Some of the most beautiful versions of any dollhouses made are those colorful lithographed examples made by the Bliss firm. These are highly prized by collectors all over the world. But the houses made by Dad, Grandad, and Uncle James are individually far superior, considered to be folk art and treasured for the memories they hold.

The interiors of dollhouses made during the Victorian era are filled with miniatures—tiny replicas of furniture, books, paintings, kitchen utensils, and people. The interior of the dollhouse Daddy made during a cold winter in the Wisconsin farmhouse would be filled with "make do" items. The child's imagination would make Mama's old thimble into a dining room table or, by simply placing it in another room, a cooking kettle. The dolls who inhabited the house would probably be made out of cornhusks, and only a discerning eye would be able to see the subtle differences between Mr. and Mrs. Husk. Buttons, pieces of thread, stones, and twigs would be used to make furnishings for the house, and imagination would rule over all.

The Bliss Manufacturing Company of Pawtucket, Rhode Island, made the houses that were most popular with America's children during the late 1800s. The company was established in 1832, incorporated in 1893, and produced the lithographed dollhouses for which it became famous in 1895. Bliss houses were inventively designed and decorated outside, but inside they usually had only one room upstairs and one downstairs. Larger versions have mica windows, while small ones have painted windows.

A "Combination Doll House" was patented in 1881 by the Stirn and Lyon Company of New York. The house was a folding example packaged in a large box, which was the foundation of the house. Other companies, such as Grimm & Leeds of New Jersey and the McLoughlin Brothers of New York, also made folding houses and rooms.

Dolls

Dolls were made out of any odd materials, and through the years, Appalachian children have owned rock dolls, stick dolls, potato and applehead dolls, cornhusk, corncob, cucumber, cloth, and rag dolls—all of them equally adored.

The ones most country collectors add to their hoard of treasures are often the ones made of bits of cloth. When the woman of the house was making clothing or quilts, there were always small pieces of material left over. These were usually handed over to the younger women of the house, and they would make dolls out of them, accomplishing two feats at once: honing their sewing skills and making something they could play with.

The Amish made their dolls without faces, the people who lived in the Midwest might stuff the bodies with cornhusks, and a black woman living on a plantation might stuff her doll with cotton. Each version was special to the child for whom it was made, and they were often so well loved that they didn't make it through the child's adolescence.

The dolls that have survived are highly collectible. The ones that show more artistic ability have turned into folk art items treasured by collectors who have long passed their childhood.

One might find dolls from New England with fur hair and leather hands or black dolls from the South wearing quaint hats and finely embroidered smiles. Some dolls are made of oilcloth with sternly drawn faces, complete with arched eyebrows. They may have miniature brooches sewn at their necks, lacy pantaloons peeking from underneath a gingham dress, or finely carved and movable joints.

My small collection of cloth dolls includes a number of Raggedy Anns made through the years, some black dolls, a few topsy-turvy dolls (white on one side, black on the other—they hide under each other's skirts), and two Cherokee versions with beaded necklaces. All have names and are special, but the Raggedy Ann that has no clothes and stuffing coming out from under her armpit is the one I love most—and, you know, I bet her previous owner loved her too.

Hobbyhorses

An English nursery rhyme claimed the hobbyhorse written about was dapple gray with a tail made of hay. Dapple gray mares were made with or without wheels, their heads were placed atop sticks so that the child could simulate the horse's pace, and the horse's figure was also scaled down so that the child could push or pull it wherever he or she deemed exciting. With a hobbyhorse and a lot of imagination, the child could go anywhere, be brave and adventuresome, and still be home in time for supper.

Jumping Jacks

Jumping jacks were designed by those whittlers or carpenters whose talent was such that they were able to carve human form. Jacks were carved in parts so that when they were tied together, each would jump independently.

Though jumping jacks were usually made of wood, some cardboard ones have been found that are not as old as their wooden cousins. Each of the old wooden versions is different because they were made one at a time. But somewhere along the line, a maker got wise and made a pattern to follow so that more than one part could be cut out at the same time.

Especially collectible today are the black jumping jacks. Again, their popularity caused the manufacturers to sit up, take notice, and start producing them in quantity. Today, jumping jacks are being reproduced on a regular basis and the buyer should take note of this fact.

Kachinas

The Native American culture made dolls long before the European settlers did, but for different reasons. Some were made for children, but others were made as celebrations of culture.

Kachina dolls, made by the Hopi tribe in the Southwest, were replicas of the many supernatural beings in which the tribe believes. Kachinas are not given to the children strictly as toys but as educational tools to teach the young members of the tribe about their heritage. These dolls are highly valued and treasured by Hopi youngsters and have become just as highly regarded by collectors, who recognize the social as well as political significance of the figures.

Kachinas are usually made of cottonwood. The older versions can be many different sizes (I saw one in a trading post in Arizona that was quite old and almost three feet tall), but they are fairly stiff in appearance. Versions made during the late nineteenth and early twentieth centuries are often clothed and decorated with feathers, beads, and other materials. Today's Kachinas are highly carved action figures, which may or may not be painted. They are beautiful works of art that bring prices in today's market comparable to those being paid for new cars.

There are hundreds of different types of Kachinas, and few collectors are familiar with all of them. The variety available to collectors, however, makes them an easy, if expensive, item to accumulate.

Rocking Horses

Rocking horses were made by a few American manufacturers in the late 1800s, though the majority were made in Europe, and

American manufacturers generally followed European designs. Some of the manufacturing companies were Asham and Son (Philadelphia, 1860s), E. W. Bushnell (Philadelphia, 1847–57), A. Christian (New York, 1856–1880s), Morton E. Converse (Winchendon, Massachusetts, 1880s), Benjamin Crandall (Brooklyn and New York, 1840–1890s), William Long (Philadelphia, 1785), and W. A. Marqua (Cincinnati, 1880).

Rocking horses also were made by the men of the family in many country cultures, including the Amish. When traveling to take the photos for this book, we encountered an Amish rocking horse that was not only exceptionally large and heavy but could be used as a storage chest when its upper body was lifted off.

Rolling the Hoop (Hoop and Stick)

Rolling-the-hoop games are highly recognizable because they have been depicted in illustrations of country and city life of the late 1800s, but few know that the game was actually an American Indian invention.

Anyone familiar with Tom Sawyer remembers the fun he and his friends had with a simple hoop and stick. The stick was used to get the hoop spinning faster and faster as the child followed its progress down a dirt road or country street.

Sleds

Sleds were owned by nearly every child, though some were improvised and others lovingly made by hand. They were made of boards or broom sage or a piece of cardboard. They had runners or flat bottoms. Some were painted; some weren't. But you could bet that if the children lived in an area where they had snow, they had sleds of some kind.

Sleds were used in both the winter and summer by country children. The snow scooter's runner was made from a barrel stave, and a slim piece of wood served to hold a seat. A real challenge, the scooter probably served to knock out more than one child when it hit a tree or a rock.

The grass sled was made of hogshead staves, with an upright piece of wood in the front of the sled serving as the place where the rider would rest his or her feet. The sled was used in a long hilly meadow area where the grass was high enough to provide a good cushion on which one could slide.

Soft Toys

Soft toys, such as dolls, teddy bears, and other stuffed animals, have been made by parents for their children for many centuries. We will talk only of homemade American soft toys in this volume, as many other books deal with those toys made in factories or in other countries. While recognizing that many of these children's toys (e.g., Steiff bears and other animals) have found their way into the American country collector's heart, I feel we have to define what we will discuss in this volume or my research work could go on for many years.

Besides, teddy bears were made in celebration of our own President Theodore Roosevelt. Cartoonist Clifford Berryman drew the president with a bear cub at his feet (Roosevelt had refused to shoot the bear for political reasons) in a 1903 edition of the *Washington Post*. Morris Michtom, founder of the Ideal Toy Corporation of America, used the cartoon as his model for a toy bear with button eyes. The toy was immediately successful, was named a "Teddy Bear," and has been made in many different versions since that time. In fact, it is said that Margrete Steiff was shown the same cartoon and produced a jointed bear that ultimately garnered the interest of collectors throughout the world.

Other soft animals, such as horses, rabbits, and dogs, have been made for children by their parents, or manufactured versions were given to them at holidays or birthdays. The ones that are hand-stitched with embroidered features are worth the most from a collector's viewpoint, and the manufactured examples are worth the least.

Stilts

Stilts were simple, long, sturdy pieces of wood into which Dad or Grampa cut ridges for a child's foot. The sight of a group of youngsters trying to walk across a newly cut meadow on tottering stilts was sure to send more of the children giggling to the ground.

Wagons

Wagons were also commonly enjoyed by children and were usually made with four wooden wheels of basically the same size (though not always, especially if handmade by someone in the family). The wheels could be pieces cut down from a log or an old bucket lid or a tin rim.

Unlike the adventurous times had with a sled, wagons offered a more sedate ride and were often used to tote toys or a younger sibling. Only in the hands of a true daredevil did wagons travel at the same breakneck speed as did sleds and then at the risk of losing a wheel when going over a bump or rock.

Wagons and sleds proved so popular that factories began making them in quantity. Ones made by American Flyer or Express were especially popular, and certain examples of specially made sleds (e.g., the "Rosebud" made for the movie *Citizen Kane*) have brought record prices when put up for auction. Because of this fact, it is not as easy as it once was to find exceptional sleds or wagons, and many country collectors have had to satisfy themselves with the "plain Janes."

Whip Tops

The whip top was a spinning toy that the child started with his or her hands, then whipped into speed by a long cord, leather thong, or eel skin. The first whip tops were made by Native Americans.

Whistles

Whistles are one of the simplest childhood toys to make. Examples have been made from bamboo, willow, and maple, and others, less likely to withstand the test of time, have been made from corn stalks, river cane, and even rolled-up newspapers. Again, manufacturers recognized the whistle's popularity and continue to make them to this day.

Country Men

EARLY AMERICAN MEN, such as those who came here on the *Mayflower* and were part of the first communities built on these shores, learned how to hunt and fish through the tutelage of Native Americans. Indians had long been trapping animals for food, clothing, and other materials. Skins were used for clothing and bedding, the innards for food, and the claws and teeth as decoration, jewelry, or in making tools. Nothing was wasted, the white man quickly learned.

By the end of that first New England winter, ships were being sent back to Europe bearing cargoes that consisted of beaver and otter skins acquired through trades with the Indians. When the boats returned, it was with the suggestion that more of the same be sent, and international fur trading began. Even then, Americans were savvy enough to know the meaning of trade and capitalism. Soon men learned how to build their own traps, sometimes improving on the Native American's basic design but always using the same premise.

Typically, men were the leaders of the clan, taking care of their families the best way they knew how and often bringing them across country or into new territories to settle. One such family was the Hubbell family of eighteenth-century Connecticut.

The move from Connecticut to Vermont was a long and tedious one for Seth Hubbell, his wife, and five daughters during the cold winter of 1789. He worked his team of oxen until noon every day, then put the yoke on himself, pulling the load to within fourteen miles of Wolcott, Vermont.

By mid-March, the ox team was too ill to continue, so Hubbell left it with a gentleman in Johnson. The family continued for eight miles on snowshoes, following marked trails where no roads had yet been cut.

By the end of their journey, Seth knew it would be necessary to do some trapping, for the family had no food or money left. He caught a sable and carried its skin fifty miles so that he could exchange it for half a bushel of wheat. Once he had the wheat, he had to turn around and carry it home to his hungry family—round trip of one hundred miles on foot.

The winter was a hard one, though Hubbell was fortunate enough to find an Indian with moose meat to sell. Surprisingly, the family made it through the winter even though the fifty acres promised Hubbell was not forthcoming, and the oxen they had left in Johnson were sold, leaving the family without a cow to help feed them through the summer.

Seth's tools consisted of an ax and a hoe. With these two tools, he cleared two acres and planted the land with corn. An early frost took the crop, and Hubbell was forced to travel another twenty miles (again on foot) to buy new seeds.

Catching and selling sable brought the family through their second winter. Seth learned the hard way that hunting would be the only way he could supply his family with food for another winter, for he was forced, yet again, to purchase a moose from another hunter. Since money was in scarcer supply than a rifle and bullets, Hubbell learned how to take care of his family in his own way.

Life was hard and nature unforgiving, yet Seth Hubbell lived to the ripe old age of seventy-three, having sired sons to whom he could leave his "rich, beautiful farm."

The city people who took it upon themselves to make long, arduous journeys to those early American settlements would write in their journals that, though the families were poor and had little or nothing to eat, they were serene, content, loved their mates, and never wanted to return to the city from whence they moved. "They set much more store by one another than in ye old settlements," wrote Reverend Nathan Parkins, pastor of the Third Church of West Hartford, Connecticut.

Clothing

Men's clothing emphasized the difference between those males who were well-to-do, settled in populated areas, and those who barely made a living in rural areas.

Breeches were popular with both city and country men until around 1830, when close-fitting trousers with straps that fit around the bottom of the man's shoe (to hold the trousers down) came into fashion. Before this time, the only men to wear protection over their whole leg were soldiers, hunters, or pioneers.

Pioneers and farmers immediately knew city men by their effeminate way of dress—the slim, elaborate waistcoat and ruffled shirt—as well as by the citified man's dainty white hands (often clutching a handkerchief over his nose). Though a country man might own a plain "Sunday" jacket, it was never the tailored, elegant style his city brother sported.

Through the middle of the century, men's clothing went through minor changes (i.e., slacks became looser and jackets broader and less form-fitting, and the silk stock once worn closely around the neck slipped down a little and resembled a bow tie rather than an ascot). By the Civil War, men looked less effeminate and more businesslike, often completing their outfits with top hats like the ones Abraham Lincoln chose to wear.

A country man's clothing depended largely on where he resided. Those stalwart pioneers who forged a land west of the Mississippi were more concerned with warmth and durability than with fashion. They borrowed the Native American's idea of utilizing animal skins and furs; however, with the advent of the railroad and more accessibility to imported fabrics, they soon had their wives working to make less bulky jackets and pants out of wools and cottons. By the end of the 1800s, only those men who lived far from civilization were still tanning hides to make warm winter jackets, chaps, and waterproof boots.

Wool drawers were first worn by men in the late 1700s. Resembling children's "feet pajamas," the long underwear was first called "draw-ons" because it had a long drawstring that was doubly wrapped about the wearer's waist.

Decoys

Country men soon learned that they would have to hunt their own food, and that task was not always easily accomplished. Decoys were used in duck hunting to lure the fowl in to shore. Today they are settled on mantels and seen as folk art in the country antiques world.

The Native American of the southwestern United States was the first to make a replica of the canvasback duck over a thousand years ago. His decoy was made of reed, rushes, and feathers. The device was used by the ingenious Tule Easter, a predecessor of the Paiutes, to attract wildfowl close enough to him so that he could shoot them with his bow and arrow.

The experiment worked. The Indian's ingenuity attracted whole flocks of wildfowl and opened the doors to duck hunters for many years to come. The earliest of these decoys can be viewed at the Museum of the American Indian in New York City.

American settlers followed the Native American's use of decoys when hunting wildfowl. Because the first decoys or lures were too fragile, village whittlers began carving decoys from wood. The earliest of these were made of cedar. Later, as that type of tree became less plentiful, white pine was used.

The story of Natty Bumppo, written by James Fenimore Cooper, describes a scene in which a group of hunters waits for a flock of pigeons to fly overhead. Driven into the hunters' sights by noises made by other hunters and Indians behind the flock, the birds are shot out of the air by rifles and cannon shot.

During that period in our history, there were thousands of passenger pigeons in the Northeast. Because of the indiscriminate hunting by the early settlers, this bird is extinct.

Pigeons were part of the menu on which the pioneers subsisted. To help in the hunt for supper, carvers made decoys in the form of pigeons that were called "blocks" (because they lacked detail). Another name used was "stools" derived from the European practice of attaching a live pigeon to a movable pole in order to attract other pigeons; thus, the term "stool pigeon."

Bird hunters soon realized that it didn't quite matter whether the blocks really looked like wildfowl, but the more blocks that were set out, the more birds came. At times they used two hundred to five hundred decoys at a time, and those had to be constantly replaced because of loss or because they were shot to bits.

By the mid-1800s, carvers began being more artistic when making their blocks. No longer were the pieces of wood plain, square resemblances of the bird's shape. Now the blocks truly took on the likeness of the fowl, incorporating painted plumage, eyes, and bills. The carvers took pride in their work and began to sign their pieces. Regional types, such as the two-piece decoys from the Barnegat Bay area of New Jersey and the fine decoys out of Stratford, Connecticut, became more developed.

The smallest decoys were made by New England carvers because those hunters violated "no hunting on Sunday" laws and needed decoys small enough to fit into their pockets.

The first rubber decoy appeared in 1867, and tip-up decoys, which imitated a duck's feeding action, were also made.

As the number of hunters increased, so did the need for decoys. Factories, such as the Stevens Company in Weedsport, New York; the Dodge Co. and the Mason Co., both of Detroit; and the American Company of Illinois, began supplying thousands of decoys a year to meet the demand.

Overshooting caused Congress to pass the Federal Migratory Bird Law in 1913. This law prohibited spring shooting and shipping waterfowl for sale, then limited the hunter to twenty-five ducks per day in 1918. In 1919, the Federal Migratory Bird Treaty was enacted between the United States and Canada, and in 1920, the Supreme Court prohibited the sale of wildfowl between the two countries. After that time, the market gunners went out of business and the decoys being made were not as well done as the ones made before those laws were enacted.

Master decoy carvers like Harry Shourdes of Tuckerton, New Jersey, and Charles E. Wheeler (1872–1949) of Stratford, Connecticut, began to be recognized as knowledgeable artisans once the factory-produced decoys were not flooding the market anymore.

Wheeler was a sportsman, naturalist, senator from Connecticut, and member of that state's game commission. He made the bulk of his decoys in the 1920s, and collectors state that his examples are the most highly sought after.

Charles H. Perdew of Henry, Illinois, carved decoys even into his early eighties and was so skilled in both carving and painting that hunters and collectors prize his work.

A. Elmer Crowell (1862–1952) of East Harwick, Massachusetts, is a well-recognized maker, whose name attracts dealers and collectors alike. He carved the wings of his birds separately and also detailed the tail feathers.

Shourdes (1871–1920) was a painter by trade but used his skill to make decoys during the height of waterfowl hunting. He guided hunting and fishing excursions at first but soon found that carving decoys was a more lucrative trade. The only assistants he had were his two daughters, who occasionally sanded a body. The rest of the work was done by Shourdes personally. Because of the enormous amount of work he did, his hometown became recognized as the decoy capital of the United States.

Fishing Collectibles

America's anglers have long been romanticized. Paintings from the early eras of our history often depict a lonely country road following a stream. On the banks of that babbling brook stands a young gentleman in a soft, flowing white shirt, a slouched canvas hat framing his peaceful face. A wicker creel is hanging at his side, and a bamboo trout pole is held above his head.

Huck Finn had a fishing pole, as did Tom Sawyer. New England is recognizable by the covered bridge scenes, with a barefoot boy fishing with a long curved branch. The very act of fishing somehow conjures up the bucolic days of young America.

One of the first recreational groups to spring up in Pennsylvania was the Schuylkill Fishing Company, founded in 1732. Everyone, including women, enjoyed the popularity of fishing, though there were few serious anglers at the time. Those who belonged to groups like the Schuylkill would search for perch, striped bass, shad, and catfish, primarily so that they could enjoy a meal on the riverbank that evening.

Angler knowledge and technique did not advance until the mid-nineteenth century. Dedication varied in each fisher, and America was now so well settled that fishing areas varied greatly. Though there were a few books published on the subject (notably *The Compleat Angler* by Izaak Walton, an Englishman), Americans used their own ingenuity and trial-and-error way of learning to catch fish.

The Fly Fisher's Entomology, published by Alfred Ronalds in 1836, served to change the attitude and techniques being used. The writer challenged the fishers to learn their craft, and the science of it, and the book sparked discussion and experimentation. Other books began to change the way people fished in that a dry fly was suggested for trout fishing by *The Vade Mecum of Fly-fishing for Trout* by George Philip Rigney Pulman in 1846, and William C. Stewart's *The Practical Angler* (1857) stated that upstream fishing was the best method for fly fishers.

Mary Orvis Marbury, a noted American fly tier during the Civil War period, wrote: "As streams have become more depleted and fish more shy, they need to be fished with greater caution and skill, and there is therefore a greater demand for smaller flies delicately tied in colors less gaudy than those now needed for the flies used in the wild, unfrequented rivers and lakes."

In 1886, Frederick Halford converted the fly caster from the sunken fly to the floater, with great impact on the fly fisher. It was said to alter both the practice and temperament of the angler.

Bass, a genus of fish strictly American, gives the fisher almost as much of a fight as do trout and salmon, making bass fishing attractive to those early fishers. They used live bait to catch the fish with long rods, which could be used for both still fishing and trolling. Colorfully patterned artificial flies might be tied at the end of a long line.

The first factory-built bamboo rods were made by the Charles Orvis Co. of Manchester, Vermont, in 1856, and that company continues to make well-built rods to this day. However, the work of Hiram Leonard of Bangor, Maine, earned more respect for the split bamboo rod than any other maker. By the end of the century, rods were no longer twelve feet long, as Orvis had designed them, but were under ten feet in length and weighed a maximum of seven ounces.

In 1875, Orvis used the suggestions of a Dr. Henshall for making a bass bait-casting rod, and nationwide use of the shorter rod resulted. All of eight feet long, the rod weighed eight ounces. The butt section of the rod was ash; the other two joints were lancewood. Collectors who are looking for these early rods will have a tough time finding them and, if they do, will pay dearly for the pleasure.

More than a decade before the Civil War, the first commercial bait-casting lure was used. A triangular piece of metal on a shaft, the Buel spoon was made in Whitehall, New York. Its treble hook was covered with red and white feathers, though they did not help the lure "fly" a great distance. Suddenly, a number of spoon lures entered the market, and Jim Heddon, first credited with devising the top-water bass lure, became a name to be associated with fishing lures.

These spoon lures and spinners, made between 1852 and 1880 by Julio T. Buel and W. D. Chapman, are coveted by collectors, as are the wooden lures made during the latter nineteenth and early twentieth centuries. The more affordable lures are those made in the 1930s and 1940s, such as Johnson's Automatic Striker Minnow, the Heddon Punkinseed, and the earlier Chippewa pike lure (ca. 1910).

The most important thing to remember when collecting lures is that rare colors and details, such as glass-beaded eyes and hand-painted gills, enhance the value of the lure as much as or more than the maker's name.

Ice fishing decoys, used along the Great Lakes states by spear fishers to attract fish, were fish-shaped pieces of wood. Each decoy has a lead weight in its body and is suspended by a jig stick through the ice. This type of fishing gear slides easily into the folk art category because decoy carvers often worked on other items, such as bird decoys, or had a particularly naive style that is attractive enough to convince country collectors to group them on their fireplace or hang them on their wall. As with folk art, prices for fish decoys range from the low hundreds to several thousand, mainly because they are being collected by several different groups of people: collectors of fishing gear, country collectors, and folk art collectors.

With the image of George Bush as the American fisherman, collectors of this type of item may find some pretty stiff competition during the next couple of years, and those who have long admired the many different types of tackle one might collect will find they are newly excited by the prospect.

Skis and Snowshoes

As with many other winter sports, the credit for making skis and snowshoes goes to the American Indian. In fact, most hand-tied snowshoes are Amerind, and they are long-lasting as well as attractive. A pair hangs in my back hall. The only thing repaired since their making is their bindings, and I still use them to traverse my property when giving the dogs their workout during winter months.

The first American-made snowshoes were made in 1790 and were an egg-shaped ½-inch ash plank with a strap attached through which the wearer could place his or her shoe. Later, snowshoes (ca. 1800) were made of hickory splints. The Indians were making snowshoes of bentwood and rawhide at that time, which proved a far lighter and more effective shoe for snowy conditions.

Early skis (ca. 1825–60) were long, curved wooden planks, which often employed a thong to hold the curve of the front of the ski in place.

Tramp Art

I am including this category in the men's section because it has been proved that almost 100 percent of the pieces we call tramp art have been made by men—that it was a male passion and hobby.

Just recently "discovered" as a country collectible, tramp art is defined as wooden pieces that were not necessarily carved out of one piece of wood but made of different levels and facets of wood. For example, the artisan creating a tramp art frame may use a simple frame as a base, then nail, staple, or glue layers of spruce gum on top of the basic frame. Each layer would be gouged or notch-carved—stars, hearts, and diamonds being favored designs—until the surface was covered with jagged geometric designs.

This type of work was popular around the turn of the century and continued until the beginning of World War II. Chip carving, done in Europe throughout the sixteenth century, is thought to have been central to this craft, though it took a long time for it to evolve into tramp art. The only other place in the world known to produce this type of work was Germany—thus, we credit the Pennsylvania Dutch settlers as being the ones to introduce the art here.

Vermonters were introduced to chip carving or tramp art in their logging camps. The long winter evenings were boring without an activity to keep the men occupied. What easier task than to whittle or chip-carve the one commodity they had in abundance: wood.

Europeans from Finland, Sweden, and Russia worked as loggers during the late nineteenth and early twentieth centuries and probably were responsible for bringing the art to their American friends in the logging camps. For instance, Scandinavian carvers were known to whittle fans from one piece of cedar. Some of these fans are known to have been made by Vermonters, and the talent and style of carving was passed from the European to the Vermonter and, through the Vermonter, to his family. The Crown of Thorns technique was typical of Russian work and was passed to the Vermonter through a friendship made in one of the logging camps.

Many of the tramp art pieces in today's collections or museums were constructed from dismantled fruit crates and cigar boxes. The carver needed a minimum of tools to create their "hobo masterpieces." Though the theory persists that such pieces were made by traveling artisans, the truth of the matter is that a hobo could not possibly have carried all of the materials and tools needed to create such things as doll furniture, sofas, bureaus, tables, pincushions, boxes, and the like. In fact, some of the tramp art collected today shows the marks of a jigsaw, a tool that definitely was not carried by a hobo on a regular basis.

The reason for the death of this art is largely the fact that, after the first third of the twentieth century, more and more craftspeople were working with electrical or power-driven tools. Factories were producing more and more decorative items for the home and were able to do so much faster than hand-carvers were able to.

Whittling

Who can think of a country summer evening on the porch of an old farmhouse without envisioning someone whittling? Whittling is a country craft that has enticed people who can work a whittling knife to produce an art object.

The craft, which served to occupy country people for many quiet hours on the porch, was brought to a higher level by those whittlers whose skill was so great that their work was in demand.

Carvers, such as Wilhelm Schimmel of Pennsylvania, who worked during the latter half of the nineteenth century, used their penknives to produce toys, little animals, birds, and geometric forms. Sometimes these treasures were sold to whoever would buy them, or they would be used to barter for room and board.

Today, wooden pieces made by carver Schimmel or any of his compatriots are worth hundreds (sometimes thousands) of dollars and fall into the category of country crafts that we consider folk art.

Country Women

LIVING IN THE COUNTRY meant spending a lot of time alone. If a woman was married, her husband was often hunting something for supper or winter's meals, fishing (again, for food), maple sugaring, cutting wood, farming, or taking care of various animals. The women learned to be self-sufficient, much more so than modern women give them credit. The women also were the ones to defend the homestead during those lonely periods, often becoming just as accomplished with a knife, rifle, or ax as were their menfolk.

They learned how to listen to the sounds and smells of the season—the howling of a wolf by the edge of the forest signaling the dead of winter, the buzz of a swarm of bees or hummingbirds during a hot midsummer's day. The honking of a gaggle of geese overhead would make them realize that autumn was almost over, and the smell of mud and rushing water indicated that winter had finally released its icy grip and spring was on the way.

Country women knew the pleasure of a night when the sky's black blanket would be studded with thousands of diamond-like stars. They shared the joyous birth of a calf, lamb, or colt and that heart-wrenching wonder when the animal first tested wobbly legs. Their nostrils would swell with the clean, woodsy odor of a forest where timber has been cut to warm the house all winter. And their pleasure was never greater than after a long, hardworking day when, muscle-sore and eye-closing tired, they could sit next to a dying fire to share some peaceful moments alone.

Their clothes were scrubbed clean and kept their bodies warm. No makeup highlighted their features, no nail polish enhanced hands rubbed red and raw by hard work. Their life was hard, their rewards few, but country women knew where to look for the lilting sound of a mockingbird or the touch of a newborn kitten's soft coat.

Country women were strong, independent souls, like the Vermont woman Hepzibah Barnam. She's not someone you'll read about in a child's history book. Her life story won't make a Hollywood multimillion-dollar movie, but it was an exciting one, full of challenges, daily disasters, births, deaths, and a lot of backbreaking work.

Hepzibah and Barnabas built a log house for themselves, raised their children within its 20-by-30-foot frame, grew their own food, raised their own animals, and braved nine Vermont winters together. Hepzibah died after getting lost during her trip home after a visit with some neighbors.

It had gotten dark. She wandered out of her way and spent many hours wet and freezing before finding her way home via the assistance of the North Star.

The cold Hepzibah developed after her misadventure grew worse through the spring and into the summer. The couple left their mountain home in the early winter because she did not improve. They promised each other to return in the spring and that matters would improve. But things didn't improve, and they never returned.

Country women have always been fairly independent, and there was a time when Vermont women who had the knowledge required to teach were heading west for Oregon. The sum of $500 was promised to each teacher-to-be if she remained single during the first year of teaching.

That sum was a rather large one but didn't quite meet the worth of a 320-acre parcel that marrying would bring her. The Oregon Land Bill stated that their promise of 320 acres would be kept only if the woman married within a year!

Speaking of marriage, bringing a woman into your household constituted a pretty good deal for most country men. For example, one woman from the Green Mountains brought the following items to her new home: treenware items of all shapes and sizes, steel knives, linen tablecloths and towels, woolen blankets, coverlet made from her own loom, and thirteen quilts in different designs (all hand-pieced).

A dowry was planned from the birth of each daughter—the larger the dowry, the better "catch" the daughter was. Think of how desirable she'd be if she owned a couple of cows!

Each girl learned needlepoint, quilting, and knitting at an early age and sought to produce as many creations as possible by the time she was fifteen or sixteen, marrying age. A sampler or two would be made early in a girl's sewing career; it was the tool used to teach the young lady her stitches, as well as her alphabet. Each bedroom in the home had three to five quilts of different weights and designs. An unmarried girl would dream of her married life as she spent hour upon hour with quilt pieces spread on her lap while the firelight died in the hearth.

I wonder just what went through her mind as she lovingly made piece after handmade piece, storing them all in a large box or trunk for her future marriage. Did she realize how hard her life would be? Was she wondering about her future? Of course! And wouldn't she be surprised if she knew how many of us, with all of our modern conveniences, *choose* to work the land in the same way she did.

History

Eight hundred thousand women joined the men, children, and caravans of animals who headed west in the early days of expansion. Those women had a hard life, often surviving harsh, cold winters in tents barely secure enough to withstand the wind, working alongside the men in forging a way through to the Pacific Coast. Through their letters and diaries, we have learned a great deal about the history of our land, what home life in the early West was like, what tools were used, what food was cooked, and what kind of communities grew as a result of the strong, fearless pioneers who carved a living for themselves on land that often must have appeared uninhabitable to human beings.

These women taught the children; cared for their own and

other families' ills; made and washed all of the clothing; tended the gardens; hauled water and boiled lye for soap; endured pestilences, famine, drought, and wild animals; worked alongside the men in all kinds of circumstances; often had four or five children before their twentieth birthday; and sometimes watched helplessly as some of those children died. They worked as homesteaders, housekeepers, cooks, prostitutes, midwives, teachers, missionaries, actresses, maids, postal clerks, or laundresses. It was not an easy life, and it isn't difficult to realize why most women looked old before their time. But, most certainly, it was a character-building life and one that can be fondly termed "country."

In a journal written in 1838 by a woman traveling to Waiilatpu, Oregon, from Westport, Missouri, it is noted that the woman had finished her washing before eating breakfast. You can be assured there were no Maytag machines on the Oregon Trail and that the woman probably washed her (as well as everyone else's) clothes against a rock down by the river. The addition of a washboard to the objects a family carried across the prairie was more of a necessity than a luxury.

She reports being visited by Indians, that she had spotted buffalo, had seen the snow-capped mountains for the first time and the changing colors of a western sunset. The woman also tells of sitting down to a supper of vegetables, salt salmon, bread, butter, and cream, the bulk of which was more than likely cooked in iron pots and skillets over a low-burning fire.

Pictures of this woman, Mary Richardson Walker, taken at age sixty in 1871, show a thin-faced, large-eyed woman with big ears and a long nose. Though her hair was sternly parted down the middle and wound into a bun at the back of her neck, Walker does not look as old as you would think one would who had had such a hard life.

One spring day in 1841, with two children under the age of two to take care of, Mary cast wicks and dipped nineteen dozen candles (that's 228, for those of you without a calculator). And that was, more than likely, not the only thing she accomplished that day.

She noted in other parts of her diary that she sweeps, washes clothes, and irons immediately upon arising, trying to get those chores done before the babies awake—not to mention tending the fire, cooking the meals, changing dirty diapers, washing dishes, and so on.

When a thorough housecleaning was done (usually twice a year), all of the bedding, quilts, coverlets, sheeting, blankets, and pillows were brought out of the house and hung on lines for airing. At that time, it was also important for the women to inspect the coverings for fleas, ticks, and lice. The women, who made the mattresses, pillows, and quilts, were now responsible for their cleaning and repair. To that end, they used rug beaters to clean them, homemade lye soap to wash them, homespun thread to repair them, and, possibly, homespun wool from their own sheep to stuff them.

Though not understood by the white women who went west during the Victorian era, Indian women were often better off than their white sisters. Depending on the tribe, many Native American women held their own possessions and had places of power in the tribe and more freedom than the white pioneer women who looked down their noses at the dark-skinned "savages" whose land they were taking over.

Having lived off the land all of their lives, Indian women were knowledgeable about the roots and herbs that could be found during the long, harsh winter months. They were capable of curing meat, they knew what kinds of vegetables to eat so that they were immune to the diseases that robbed so many new settlers of their lives, and they were trained to utilize every part of a killed animal so that nothing in nature was ever wasted.

Black women often had just as difficult a time assimilating to their new homes as Indian women had in adapting to the takeover of their land by whites. Their African heritage had been overshadowed by their slavery, making it hard for black families to adjust to their lack of freedom, and it put up roadblocks when it came time to learn how to physically sustain themselves once they were able to have homes of their own.

Although the West offered African-American women an opportunity to settle their own land and start anew, it was no easier for black women to battle the West, with all of its pitfalls and problems, especially when they had to contend with the prejudice of their neighbors as well. Black women often worked as laundresses, maids, or governesses but found that, with the influx of Chinese workers, they often lost their jobs to those who would work for less.

Arts

Virginia Woolf was probably the first writer to suggest that "Anonymous was a woman." In her book, *A Room of One's Own,* Woolf discusses the fact that women who were artistically inclined were often suspected of being witches, crazy, or possessed by devils. Artistic women who wanted to continue enjoying a bent that was not easily understood by others probably felt that it would be safer if they didn't sign the artistic work they did. Yet it is American women whom we have to thank for a good portion of what collectors term folk art today.

Those magnificent quilts, hooked rugs, needlepoint samplers, and naive paintings were usually the work of unskilled female artisans, artists denied their calling because others thought it wasn't "proper" for women to pursue such "base callings."

It wasn't until the Victorian era that the female artist was finally observed. In fact, she was given her own building, appropriately called the Woman's Building, at the World's Columbian Exposition of 1893. Included in that exhibit were paintings, sculptures, needlework, and quilting, as well as other artistic ventures. Some were trained; some were not—but none had to sign "anonymous" to their works.

Women portrayed life around the house, capturing special small moments such as a group of women quilting, a family around a kitchen table, the Thanksgiving dinner, or the garden's harvest. They painted portraits or pictures of memorable occasions. They recorded the way their houses looked, what the fashions of the day might be, and the way people of that time spent their leisure moments. Their art was transformed by their needles and by pen, pencil, watercolor, and oil. They used the tools they had and spoke through the pictures they made with those tools. I am sure that few of them realized their talents would make them immortal and that we, at the turn of the twentieth century, could be learning from them.

Clothing

Though it would seem to make more sense for country women to dress as did their male counterparts—for ease in getting around, especially when working on a farm, as well as for comfort—they still attempted to follow the styles of the day. Bustles and draped fabric did little more than make the country woman's tough job of living just a tad tougher, which is probably the reason that bustles and petticoats were considered so dispensable by those pioneers who needed to lighten their loads while on the road west.

The Empire style of high-waisted, pouf-sleeved, straight-skirted gowns was followed by American women in the early 1800s. Originated by Napoleon's Josephine, the dresses were made of flimsy material and were worn with little underwear and flat slippers.

Soon the Puritan ethic of the original settlers fought its way back to the surface, and women were back to wearing long-sleeved, full-skirted gowns with corsets that were uncomfortable and restraining.

The nature of fashion during the early to mid-1800s produced clothing that both constricted and exaggerated a woman's body. Corsets held a woman's middle in so tightly that miscarriages were often caused, yet the skirts of these dresses were so full and bustled that one could scarcely tell whether the woman was slim or exceedingly heavy from the waist down. Heavy satin fabrics made the dresses so cumbersome that it is no wonder many women had fainting spells.

Thus, the mid-1800s was a step back in time, putting women back into the constraints they had so recently enjoyed discarding. Several petticoats served to make women appear to have hips three feet wide, thus covering up what the body really looked like. Needless to say, it was difficult to get comfortable, and wasn't that the point?

For these reasons and because rural areas waited long for the arrival of new European imported fabrics and designs, the women whose lives centered around farm and ranch life opted to use lighter fabrics, like cottons and calicos, and to forgo crinolines, bustles, and other action-impeding garments. It wasn't until after the turn of the century that city women realized that they too needed to be able to breathe and that waists did not need to be 15 to 19 inches in circumference to prove a woman's attractiveness.

By the Civil War, necklines had risen even higher, and hairstyles were severe—drawn straight from a center part over the ears into a knot at the back of the neck. Bodices were tight, and skirts were full. A "bertha" or shawl-type attachment was added across the shoulders and busts of dresses made from silks, taffetas, wools, and calicos. It is this style most commonly seen in photos of country women at work in the field or at home.

The dress would be fancied up for social events or church gatherings by the addition of a small brooch or piece of black velvet tied at the neck of the dress.

Bonnets of straw or silk, trimmed with ribbons, plaitings, and feathers were commonly worn to keep the woman's face protected from the sun. Sunbonnets were worn by women for hundreds of years, both because women of that period treasured pale skin and because they were afraid of getting sunstroke.

Once the cold weather set in, women pulled on long drawers (invented in 1790) and dared not remove them until spring arrived. Made of flannel or homespun wool, these undergarments were as heavy as modern overcoats and quite uncomfortable.

Clothes were one of the last luxuries to be packed for a trip west and the first to be discarded should the trunks or the wagon be too full. In 1856, one woman reported that she had burned the bottoms of her dresses around an open fire and would probably have to don the "bloomer costume" soon. Approximately a month later, she was wearing bloomers and found that they were "well suited to a wild life" like hers.

These days when a large, roughly cut, antique seal coat is found, it is often expected to have belonged to a man, but that isn't necessarily so. It was common for the women who traveled west to own a seal coat or for those who were in Alaska during the Gold Rush to dress much like the Eskimo women who inhabited the area. At a later time, seal coats would be regarded as a sign of wealth. Those women, however, just considered the coats the most logical way to stay warm.

Instead of getting a new dress or coat every year, the American woman prior to the turn of the century may have changed a coat's collar from brocade to fur, put some new fringes on a cloak, trimmed the bottom of an old dress with a new piece of cloth or lace, or in any number of other imaginative ways rejuvenated and lengthened the life of their old clothes.

Western women in the mid to late 1800s wore cloaks that were two or three layers deep, hats that resembled the ones worn by contemporary men, calico dresses with blousey tops, full long skirts, and high collars. Their shoes were often saved for special occasions, and they spent their days in the house barefoot to save on precious and expensive shoes. One woman reports that the material to make her first blue calico dress cost $.125 per yard. Later she reported that she made her own flannel and that, after supper, the girls in the family would spin flax or knit till bedtime.

The turn of the century gave women the opportunity to have a little more fun—to ride a bicycle, legs up and pumping, wearing lace-trimmed bloomers, the forerunner of women's trousers. Women borrowed straw hats and bib-front shirtwaists from men's styles, recognizing that these items were not only neat but comfortable. Perhaps we can say that getting rid of restrictive clothing was one of the first positive steps on the road to liberation (and freedom)!

By the late Victorian era, most women were at least partially relying on the sewing machine to help make the family's clothing. It certainly seems to make sense that the already overstressed women of that era would long for help when hand-stitching the five or six yards of fabric that made up the skirts of their dresses. It was hard enough to *move* in such a costume, never mind *make* it.

Cleaning such voluminous outfits required special care, though clothing was not washed as often before the advent of the washing machine as it is today. The Victorian women who had to contend with their clothes being more susceptible to becoming dirty (e.g., dress trains dragging along behind them in the dust, mud, rain, or snow) were surprisingly scrupulous about the care given to their several outfits. Not having the benefits of dry cleaning or the ease of cleaning manmade fabrics, yesteryear's women attended to each and every stain on an individual basis. Each one was identified, and different remedies were used for its removal. It's not difficult to realize what a long and tedious process this was.

Body dirt or stains were minimal even though the outfit or dress would be worn many times before being cleaned. The women wore a large quantity of underwear, which seemed to serve as protection for outerwear.

In etiquette books of the day, women were warned to be careful of the way they sat, of where they stood, and of any closeness to fire. The crinolines worn under skirts often caused more accidents than they were worth. Many women fell down stairsteps or off chairs of suffered burns because their skirts were simply too unwieldy.

Out of this era came "Victorian whites," white cotton clothing and underwear that has become a favorite clothing collectible, especially among country aficionados. White cotton shirtwaists trimmed with ribbon and lace and camisoles once worn as underwear are serving as summer blouses for today's women; roomy bloomers are hung on bedroom walls as clothing art, and white skirts or petticoats are favored pieces of cool garden clothing. Chemises, which usually stretched well below the knees before 1860, were shrunk to waist-length and were no longer plain. By the end of the century, the chemise had become extremely pretty, with a round or heart-shaped neckline, a ribbon trim, and embroidery or lace trim around the edges.

Even though their outfits were long and heavy, women realized that they needed underwear that would keep them warm in the colder weather. Wool, flannel, or silk long drawers, chemises, and petticoats found popularity in the 1880s.

The old saying "a woman's work is never done" must have

been written by a country wife. Often up before dawn, she seldom got to bed before the sky was once again dark. In spite of all of her hard work, the woman was also expected to be beautiful and ready to please her husband at the drop of a hat (among other things). She wore lacy collarettes designed to lie on top of her dress, removable so that they could be cleaned easily. The collars were easily laundered, but ladies' dresses were not—no dry cleaners down the road in those days.

Frilly and feminine, the collars spread out to the shoulders and had high, buttoned necklines. They could often be ordered from Sears, Roebuck and Company ("the cheapest supply house on earth") for $1 to $3 each.

Shoes forced the foot into a narrow space, causing maidens to mince. Most women could not afford to buy more than one or two pairs of shoes in a lifetime, so it was tough luck if their feet grew!

Folk Medicine

It was the woman's position in the family to learn about natural herbal medicines, the names of flowers and what they could be used for, and what fruits and vegetables would grow in her area of the country. It could be said, at this point, that women were often the diplomats of the family because much of what they learned about living off the land was acquired knowledge obtained through their contact with local Indian tribes.

It was the Amerind who taught the first settlers about growing corn, about herbal remedies, even about vegetables like wild peas and beans that would make coffee. Indian blankets were used by early settlers, and Native American women taught some of their white sisters the secret of cleaning and tanning buffalo skin—a skill that kept many a settler warm on a cold prairie night.

Housekeeping

Country women who settled the lands both east and west of the Mississippi loved the convenience of their black iron Dutch ovens.

Placed right in the fire, these pans were used to cook bread over an open fire and could double as casserole ovens. They also were used to cook many different combination meals that today would be cooked in an oven or double broiler.

Other devices were concocted in order to make "special" dishes, such as Graham pudding. For example, one woman in the Northwest Territory described stringing a tea kettle onto a broom handle that was then stuck into the cabin's log walls so that the kettle was suspended and could be used to cook the meal of Graham pudding.

Marriage

Women came well prepared for marriage, having concentrated their single years on making quilts and preparing a selection of sheets, pillowcases, tablecloths, towels, and trousseau clothing. It might also be mentioned here that they made their own wedding dresses and that they were generally not white—one account mentions a pretty, sky blue, figured-lawn wedding dress.

Once married, the woman was considered the man's property, his chattel. She was under solemn obligation to work with him, to do as he said, and to adhere to his rules of the house. Thank goodness, that has changed!

Sewing and Quilting

Women learned sewing at a very early age. They made samplers before the ripe old age of ten, learning their alphabet as they learned different stitches. Throughout their teenage years, country women spent all free time making items that they would put away in a box for their dowries. Quilts, sheets and pillowcases, tablecloths and samplers were kept for the day they would get married.

Today's country collectors usually have at least one quilt, hooked rug, or sampler in their collections—all the work of artistic women. (See other information on this subject throughout this volume.)

Wash Day

Washing was the woman's job and one that required a lot of time. If she just washed fortnightly, the amount of washing, drying, and ironing she would have to do might spread over several days. Yet most households did not own enough clothing to let the wash go that long and the wash was done every week.

Washboards were the first step toward civilization; they were a close cousin of the ancient method of bringing clothes to a riverbed and beating them against the rocks. By the Victorian era, early washing machines were wooden tubs that were rotated or rocked so that the water and soap would circulate throughout the clothes. The sides and bottom of the tub were usually corrugated or spiked so that when the tub was turned, the clothes inside would rub against them. A later version had two rollers through which the clothes were pushed backward and forward.

As you can probably tell, neither of these washing techniques was necessarily kind to finer fabrics, buttons, or lace pieces; thus, the woman was back to square one: hand-washing her most delicate pieces of clothing.

By 1880, wringing machines had replaced washboards and most other washing devices in many homes. I guess you could call that invention one of the first forms of women's liberation.

Those first wringers were attached to washtubs with the help of clamps that held the wringer tightly to the tub so that clothes could be passed between the rollers. Many country homes have used the wringer and tub strictly as a decorative accent, for modern women don't have the back-breaking memory of using that device. I'm sure our great-grandmothers would laugh at our folly.

Other washday items, such as soaps, powders, and bleaches, are now crowding collectors' shelves as advertising collectibles.

Weaving

In May, the sheep were sheared. Then the wool had to be washed, picked, and carded by the women. Many of the diaries mentioned that the women considered this task to be their summer's work.

Once the task was completed, they used the rest of the year to spin the flax and make material or clothing out of the spun wool.

When you consider the fact that a small flock of sheep was usually twenty-five to fifty head and that all of this work was done by hand, without benefit of machines or electricity, it is fairly easy to imagine what a large job the women had before them and also to realize that if they didn't get their job done, their families would probably go without new or repaired winter clothing.

In one woman's journal, an entry dated July 1, 1842, mentions that her wool has been carded and that she's ready to spin. Planning to do her stocking wool first, she figured she would spin two skeins a day, utilizing her evenings to double and twist it while her husband read the Bible to her.

By November, the woman had woven a small plaid flannel material, a new dress for herself out of the red and blue material, two pairs of jeans for her husband, and two pairs of stockings for each of them.

Another woman mentioned that her husband had asked her to make him a bottle-green suit because he was sick of all the gray suits he saw while on business trips (you can certainly learn one thing from this account—that men's clothing has not changed very much in the last hundred years!). She made the suit by buying the wool, carding it into rolls, spinning it, then preparing to dye it by first scouring it white. Then she added indigo, yellow flowers, and a liquid made from rabbit brush, letting the color set.

After the yarn had stayed in this mixture for a while, it came out a dark bottle green. She took the yarn to another woman who wove it into cloth, then ripped up one of her husband's old suits so that she might use it as a pattern.

When done, she made the suit by hand, backstitching every stitch. For his hat, she traced a large dinner plate, cut the crown of a cap, lined it, and put a band on it. Her finished results made him look (in her words) "surely swell for these days."

Prices

If an item is not indicated as being specifically Shaker, Indian, Amish, etc., then it should be considered strictly a "country" piece. For items specifically made by the country groups spoken of in the first section of this book, consult that chapter.

CHILDREN

Bear, straw-stuffed, ca. 1890s. *$175–$225*

Youth chair, ca. 1820, old blue paint over yellow, great wear. *$250–$275*

Courtesy of Pumpkin Vine Line Antiques, Buddy and Atha Wallin, Fairfield, Ohio; photo by Donald Vogt.

Blanket chest, child's size, complete with till, poplar, nice dovetailing and beading, ca. 1830–50. *$450–$550*

Blue hooded cradle, ca. 1870s, two hood panels have been replaced. *$400–$500*

Doll's quilt, red, white, blue, 29″ × 44″. *$175–$200*

Victorian children's blocks, 2″ × 2″. *$4–$5*

Courtesy of Alice Kempton, Kempton's Country Classics; photo by Donald Vogt.

Buffet, blue, child's, ca. 1940s. *$45–$55*

Wooden top. *$8–$120*

Wooden red top. *$9–$13*

Courtesy of Eileen Russell, Worthington, Ohio; photo by Donald Vogt.

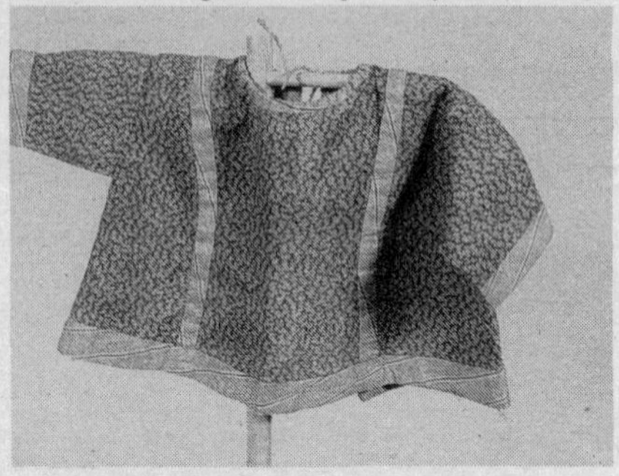

Calico shirt, red with beige trim. *$25–$35*

Cannon Ball, child's wagon, original yellow and green paint on body and wheels, ca. 1930, fine condition. *$170–$200*

Carriage, with original green paint and white striping, 3 wheels, 2 large and 1 small, 37″ high, 51″ long, collapsible leather roof as is. *$330–$400*

Chair, childs, Windsor, 1930s. *$125–$135*

McGuffey's primer books, set. *$38–$45*

Teddy bear, 1943. *$63–$70*

Courtesy of Danby Antiques Center, Agnes & Bill Franks, Managers, South Main Street, Danby, Vermont; photo by Ginger Gamadge.

Chair, country Sheraton, original black paint with gold stenciling, ca. 1850, seat replaced. *$295–$325*

Courtesy of Kay Previte, Antiques of Chester; photo by Donald Vogt.

Children's dresses, made in Southern Ohio ca. 1900–1910, good condition.

Long dress. *$28–$32*

Short dress. *$24–$28*

Clothing, child's dress, blue/white wide-striped material with long sleeves, 29″ long, late 1800s–1900, button back. *$68–$75*

Child's dress, blue/white striped, long-waisted and long-sleeved, 24″ long, probably 1900, button back. *$68–$75*

Mittens, pair, white wool, hand-knit, cable and shell knit backs with shell knitting as cuff on inner side, 8″ long. *$25–$30*

Courtesy of Alice Kempton, Kempton's Country Classics; photo by Donald Vogt.

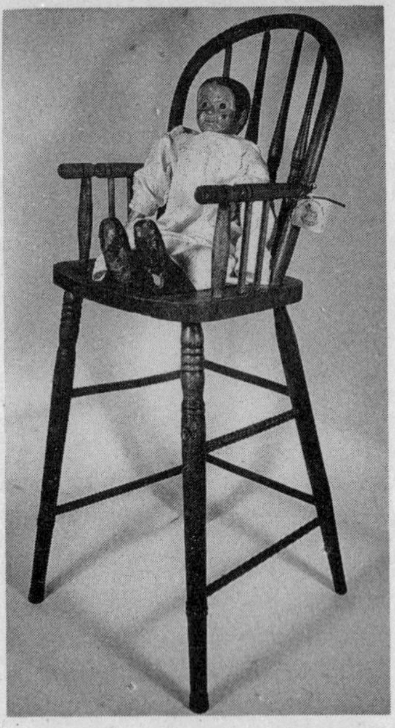

Contemporary folk art doll in bentwood youth chair, ca. turn of the century (price is not for doll). *$90–$110*

Cow and wagon toy, green, red, and yellow cow, ca. 1900. *$60–$80*

Cradle, hooded, pine, 27″ high, 40″ long, partially refinished. *$110–$200*

Crib blanket, unusual, with central American eagle and shield in red, white, and blue stripes, 32″ × 44″, faded, needs minor restoration, ca. late 19th/early 20th centuries. *$55–$75*

Doll carriage filled with blocks, 1920s. *$60–$70*

Hand-crank toy washing machine, iron and glass, 1930s. *$55–$75*

Doll's dress, handmade, red with orange trim, ca. 1900. *$55–$70*

Courtesy of Danby Antiques Center, Agnes & Bill Franks, Managers, South Main Street, Danby, Vermont; photo by Ginger Gamadge.

Dress, paisley stripe, muted tan, brown, gold, and blue, ca. 1865, very good condition. ***$65–$85***

Teddy bear, light tan, good condition, ca. 1920, 11″ high. ***$350–$400***

Courtesy of Grandad's Attic; photo by Donald Vogt.

Elephant pull toy (handmade). ***$35–$45***

Small stuffed dog inside pull toy. ***$65–$95***

Larger dog outside pull toy. ***$195–$235***

English bear (not priced) in American hand-carved children's chair, ca. 1900. ***$125–$175***

Courtesy of Grandad's Attic; photo by Donald Vogt.

Farm animals, cardboard, mint condition, ca. 1930s. *$12–$20*

Game board, folk art, in black and yellow paint, 23″ × 16″. *$154–$175*

Homemade sock doll with blue jumper. *$30–$45*

Shoes, child's, black leather. *$45–$60*

Socks, long, white, child's. *$20–$25*

Undershirt, child's, white. *$22–$30*

Mittens, child's, suede. *$20–$28*

Horse, large, on wheels, black and red decoration, late 1800s. *$600–$800*

Horse-and-buggy pedal cart, 90% of original paint decoration remaining, label on back, "patented July 6, 1909, Anthony Arney Specialty Co.; Port Huron, Michigan"; 5′ long, front tire probably not original, ca. 20th century. *$1,980–$2,000*

Courtesy of Summer House Antiques, Antiques of Chester; photo by Donald Vogt.

Horse scooter toy, flexible front, turn of century, ca. 1910. *$275–$325*

Courtesy of Pumpkin Vine Line Antiques, Buddy and Atha Wallin, Fairfield, Ohio; photo by Donald Vogt.

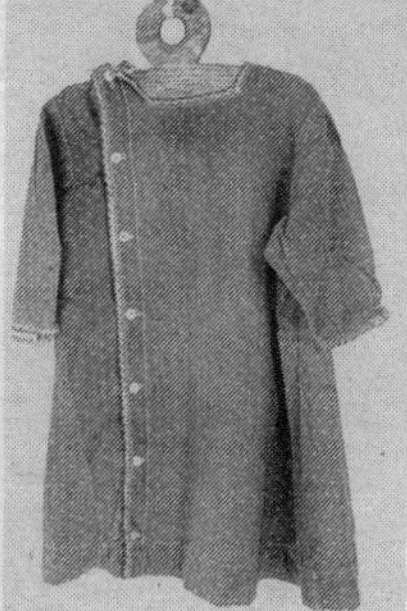

Indigo blue children's dress, made in Ohio, ca. 1900–1910, good condition. *$24–$28*

Ladder truck, wooden, fire department, consists of ladder bed, wheels, portable ladder, and mechanical ladder, possibly needs restoration, incomplete, ca. 19th century. *$300–$400*

Courtesy of Chester Freeman; photo by Henry Peach.

Pull toy, horse, hide-covered, excellent condition. *$700–$900*

Collectible artist-designed bears by Chester Freeman. *$200–$250*

Push-me/pull-you cart, original stenciling, iron wheels, ca. 1880–90, green background, red trim, gold stencil. *$175–$195*

Puzzle, Victorian, 6-sided, with original box, scenes include an elephant, kittens, horse, and other animals. *$350–$650*

Courtesy of Alice Kempton, Kempton's Country Classics; photo by Donald Vogt.

Road grader, steel, Tonka, ca. 1940s. *$75–$85*

Rocking horse seat, original decoration 95% intact, 25″ high, 35″ long, ca. 20th century. *$165–$250*

Courtesy of Mary Calder, Antiques of Chester; photo by Donald Vogt.

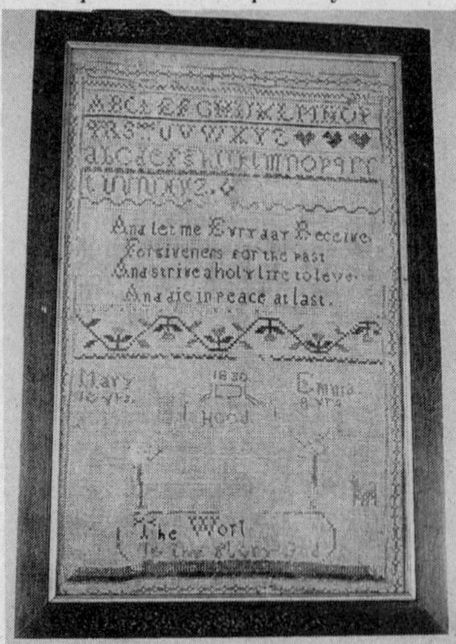

Sampler, made by Mary (10) and Emma (8) Hood, dated 1850, excellent condition. *$400–$500*

Sawbuck, mid-19th century, painted tan, New York. *$150–$200*

Banks, tin, set of 4, First National Banks (each). *$30–$60*

Courtesy of Mary-Lee Muntz, Bonneyville Knoll Antiques, Middlebury, Indiana; photo by Donald Vogt.

Scooter, blue and orange, ca. 1900, all wooden, bought in Nebraska. *$100–$125*

Courtesy of Chester Freeman; photo by Henry Peach.

Scooter, excellent condition. *$50–$75*

Artist-designed teddy bear by Chester Freeman. *$150–$175*

Seat/pen, wooden, 19″ high, 24″ long, ca. 19th century. *$175–$200*

Shoofly horse, ca. 1850, red paint. *$175–$225*

Boy doll, composition head, foot missing. *$55–$65*

Child's shoes, ca. 1900s, tan, with design on side. *$20–$25*

Sled, girl's, ca. 1880, original paint, red, with flower, good condition. *$395–$450*

Skates, ca. 1850. *$200–$250*

Sled, boy's, racing, old red paint, late 1800s. *$125–$175*

Sled, old, green, 30″ runners. *$225–$250*

Courtesy of Pumpkin Vine Line Antiques, Buddy and Atha Wallin, Fairfield, Ohio; photo by Donald Vogt.

Sled, with red background, gold scrollwork, and hand-painted scene of mountains in inset, ca. 1880–90, not signed. *$575–$675*

Courtesy of Grandad's Attic; photo by Donald Vogt.

Stuffed dog on wooden tricycle. *$45–$75*

Surrey, cast iron, by Stanley Toys, with original paint, excellent condition. *$225–$275*

Courtesy of Sign of the Dove and Antiques of Chester; photo by Donald Vogt.

Table, primitive, child's, gray paint over mortise-and-tenon construction, old, repair to top. *$185–$215*

Child's high-top shoes, ca. 1870, leather, three-color (blue, white, and red). *$35–$45*

Courtesy of Chester Freeman; photo by Henry Peach.

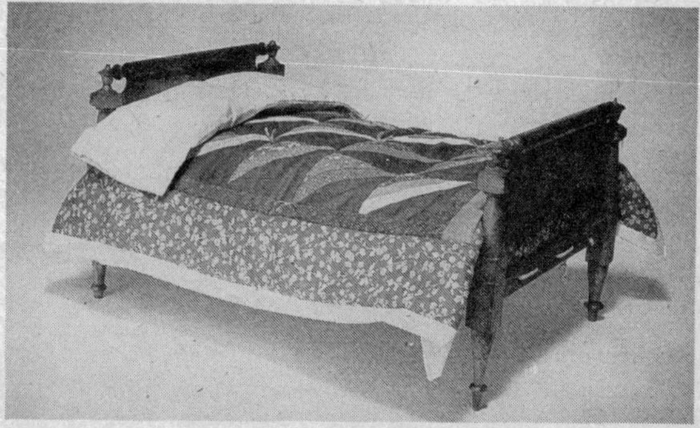

Toy bed, rope, ca. 1870, handmade, in excellent condition. *$600–$800*

Toy, carved wooden horse on wheeled platform, painted black, 10″ high, 11″ long, ca. 19th century. *$150–$250*

Toy, cast iron, "Fire Patrol" with driver and horse, 18″ long overall, paint in good condition. *$385–$400*

Toy, elephant pull, painted green, gray, and red, 8″ high, 10″ long, ca. 20th century. *$40–$75*

Courtesy of McFarland Auctioneers, Williamson, New York 14589.

Toys (left to right, top row), 19th-century penny dolls in original dress, ca. 1880. *$580–$600*

Friction engine, original surface. *$495–$550*

(Bottom row) *German balance ornament.*

Courtesy of Jeannine Dobbs' Country/Folk/Antiques.

Village, 9 of a 15-piece handcrafted recreation of a northeastern village, ca. 1930, made as a setup for a model train, tallest building is approximately 13″ high. *Price not available*

Courtesy of Pumpkin Vine Line Antiques, Buddy and Atha Wallin, Fairfield, Ohio; photo by Donald Vogt.

Wagon, Coaster car, wooden, No. 1, roller bearing, stenciled, ca. 1890, bit of red on the trim. *$550–$700*

Wagon, painted in old blue paint, with removable side boards, 25″ high overall, 44″ long plus handle, 29″ wide, 19th century. *$330–$500*

Wooden buildings, made originally for railroad toys, 1930s–40s *$125–$150*

MEN

Beading plane, 5/16″, old mark. *$13–$15*

Courtesy of Alice Kempton, Kempton's Country Classics; photo by Donald Vogt.

Checkerboard, Michigan, with original checkers, 18″ × 24½″, ca. 1880s, buttermilk paint. *$90–$125*

Cooper's tools, grouping: draw knife, 7″ blade, signed "L & White." *$18–$22*

Old-style bung reamer, 9″ blade, 14″ handle. *$17–$23*

Bung lifter, hand-forged, 7½″ × 7½″. *$14–$20*

Decoy, black duck, by Ferman Ayer, used near Gánonque, Ontario, on the St. Lawrence River, paint 95% complete. *$120–$200*

Decoy, broad-billed drake, by Jean Boucher, Lake St. Peter, Quebec, 95% paint. *$100–$150*

Decoy, carved, bluebill drake, stamped "Cape Cod Decoys H.A. Davis, Waquoit, Mass." *$110–$150*

Decoy, carved, curlew, mounted on driftwood, brand of "K. Blakely Decoys, Wellfleet." *$175–$200*

Decoy, curlew, with turned head, by Byron Bruffee. *$75–$125*

Decoy, godwit, by Byron Bruffee. *$85–$100*

Decoy, pair of primitive carved goldeneye. *$130–$150*

Decoy, pair of primitive carved merganser. *$150–$200*

Decoy, primitive carved merganser hen. *$50–$100*

Decoy, primitive Cape Cod brant, length 23″, as is. *$100–$125*

Decoy, primitive carved merganser drake. *$75–$125*

Decoy, primitive carved brant. *$150–$230*

Decoy, 2, ducks, carved and painted. *$50–$100*

Decoy, whistler drake, by J. N. Dodge Factory of Detroit, head reglued and paint worn. *$66–$100*

Decoy, wooden duck, 17″ long, paint worn. *$286–$300*

Decoy, goose, working, cork-bodied. *$50–$100*

Courtesy of Mill Village Antiques, Francestown, New Hampshire.

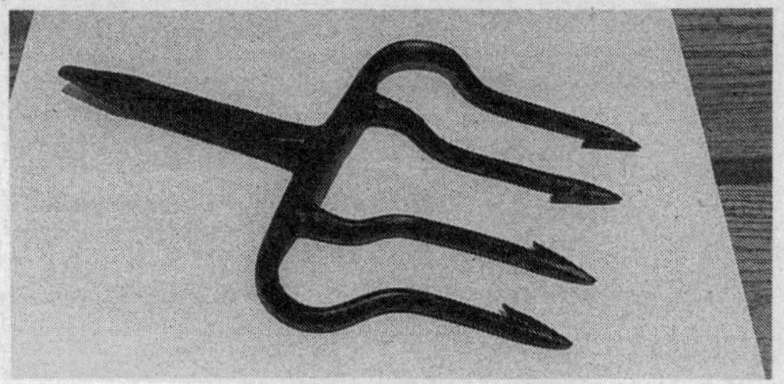

Fishing spear, 9″, handmade, ca. early 1900s. *$75–$95*

Courtesy of Mill Village Antiques, Francestown, New Hampshire.

Fishing spear, 13″ handmade, ca. early 1900s. *$75–$100*

Courtesy of Mill Village Antiques, Francestown, New Hampshire.

Fishing spear, 17¼″, handmade, ca. early 1900s. *$75–$100*

Game board, green and black, with decoration, from Woodstock, VT, ca. 1900. *$175–$200*

Game board, double-sided, painted decoration, 28″ square, ca. 20th century. *$150–$175*

Gentleman's chest, Kentucky, mid-19th century, 43″ wide × 22″ deep × 50″ high. *$1,200–$1,500*

Courtesy of Louisville Antique Mall, Louisville, Kentucky; photo by Donald Vogt.

Grappling tongs, old red and green paint still on the hand-forged iron. *$22–$25*

Courtesy of Rampant Lion, Antiques of Chester; photo by Donald Vogt.

Group of tools (center), apple tray with cutout handles, mid-1800s, marked "W D W." *$275–$300*

(Left) *thread box,* handcrafted (used to cut threads on wooden dowel). *$75–$85*

(Center) *shoe sizer,* folding maple, brass foot, mid–late 1800s. *$58–$65*

(Right) *small curved carpenter's clamp,* maple, mid-1800s. *$45–$60*

Courtesy of Rampant Lion, Antiques of Chester; photo by Donald Vogt.

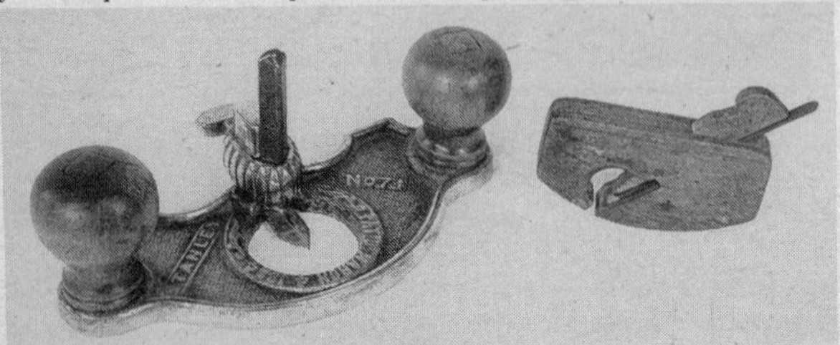

Group of tools, large plane with two kinds of knobs, Stanley Model 71, router plane. *$68–$80*

Miniature curved maple plane, mid-1800s. *$55–$70*

Courtesy of Rampant Lion, Antiques of Chester; photo by Donald Vogt.

Group of tools (left), pair of unusual matched rosewood and brass scribes, mortise gauges, ca. 1870. *$110–$125*

(Center) *leather knife,* walnut, brass, and iron, ca. 1870, marked "Francis & Ward, Newark, N.J." *$65–$85*

(Right) *mortise gauge,* early Stanley, brass and walnut, patent 1857. *$110–$125*

Courtesy of Rampant Lion, Antiques of Chester; photo by Donald Vogt.

Hunting accessories (center rear), pewter military canteen, mid- to late 1800s, replaced strap. *$45–$60*

(Left) *powder flask,* ca. 1870, Sykes patent. *$80–$100*

(Center) *powder flask,* shell design, copper and brass, ca. 1860. *$110–$125*

(Right) *powder flask,* Hawksley overall, ca. 1860. *$110–$125*

Courtesy of Mill Village Antiques, Francestown, New Hampshire.

Ice spearing decoys, carved by Otton Fane (1881–1954), Hanover, MN (rear) 10¼″ long, crazed paint, light green face, medium green on back, white belly, painted eyes, shows good in-use wear, ca. 1930s. *$600–$700*

(Front) *10″ long,* medium brown back to light brown sides with white belly, small white slash marks on sides, painted eyes, excellent overall wear, ca. 1930s. *$600–$700*

Courtesy of Mill Village Antiques, Francestown, New Hampshire.

Ice spearing decoys, carved by Earl Kielmeyer (1902–1984) of Nerstrand, MN, 10½″ long, varnish over natural wood, burned slash marks on body, burned-out holes for eyes, slight in-use wear, ca. 1940s. *$50–$75*

Courtesy of Mill Village Antiques, Francestown, New Hampshire.

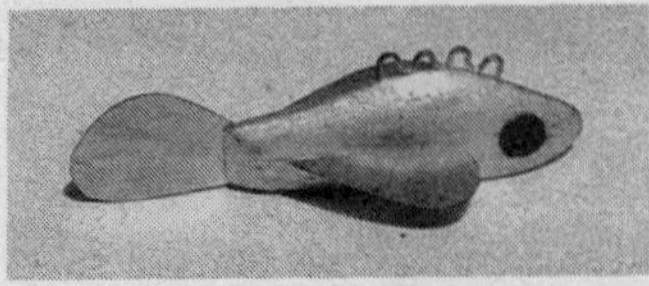

Ice spearing decoys, carved by LeRoy Howell (1899–1988), Hinkley, MN, 3¼″ long, silver with painted red eye/black center, ca. 1930s. *$350–$400*

Courtesy of Mill Village Antiques, Francestown, New Hampshire.

Ice spearing decoys, unknown carver, turtle, 14″ long, wooden body and head, tin legs and tail, ca. 1930s. *$300–$400*

Courtesy of Mill Village Antiques, Francestown, New Hampshire.

Ice spearing decoys, unknown carver, frog, 6¼″ long, wooden body, tin legs, glass eyes, mottled green and black body with yellow undersides, ca. 1930s. *$350–$400*

Courtesy of Mill Village Antiques, Francestown, New Hampshire.

Ice spearing decoys, unknown carver, sunfish shape, white body with red face and red body stripe, buttons for eyes, tin fins, well used, ca. 1940s. *$150–$200*

Courtesy of Mill Village Antiques, Francestown, New Hampshire.

Ice spearing decoys, unknown carver, supposed to look like a fish decoy, carved by Oscar Peterson of Cadillac, MI, 14″, gold with black "squiggles" and red and black dots, painted red gills, tack eyes, contemporary. *$100–$150*

Courtesy of Louisville Antique Mall, Louisville, Kentucky; photo by Donald Vogt.

Planes, group of four wood-molding planes, 7/8″–1 7/8″ wide, most from Ohio (each). *$13–$20*

Courtesy of Louisville Antique Mall, Louisville, Kentucky; photo by Donald Vogt.

Planes, two wood-molding grooving planes, one (1 7/8″ wide) marked "F. Seybold, E. Cin., Ohio" and the other (1 1/4″ wide) marked "F. Seribo." *$16–$20*

Powder horn, carved, with half-circles where base is attached, wood base marked "I.B.," 12" long, ca. late 18th/early 19th centuries. *$88–$100*

Courtesy of Louisville Antique Mall, Louisville, Kentucky; photo by Donald Vogt.

Rim sifter, for rocks, 4 handles, late 1800s. *$45–$60*

Courtesy of Louisville Antique Mall, Louisville, Kentucky; photo by Donald Vogt.

Spoke shave, handmade, 13", brass and bird's-eye maple. *$20–$25*

Courtesy of Alice Kempton, Kempton's Country Classics; photo by Donald Vogt.

Tool tote with covered box, old red paint, turn of century. *$100–$125*

Courtesy of Country Cottage Antiques; photo by Donald Vogt.

Utensil box, New England, old blue paint, 11½″ × 8″ × 8″, cut-out edges. *$235–$250*

MISCELLANEOUS

Courtesy of Kay Previte, Antiques of Chester; photo by Donald Vogt.

Pine clam bucket, with iron staves, Maine, ca. 1900. *$125–$165*

Rare and unusual sled, designed in chair form so that a single person can be pushed along the ice or snow, old salmon color paint, yellow lining, 34″ high, 48″ long, 21″ wide, 19th century. *$330–$500*

WOMEN

Courtesy of Eileen Russell, Worthington, Ohio; photo by Donald Vogt.

Apron, blue and white gingham, midwestern. *$70–$80*
Bonnet, blue and white gingham. *$50–$60*

Courtesy of Louisville Antique Mall, Louisville, Kentucky; photo by Donald Vogt.

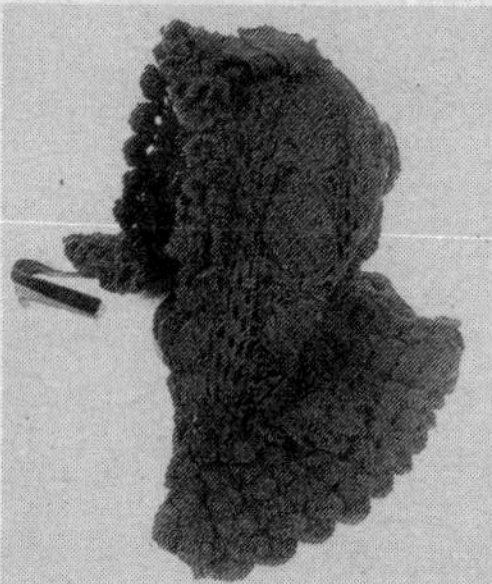

Bonnet, hand-crocheted, black, church bonnet. *$22–$28*

Courtesy of Elizabeth Enfield, Mount Vernon Antiques, Rockport, Massachusetts.

Bonnet, silk flowers around back, ca. 1830s. *$650–$700*

Elvirah Evans sampler, 1851, flowers and birds, 21½″ × 27½″, with frame. *$695–$750*

Courtesy of Elizabeth Enfield, Mount Vernon Antiques, Rockport, Massachusetts.

Hat, straw, ca. 1910, lilacs and netting around brim. *$275–$325*

Hat box, oval, paper, made from Concord, NH, and Albany, NY, newspapers, 1836, 18½″ × 15″ × 12″. *$138–$200*

Quilting frame, rare, in old green paint, 30″ high, 98″ long, 27″ wide, ca. 19th century. *$138–$300*

Sampler, framed needlework, "Almira Foster's work wrought in the tenth year of her age," executed mainly in blue, green, and yellow stitches on woven linen ground, a floral-decorated border framing a poem and alphabet, 21¼″ high, 17½″ wide, some stains throughout. *$300–$400*

Sampler, framed needlework, "Eliza Jane Foster, Dorchester aged 11," executed in green, blue, and yellow stitches on woven linen ground, wrought with alphabets and verse, scrolled borders, 21½″ × 16½″, ca. 19th century. *$400–$500*

Sampler, framed needlework, "Almira Morse Roxbury 1844," executed in navy blue stitches on woven linen ground, 6 bands of alphabet and numbers, 11¾″ high, 10¾″ wide, some staining lower right and upper left, ca. 19th century. *$150–$200*

Sampler, framed needlework, "Elizabeth Foster Morse Roxbury 1842," executed in brown stitches on woven linen ground, three bands of alphabets, 8″ high, 16″ wide, ca. 19th century. *$100–$200*

Sampler, framed needlework, "Anna C. Frost Wayne," 4 rows of alphabets executed on loosely woven linen ground, 10″ high, 14″ wide, hole lower right side, loose threads, faded, no date.
$100–$125

Sampler, important, American, "Mary Coffin, AE. 10, 1801," light brown linen backing with superb needlework decoration of flowers, figures, trees, verse, and partial alphabet, "Here is this green and shady bower, Delicious fruits and fragrant flowers, Virtue shall dwell within this seat, Virtue alone can make it sweet." The bottom scene, from left to right, reveals a grape arbor, a young black servant holding an umbrella for a lady in a pink dress, a willow tree, a duck pond, a man fishing in the pond, a young girl, a tree, and another young girl; superb colors and condition, one minor hole. This piece has apparently been kept in a box for most of its life; it is related to the well-known group of samplers done in Newburyport, MA, family tradition also points to that area, 15″ × 20½″. *$46,200–$48,000*

Sampler, unusual, framed, with verses and a large basket of fruit, flowers and alphabets on a linen ground, 19″ × 26″.
$358–$500

Sampler, framed, with alphabets, numbers, "Betsey Fisher's Sampler wrote in the year 1813," 10″ × 11″. *$110–$150*

Samplers, done by sisters M. E. Cannon (May 1877) and Louisa E. Cannon (1881), 8¼″ × 8½″ (each). *$225–$275*

Courtesy of Janice Derrick Collection.

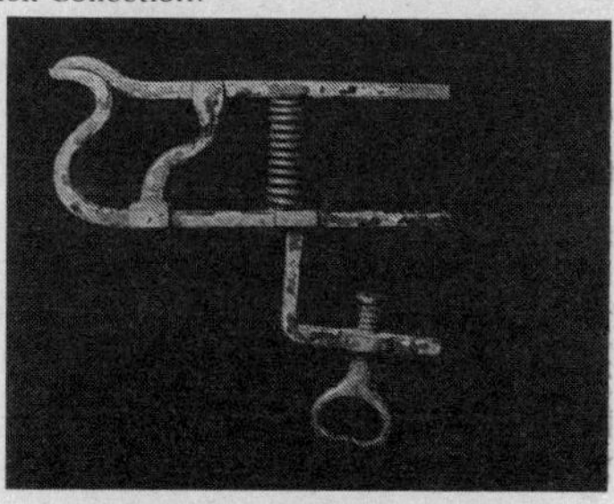

Sewing bird, primitive bird shape, iron, 4½″ high, 19th century.
$100–$125

Courtesy of Janice Derrick Collection.

Sewing bird, "A. Gerould & Co. Patent," brass and iron, 4½″ high, 1853. *$250–$300*

Courtesy of Janice Derrick Collection.

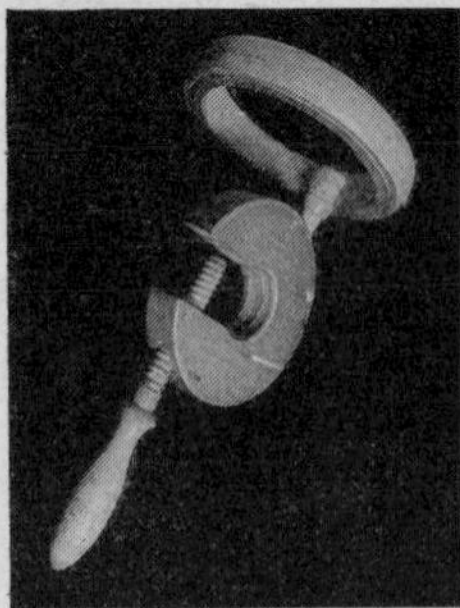

Sewing clamp, with embroidery hoop, wood, 11″ high, possibly Shaker, 19th century. *$150–$200*

Courtesy of Janice Derrick Collection.

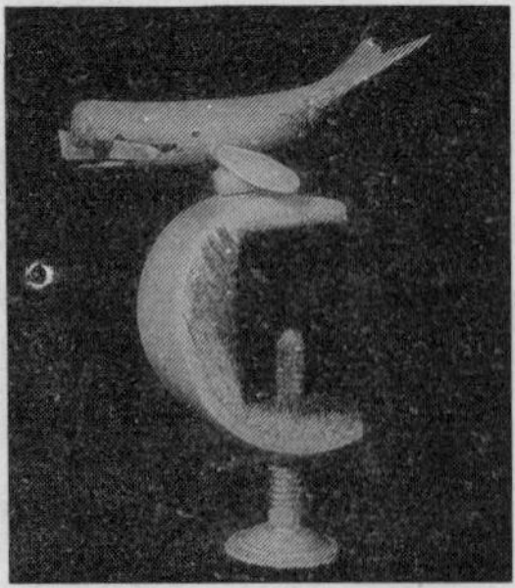

Sewing clamp, scrimshaw, carved figural whale, bone, 3¾″ high, 19th century. *$600–$650*

Courtesy of Janice Derrick Collection.

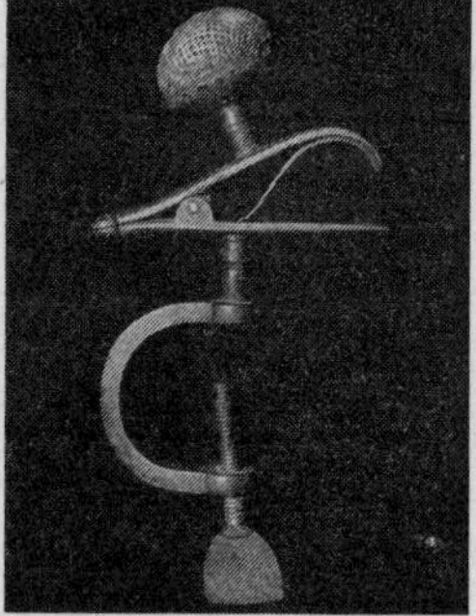

Sewing clamp, with snake motif and original needlepoint pincushion, iron, 7¼″ high, late 18th or early 19th century. *$300–$350*

Courtesy of Janice Derrick Collection.

Sewing clamp, wood, 9¼″ high, 19th century. *$125–$175*

Courtesy of Elizabeth Enfield, Mount Vernon Antiques, Rockport, Massachusetts.

Straw hat, decorated with cherries and velvet ribbon around crown, ca. 1910. *$225–$250*

THE COUNTRY HOME

WHENEVER I THINK of a country home, I think of bright flames in a brick fireplace, the smell of a beef stew simmering on the stove, the sound of a babbling brook going past a bedroom window, fireflies on a warm summer night, and cookouts with friends and family. I think of the Christmas season, when neighbors go from house to house, relaxed enough to visit and enjoy each other's company. Or of haying season, when everyone, young and old, hops on the back of the wagon and works together to get the bales in the barn before the end of the season. Gardens come to mind, and I think of starting the seeds indoors when it's still cold outside, planting those struggling green shoots in cool earth, watching them grow, mature, and produce fruits and vegetables for the August dinner table.

I think of harvest tables, pitted and vallied with age, in the kitchen and the large group of people that sits around them. Or of cupboards, filled to the brim with jellies, jams, and preserved pickles and fruits. And the brightly colored hooked rugs to warm the floor beneath your toes on a frosty winter morning or fresh-smelling quilts to throw over a newly made wedding bed.

A country home is comfortable, something you want to come back to after a long day at work. It is a safe haven from the rest of the world where you can stretch your limbs, warm your toes, and relax.

Growing up in a country home meant being responsible for scouring the large iron pots that sat in the fireplace all winter and enjoying the springtime chore because it gave you a chance to go down by the river. It meant reading school texts by the soft light of an oil lamp, proud of being the first in the family to go to school.

This section is divided into different parts of the house. Though there are furniture prices in each section, they were not paramount in my thinking when putting together this book. I wanted to concentrate more on the smaller country-oriented items. However, there is information about certain pieces of country furniture, such as cupboards, dry sinks, rope beds, and other items most commonly found in country homes.

Some of the items you find in one "room" in this chapter can also be found in other parts of the house. For instance, all information on lighting is included in the parlor section, but each room needed lighting, and because lamps were commonly carried from one place to another, I saw no reason to spread the facts too thinly throughout the chapters. Occasionally, I will mention that other details about certain country collectibles may be found in different chapters of this book. If you are looking for a particular item, it might be best to start where you find the largest body of information and then to check the index to see whether I might have mentioned your item anywhere else in the book.

As in the section on country items found in the kitchen, there was a plethora of collectibles from which to choose. I hope I made the right decision when selecting the objects and that I have chosen the ones that are most popular. If not, let me know what you would like to see covered, and perhaps we can add it to the next volume.

In the meantime, let me take you into the country home I have designed in my mind to show how our ancestors lived and what they used on an everyday basis.

The Kitchen

EARLY AMERICAN KITCHENS were large rooms. The fireplace took up the better part of the room and, as we've mentioned before, was the place where the family gathered.

In larger homes, the kitchen was almost a separate part of the house—the servants' domain. Often the room would be in the basement or lower regions of the house, where it was cooler in the summer and warmer in the winter. The heat generated by the large fireplace and/or Dutch oven would rise and circulate throughout the rest of the house.

Long, roughly made tables were used when preparing a meal, kneading dough, cutting and stringing apples, or preparing meat for cooking. Hooks on the fireplace wall held large pots, kettles, spoons, and strainers. Some of these brass, copper, or iron pots weighed approximately forty pounds when empty and much more when full of a soup or stew. One could definitely gain arm strength working in such a kitchen.

Herbs, dried meat, and poultry hung from trammels, or hooks, attached to the ceiling beams. Dried apples and other fruits would be strung across a window or hung near the fireplace. An open-shelf cupboard might hold the family's pewter plates or additional cooking utensils. Wooden boxes in graduated sizes were used to hold flour, sugar, salt, and other spices.

Every item had a place in those early kitchens, and most articles of kitchenware were meant to last. They were made of durable metals or woods and often passed on to other members of the family.

As America went into the nineteenth century, kitchens became smaller. No longer were they dark rooms built of stone and relegated to the back or basement of a house. Victorian kitchens had one or two sunny windows, a small wood stove or cook stove to provide heat, and smaller, space-economical tables and chairs. A pantry was utilized to store supplies, dried or canned foods, the flour barrel, the sugar bucket, and spices. It was where the cook might store her towels, aprons, broom, mop, and other cleaning utensils.

Victorian cooks continued to use cast-iron cookware, but other, lighter pots and utensils were also popular. Graniteware kettles and pots, tinware pans, and earthenware mixing bowls were commonly found in nineteenth-century homes. "Modern" conveniences such as refrigerators, water coolers, and ice cream freezers were in use toward the latter part of the century, and every housekeeper/cook wanted one.

By the twentieth century, everyone agreed it was imperative for a kitchen to be sanitary. Everything had to be clean and efficient, and the totally white, antiseptic look was born. Wooden floors were covered with linoleum or tile, wallpaper was hung, and all kitchen accessories were painted white. Gas ranges replaced fireplaces, coal stoves, and wood stoves because, as the ads said, gas was "cleaner." Pots and pans were still being made of cast iron, graniteware, and tin but also of aluminum. No longer did they weigh forty pounds empty.

Kitchenware

Items made specifically for kitchen use during the last century are still affordable collectibles. Some of my friends in the antique business have started to specialize in kitchen items, figuring they are still fairly easy to get and priced so that most country collectors can afford them.

Kristin Duval of Irreverent Relics in Allston, Massachusetts, was putting together sets of wood-handled utensils, made in the 1920s–1940s, for her customers a couple of years ago, but she doesn't do it quite so often today because the pieces "just aren't as easy to get." Other friends of ours are rescuing 1950s kitchen items from the trash pile, reviving those that could be dangerous (e.g., frayed electrical cords are replaced), and resurrecting them for use in today's microwave-equipped country home. I bought a waffle iron from them a couple of years ago and have been creating golden, toasty waffles covered with Vermont maple syrup ever since—the good things never die.

Last summer I resurrected two cases of old Ball canning jars from my basement and, with a friend's help, had them filled with pickles, relish, and jams by the end of harvest. Those jars will still be in working condition ten or twenty years from now, and they look much more attractive in a farmhouse pantry than do the modern screw-top versions. Because of those facts, canning jars that sold for less than $1 apiece a couple of years ago are now selling for $3–$4 (or more, depending on their color). They can be used for storage of all types—for leftovers, dimes and pennies, buttons—or for their original purpose: canned fruits and vegetables harvested from a country garden.

Apple Processing Tools and Cherry Stoners

Although odd and often awkward to use, apple processing tools and cherry stoners were essential for those country homes lucky enough to have either type of tree on their land. Apple processing tools were common on yesterday's farms and continue to be used by those who wish to get back to the land.

Peelers were originally made of all wood and employed a crank-turned device for removing the apple's skin. A revolving wheel would turn the apple to a blade, which then peeled off the outer skin. Peelers might sit directly on a table, screw onto the table's edge, or be constructed to stand by themselves on the floor.

By the nineteenth century, the wooden parer was replaced by an all-iron one. Some parers did more than one job; for example, the Vermont Apple Parer and Hudson Parer not only pared but cored and sliced apples as well. Even some left-handed versions were made toward the end of the century.

Cherry stoners were intended to make the job of removing the stones from the tiny fruit a little easier. The cherries were dropped into a scoop at the top, and as the handle was cranked, the pit came out a vent and the whole cherry was dropped into a bowl below. Stoners were usually made of iron and were meant to be clamped onto a table. The Enterprise Company made a number of different sizes of cherry stoners in the late 1890s.

Beetles

Beetles look like pestles, only their ends are flat. They have a stout pounding or tenderizing end and a long handle end. The tools are used to tenderize meats or to crush vegetables.

Blancmange Molds

I never knew the name for those decorative molds, made of tin, copper, porcelain, or pottery and hung on the walls of some country homes I visited. I just called them molds. But the proper term is blancmange molds.

The molds are sometimes in the form of flowers, vegetables, or fruit, sometimes in geometric shapes. They are used when making blancmange, another term for gelatin or gelatinous dishes.

Bread-Making Collectibles

Every country family made its own bread—some still do. Though it's been at least ten years since I've combined shortening, flour, and yeast and waited for that mixture to rise, we have almost fifteen different types of breadboards on our kitchen wall. Because they were used almost every day, it's extremely difficult to tell which ones are the oldest boards in our collection.

Most were handmade from scraps of hardwood like maple and birch. Most makers seemed to prefer maple, probably because it's a hard wood that was readily available throughout New England and the Northeast. The most recently made breadboards are of thinner pieces of wood, sometimes painted or decorated with decals and of a uniform shape and size.

Bread boxes were usually made of ventilated tin, though I have seen wooden, screened, and stoneware versions. One particularly unusual one, which we photographed for inclusion in this book, had a granite base—not what you would call a "portable" bread box.

Bread graters are large and used to make crumbs of dried bread. (See "Choppers and Graters, below.) Bread coolers are wire racks where bread was placed to cool. They are often footed, holding the rack off the surface in order to allow air to circulate.

Knives specifically designed to cut bread slices are scalloped or flared, while their points are blunt or truncated.

Tin pails with attached crank paddles were used to mix bread ingredients and were made by such companies as Universal or Eclipse.

Tin or black sheet iron was used to make pans for baking bread. These were made in many different sizes and shapes by such companies as Matthai-Ingram, F. A. Walker, and Ideal. Some bakers used a bread riser, a large, covered tin bowl with a ventilated lid, to help their bread rise.

Dough boxes or trays were wooden troughs in which the dough was mixed, kneaded, and left to rise. Some dough boxes stood on their own legs, while others were placed on the kitchen table for easy use.

I have sold two or three dough boxes that were one-piece units with removable tops. They stand on the floor and are about waist high, a perfect size for kitchen storage. A friend has hers under a hanging wire frame that holds pots and pans, and it serves both as a center island in her kitchen and as a receptacle for her extra pans.

A dough scraper resembles a small iron hoe and is used to scrape dough from a board or box. The oldest versions were fashioned completely out of iron (18th century), while newer ones might have wooden handles.

There were a number of types of flour bins and sifters made during America's history. They came in sizes ranging from 25 to 100 pounds and were usually made with a pan or a tin removable bowl at the bottom to catch the sifted flour. Some companies that produced flour bins and sifters are the Matthai-Ingram Co., Perfection, and Geuder, Pesche and Frey.

Hand-held sifters are sieves with mesh bottoms and hand-worked cranks. The cook could put a cup or two of flour through the sifter at a time, making it easier to use just the amount of flour she needed at that moment.

Measuring vessels are extremely important when making bread. Though the earliest versions were made to measure ale or beer in taverns, I'm sure that all cooks would agree that they are most often used in baking. Measuring cups have been made of pewter, tin, copper, porcelain, glass, wood, and brass. They come in sizes ranging from a quarter pint to a gallon.

Butter-Related Items

Butter-related items were plentiful on farms during the early 1800s and through the 1940s, though butter was produced in centralized creameries beginning in about 1918. The majority of butter-related items you may find on the market today originated in the Midwest because that's where the largest dairy farms were. However, you will find items from the eastern states, particularly those that were farm-oriented (e.g., Vermont, New Hampshire, Pennsylvania).

Mixing bowls, used to work butter, are most typically wood but may be ceramic, spatterware, or spongeware. Some of the wooden examples had a copper strip tacked to the rim so that the bowl would not easily split. The spatterware or spongeware examples are the most highly collectible and are valuable even though they may have some slight imperfections or damage.

The small wooden tubs used to keep the milk cool until the cream rose to the top were called "keelers" or "keels." Also used to store milk, both fresh milk and cream, were open-topped stoneware crocks (more on stoneware in The Country Market chapter). Some companies, such as Wesson, made the crocks for butter storage and stamped their name on them so that they would be returned. Such stoneware is collected for both its advertising significance and because it fits into the category of kitchen items.

Butter molds come in all shapes and sizes, though the most recognizable are the round plunger style and the rectangular factory-made examples. They were used to compact or decorate the butter once it was agitated into one large yellow mass. Most simply pressed a pound at a time and could be used to market the product by the general store or dairy farm. The majority of butter molds are made of hand-carved wood, though glass, pottery, and even metal examples may be found.

Miniature butter molds also were made, though some collectors appear to be confused by the difference between them and maple sugar molds. One way to determine which is which is that butter molds usually work one at a time, and maple sugar molds may have several small designs on one long mold. Another distinction is that butter molds have a hollow body to hold the butter, and maple sugar molds were shallower because they were pressed *onto* the sugar to make candy.

The designs carved into butter molds were typically flowers, stars, hearts, sheaves of wheat, and the initials of the company or farm family. Rare examples may have fish or animals on them, and some molds have hinged sides.

Paddles are usually 8 to 10 inches long with a thin, wide blade that is straight or slightly curved. The paddle's handle may be curved so that the worker could hook it onto the side of the bowl or hang it when finished. "Scotch hands" resemble paddles, except that one surface is ridged. They were made in pairs and were used to produce butterballs by rolling the butter between the two corrugated sides of the paddles.

The butter tamp looks like a kitchen masher, though its handle is a lot longer and the head averages 3 inches in diameter. Used to pack butter, the tamp is made of a hard wood, perhaps maple. If in doubt about whether or not your tamp was used for butter, smell it. Years of packing butter leaves a distinct aroma.

Butter tubs were made in several different sizes by manufacturers who often used soft woods, like cedar or pine. Stave-constructed and iron-strapped, these tubs held butter for storage or shipping. Most butter tub manufacturers were out of business by the first quarter of the twentieth century, signaling the beginning of the refrigerated era as well as the advent of different types of packaging.

Churns were made in assorted styles and shapes, though the ones most people are familiar with are tall, wooden examples, stave-constructed and wrapped with wooden (early examples) or iron (later examples) hoops. A round wooden cap sat over the top opening, and a plunger was put through a hole in the center so that the agitating pole could move easily.

Early butter churns might be painted blue, red, or yellow. If you are lucky enough to find one in a color, consider it more valuable than its plainer cousins.

The later butter churns were table models made of glass. Round or square, these churns usually had a metal top, wood handle, paddles and dashers, and circular toothed gear.

If a large quantity of butter was to be churned, a "rocking" floor churn was used. Resembling a barrel sitting sideways on four legs, these churns would be rocked until the butter "came."

A cooper who made barrels, buckets, kegs, and other types of wooden containers was a necessary person in country towns. Items such as pickles were stored in wooden barrels over the winter; nails, cornmeal, and salted meat were a few of the other things stored in buckets or kegs. Coopers were also responsible for making butter churns, a necessary ingredient for women who wanted to turn their excess milk into butter.

Churns and other wooden containers are usually made out of cedar because it doesn't shrink when wet, but poplar is also used because it's easy to work with. Because most barrels, churns, and buckets were not painted, those you may find with old milk paint (red, blue, yellow) on their exteriors are usually highly prized and worth far more in the antiques market.

To make a churn, the cedar was cut into staves, measured, and sawed to the same lengths. The staves were tapered to be narrower at the top than at the bottom and thinner in width at the top by about a quarter inch. They were then fit into two temporary hoops, and a straw-filled bag was placed between the hoops so that the staves could be added one at a time. Once the staves were tightly fitted, the bag was pulled out and the staves hammered until even. Any excess length was trimmed off the bottom with a pocketknife, and the bands were then adjusted higher or lower for a better, tighter fit.

The bottom and top, with its dasher handle, were the last parts of the churn to be made. They were measured carefully so that the bottom fit securely and would not detach with the slamming of the dasher and the weight of the butter. The top had to have a hole in it through which the dasher would slide with ease.

Cake Spoons

Cake spoons are perforated metal, plastic, or wooden spoons that were made to stir cake batter. They were introduced in the Victorian era, when women's magazines were fond of touting "ways to make milady's life easier." Makers of such utensils include Ekco, Ideal, Favorite, and Rumford.

Cake Turners or Flippers

The flat, solid, or perforated utensils are called cake turners even though they are used in turning other items, like eggs, pancakes, and hamburgers. The older versions are made of much heavier metal than the newer ones.

Can Openers

Can openers were in use from about the 1830s in the United States, but they didn't resemble the ones we have today. Instead, many forms had only two things in common: a puncturing point and a cutting blade. The earlier versions did not have a turning crank but were simply pushed into the can and turned by hand.

Some brand names of can openers were Yankee, Tilt-Top-O-Matic, Peerless, Standy-by, and Star.

Canister Sets

Canister sets are not only collectible but highly usable, even in today's high-tech kitchen. Though the oldest versions were made of tin and designed strictly to keep mice, weevils, and other pests out of flour, meal, and sugar, I favor the porcelain and pottery versions, which are newer (late 1800s/early 1900s versions).

Some sets made for the household were meant to sit atop each other and are called "nested" sets. Each one will be labeled as to its purpose (e.g., the largest for flour, the smallest for tea), and the set often will include a bread box.

Do not be confused by a cracker box or humidor that appears to be part of a canister set. Some companies began packaging their goods in tin containers by the end of the nineteenth century, in the hope that the packaging would entice homemakers to purchase their product. These containers were often cleaned out and used over and over again for other purposes. Today's homemaker could learn some valuable lessons about recycling and conservation by studying what the homemakers of yesteryear saved to use again.

Cheese-Related Collectibles

Cheese-related collectibles appear to be more commonly found in Pennsylvania and the Midwest, though cheese was made wherever cows produced milk. Today's country collector may like to hang pierced cheese colanders or molds on kitchen or dining room walls. Made of metal or wood, the molds were used to make different cheese shapes.

Cheese presses, on the other hand, were used to press the curds after the whey was drained. Some presses were freestanding; others sat on tables.

Cheese toasters were used to melt cheese on toast or other foods. Cheese scoops and triers were tools used in the cheese-making process (scoops for scooping cheese from the vat, triers for taking cheese out of the vat for testing).

Chocolate Mills or Pots

Chocolate mills or pots are often misidentified by collectors of country items. They look like small coffeepots, but there is one major difference: a wooden muller is inserted through the lid of the pot, and the muller slides up and down to froth the chocolate. Usually, the pot's handle is at an angle on the side of the pot, about one third of the way down.

Chocolate Molds

Chocolate molds have been popular with more than one type of collector. Some people like to hang the tin or pewter molds on the wall of a country kitchen. Others collect them because of their shapes: animals, eggs, geometrics. Still others collect them because they fit into the category of "kitchen collectibles." And then there are those who hunt the molds out so that they may fill them with contemporary chocolate and carry on the tradition.

Choppers and Graters

Each kitchen, from colonial days to today, most likely had a chopper or grater in a cabinet or drawer. No cook can be without one when chopping vegetables or mincing meat. They were made of wrought iron in the early days of our country and were usually one piece. Steel choppers came of age in the Victorian era. In the nineteenth century, many of the wooden-handled choppers were factory-made, and most are stamped with a patent and date or the maker's name and address.

Mincing knives have a curved blade that can be rocked back and forth during the cutting process. Some were made with double blades for easier chopping.

Choppers look like mincers. Some, however, may use four blades, shaped like an *X*.

Graters were made in various sizes and shapes, depending on

their purpose. Nutmeg was grated on very small graters, while larger versions were used for fruits and vegetables.

Cabbage was sliced on a slaw, or kraut, cutter. The slicer was a flat piece of wood with one or two cutting blades attached to the wood at an angle. The head of cabbage would slide up and down the board, against the knife.

There are many different kinds of graters to collect. The smallest were meant for grating lemon, nutmeg, and bread. Others were used for vegetables, cheese, bread, and herbs. Nutmeg graters were small enough to be carried by travelers in the seventeenth and eighteenth centuries and were made in a variety of styles.

Larger graters were not meant to be carried. Some had a handle on top by which they can be held in place while an object is grated against them.

Certain companies, such as Matthai-Ingram and Dover Stamping Company, sold grater "blanks" to tinsmiths or homeowners so that they could make their own. Companies that made graters include the Lorraine Metal Mfg. Co. and Cream City Ware, and Geuder, Paeschke and Frey Co.

Colanders

Colanders resemble bowls but are usually handled and perforated. They are used to separate solids from liquids (e.g., draining pasta or vegetables). Some are footed or have a ring base. A soldered ring is called "foot fast"; if not soldered, it is called "foot loose."

Cookie Cutters

Cookie cutters are tin or metal cutters that, when pressed into cookie dough, recreate their own shapes. Some cutters have handles; others do not. The earliest versions were made by a tinworker from the scraps they might have left over from other projects. Old cutters are often more unevenly soldered and cut than their factory-produced cousins.

The cutters I have in my collection include the standards—hearts, clubs, diamonds, spades, Santas, a gingerbread family—as well as a horse, chicken, rooster, etc. There are many different shapes of cookie cutters, as you can imagine; it is one collectible that offers infinite possibilities. And think of all the goodies you can create!

Cookie Jars

Cookie jars have been avidly collected by country aficionados for many years, though they are fairly new to the antiques market. Jars have been made in many different shapes and sizes, and continue to be made today. Nursery rhyme figures are a common cookie jar subject, as are animals, houses/cottages, and black figures (e.g., "Mammy" or "Chef").

A company that is well known for hundreds of styles of cookie jars it has produced throughout the years is the McCoy Pottery Company. They are still in business and still producing pottery cookie jars for today's market.

Some cookie jars to keep an eye out for include any Disney characters or contemporary movie figures (e.g., "Star Wars" figures).

Egg-Related Collectibles

Since my husband and I collect advertising items, we are naturally drawn to cardboard egg cartons that are decorated with farm scenes or poultry. A fair supply of them are still available, most at prices of $5 and under. We hang them on the kitchen wall, next to cardboard butter cartons and early lithographed ads for cream.

Prior to the use of cartons, eggs were stored in stackable wire boxes that held a dozen or two on each level. These were generally held by the general store or housekeeper until it was time for a "refill." No need for foam containers in those days, when *everything* was recyclable.

Because eggs were a part of almost every American's diet, the number of different egg-related items one might collect is infinite. For instance, egg beaters have been made for hundreds of years. The first patent for a Dover rotary egg beater was entered in May 31, 1870, and the Dover beater was not the first—there were at least 140 egg beater patents granted earlier.

Before rotary egg beaters, the cook relied on a whisk of wire or wood, a fork, turkey wing bones, or the hand. Even egg whips differ in design, with some resembling twirled wire spoons, some that look like spatulas made of wire, and some resembling a whip itself.

Other egg beaters are attached to a pitcher or measuring cup, making it a little easier for the cook to add the beaten egg mixture to whatever dish they are concocting and a lot less messy than beating the egg in a bowl.

Other egg-related collectibles may include egg baskets (made of wire, like early store egg "cartons"), egg candlers (used to determine an egg's freshness), egg fryers (cast-iron pans with egg-sized depressions, used to cook sunnyside eggs), egg poachers (made in a variety of styles but usually of tin with perforated bottoms so that the poacher can be set in water and each cooked egg separated from the others), and egg stands (wire racks with a handle in the middle).

Furniture

Because most American homes did not have built-in cupboards until the turn of the century, freestanding cupboards were used to store dinnerware, pottery bowls and jugs, pewter mugs and plates, and spongeware platters. Today's country home's decor usually incorporates a country cupboard into its design.

Open cupboards are early, often found in New England, and have open upper shelves, which normally held dishes, and drawers, shelves, cubbies, or a combination of two or more of those elements as part of the bottom half. Stepback cupboards are one piece, with the lower half jutting out from the shelves of the upper half. Hanging cupboards are commonly open or closed shelf units used to hold spices in the kitchen or other types of articles in the parlor, pantry, bedroom, and bath.

In my house, a tall, skinny cupboard called a chimney cupboard—because it was usually the same width as the chimney against which it was built—holds our collection of nineteenth- and twentieth-century tins. A friend of mine filled her red nineteenth-century New England stepback with a collection of teddy bears and stuffed Victorian rabbits. Another friend fills a double-door linen cupboard with her clothes and uses it for wardrobe storage in her bedroom. Many of my country-collecting friends actually use the cupboards for their original purposes—one even has her jelly cupboard filled with homemade jams, jellies, pickles, and relishes, which she made in the old-fashioned way.

Originally, the dry sink, a rectangular, low, boxy type of cupboard, was used to hold the wash bucket and household utensils. Every country home that did not have indoor plumbing utilized the services of a dry sink.

Dry sinks were usually made of pine, poplar, or oak and are most valuable when still wearing their original coat of blue, red, yellow, or green milk paint. Though not a fanciful item, but rather one that was continuously used, the dry sink was often built into the wall and characteristically shows its years of wear and tear by being well scarred. Many country collectors like this kind of look for many reasons—it speaks of years of family use, hard work, days when life was not as easy as it is now.

Collectors can acquire dry sinks that still have a zinc liner installed in the recessed trough at the top of the sink. This style was made until after 1870, when commercially made examples came on the market.

Later, in the late eighteenth and early nineteenth centuries, dry sinks were built into the walls of new kitchens, along with cupboards. However, the hutch dry sink, which is exactly what it says—a combination of the two pieces of furniture—was also used. It helped to solve the space problem in one- or two-room homes by giving the family storage space above as well as below the sink area.

Dry sinks were normally waist-high pieces of furniture that basically were used for the same purpose as our sinks are today, the biggest difference being that dry sinks were made prior to the days of indoor plumbing. They are popular with country home owners/decorators because their size (35″–50″ high and 30″–50″ wide) is such that they can be used for a variety of purposes. For that reason, as well as because they have not been made for almost one hundred years, the price of dry sinks is usually $300–$400 and up.

Hoosier cabinets were made in the early 1900s and were, as the early advertisements state, designed to store almost everything a housewife needed in a most economical fashion. Like their older cupboard counterparts, Hoosiers stored food and dinnerware. However, the new design might also include a flour sifter tucked neatly behind a shelf, a potato bin hiding behind one of the lower doors, compartmentalized drawers and shelves for easy storage, as well as many other helpful features.

They are just as economical (spacewise) in today's homes as they were in our great-grandparents' days and are highly popular with those of us in limited space. I've sold quite a few Hoosier-type cabinets, but the one I remember most fondly was a monster of an example.

Whereas most Hoosiers were factory-made, this one was handmade—by a carpenter who put his best foot forward. Not only did the maker use a beautiful grain of oak (which had been painted a hideous shade of brown that my husband immediately stripped off), but he put every ounce of his carpentry knowledge into the design of the cupboard. Each door was cross-hatched, each drawer rolled smoothly on hand-rubbed rails, and the cutting board (which was tucked away under a drawer) was 2 inches thick and well used.

We sold that cupboard on the field of Don Mackey's Farmington, Connecticut, show to a couple who raced down our aisle as soon as the gates opened on Sunday. They had seen the cupboard on Saturday, as had many other thousands of people, and had gone home to measure to see whether it would fit.

"We haven't been able to stop thinking about it," they said breathlessly. When we loaded the cupboard into their wagon, they couldn't believe how heavy the piece was and how well it was constructed.

I often think of pieces like that cupboard and of customers like that couple, and wonder if they're getting as much pleasure out of the country pieces they purchased from us as we did when hunting for those treasures.

Harvest tables are long tables, often well worn, with wormholes and wood splits showing how well used the tables were. They were large enough to comfortably feed a family of eight yet were used for many other purposes besides eating. That was where the canning for the winter was done, where vegetables were sorted and prepared for dinner, where fabric was cut to make a Sunday-go-to-meeting dress, where babies were changed, and where bread was rolled out by firm, rounded arms covered in flour.

As I write this page, I am seated at a soft-pine harvest table with chunky turned legs and a long hidden center drawer. The table has chips of wood missing from one corner, where a sewing bird had been clamped time and time again. The legs are nicked and scarred with almost two centuries' worth of "boot kicks." Not every board is straight; there are many hills and valleys in this old table's surface. But I love it this way. It has character and speaks to me of more history than I'll ever live to see.

Some harvest tables have one-board tops, others have two, three, or more. Some are painted red or yellow. Some have soft wood tops; others do not. Some harvest tables have a sawbuck-shaped base. Others, like mine, have turned legs, and some tables' legs are straight.

Each one has its own personality, its own history, and each speaks to us in a different way. But there is a similarity to all harvest tables: they were one of the most consistently used pieces in any country home, either now or long, long ago.

I must say that pie safes are one of my favorite pieces of furniture, not because of their decorative exterior of punched tin or wire but because of their many uses and the warm feeling I get when thinking of how they were *originally* used: to store home-baked pies and cakes.

Because a country woman often did all of her baking for the week on one or two days (depending on the size of her family), the pie safe was invented to store all of those pies, cakes, cookies, and breads in a dry place, safe from mice (built a little off the floor) and with punched-tin or screen doors that would let the air circulate but stopped the flies from coming in.

Pie safes, especially those primitive ones in blue milk paint with punched-tin hearts or stars on their doors, are getting more and more difficult to find. The punchwork has often been considered American folk art because the design was usually the brainchild of the carpenter who made the piece. As we already know, quite a good portion of the furniture we call "country" was made by the homesteader, the pioneer, the farmer, or the owner of the house, not by a professional furniture maker. Thus, the work is considered a one-of-a-kind piece made by an untrained artisan—folk art.

Though pie safes were often handmade, there were many factory-made examples produced from 1870 on. The way to tell the difference between handmade and factory-made safes is to study the punched tin closely. If the piece is factory-made, all squares of punchwork will be exactly the same. Needless to say, the punching done by an amateur will not be perfect because *we* are not. But those handmade pieces sure have more character, and they're worth a lot more to any antiquer.

Pie safes that used screening on their doors instead of punched tin were made and used well into the twentieth century. In fact, I believe I would be safe to say you could probably still find some being used on a daily basis on some Amish farms throughout the Midwest. These versions are not valued as highly as their pierced-tin cousins.

Meat-Related Collectibles

The first cranked meat choppers date from the 1860s. They consisted of a revolving wooden barrel with a heavy cutting blade that moved up and down while the barrel turned. The more common type is the iron version, which clamps to a table or sits splay-legged so that a vessel can be placed underneath to collect the chopped meat.

Homemakers used meat choppers/grinders to make ground sausage, hamburger, lamb, pork, and other ground meats. Companies that made choppers or grinders include F. A. Walker, Montgomery Ward, and Steinfeld.

Meat hooks were used to hang large slabs of meat in a smokehouse or chimney where the meat was being smoked or preserved. Most were made of iron.

A meat press was used to get the juice out of the meat. The juice might then be used as a gravy or soup base.

Meat screens were often placed in front of the fire on which a piece of meat was being cooked. They acted as reflectors for the heat thrown by the fire and helped the meat to cook more evenly.

A wood-handled mallet with a grooved, pointed surface was used to tenderize meats such as steaks, chops, or chicken breasts. Pounding the meat with such a tool could tenderize a tougher cut, making it tastier.

Pewter Collectibles

Pewter is an alloy of lead and tin. Though most amateur collectors think that pewter is marked, a lot of good pewter is not. That doesn't make those pieces any less collectible, just harder to attribute to a maker.

There was much more pewter manufactured in England than in America, but even in England the good pieces seldom surface. Perhaps one of the reasons good pewter is hard to find is that it was most commonly used domestically for little more than a hundred years (1650–1780) during the beginning of this country's history. Boston was where the bulk of American pewter plate was made, and it also was known for distributing English pewter.

The use of pewter died out in the first third of the nineteenth century. It was replaced by other metals, such as silver, and by earthenware.

American pewter makers worked in much the same manner as the English, though the metal itself may have weighed less. By 1780, American craftsmen's work was on a par with that of the English, who had been working with pewter for much longer.

This might be because the Americans had brought the craft with them from England or had learned from English makers.

Because so much pewter was *not* hallmarked and because English hallmarks were often counterfeited, it is best to rely on being able to recognize the American *style* of pewter-making.

It appears that pewter oil lamps were pretty much an American product, made simply and modeled skillfully by pewter craftsmen of the early nineteenth century.

American pewter makers of note who marked their wares include Roswell Gleason of Dorchester, Massachusetts (ca. 1830s), R. Dunham of Boston (after 1825), Thomas D. Boardman of Hartford, Connecticut (after 1825), and F. Porter of Connecticut (after 1825).

Pie-Related Collectibles

Pie-related collectibles have interested many country collectors. You might want to use a pie safe, a cupboard with punched-tin or screened doors (see "Kitchen Furniture"), as extra shelf or storage space.

Pie birds are pottery or tin "birds" with stems that are inserted into a pie while it's cooking. Not only did these gadgets serve to keep the piecrust from collapsing, but they allowed the steam to escape from the cooking fruit.

A large, fork-type device used to lift the pie from the oven was called (understandably) a pie lifter, while a pie pricker was an implement made of wood or metal and used to prick holes in the piecrust.

Pie racks made of wire were used to allow the pie to cool. Pie plates, molds, and pans were used in the actual baking process.

Pottery

Though pottery was produced by American craftspeople or settlers very early in our history, the first European colonists to be recognized as influential in the field of pottery were John Remney and William Crolius, both New Yorkers, who did the bulk of their work in the mid-1700s. They produced stoneware jars, butter churns, and teapots that were salt glazed and decorated.

Most pots of this age were wheel-thrown utilitarian pieces that were not signed. The only marks that might be found on such early pottery were the name of the person to whom the potter was giving the pot and the date it was given.

Early potteries were small and produced only what was essential for life in the colonies. After 1776, potteries became more inclined to produce decorated pieces because utilitarian needs had been met. The country's new independence and national pride was reflected in pottery. Pieces were decorated with flags, stars, the American eagle, or the portrait of a patriot.

Each area that produced pottery is recognizable by certain styles or decoration, which we will discuss in this and other chapters. Naturally, we cannot describe in detail each and every type of country pottery, but we will attempt to give enough information to provide an overview of the field for you, the American country collector.

Bennington Pottery

When someone says he or she has a Bennington piece, your immediate response should be "Bennington what?"

The company, located in southern Vermont, has made well over two thousand different types of items, and only a small portion of the pottery is the mottled brown and gold we call "Bennington." The company also made stoneware (identifiable by the incised name of the Norton Company, Bennington, Vermont), yellowware, graniteware, parian ware, flint enamelware, slip-covered redware, and other porcelains and pottery.

Flint enamelware (see The Country Market chapter; graniteware also) was brown with specks of color throughout; graniteware is glazed white pottery; scroddled ware, the rarest of the Bennington pottery, is a variegated pottery that usually has a cream-colored background with dark brown streaks running through it; Rockingham is mottled brown; and Bennington majolica, though not true majolica, has the same high-polished glaze.

Moravian Pottery

Another religious group that not only contributed to the social differences that make America the melting pot it is, but also gave us the benefit of their artistic skills, was the Moravian community of North Carolina. They brought their unique, highly organized system of community life with them from Bohemia, Moravia, and Poland, settled in Pennsylvania, and then moved to North Carolina in November 1753.

Colonists built a temporary log settlement, dubbed it "Bethabara" (house of passage), and maintained that stronghold for almost two decades. The tract of land had been sold to them by Lord Granville of England and was named Wachau by the Moravians in honor of the ancestral estate of the ancesteral estate of Count Zinzendorf of Austria. By 1772, a new town was built and called Salem, the Hebrew word for peace.

The new town functioned as a congregating place for Moravians and was the nucleus for a number of major businesses the people owned and operated. One such business was a pottery, and it is that industry for which the Moravians are best remembered.

Thanks to the incredibly complete records kept by this industrious group, we have been able to understand the development of their society, as well as the extent to which industries such as pottery-making were influential in Moravian life. Through these records and the archeological excavations in and around Moravian settlements such as Bethabara and Salem, we are able to piece together a picture of the quality and workmanship of these master potters.

The 1968 discovery of wares that were exact duplicates of eighteenth-century British creamware and of tin-enameled pottery similar to pieces made in central Europe was extremely important because it had not been known that either type of pottery was being made to any extent in the United States. The discovery thus served to help us understand the abilities and inventiveness of Wachovia potters.

In half-timbered dwellings with sloping roofs and multipaned windows, which resembled those they had left behind, Moravian potters such as Gottfried Aust, Randolph Christ, John Holland, and Gottlob Krause created pottery that was both simple and sophisticated. The masters not only followed the designs they brought with them from Europe; they also looked to the future, building new kilns for faience when that type of pottery was popular, and they always paid attention to what type of ware was selling. If not remembered for any other reason, the Moravians will leave their mark in history books as being good businesspeople.

As with most pottery, a good many of the pieces made by Moravians were meant to be utilitarian or used in the kitchen. Simple earthenware pieces were created to be used on a daily basis, and if the piece broke or cracked, its owner threw it away. Bowls, mugs, jars, pots, plates, and jugs were made in quantity and were the bulk of production in any pottery-making factory.

Decorated pieces, meant to last longer, were displayed rather than used. Since decorated earthenware was not what the potter could easily sell, it has often been noted that these pieces were especially made for customers or created by the potters only after they had completed the rest of their work. Such work was called "slipware" by potter Christ and "flowered dishes" by potter Holland.

Like many pottery-making communities of the eighteenth and nineteenth centuries, a "school" was developed by the Wachovian potters. Details of work done by the masters were shared by the apprentices and journeymen, passed from teacher to student for many years. The influence of Gottfried Aust's work was passed on through his apprentices, and the English influence on Christ's work was transmitted to others, with at least one potter carrying his "schooling" away from the Wachovian community.

It is difficult to tell which potter might have made a thrown piece but much easier to identify a molded piece because each piece would be the same. Details, such as how feathers are delineated or how eyes are expressed, are often a potter's trademark or signature. In another category or way of thinking, Moravian pottery done by the masters might be considered folk art. An example of a piece of pottery that can be immediately identified as having been made in Salem is a molded fox clutching a dead hen in its paws.

Wachovian glazes tend to be similar to those made by other earthenware-pottery-making communities of the era. Browns and greens were the basic colors used, with green most likely to be used over a white slip to make a lighter coloration. The interior of a vessel with a clear exterior glaze will be different colors (i.e., red, pink, yellow) depending on the type of clay used in making the piece.

Some Moravian pieces, with thin walls and sometimes an Oriental influence (seen most often in Aust's early work), approach the "fine pottery" category. The influence of English Queensware pottery on Wachovia is seen clearly in the rib-thrown mugs made by Christ. Such patterns were popular in England from 1750 to 1800. The reeded handles on these mugs were also similar to their English counterparts.

Each potter had his signature, and most have been identified by archeologists working at the Moravian sites. Examples of each are held by the Wachovia Museum in Old Salem.

Some of the ways to distinguish Moravian pottery are (1) handles: a scrolled handle terminal on a water jug was one of Aust's signatures; (2) apothecary jars had a concave shoulder and foot, as well as a well-defined rim over which a cloth secured with string could be placed; (3) some potters, such as John Butner of Bethabara, used a stamp indicating the potter's name; (4) mug sizes were quart, pint, half-pint, and gill and show heavy English design influence; (5) teapots had an Oriental or English influence.

Rockingham Ware (see also Bennington Pottery)

Rockingham Ware was made in England as well as at the Bennington factories, so one should be extremely careful in identifying pieces as either American or English. The easiest means of identification, of course, is to find the potter's name imprinted or stamped on the piece. If there are no marks on the piece, the next step would be to consult the book *Bennington Pottery and Porcelain,* a guide written by the director-curator of the Bennington Museum. It should be noted that Bennington Pottery is not easily identifiable, as there were often a number of variations of certain styles of pots, figurines, and pitchers.

One of the ways to tell whether a bowl or pie plate is Bennington-made is to check for raised supports or notches on the bottom rims of the piece. If you *do* find supports or notches, your bowl or plate was not made in Bennington.

There are many identifying features that delineate pieces made at Bennington—too many, in fact, to note them all in this chapter. That fact leads us to comment that Bennington collectors must enjoy the challenge of adding pieces to their collection that meet every one of the features that make them Bennington-made.

Shenandoah Valley Pottery

The pottery produced in the Shenandoah Valley of Virginia was so distinctive that it is considered folk art. Most well-known potters from this area were working during the 1800s, thus their work was not considered significant until much later than the pottery produced in other parts of the country.

The people of the Valley were largely of German descent—honest, diligent citizens who contributed much to the communities of which they became part. Most of the pottery was made for use by family members, friends, or oneself, utilitarian objects used everyday or pots meant to be gifts.

Potters such as the Bells of Hagerstown, Anthony E. Baecher of Winchester, and the Eberly family of Strasburg were active in the Shenandoah Valley and are among the potters collected today.

Certain design idiosyncrasies identify some of the Shenandoah potters. For example, the lion motif was often used by Solomon Bell; Baecher made quite a few pottery animals; the Eberlys' device was to make handles in the shape of a bird's wing. Slipware was produced by Pete and Solomon Bell, as well as by the Eberlys, but other Valley potters did not produce much slip-decorated pottery.

White clay was available in abundance to the potters of the Shenandoah Valley, but it is the deep, deep red of Valley redware that distinguishes the pottery from that made in other areas.

Valley potters processed their clay in a horse-powered pug mill, the clay kneaded and worked into blocks before being stored under wet burlap, until finally being used to create some kind of pottery. Thrown hollowware pottery was produced, as well as molded pieces and sculptured ware. The glaze used by Shenandoah potters was usually multicolored with a mottled appearance, which gave the pottery a look of its own.

Southern Pottery

The Southern pottery makers naturally clustered near each other, creating what came to be called "jugtowns," the term for towns where half a dozen or more potters produced their wares. Though each potter had his or her own specialty, the tools they used and the basic production process was pretty much the same throughout the South.

The best and most productive years of the Georgian potters were those before the turn of the century. After 1900, glass and tin containers were produced in large quantities. These new containers soon replaced the pottery jugs, stoneware crocks, and churns that had long been used to hold milk, pickles, cream, butter, and all sorts of other perishables.

Country folk hung onto their traditional pottery for a while longer (into the 1920s), probably because the new types of containers were not readily available to them. Part of the reason the pottery market declined was the fact that Prohibition was enforced in Georgia as of 1907.

Though pottery families have continued to produce their wares up to the present, the need for such wares dwindled after the turn of the century. As a result, today's potter makes more decorative items than utilitarian ones.

Potters such as the Meaders family of Georgia might produce 300 medium-size gallons during a good day or an average of 200 gallons in churns or 150 in jugs. For their efforts in the 1920s, the best workers might make 3 cents a gallon. However, once the Depression hit, the potter was lucky to make one-third of that amount.

Most potters would pack a load of pottery per week and haul it all over the state and into North Carolina, where they would attempt to sell their product to hardware stores, country markets, and private customers.

Spongeware

Spongeware is the type of pottery that has a sponged or "mottled" surface. The ware was made in the same manner as yellowware, but the clay used was different, coarser and less refined than that used for yellowware.

Spongeware was not made until the turn of the twentieth century, almost seventy years after yellowware was introduced. Rockingham ware was similar in appearance to spongeware, the difference being basically that Rockingham ware was made by glazing a yellow clay body, while spongeware was stone-bodied. The ware was made primarily in kilns located in Ohio, New Jersey, Pennsylvania, and Minnesota.

Often confused with other wares, spongeware is distinguishable by the sponged decoration, different from piece to piece. The decoration is not spotted as in spatterware or streaked as in flint enamelware but smoother and almost uniform.

Spongeware forms include bowls, teapots, dinnerware, platters, canisters, banks, washboards, planters, cookware, mugs, pitchers, casseroles, water coolers, and jugs.

Companies that manufactured spongeware include the International Pottery Company in Trenton, New Jersey (1853–88); Etruria Pottery, New Jersey (1865–82); W. L. Leake, Trenton, New Jersey (1878–87); Bennett and Brothers (one of the earliest spongeware manufacturers, 1841–44); Union Pottery, Ohio (1844–1910); Red Wing Pottery, Minnesota (1890s–1940s); and Western Stoneware Company, Monmouth, Illinois (1906–40). Some of the above companies are described in further detail elsewhere in this chapter.

Yellowware

Yellowware was more durable than the redware bowls, canisters, jugs, and bottles that early America's homemaker used until (and after) the mid-1800s. Even more than its durability, what made the ware popular was the fact that it was mass-produced at a low price.

Homemakers brought the attractive and sturdy yellow pottery into their homes in many different guises: bowls of all types, clips, pitchers, baking dishes, colanders, casseroles, preserve jars, crocks, molds, and even rolling pins.

The major portion of the yellowware industry was located in New Jersey and Ohio, where yellow firing clay sources were abundant.

Yellowware is glazed, in most cases, with a clear lead- or alkaline-based glaze, producing a shiny, glasslike effect on the pottery's surface. Later pieces, however, have a different glaze (a mixture of kaolin, ground flint, and white lead) because the lead-based glaze was toxic.

Though some yellowware was hand-turned or drape-molded, most pieces were mold-cast. The molds were usually made of plaster or baked clay. The process of pouring liquid slip into a hollow mold is called slip casting. Yellowware was usually fired twice—first to vitrify the body and then to fix the decoration or glaze.

Decorations or banding differ widely on yellowware, depending on the maker's preference. The colors usually used to decorate the pottery were white, blue, or brown or any combination of the three.

Yellowware decorated with designs we now call pinetree, feather, thistle, and seawood are referred to as Mocha or Moco decoration because the designs are similar to those found on earthenware from Mocha in the Near East. Companies/potters that made Mocha ware include Edwin Bennett of Baltimore and (in the 1880s) C. C. Thompson & Company of East Liverpool, Ohio.

Other makers of yellowware products include potteries in Red Wing, Minnesota (1930s–1940s); Washington Pottery of Philadelphia (early 1800s); the American Pottery of Jersey City, New Jersey (early–late 1800s); Swan Hill Pottery of South Amboy,

New Jersey (mid–late 1800s); Tivoli Works, New York (early–mid-1800s); Charles W. Coykendall & Company, New York (1868–71); Norton/Fenton, Bennington, Vermont (1844–58); J. E. Jeffords, Philadelphia (mid–late 1800s); and Market Street Pottery (early–late 1800s, under several different names).

For more information about yellowware and manufacturers who made it, refer to William Ketchum's book *American Country Pottery*.

Refrigerators and Ice Boxes

Refrigerators were not powered mechanically until the mid-nineteenth century, when examples were found in railroad cars. The mechanized version did not reach the average household until much later. Though they are not highly collectible because of their bulk, perhaps the old GE "monitor tops" will find their way into the country home as a conversation piece.

Old oak iceboxes, on the other hand, were made prior to the twentieth century and are a much more attractive piece of furniture than their electrified cousins. The oak versions were kept cool by large chunks of ice cut out of frozen bodies of water or, in later years, delivered by horse-drawn wagons. The inside of the box was lined with zinc or tin, alloys that served to maintain the ice's solid form as long as possible.

Salt Dishes

Salt dishes, or "salts," were used by our ancestors but are seldom seen in today's country home unless as an ornament or part of a displayed collection.

Salt has been used since Bible days in cooking and enhancement of food. Before shakers there were salt cellars or cups and footed bowls equipped with tiny spoons that were used to dispense the salt.

Pewter salts were the most widely used in America because pewter is highly resistant to salt corrosion. They were low, open, footed dishes approximately 2¼ inches wide by 3 inches long by 1¼ inches high. Other salts may be found in glass, silver, and china.

Salt and Pepper Shakers

One of my fondest childhood memories is of my aunt's salt and pepper shaker collection—she had amassed hundreds of pairs. They marched along a windowtop ledge encircling her dining room and filled the built-in china closet. I spent hours counting them or just studying the figurals, animals, and fruits and vegetables, which made often incongruous pairs. One of my favorites was a squirrel who held a fat nut under each arm.

Though pepper and other spices have been used since European explorers brought them back after their trips to "exotic" lands, the salt and pepper shakers found in most country collections were made during the twentieth century. Receptacles used to hold dinner table salt prior to that time were small plates or "salts." They, too, are collectible and covered under the heading "Salt Dishes" in this chapter.

Some salt and pepper shakers are highly collectible, such as those made in Occupied Japan or any shakers included under the heading "Black Memorabilia." Yet most are still highly affordable, with prices ranging from under $10 for a pair of 7-Up bottles to $100 or over for the F & F Plastics seven-piece spice set featuring Aunt Jemima.

Salt and pepper shakers have been made from many materials, including plastic, glass, metal, tin, porcelain, and chalkware. Some of the companies known to make salt and pepper shakers include F & F Plastics, McCoy Pottery, Avon Products, Bakelite, Walt Disney, Shawnee Pottery, and Ceramic Arts Studios of Wisconsin.

For an in-depth look at hundreds of shakers, Melva Davern's *Collector's Encyclopedia of Salt and Pepper Shakers* is an invaluable guide.

Silverware

Though I believe pewter ware fits better under the umbrella term "country collectibles" than silverware does, I feel obliged to give a brief history of American silver and of one of its foremost craftspeople, Paul Revere.

Silversmithing was one of the most widely practiced trades of the seventeenth and eighteenth centuries. The major names in the field are from New York, Boston, and Philadelphia, and one can reasonably assume the reason is that those eastern cities were the cradle of development in the United States. Though most people have believed silversmithing to be largely an English art, it was proved by major museums, experts, and collectors in the early part of our century that there were quite a few American silversmiths who had literally carved their own style and a place for themselves in American history.

One such person was Paul Revere, goldsmith, engraver, and publisher of political cartoons. A multitalented Bostonian, Revere is more often remembered for his exploits rather than his incredible silversmithing talents. He learned his trade from his father, designing and engraving silver pieces until, at age nineteen, he inherited his father's shop. After a stint in the artillery (not an exciting one, I might add, since he saw no action), Revere came home to build his business and to use his discernible talent to create designs uniquely his own. He was experimenting with copper by the time he was involved with the American Revolution and his historic midnight ride to Lexington.

During those turbulent years, Revere was more inclined to inspect and repair military equipment than to design tea sets; however, he was back in Boston by 1780, and his friends did not forget him. He was asked by John Adams and Benjamin Franklin to do the engraving and printing of our first national paper money, and he also designed a state seal for Massachusetts.

His interest in silversmithing led him to open a jewelry store in 1783, to start a brass and iron foundry in 1789, to begin casting brass cannons and metal ship fittings by 1794, and to make various pieces for the frigate *Constitution* by 1798. He was also responsible for the copper dome on Boston's State House.

A good selection of his silversmithing can be found at Boston's Museum of Fine Arts, but not many pieces are owned or sold by private collectors. As you can figure from this brief history, Revere had many other things to do besides making tea sets; thus, there simply are not many Revere pieces of silver in today's market.

Tinware/Toleware
(See also "The Country Market" section)

Tinware, originally called "poor man's silver," has been welcomed into country homes because its unassuming charm allows it to blend in well with the pine, oak, and maple furniture that usually fills them. It came into vogue at the beginning of the nineteenth century because the other metals (iron, brass, copper, and pewter) were, for one reason or another, difficult to work with.

Tinware was made from tinplate, thinly rolled pieces of iron or steel that were cleaned and dipped in molten tin at the plating works. Each sheet was dipped several times, depending on how thick a piece of tin the smith wanted. The standard size of early tinplate sheets was 10 inches by 14 inches, and tinware trays were sized by how many sheets were used to make them (i.e., quarter sheet, half sheet, or full sheet).

The need to decorate furniture, tinware, boxes, and the like came to Americans in the 1700s. Paint was used to protect interior woodwork, wall surfaces, and any woods exposed to the weather. Soon that need led Americans to paint their furniture, boxes, and tinware—not just to cover them with coats of paint but to create designs that would enhance the pieces.

The New England colonies, New York, New Jersey, and Pennsylvania employed the custom of decorating furniture in a much stronger fashion than the rest of the country. In fact, the art became so popular that there still exist some furniture companies (e.g., Hitchcock) who continue to produce decorated items.

Painted tinware falls into two categories: baked and unbaked. Early tinworkers learned quickly that just painting a piece did not ensure a lack of rust, but if the piece were varnished and fired, one could be relatively assured of a hard and enduring finish.

History

In 1730, Boston's Old South Church was finished, its vane, or weathercock (the crowning glory), made by Shem Drowne, a tinman. He was also responsible for making the weather vane for the North Meeting House in Boston, a 6-foot, 117-pound vane that was the object of some complaint from Pastor William Croswell, who noted that the vane was "not so light a matter as weather vanes are supposed to be." Also made by Drowne was the famed grasshopper vane that resides atop Boston's Fanueil Hall. A master tinsmith who made his mark in Massachusetts, he died at ninety-one in 1774. (For more on weather vanes, see The Country Barn chapter.)

The first tin-cutting machine was designed by Eli Parsons, a smith from Dedham, Massachusetts. His invention was patented in 1804 and was later discussed in a paper written by Calvin Whiting, Parsons's partner. The pair sold the rights to the machines to many tinsmiths throughout the colonies, yet Connecticut seemed to be the state where tinsmithing was raised to an art. During the 1800s, more than three hundred workers and firms were involved in tinware or related industries in the state of Connecticut.

It is thought that a Scottish immigrant named Edward Patterson was probably the first tinsmith in Connecticut, making the first American-made tinplated kitchen utensils around 1750.

Some of the most recognized Connecticut tinsmiths include the Upsons of Marion, who began making tin items prior to the Revolution; the Filleys of Bloomfield, whose business and personal papers have served to tell us much about Connecticut's tinsmithing industry; and the Norths of Berlin, a family involved in many different kinds of metalworking.

In New England, one tinsmith, Zachariah Brackett Stevens, stood head and shoulders above the rest. He produced tinware from 1798 until 1842. It is said that he once studied his craft at the side of the legendary silversmith Paul Revere, but that fact is not a provable one. Yet we can definitely attribute decorated tinware to Stevens and his two sons, Samuel and Alfred, who took over his business in 1832.

At first (prior to 1830), smiths imported their tin from England, but that practice was halted in 1890 because of heavy tariffs placed on international trade. It was at that time that American tinsmiths realized they needed to make tin themselves.

It was an easy process to make the ware. All that was required were wooden mallets, tin shears, or snips (of varying sizes), chisels, and a soldering iron. The soldering iron was used to solder the already cut tinware templates together. Seams were folded over and hammered, and outside edges were often reinforced by being folded over wire and again hammered. If the piece was to be curved, it was shaped over a form or any other stable surface that would give the desired curve.

During the Gay Nineties, the tin peddler loaded his clanking goods on a wagon and took his wares from house to house. It was a convenience for country families who would rather not make the long trip into town, and the peddler's visit was a welcome one, a treat for the woman of the house as well as for curious children. I suppose the children were more curious about the peddler himself than about his wares, and well they might have been. This mysterious stranger often traveled from one end of the country to the other, getting into trouble, having adventures and love affairs, and making a living while doing so.

Besides carrying larger, fanciful pieces of toleware, a peddler's inventory might also list pins, scissors, needles, combs, thread, cookware, dinnerware, brooms, and many other household items. The peddlers' way of selling varied as greatly as the goods they carried on their backs or in their carts, and so do the stories passed on through the generations.

It is interesting to note that one of America's largest and best-known companies, Proctor and Gamble, was the result of a two-peddler team: William Proctor and James Gamble. The team founded their company in 1837 and peddled their homemade soap from a wheelbarrow.

Types

Tinsmiths were responsible for making a lot of household items (e.g., lighting devices, plates and cookware, boxes, trays), but their work was not restricted to domestic items.

Some articles of tinware decorated by notable tinsmiths include pincushion boxes, all types of trays, flower holders, moneyboxes, teapots, coffeepots, tea and coffee canisters, and many other household items. Some were extremely fanciful, while others may have had a simple geometric design on the body of the piece.

Certain distinctive touches might enable you to distinguish a tray made in Pennsylvania, for example, from one made in New England. A Pennsylvania tray was usually decorated in strong, bright colors with characteristic designs such as unicorns, tulips, pomegranates, angels, birds, people, and geometric patterns. New England's decorators used mostly native flowers and fruits in their designs.

Though tinware was often stenciled, it was sometimes decorated in a freehand fashion, making each piece a little different from the one before.

Toleware designs are the most elaborate and finely executed, usually enhanced by shades of gold and excellent coloring. Scenes may include villages, houses, churches, fountains, people, animals, and nature.

Treenware

Treenware dates back to the *Mayflower,* and it certainly makes sense that this country's earliest inhabitants did not fill that seagoing vessel with breakable china and glass. Though the woodenware is not pretty, it was commonly used by early settlers because the cups, bowls, trenchers, and plates were durable and easy to care for.

Wooden eating utensils or treenware were made from poplar or maple—the maple knots made great burled bowls. Children who unceremoniously dumped their dishes to the floor could not break this durable ware.

Treenware was usually made by the men of the family, utilizing their trusty jackknives and turning the piece by hand, chipping away at it until perfect. Later, walnut or maple objects were turned by machinery and finished by hand.

Salt cellars were made of treenware, as were toddy stirrers, butter molds, pie boards, and many different types of boxes.

Vegetable Bins

Vegetable bins were used to store root crops that needed no refrigeration. They were open bins, usually made of tin or mesh, to allow the air to circulate. Baskets made of wire or mesh were also used to wash and drain vegetables.

Wood Stoves

The American home was first heated by the central fireplace, and though the all-iron fireplace (wood stove) was in use in England during the early part of the eighteenth century, Americans did not begin to use it until later in that century.

We all know that Ben Franklin was responsible for refining the cast-iron stove. His invention of 1744 was the beginning of a new batch of stove designs, led by the Pennsylvania Germans, who were responsible for both five-hundred-pound monster stoves and small parlor wood stoves.

Wood stoves were popular until the end of the nineteenth century, when Americans learned to pump hot water from large central radiators through pipes to room-size radiators to heat their homes. These central heating systems were fired by coal furnaces, a messy, unromantic way to provide heat. Gone was the warm, red glow of the wood stove or fireplace. In its place came clanking iron radiators and a black layer of dust on everything in the house. But, to be optimistic, at least the bathrooms were warm!

The twentieth century saw the introduction of the oil-burning heater, a cleaner, more efficient way of heating. The thermostat made heating automatic—a word that Americans have loved for years.

The Bedroom

BEDROOMS WERE NONEXISTENT in most early American homes. Houses consisted of one large room, which was divided into parts indicated only by the type of furniture that occupied each section. Often the whole family slept in one bed set in the main room or in what was called a jack bed, a wood-framed unit built into the wall. It wasn't until the eighteenth century that rooms were made specifically to house a bed.

In this section, I have included some furniture that was made strictly for the country bedroom. Some of the other information in this chapter, such as quilts and samplers, is also covered in other portions of this book, so you might want to check the index if you are looking for a particular item.

Decorating a Country Bedroom

The bedroom is the place where country collectors often have to dip into other eras when completing the country "look," simply because if you are concentrating on furnishing your house in pieces made in the early years of our country, there simply weren't enough bedroom pieces made to service the whole antiques community. For instance, though I have samplers on the wall and a quilt over the foot of the bed, my bed is a high-backed Victorian oak, and my bureaus are from the Empire period. Eventually, I would like to replace them with cupboards, but sometimes it is difficult to do exactly *what* you would like to *when* you would like to.

The rustic bedroom look and the simple handwoven textiles made for the sleeping area (becoming harder and harder to find) are complemented these days with Victorian touches. The use of chintz (often used in the early 1700s, then neglected for a long, long time) in decorating a bedroom, as well as other rooms, has been revived by some who want a brighter, more feminine look. The pale pinks, purples, and blues of flowered chintz fabrics go well with almost any kind of country furnishings—from the more formal, mahogany Colonial look, to the gnarled branches and rough surfaces of rustic Adirondack furniture, to the soft golden-beige tones of pieces made from pine or oak.

Use your own judgment and decorate your sleeping area in the style that makes you most comfortable. However, be careful when buying old beds because they are often not standard sizes, and you may have trouble finding coverings to fit them—or, worse yet, your feet will hang off the ends and your husband/wife will complain that the bed's not big enough for the two of you!

Bedsteads

Bedsteads were often laced with rope, an early form of the spring, to keep the mattress off the floor and comfortable. It took approximately 120 feet of rope to lace a bed, and the rope was periodically tightened with a wooden bed key, which looked like a large clothespin.

Coverlets

Woven on a loom, coverlets had a border design or fringe on three sides. The fourth side would cover a pillow or be tucked under the mattress. Early coverlets were made in colonial homes on looms with two harnesses: the loom was placed in a "working" room, and because early homes were small, so were the looms. As a result, the coverlets were made in two sections, then sewn together.

Four harness looms replaced the original two harness looms by the early 1700s, and by the turn of the nineteenth century, professional weavers took over, using six to eight harness looms.

Jacquard coverlets were made possible by an invention of the 1820s called the Jacquard attachment. It enabled the loom to weave complicated curvilinear designs into a coverlet. Before that time, patterns were geometric.

Overshot coverlets originated in New York, for the most part, though there have been examples made by country weavers in other parts of the United States, including those made by Mennonites and by country people in the South.

The warp of an overshot coverlet was usually a natural linen-color thread, and the weft thread was colored wool homespun. Patterns are generally geometric (squares, stripes, diamonds), and the weft floats over the plain background weave. There was always a middle seam, which might not have been perfectly matched on both sides. However, like some Native Americans, Southern weavers often believed that the break in design would give the spirits a chance to escape the piece and guarantee good luck for its maker.

Crewelwork Spreads

During the eighteenth and nineteenth centuries, when bedcoverings were decorated in every way possible, small-town weavers were producing a coarse linen homespun that was sold to be "workt," or embroidered. Though Englishwomen used crewelwork to decorate linen (utilizing finely twisted, colorful wool to make their stitches), American women used whatever was available, often cotton or silk thread.

American crewelwork differed from the traditional European style—stiff, dark designs with the background completely stitched—in that the New World designs were open and freely formed, with no confining borders around them. As with other needlework, the independence and free spirit of American women resulted in naive, unschooled patterns or designs that are charming.

Most early crewelwork was done in shades of blue and natural colors made from herbs, barks, and flowers. The art of embroidering on wool gained popularity during the mid-1800s and continued throughout the Victorian era, but it is not considered true crewelwork in that there are fewer types of stitches and the overall effect is coarser.

Hooked and Braided Rugs (See also "The Kitchen" and "The Parlor" in this section)

Like quilts, rugs were made by almost every woman who lived in a country household. Besides offering members of the household a warm place to put their feet, rugs are also artistic examples of the maker's world. Collectors who buy rugs now have more respect for them than the families who originally owned them did; they hang the rugs on the wall, treating them as folk art rather than walking on them.

Though some folk art is better than others, it all fits the description of being "naive." And folk art need not be a picture of sorts. It can be a household object (e.g., quilts, rugs, stoneware) that has been elevated from its lowly position by the decoration the maker created upon it. Color and the juxtaposition of colors is what sometimes makes the difference between an ordinary piece and an exceptional one. Crude drawings, dull or unimaginative colors, and rugs that are poorly hooked also serve as attributes determining the difference between a good rug and a bad one.

Hooked rugs were made by attaching the burlap fabric, onto which a design was drawn, onto a frame. Fabric strips were then pulled through the burlap by a thin, hooklike device. Hooked rugs with burlap sacking backs were considered commonplace by the late 1850s in the United States but did not catch on in England until the end of the nineteenth century. In fact, in England a hooked rug with a burlap back was usually made after 1850.

Mail order catalogs (e.g., Sears, Roebuck and Company and Montgomery Ward) offered hooked rug patterns by the 1890s, but the origins of the craft have been traced back to northern

New England, particularly Maine and New Hampshire, and northeastern Canada. All of New England, the Atlantic seacoast, and some parts of Pennsylvania had adapted to rug hooking by the 1860s, with the rest of the country sharing their enthusiasm by the end of the nineteenth century.

Perhaps one of the reasons the maritime communities were the first to practice the art is that families who were involved with fishing or farming had both the time to spare on cold winter nights and the need for warm rugs beneath their feet. Usually, families such as these did not have the ready cash needed to buy the Oriental or Victorian carpets popular at that time, and homemade rugs were their way of following the fad while keeping warm and busy. Needless to say, it also served as a way for artistic personalities to stretch themselves in a useful manner.

Linsey-Woolseys

Linsey-woolseys are quilted spreads made of wool, one of the earliest forms of quilting found in the colonies. They were almost always made for country homes in the colder regions of the nation. The term linsey-woolsey originally came from the Middle English term "lynsy wolsye"—lynsy standing for Lindsay, a Suffolk, England, village where the fabric was originally made.

Most linsey-woolseys were made for four-poster beds, with slits cut at the two end corners so that the bed covering could hang to the floor, unimpeded by the bed's posts. Surprisingly, these coverings are quite large because beds at that time were wide enough to sleep three to five people.

Linsey-woolseys found by today's collectors are often indigo blue in color and were made by German settlers from Pennsylvania. This color held well throughout washings and was dark enough not to show dirt. Though blue is the most common color, linsey-woolseys were also made in browns, reds, deep blue-green, yellows, and pinks; the Shelburne Museum in Vermont has even unearthed a white example as well as a plaid one.

Because the fabrics used were woven at home, they are coarse and were probably itchy because of their wool stuffing. The sculptured quilting was often done in floral and vine designs encased in geometric blocks. The actual quilting was done with the same color thread as the material, though certain red examples were quilted with white thread.

Some linsey-woolseys were "glazed," before they were quilted. A smooth, soft stone was rubbed over the fabric until the material began to shine. Woolen materials were glazed with a mixture of egg white and water, which was brushed on, dried, and later polished. Gum arabic or other resinous substances were also used to give material a high gloss.

Quilts
(See also "Amish Country" in the "Country Places" section, as well as other sections of this book)

Quilts were produced in American homes on all social levels throughout the nineteenth and early twentieth centuries. They replaced blankets and bed rugs as bed coverings, but became much more, mostly because of the artistic leanings of their makers.

The art of quiltmaking has been studied by leading historians, art critics, and textile experts for years. It has been determined through these studies that certain country people have left their trademark on the quilts they designed. We are aware of the Amish and Mennonite quilt-making style, so it is not difficult to realize that other areas of the country also followed their own patterns.

Quilts are made in three layers: top, middle (or filling), and back. The top piece determines the pattern, the middle determines the weight and warmth, and the back is the part that lays face
down.

Before the advent of the sewing machine, making a quilt represented a rather large project. It took the maker many hours of tedious piecework, sewing, and binding to complete. Because some quilts needed to be made within a certain period of time (i.e., for a wedding or birth), it was easier for groups of women to get together to work on one quilt than for each of them to slowly make her own. When a quilting bee resulted, the women found they enjoyed the socializing almost as much as the satisfaction of finishing the piece.

Even after women became accustomed to sewing quilt tops by machine, they still continued to do their quilting by hand. Prior to 1860 (before the invention of the sewing machine), quilts were made in block-by-block fashion. Each block was approximately ten to twenty squares, and they were either pieced together or appliquéd, depending on the whim of the maker. Templates, cut in designs or patterns and made of cardboard or metal, were traced so that each part of that particular design would be uniform. For instance, if a quilter was making an appliqué quilt, she might have four or five different tulips or borders to choose from. If she used the same template to cut tulips from different colors of fabrics, they would fit into a design nicely because they would all be the same size.

Once the quilt top was completed, all three pieces (top, filling, and back) would be joined by quilting or stitching the layers together. A quilting frame, a rectangular device made of four rods held at the corners with clamps, helped hold the three layers together during the quilting process in much the same manner as an embroidery hoop holds and stretches the cloth that is being embroidered. The designs to be quilted were marked on the quilt top, sometimes with the use of templates. Rarely were the designs drawn freehand. The actual quilting was begun on the outer edges of the quilt, working inward, the center being done last.

The rule of thumb used to tell the quality of the quilter's stitches was to measure how many stitches there were in an inch—twelve to fourteen stitches to the inch meant the quilter was highly skilled.

Quilt bindings were the last part of the piece; they were attached to hide the ragged, frayed edges, a normal result of the quilt's being held in the frame. Bindings were usually bias tape or narrow pieces of cloth that matched some part of the quilt.

Tennessee Quilts

In 1983, a quilt expert named Bets Ramsey and a college English teacher named Merikay Waldvogel joined forces to begin an investigation into quilts made in Tennessee. They, like others before them, embarked on a research expedition that brought them into contact with quilt owners and quilting history. As a result, they were able to piece together a chunk of women's history as well.

Tennessee was originally part of the North Carolina Territory. In the 1760s, colonists moved into the area, coming from the north and the middle Atlantic states. The name Tennessee was the American version of Tanase, the name of an Indian town. In 1796, Tennessee became the sixteenth state in the Union.

The beautiful mountains, rivers, and valleys of that state were home to many strong and talented women, who fed and clothed their families—it's amazing that they had enough time to craft memorable quilts. This state was settled during the years prior to the Civil War, which was one of the times when quiltmakers pulled out all the stops and created some extraordinary quilts. Tennessee women buried many of their masterpieces when Northern soldiers invaded the area. The soldiers were in need of blankets and quilts to keep them warm, and the women of Tennessee made sure (for the most part) that Union soldiers remained cold.

Southern states were agrarian; thus, the women who quilted were often also responsible for growing and carding the cotton they used to stuff their quilts. They also spun their own thread and wove and dyed their own cloth because commercial products were neither readily available nor affordable to most Tennessean families. Out of this period of economic necessity came scrap quilts with a distinctive character. This is one of the earmarks of a Tennessee quilt.

Quilts made in other states, such as Pennsylvania or Virginia, were similar in pattern to those made in Tennessee. However, Pennsylvanians were able to purchase cloth at a reasonable price. Their scrap quilts, though designed in the same fashion as those made by Tennessean women, are identified by the store-bought cloth from which they were made. Tennessee quilts, on the other hand, were "built" by women who saved every possible household scrap of material. Only quilts made for company (of which there are few) were made with purchased material.

Out of the 1,425 quilts documented by the Ramsey/Waldvogel survey, the majority were pieced (1,050). Another category common to Tennessee quilts was the appliquéd quilt, with only 199 recorded versions. Of the pieced quilts, 47 were made using the string quilt technique, and star patterns were the prominent design.

All of the photographs of the quilters included in the Ramsey/Waldvogel volume show women with plain faces—strong, thin-lipped women whose determination reaches out of the photos and into our hearts. Some of those women had help from sisters, daughters, or female friends in making their quilts. Others did the intricate design work and quilting alone. It is not surprising that a good portion of them wore wire-rimmed glasses. Quotes from the quiltmakers show that most of them learned how to piece quilts at a young age and continued quilting into old age. With poor lighting the norm back then, eyesight was one of the first things to deteriorate.

The most pleasing aspect of the study was that most of the quilts Ramsey and Waldvogel discovered had remained within the family for many generations. It is my hope that if you own a quilt made by a member of your family, you will do your darndest to pass it on to a daughter or son who will treasure it as you have.

Samplers

Women used the sampler format to practice their embroidery. In fact, girls as young as age seven learned how to hold a needle and push it through unbleached muslin. In this manner, they were learning to sew as well as learning the alphabet.

Alphabet samplers are the most common found; Biblical verses are the second most popular form. Any samplers that divert from the use of letters, showing scenes illustrating the verses taken from the Bible, are considered highly collectible.

Samplers were commonly made in England, and that influence defined what American samplers would be like. English samplers were made on textiles imported from India, China, and Persia, but American samplers (particularly after the first fifty years of settlement) were normally made on American fabric, like cotton. Many sampler makers used unbleached linen. Metal thread and spangles were popular in the eighteenth century, but that popularity died out in the nineteenth century. Pattern darning was used to fill in backgrounds, and stitches were varied to make landscaped scenes appear three-dimensional.

Most samplers are signed and dated, making it easy for the collector to add that information to their knowledge of the piece. A girl's diary in the late 1700s may include information about what she had sewn (e.g., borders on handkerchiefs or lawn aprons). By 1750, American girls were using their imagination and a certain degree of flair when designing their samplers, which were less formal and symmetrical than British examples from the same period.

By the second half of the eighteenth century, samplers were often small squares on which a verse or inscription was embroidered. A wide border surrounded the verse and was the major part of the work. The border could enclose a landscaped scene, figures of animals, minutely detailed houses, or biblical scenes. Flowers or floral designs often made up the sides of the border.

By the late eighteenth century, cross-stitch samplers were more popular, and many patriotic themes and emblems were used. The War for Independence affected the way samplers were used in the school curriculum, with teachers urging their girl students to show their patriotism in their needlework.

Schools, such as Mrs. Leah Meguier's in Pennsylvania; Balch Academy in Providence, Rhode Island; and a Quaker school called Westtown in Chester County, contributed their versions of samplers to the world by teaching the girls who attended them different styles of sewing.

Meguier's early-nineteenth-century samplers were divided into as many as twenty-two squares, each containing different motifs or geometric patterns. The center square would be a scene with one or two figures, one of which might be a woman holding flowers. Girls from Balch Academy, operated between 1785 and 1799, produced samplers with large landscaped scenes featuring public buildings. The scene was decorated with borders of large flowers, and short inscriptions of verses completed the samplers.

Westtown samplers were sober because of the Quaker ethic. Most commonly made were alphabet samplers with simple motifs, vine and leaf work.

Some Quaker samplers (and some schoolgirl examples) were made in the shape of a map. Though there were other types of samplers made (e.g., puzzles, arithmetical charts, and acrostics), map, darning patterns, and holy point-stitch samplers were the only ones that enjoyed a long period of popularity.

Darning pattern samplers were extremely difficult to embroider. The subject was taught at what would be considered an upper level at girls' schools. In fact, needlework was so important that an 1821 regulation stated that schools must allow "time . . . for needlework." The main principle in darning was to fill a hole in the linen piece with two or more colors darned into a pattern.

Symbols were used in samplers, the most common of which were flowers and fruit. Flowers symbolically represented love, while fruit, especially apples, represented Christianity's forbidden fruit. Trees stood for the biblical Tree of the Knowledge of Good and Evil. Verses, also largely biblical, were chosen by the maker to be highly moralistic, amusing, or celebrations of the woman's role in life—as if she needed to be reminded to be virtuous, hardworking, and loving.

During the nineteenth century, most samplers were indifferently done, with cross-stitch being more consistently used than any other style. Sampler patterns were used by needleworkers much more than was done in the eighteenth century, and the test of using as many original designs as possible in a sampler was dying by the mid-1800s.

Landmarks in social progress and scientific inventions, such as steam engines, railways, telegraphs, telephones, gas and electric lighting, and typewriting, influenced the embroiderer's surroundings. The days when a woman needed to cultivate her needlework skills above all else were changing. Women were becoming more educated; novels had become popular, and as a result, samplers of that period indicated a growing number of inscriptions or alphabets on samplers. Alphabets and quotes tended to take up the greatest amount of space on a piece of linen, leaving little room for anything else.

Lack of room was also one of the reasons women were using a more limited variety of stitches in their work. After 1750, the cross-stitch was the most popular. Before that time, other stitches (like eyelet or satin) were used to embroider a letter.

Sleigh Beds

The sleigh bed is often spotted in today's country rooms where lack of space is a factor. Made in America between 1835 and 1845, the curved head and footboards of this type of bed resemble a sleigh. However, the bed was originally called a scroll bed and was copied from one that Napolean used at Trianon.

Most sleigh beds have the immense, lumbering form recognizable as being of the Empire period and, more often than not, were made of crotch mahogany. There were some made of pine, and I have even possessed, at one time, a nice sleigh bed made of oak. However, the prettiest example I've seen was a pine version that had dainty hearts and flowers stenciled over the graceful curve of its head and footboards.

Textiles

The fibers used by colonial Americans and by early "country folk" were natural ones—cotton, flax, silk, and wool. To be spinnable, fibers must be long, pliable, strong, and cohesive enough to form a yarn.

You can identify fibers in old textiles by taking one or two small samples and burning them. Wool and silk burn briefly, then char, leaving the odor of burning hair; cotton and flax also burn and char, leaving the odor of burning paper. Man-made fibers have chemical odors and melt while they burn.

When collecting textiles woven in the past three hundred years of America's history, it is important to remember that we are dealing with relatively recent examples of woven material. If we understand the art of weaving, it will become easier to identify when and where certain weavings were made.

Scholars have ascertained that primitive man was making coarse cloth over twenty thousand years ago, but we have few of those early textiles available to us for study because they are relatively perishable.

Some Terms Used in Working with Textiles

1. Warp simply means ends.
2. Fillings are picks or weft loom parts.
3. The warp beam is the part of the loom on which the warp yarns are wound.
4. The cloth beam is the part on which the cloth is wound as it is woven.
5. The harness frames carry the heddles and move up and down to form the weaving shed.
6. Heddles have an eye through the center and are the parts of the loom through which the individual yarns are threaded.
7. The reed keeps the warp yarns separated and determines how wide the cloth will be.
8. The shuttles or bobbins carry the filling yards from side to side.

The Parlor

AS MENTIONED in previous sections, early American homes were just one large room. Parlors, as we now know them, were just the area around the fireplace where the family gathered in the evening to share the events of the day and to work a little before retiring.

For that reason, I have included fireplace equipment in this chapter, as well as information on lighting because it was normally lamps lit from the fireplace's flames that were carried by the family throughout the house.

It was in the parlor that the family hung any prints or paintings that might have been special to them. Hearth rugs were placed in front of the fire, benches sat with their backs toward the coldest part of the room, Mother's rocking chair was hitched closer to the warm flames, and Father's stool lifted his feet off the cold floor.

The Victorians brought a completely new and different meaning to the word parlor. Their parlors were for social occasions other than those spent with their immediate family. It was in the parlor that a Victorian matron would greet her guests, seating them on the edge of an overstuffed chair to sip tea from porcelain cups. Each wall was decorated to within an inch of its life, every space filled with some little geegaw or collectible; dark curtains covered the large glass windows at each end of the room, and rugs, equally as dark, were piled one on top of the other to cover the cold floor—certainly the opposite of a one-room log cabin.

Come with me into the country parlor and hear the whisperings of the past as we talk about what you might find there.

Benches

Benches are found in all shapes and sizes, in both formal and primitive styles, in most country homes. Windsor settees, or mammy benches, were common in the long, spacious hallways of Southern homes. Painted blue, red, or yellow, milking benches might be found throughout Pennsylvania's farmlands, while rustic pin benches were set against the cool pinks of Southwestern adobe buildings.

Benches were used to hold many other things besides people. They held milk bowls off the ground, water pails for a farmer, carpenters' tools for a homebuilder, or leather shoe forms for a cobbler.

In some churches, backless benches were designed to help keep the churchgoers awake. Railroad stations made collapsible decorative benches on which travelers could rest. Settles were the tall-backed benches meant to sit close to a fireplace in a country home—the high back was designed to cut down on drafts and to keep the "setter" warm.

Braided Rugs

Braided rugs used a family's cast-offs and were simple to make, requiring only a needle, thread, and the material. They were made in three different shapes—oval, round, and square—and could be made in almost any size, from hearth size to room size.

To make a braided rug, the fabric was first torn into lengths of 1 to 1½ yards, then torn again into strands of equal width so that they could be easily braided. Though braided rugs are made of all types of material, cotton was the easiest to work with and to wash and was the longest-lasting. Rugs made of wool were tempting to moths and also tended to rip or ravel more easily than those of closely woven cloths. Stiff materials were not used unless the maker had no choice, as it was important to work with goods that crushed up nicely into braids.

Though material of many different colors and patterns could be used in one rug, a maker would often group those of similar colors. For instance, the center might be of blue fabrics, the next section of rows might be white, and the final braiding might be black. As with quilts, the play of light colors against darks would give the rug a distinctive pattern that was pleasing to the eye.

Once the pieces were braided, they would be sewn together with an overhand stitch on a flat surface, keeping the braids even so that the rug would lie flat once in use.

Braided rugs were originally used in the bedroom; in today's country home, however, you may find braided rugs in any room.

Currier & Ives

If a country family were to hang something on the wall of their home during the mid-nineteenth century, chances are it would have been a print by the well-known American lithography house, Currier & Ives. The prints were popular in the 1840s, with some already considered rare by the 1860s.

Because of their popularity, the best-known Currier & Ives prints have frequently been reproduced and quickly "aged" with chemicals to give them a brownish tone. As with any other collectible, the best way to safeguard yourself against buying a worthless reproduction is to know that the dealer from whom you're buying is reputable and respected.

Certain Currier & Ives images are worth more than others (e.g., their "Darky" series, which features black characters caught in potentially dangerous situations) usually because of subject matter or rarity. Until recently, subjects such as the portraits of children, popular in Victorian days, were easily found and inexpensive. Today, collectors are adding such prints to their collections because the price of original art has skyrocketed. Buyers are looking to the next best, affordable wall decoration whether prints or photographs.

Doormats

Scalloped doormats were needle-made rugs that were put together, as were braided rugs, out of extra pieces of fabric. The cloth used was usually wool, and the material was cut in tongue-shaped pieces, then sewn together in an overlapping fashion on a burlap foundation. The pieces of cloth are laid out in much the same way as shingles on a roof. These rugs were not made of cotton because cotton does not wear as well in a rug made as scalloped doormats were.

Doorstops

There were hundreds of different kinds of doorstops made during our country's history; however, the ones with which most of us are familiar are those made in the mid-1900s (the 1920s through the 1940s).

Originally from England, doorstops were often called door porters. They were used to keep doors open to improve ventilation. When you consider the climate of England and the fact that few houses had central heating, it is certainly not surprising that those prudent people would wish to make the most of whatever heat they were able to produce. Keeping a door open through the use of a doorstop not only helped ventilation but also prevented the door from slamming shut when unruly drafts arose. Perhaps doorstops also contributed to keeping ghost stories to a reasonable minimum!

The Victorians followed fads closely; thus, when English doorstops hit our shores, they became widely popular. Stops shaped like animals (especially dogs and cats) were favored by most houses, though doorstops took many other forms. Once the trend caught hold, the number of themes increased, and by the 1920s–1940s, stops were sold in stores for an average price of $1.50—a small portion of what they are worth in today's market.

Cast-iron doorstops all started as sand castings, meaning that the melted pig and scrap iron was heated to approximately 2800 degrees Fahrenheit, then poured into a sand mold. The cavity inside the mold was the shape of the doorstop desired by the maker. After the iron cooled, the doorstop was painted by hand or sprayed, and the job was complete.

Some of the companies that produced doorstops from the turn of the century through the 1940s (production was halted during World War II because iron was needed for other things, like rifles and bullets) are the Albany Foundry Company of New York, which produced undecorated gray iron castings that would be decorated only if the customer ordered it; A. M. Greenblatt Studios of Boston, which made signed and dated stops such as the Lighthouse of Gloucester, Massachusetts; Bradley and Hubbard of Connecticut, a company well-known for a variety of iron products, including clocks, chandeliers, and andirons, and is considered the best of the doorstop producers; Eastern Specialty Manufacturing Company of Boston, which is known for "Owl on Books" and "Horse Jumping Fence"; Hubley Manufacturing Company of Pennsylvania, also an important producer of doorstops and many other metal/iron goods; Littco Products of Littletown, Pennsylvania, which produced many different kinds of stops; National Foundry of Whitman, Massachusetts, a company still in business today, producing gray iron machine parts; Wilton Products, Inc., of Wrightsville, Pennsylvania, the oldest manufacturer of cast-iron repros and responsible for some of today's repro stops (e.g., Aunt Jemima, the Fireside Cat, and the Bulldog); and the John Wright Co., of Wrightstown, Pennsylvania, which bought Hubley's patterns in the 1940s and has been reproducing them.

Because doorstops are reproduced on a regular basis, it is wise for collectors to be aware of the telltale signs that distinguish a new casting from an old one. Be aware of the piece's finish: if it is old, it will usually have a smooth finish; new stops generally have a rough, sandpaper-like feel to the finish. Check to see whether seams match if the stop has more than one part. Old seams will match nicely; new ones are often off kilter. You should also be aware of new paint versus old—if the doorstop looks bright and new, it probably is.

Popular shapes of doorstops include women holding flowers, black figures, children, fairy tale figures, animals (especially dogs and cats as previously mentioned), flowers, and cottages. Most stops range in value from $50 to $250, the average cost being around $75.

Fireplaces

History

The earliest American settlers were allowed to bring iron, copper, and brass items with them on their trip across the ocean to their new homes, so it is reasonable to assume that the few pieces of kitchen equipment they brought had probably been used for years before becoming Americanized.

Since America was settled by Europeans, residents of this country have used fireplaces to warm their homes, to cook, and to provide light. Fireplaces were central in the household; there families gathered to share news of their daily lives, women worked to spin wool or dip candles, and children first learned to read and write.

Naturally, it was important for fireplaces to be efficiently and correctly built. Benjamin Franklin and Count Rumford recognized the importance of such construction, and these two Americans contributed greatly to the early science of domestic heating.

We remember Franklin for his invention of the Franklin wood stove, known by many country families as a most reliable heating source. Rumford, on the other hand, is known as an innovator in fireplace design. Unlike today's fireplaces, the ones that Rumford developed did not have dampers that allowed the warm air to leave the fireplace or house. This was an extraordinary waste of heat and the major reason dampers were invented.

According to the discoveries of both of these men (as well as of others throughout American history), fireplace chimneys should rise two or three feet higher than the house's roof, and the walls of the chimney should be at least nine inches thick. Those who did not choose to follow such simple guidelines often had to fight chimney fires that threatened to destroy their homes—and they did not have fire insurance in those days. When the house burned down, all was lost, and most early Americans did not have the capital to start over again (which is one of the reasons it was nice to have caring neighbors).

Smoke chambers above the damper were most safely constructed at a thirty-degree angle. From this point, the flue was started above the center line of the fireplace and went straight up the chimney.

The smoke shelf was at the back of the chamber and the damper in front. The purpose of the shelf was to channel occasional cold air downdrafts forward, then upward with the fireplace's smoke and hot gases.

Dampers are placed as near to the front of the shelf as possible and run the full width of the fireplace. The plate opens forward and is generally adjustable through the use of a fireplace tool.

Fireplace Cooking Utensils and Accessories

The first iron pot cast in America was made in 1643 at an iron foundry in Lynn, Massachusetts. The foundry, owned by John Winthrop, Jr., produced a pot that weighed 2 pounds, 13 ounces and held one quart less one gill of liquid.

More than a century later (1760) the first cast-iron teakettle was made. All made before that time were of wrought iron and/or imported from Britain. The tables were turned when America started exporting iron to England in 1748.

Iron pots and kettles hung from a lug pole, or crane, over early fires. Pots are defined as having bulging sides and covers, while kettles had sloping sides and no covers. One of the pots or kettles hanging from the crane always held a supply of hot water, which was used for various purposes such as cooking, dyeing, or making soap or candles.

A great kettle, holding 15 or more gallons, was called a caldron. They were also made of copper, brass, or iron.

Two different types of hooks were used to hang pots: single ones, 4–16 inches in length, and trammel hooks, which could be used with double hooks, one end set into the other in notches, so that the pots could be lifted or lowered as needed.

A rachette pothook allowed an iron teakettle to be tipped as it hung over the fire, a boon to cooks, who did not have to lift the teakettle off the hook in order to get some hot water.

Handles on iron pots or kettles were called hoop handles, as opposed to bale handles, which were those attached to wooden buckets and pails. It was by these handles that pots, kettles, and caldrons were hung over the fire.

A brazier, an iron pot filled with charcoal, was used to keep the food warm, as well as to warm cold rooms. The grating on the top held pans or dishes, which, in turn, held the food that was to be warmed.

Iron toasters for bread were hand-wrought, sometimes in intricate, delicate, and beautiful designs. Some early toasters had revolving heads placed at the end of long handles. The heads would spin to allow the bread to toast evenly.

Any number of iron spoons, skimmers, spatulas, and twining forks were employed to help the cook accomplish the day-to-day job of keeping the family fed. Two- or three-pronged, long-handled forks were used to turn or lift meat; bread paddles lifted bread from hot ovens; skimmers took the fat off the top of a stew or soup.

Fireboards are decorated pieces of wood or painted metal that were meant to keep out drafts (as well as unwanted birds and animals) when the fireplace was not in use. They were made to fit directly into the mouth of the fireplace. Though hard to find, they act as decorative accessories in a country parlor. Most fireboards are considered examples of folk art because they were usually painted/decorated by the owners of the hearth they occupied.

Hearth Rugs

Hearth rugs were first used around the beginning of the nineteenth century. They were usually made of yarn and were put in front of the hearth to protect the floor from ashes, sparks, and soot.

The majority of yarn-sewn rugs were made between 1800 and 1840 of two-ply yarn sewn on a grain bag or piece of homespun linen. The design was created by sewing the yarn through the base piece (linen or grain bag) in a continuous fashion. The surface of the rug was formed by loops that followed the shape of the design. Sometimes the loops were cut, creating a soft surface pile.

If the height of the loops is regular, it can be ascertained that the rug is reed-stitched, a term used when a quill or reed was used to regulate loop height.

It has been said that sailors on long sea voyages created some yarn-stitched rugs.

Hooked Rugs
(See also "The Bedroom" in this section)

Hooked rugs are different from yarn-stitched rugs in that burlap was used for a backing. The underside of a hooked rug repeats the design on its surface; the back of a yarn-sewn rug has a dotted appearance, with most of the linen backing showing.

Different designs were popular for rugs at different periods of time—for example, patriotic motifs were prevalent after the War of 1812 when Americans no longer relied on English designs, and floral or geometric designs prevailed in the seventeenth and eighteenth centuries. In the mid-1800s, American rugmakers began to be more imaginative, boldly using space and weaving a little fantasy into their designs.

As with samplers, young girls tested their needlework talents by making rugs. Though rugs are pictorial rather than alphabetical, as many embroidered samplers were, they still served the same purpose—to help the girls learn the basics.

Flowers, birds, houses, and animals are common rug designs, though some rugs are more fanciful than others, combining two or three of these elements with an equally strong border.

Fabric mills were started in New England during the early 1800s, and they began turning out machine-made carpeting around 1830. Once rugs were readily available, it became more desirable to have your floors covered. Women began looking into their scrap bags in order to create rugs for their home, and shirred rug making was born.

Shirred rugs are made by using strips of cloth much stronger and thicker than yarn. The strips could not be sewn through a linen or cotton base so they were attached to the base with a running stitch. The backs of shirred rugs show only the thread stitches.

Lighting

Betty Lamps

Betty lamps have a wick support at the bottom of the lamp. The "pan" base of the lamp is roughly triangular, though it can be pear-shaped or resembling a cloverleaf. A half bail curves up over the top and is used for holding the lamp or hanging it up.

Double iron Betty lamps, with two wicks for single or double lighting, are very rare.

Betty lamps burned whale oil or melted animal fat, but today's Betty lamps (good to have around during a hurricane that causes the lights to go out) can burn mineral or salad oil, Crisco, or candle ends. Because the melted fat or oil did not drip over the edge of the lamp (wick drippings ran back into the font), the lamp was a popular house lamp for hundreds of years.

Betties were first used in Medieval Europe and brought to the new colonies by the first settlers. The term "Betty" was derived from an old English word, *bete,* which meant "to advantage" or "to kindle a fire."

Though it is hard to tell the age of Betty lamps, you can look for certain clues to help you determine how old the piece is. Older examples were made of hand-forged or cast iron. Except for the cover and wick support, the font was one solid piece. Soldered or brazed lamps, of any material, are probably eighteenth- or nineteenth-century examples. Tin Betties were produced till the mid-1800s. Sheet brass, copper, and pewter Betties were also made, but they are rare.

Some of these lamps are signed by their makers, thus making them more valuable to collectors. Of the lamps that have been attributed to specific makers, it is interesting to note that most are of Pennsylvania origin. One company that distributed Betty lamps was M & R Baker of New York.

Collectors should also note that the initials on a lamp may be those of the owner, not the maker. But do not despair; dealers and other collectors will share knowledge with you, and pretty soon you will know the names of some makers, as well as traits that will identify their pieces.

Brass Lamps

Brass lamps are fairly hard to find; they were not made until long after the appearance of tin and pewter examples. Collectors often find it a lot easier to locate brass candlesticks than lamps.

When brass lamps came into use, glass oil lamps were also coming into their own. It appears that the glass versions won the popularity fight because brass examples are just not as available.

Candleholders

As I have already mentioned, most country homes had a generous supply of candles near the hearth. The women were responsible for making them, often dipping hundreds in one or two short weekends.

Candlesticks and holders can be found in a number of materials, including wood, glass, brass, silver, pottery, iron, pewter, and tin. They have been made in any number of sizes and shapes, from the simple small dish with a thumb handle to the elaborately designed Sandwich dolphin.

Iron candlestands were often the work of the local blacksmith. Though some are rather plain and utilitarian, one positive aspect was that the candlestick was fairly heavy, less likely to be knocked over as easily as a wooden one, for instance. Iron also did not burn or scar as easily as other materials.

Tin was used most often for candleholders that were meant to be carried. The metal was lighter, making it easier to carry a lit candle from room to room.

People tend to forget that matches were nonexistent when our forefamilies were lighting their homes with candles. It is just as interesting to collect the means for lighting those early lamps as it is to decorate with the lamps and candlesticks themselves.

Friction matches were invented in 1827, but until that time, flint, steel, and tinder boxes were used when a person wanted something lit.

Candles

Most candles used by the country family were made at home by the woman of the house. She used one of two methods—molding or dipping—and her choice of which method to use was governed by how many candles she needed to make. Molds allowed the maker to do a hundred at a time, while only a dozen or so candles could be dipped at once. Temperature control was important when making candles—if the fat was too hot, the candle would not build up quickly enough.

She made candles from melted suet or candle ends. Paraffin, beeswax, and berries have also been melted to make candles. Of these, bayberry candles were the most highly valued by their Atlantic Coast makers. It was said that they gave off a faint odor when burning, but it wasn't their fragrance that made them popular; it was the fact that they burned well without smoking and were less likely to bend or melt in summer's heat.

Candlesticks

Solid brass candlesticks were brought to the New World by the settlers who came to Plymouth on the *Mayflower*, and they have been used by Americans ever since. The basic design of candlesticks has changed little, with a few exceptions, through the centuries.

Those first candleholders were solid brass, only about 6 inches high, with a grease cup or drip pan at the base of the stem. That drip pan gradually moved up until it was midway on the stem by the latter part of the seventeenth century. By 1710, brass candlesticks were no longer solid but made with hollow stems. They had knobs on the stick that served to raise or lower the candle in its stem, thus the term "push-up."

By the early nineteenth century, candleholders were being made from sheet iron. They were also push-up sticks and had a thumb piece for lifting the holder. This thumb piece was called an "ironmonger."

It should be mentioned that candles were luxuries in those early years (the seventeenth century) and that grease lamps and the light from the fireplace was what illuminated most houses. It wasn't until the eighteenth century that candles were used on a regular basis, and brass candlesticks, though brought from Europe by the first settlers, were not commonly made in America until the end of that century.

Chamber Lamps

Chamber lamps were swinging pewter lamps. These had a ring on the edge of the saucer that was used to hang the lamp. Their long wicks indicate that they were probably meant to burn camphene. Often the extinguisher for a lamp of this type was attached to it by a tiny chain.

Iron Lamps

Iron lamps were not in use for a long time; thus, examples are rare and hard to find. Tin lamps, on the other hand, were much more popular, perhaps because they were easily and inexpensively made, durable, and efficient.

Kerosene Lamps

Kerosene lamps are the most efficient oil-burning light. The first noted use of kerosene lamps in the United States was the result of the discovery by Peter Kalm, a Pennsylvania naturalist, of several oil seeps in that state.

Shale oil was the type burned prior to 1860, but by 1861 crude oil was more economically collected and refined because of the appearance of a "spouter" on the property of Colonel Drake of Pennsylvania. The oil business grew rapidly, and there were 194 U.S. distilleries by 1866. Obviously, the ever-inventive Americans realized that refined oil was the more efficient way to light and had decided to supply the country with the new product.

Lanterns

Lanterns were not used on a regular basis until long after the original colonies were settled. Though there has been some argument on when the first lanterns were made in America, it is generally conceded that they were not widely used until the early to middle 1700s.

Most hanging lanterns made between that time and the dawn of electricity were of tin or a combination of tin and glass. They came in many different shapes and sizes; some were decorated, some were not.

Some early examples used candles to shed light, while others held oil lamps. Most lamps had glass windows, though you might occasionally find one with a thinly scraped horn window.

There were cone-shaped tin lamps that were punch-decorated in the same manner as pie safes, which not only was decorative but also allowed a diffused light to be thrown off through the punched holes. This type of lantern was most often used in a tavern, bedroom, or other habitat where little light was needed or wanted.

One thing country collectors should be aware of when buying pierced-tin lanterns is that they can be very easily reproduced as well as counterfeited. More than one dealer looking to make a dollar has been known to take new tin lamps, throw a little acid on them, and bury them in a damp place to make them pass for old or antique.

The square lanterns with glass windows enabled settlers to throw a good deal of light where they wanted it most (i.e., along a sidewalk or at an entryway to a building). Old glass is very easily distinguished by features of imperfection, such as waves, bubbles, or swirls. Lanterns such as these have often had one or more panes of glass misplaced during long lives, so it is always wise to do a glass check before believing the lantern to be "all original."

Most early American homes had lanterns hanging in the front halls, near the base of a staircase that went to an upper floor.

Most of these lanterns had glass sides and were made from pewter or brass, both considered more "proper" and formal than tin.

Lens or Reading Lamps

Lens or reading lamps were usually made of pewter and were called such because they were expected to focus the light as reading glasses do with the sun's rays. Lens lamps have one, two, or four lenses, and, though most were made of pewter, examples have been found that were made of tin and brass.

Pewter Lamps

In the mid-1700s, pewter lamps were improved. An English company made a reading lamp that burned whale oil in a drum-shaped oil font. The most interesting feature of the lamp, however, was the two facing pieces of bull's-eye glass that sat on either side of the flame. A pewter shade was set over the glass, allowing the user to angle the light to wherever it was most needed.

Once Americans realized how useful this lamp was, bull's-eye lamps were produced by American firms. However, they were made with only one lens. These lamps are not commonly found by today's lighting collector and should be considered a treasure.

It is unusual to find an early pewter lamp or candlestick with the maker's name on it.

Rushlights

A rushlight gives off a candle-like glow because the pith of the rush is dipped one or more times in melted fats. Because rushes were soft, a harder outer core was needed for support while they burned.

Though some experts believe that rush lighting may be older than candles, there is little evidence to support that fact. Yet it is known that rush wicks were used as early as Roman times.

A rushlight is an unusual early lighting device that somewhat resembles a candlestick but has a clip to hold a piece of rush instead of a cup to hold a candle. They are not often found, except in museums and private collections, and are often not recognized for what they are.

The rush itself is as hard to find as the light. The meadow rush *(Juncu effusus)* has been found in meadows near ponds and lakes and can be gathered in late summer.

I imagine our early settlers made a day of gathering rushes. Perhaps they took a picnic lunch, which they would spread on a home-woven blanket once they had collected enough rushes to keep their home lit for the winter. There they would sit, silhouetted by the dying late-summer sun, enjoying their togetherness while they peeled the rushes. Each member of the family would take part in the activity, even the smallest child; and when they were finished, the food would be packed back into a basket, the blanket folded, and the rushes tied together in a bundle to be carried back to the family's cottage.

To prepare rushes for lighting, they were trimmed and peeled. What was left was a thin strip of green skin. After being dried, the pith of the rush was drawn through household fat, which was held in a wrought-iron container called a "grisset." Once the rush was seasoned, it would be placed in the pliers-like holder and lit at its upper end. As the rush burned down, it would be shifted forward until the piece was totally used.

Always thrifty, country people dipped rushes in kitchen grease or in the skimmings off the top of a soup, sauce, or gravy that might be kept simmering atop the fire all winter long. A pound of rushes could be dipped in six pounds of fat, giving the family a year's supply of lighting.

The plant itself was found in various wet places or meadows throughout New England, where it grows in clusters. It has no leaves and can be recognized by the cluster of blossoms that grows on only one side of the plant.

Rushes were far more available in England than in America, which was probably one of the reasons that rushlights are not commonly found here.

Rushlight was used well into the nineteenth century, making it the oldest candle-like device that was in continued use since Roman times.

Sandwich Glass Lamps

Some of the best early-nineteenth-century lamps were those blown-and-molded types made by the Sandwich Glass Company and the New England Glass Works between 1825 and 1840. Used to burn whale oil, the lamps were made with a threaded pewter collar. Two metal wick tubes were fitted into the collar. The reservoirs, which held the oil to be burned, were blown into a pattern mold. These were then welded to the pressed-glass pedestal or base.

Though the lamps first made by these companies were small, they soon grew in both popularity and size. By the 1830s, exquisite versions of Sandwich glass lamps were produced and sold. Collectors especially love the dolphins or the ones with lacy bases.

Some of the most desired patterns in whale oil lamps are the Bull's Eye, Sweetheart, Fleur de Lys, and Diamond. Most of these lamps are between 8 and 10 inches in height.

Spermaceti Candles

Spermaceti candles were made from the crystalline substance produced in the head of a sperm whale. They were common in New England from the mid-18th century forward.

The head cavities of the large sperm whale held an oil that crystallized once the animal was dead. Candles made of this substance were a translucent pearl color and were thought to be better than wax candles because they shed more light.

By the middle of the nineteenth century, a way was found to extract the smoky glycerin from stearine fat. The stearine was a better material for candlemaking because, when burned, its flame was clear, and candles made with this substance did not bend when exposed to heat.

Squat Lamps

Squat lamps are small hand lamps with bell-shaped bases. They are the same size and shape as what is commonly referred to as a "tavern" lamp.

Clockwise from top left: Victorian six-sided puzzle with original box; scenes include an elephant, kittens, horse, and other animals, \$350–\$650. *Courtesy of Grandad's Attic*. Elvirah Evans sampler, 1851, flowers and birds, \$695–\$750. *Courtesy of Country Cottage Antiques.* Game board, green and black with decoration, from Woodstock, VT, ca. 1900, \$175–\$200. *Courtesy of Kay Previte, Antiques of Chester.* Calico dress, wine color, ca. 1860, \$50–\$75. Also shown is a chimney cupboard, old mustard paint, ca. 1850, \$750–\$1,000. *Courtesy of Marjorie Staufer.* Wagon box, for tools, stenciled, old red with black, Hench & Dromgold Co., York, PA, \$225–\$250. *Courtesy of Country Cottage Antiques. All photos by Donald Vogt.*

Counterclockwise from top right: Unique child's bicycle with hard rubber wheels, ivory handle grips, and replaced seat, $600–$800. *Photo courtesy of Chester Freeman; photo by Henry Peach.* Large horse on rockers, black and red decoration, late 1800s, $600–$800. *Courtesy of Grandad's Attic.* Blue hooded cradle, ca. 1870s, $400–$500. Also shown are a red, white, and blue doll's quilt, $175–$200, and Victorian children's blocks, $4–$5. *Courtesy of Alice Kempton, Kempton's Country Classics.* Old green sled, 30″ runners, $225–$250. *Courtesy of Country Cottage Antiques.* Push-me/pull-you cart, original stenciling, iron wheels, ca. 1880–1890, $175–$195. *Courtesy of Mary-Lee Muntz, Bonneyville Knoll Antiques, Middlebury, IN. Photos by Donald Vogt.*

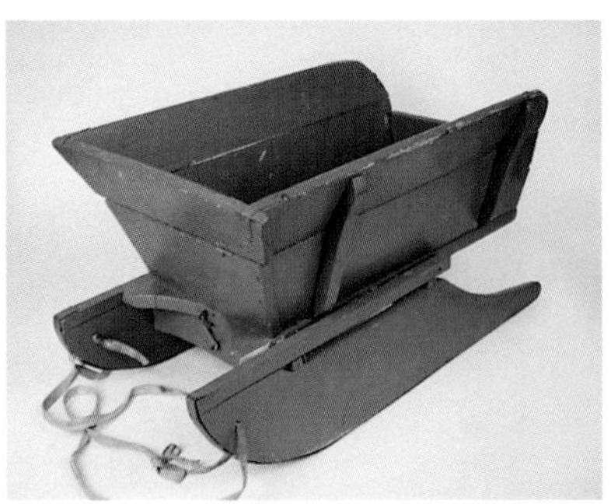

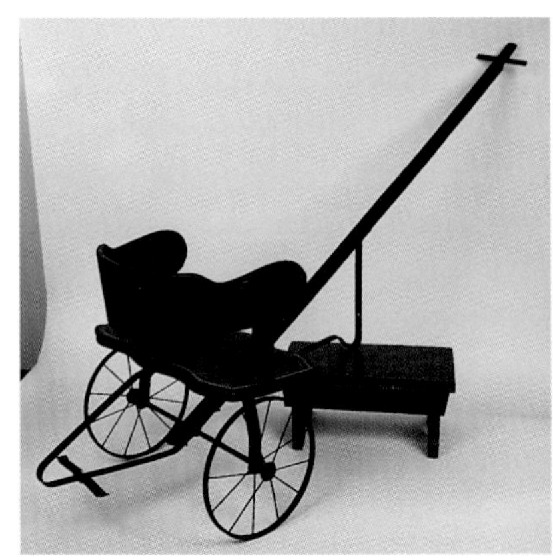

Left: Mennonite quilt, late 1800s, hand quilted, $600–$700. *Courtesy of Eileen Russell, Worthington, OH.* Right: Mennonite quilt, 1870–1880, hand appliquéd and hand quilted, $4,500–$5,000. *Courtesy of Eileen Russell, Worthington, OH. Photos by Donald Vogt.*

Amish crib quilt, 1920, hand quilted, $2,600–$3,000. Made by Mary Beachy (1893–1977) for her first son. *Courtesy of Eileen Russell, Worthington, OH; photo by Donald Vogt.*

Fireplace, with all the trimmings. *Courtesy of Grandad's Attic; photo by Donald Vogt.*

Left: White Mountain Jr. ice cream freezer, $195–$225. *Photo courtesy of Chester Freeman; photo by Henry Peach.* Middle: Cookie jar, Cottage, McCoy Pottery Company, ca. 1958–1960, $65–$70. *Photo courtesy of Shareene Hilger Collection.* Right: Cookie jar, Hen on Nest, McCoy Pottery Company, ca. 1958–1959, $45–$50. *Photo courtesy of Shareene Hilger Collection.*

Tub, tin footed with oak trim, $155–$200. *Photo courtesy of Chester Freeman; photo by Henry Peach.*

Child's desk, toy fall front, pine with natural finish, early 20th century, $150–$175. *Photo courtesy of Chester Freeman; photo by Henry Peach.*

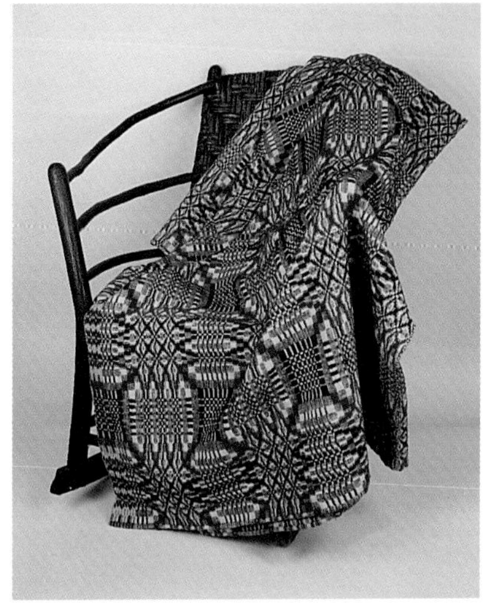

Coverlet, ca. 1898, $450–$500. Also shown is a hickory rocker, ca. 1900, $150–$175. *Courtesy of Mary-Lee Muntz, Bonneyville Knoll Antiques, Middlebury, IN; photo by Donald Vogt.*

Side table, one drawer, ca. 1860s, $495–$550. *Courtesy of Country Cottage Antiques; photo by Donald Vogt.*

Sofa, 19th century, New England, pine, $2,200–$2,500. Also shown is a homespun woolen blanket, red and brown, Vermont, 19th century, $150–$175. *Courtesy of Helen Pringle; photo by Norton/Miller Photography, Weatherford, TX.*

Left: Stepback cupboard, 18th century, New England (probably Massachusetts), pine, contains various redware, stoneware, baskets, boxes, greenware, iron and horn cups, $5,500–$6,000. *Courtesy of Helen Pringle; photo by Norton/Miller Photography, Weatherford, TX.* Right: Sheraton table, 19th century, New England (possibly New Hampshire), $1,200–$1,500. Also shown is a stepback cupboard, 19th century, New England, $2,500–$3,000. Contains various pewter pieces, mostly 19th century. Large treen dipper on door, $125–$150. *Courtesy of Helen Pringle; photo by Norton/Miller Photography, Weatherford, TX.*

Shaker basket, double-lidded fancy, mint condition, $2,500–$2,800. *Photo courtesy of the slide/lecture library of John McGuire; photo by Henry Peach.*

Grouping of Shaker strawberry baskets, $65–$125. *Photo courtesy of the slide/lecture library of John McGuire; photo by Henry Peach.*

Shaker cheese basket, Mt. Lebanon Shaker community, $550–$700. *Photo courtesy of the slide/lecture library of John McGuire; photo by Henry Peach.*

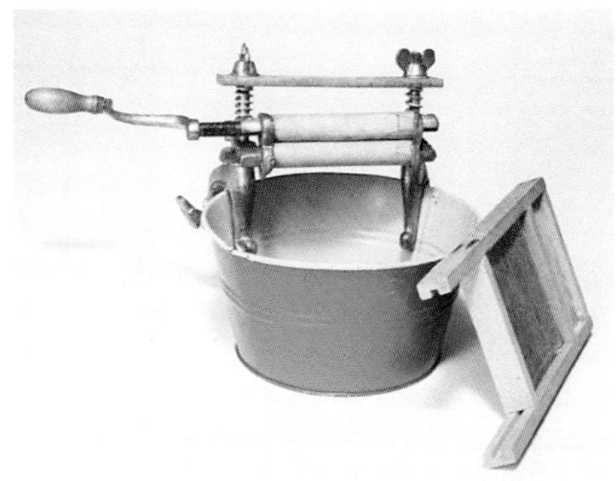

Ringer washer and scrub board, salesman's sample, wood and iron, $125–$150. *Photo courtesy of Chester Freeman; photo by Henry Peach.*

Stoneware with blue canning jars, graduated sizes; Bayliss & McCarthy/McCarthy & Bayliss, Lexington, KY, ca. 1870s–1880s, $175–$275. *Courtesy of Country Cottage Antiques; photo by Donald Vogt.*

Double-handled, eight-gallon jug, black and beige, for cider or vinegar, $95–$125. *Courtesy of Country Cottage Antiques; photo by Donald Vogt.*

Calendar, 1931, McCormick-Deering International Harvester Company; Cyrus McCormick's invention, *The Reaper*, centennial calendar, 1831–1931; from an original oil painting by N. C. Wyeth, $150–$250. *Photo courtesy of Lagretta Bajorek Collection.*

Trade card, T. M. Sinclair & Co., Cedar Rapids, IA (pork and beef packers); "Fidelity Hams," die-cut lithograph, copyright 1901 by Alfred --------, Milwaukee, WI, $30–$45. *Photo courtesy of Lagretta Bajorek Collection.*

Student Lamps

Student lamps are candlesticks with a tin (or other type of metal) shade suspended over the flame on a square rod. These lamps often had a ring at the top of the shade's rod so that they could be carried. Later, these lamps would be double candles and shades with the capability of adjusting the candle bracket (the center rod) for height.

Tavern Lamps

Tavern lamps were used in taverns. Makes sense, doesn't it?

These small lamps were given to guests to light the way down a dark hallway to their rooms. If a traveler happened to be a little drunk, perhaps stumbling a bit on the way to the room, possibly dropping the lamp, it wouldn't matter, for the lamp was pretty well contained. If the traveler forgot to extinguish the light, no matter. The small amount of oil the lamp held would cause it to go out shortly anyway.

Whale Oil Lamps

Whale oil lamps have burners that screw into the font, and they have one or more round wick tubes and slots for adjusting the wick. The term "whale oil lamp" is a general one that serves as the umbrella category under which many more specifically termed lamps (e.g., peg, petticoat, or lens lamps) are grouped.

Whey Butter Lamps

Whey butter lamps were lighting devices that employed broad wicks. They were used in country areas where cheese was made.

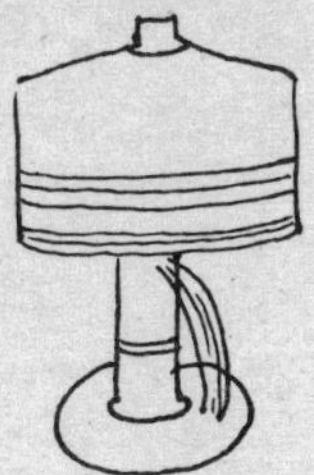

The fat used in these lamps was actually the butter fat residue from the cheese. The lamp looks like a candle holder with the addition of another, wider cylinder above the one where the candle would normally be housed. That cylinder would hold the wick and the fat, which could be lit like other types of lamp oil.

Mantels

Almost every country home had a mantel, and I'd be willing to stick my neck out to say that I imagine every country mantel in the United States is the home for a collection of some sort.

In all of the traveling my photographer, Donald Vogt, and I have done for this book, I can remember only one fireplace mantel that was being used for its original purpose—to hold fireplace tools, matches, and cooking utensils—and even that was a "collection." That fireplace, however, was the most striking of them all because, though it was in a modern house, it was set up just as it might have been in the 1700s. The modern "folk" in jeans and Reeboks didn't look quite right standing next to it.

Mantels have been highly collectible as decorative country accents, even in New York City apartments, and for good reason. Even if not used as a frame for a warming fireplace, mantels definitely "countrify" any parlor.

The Pantry/Keeping Room

THIS CHAPTER covers items that might have been used in the kitchen, on the porch, or in the pantry, keeping room, or working room. Items like "wash day" implements (see "Country Women" in the Country People section), sewing/weaving instruments, yarn winders, and spinning wheels were important instruments in a country home, and I felt they should be covered but wasn't quite sure where to put them.

When you think of a country pantry or keeping room, you think of the place where all of the canned vegetables were kept, where root crops were stored, and where stoneware crocks of pickles or liquor were saved (see The Country Market chapter for more on stoneware). All of the housekeeping products and tools were hidden there, kept out of the way when not in use.

Today's country collectors seem to accumulate such items as a way of reminding themselves of how much easier it is to live in today's machine-oriented society. Perhaps you do, too.

Wash Day

If you're anything like me, the farther you are away from an iron, the better. However, our ancestors had no choice; they *had* to use irons. As a result, old irons have become a favorite of today's country collector.

Sadirons, heavy irons with iron or wooden handles, were heated and used to smooth wrinkles out of linen and cotton washables. The irons were made by a blacksmith and not meant to be used for anything other than "woman's work." During the latter part of the nineteenth century, cold irons were used, and the designs on iron handles were more decorative and the sadirons easier to handle than their early cousins.

The oldest irons had a sliding drawer that was slid out and filled with hot coals of charcoal. These were "box" irons. They weighed about fourteen pounds and were nowhere near efficient, but they continued in use until flatirons (sadirons) were invented in the nineteenth century. (By the way, "sad" meant "heavy.")

A flatiron was usually signed by the maker on its handle, which was attached to the iron's base at two points. Late in the nineteenth century, ironers got a break when a sadiron with a handle that did not get hot was invented. Women of the world must have shouted, "Hallelujah!"

Special irons were made for distinct purposes, such as sleeve irons, fluting irons, and tailor's irons. Each was shaped for its particular purpose, some weighing more than others, depending on its use.

A gas iron was invented in the 1880s, but the invention of the electric iron was a time when all housekeepers breathed a collective sigh of relief.

Ironing Boards

The wooden kitchen table found in most country homes functioned as the first ironing board. However, it was not easy to iron something such as a sleeve so ironing boards were invented to make ironing more convenient. Those first boards were just that: a shaped, nonwarping board that would sit with one end on the kitchen table and the other on a chair. Still not a convenient way to iron, and one wonders how sturdy they were. How many of those heavy sadirons dropped through or off the board onto the homemaker's foot? How many burned a hole through both the clothing and the board?

Shirt or bosom boards were approximately three feet long, while skirt boards were sometimes as long as six feet. Sleeve boards stood on their own bases and were narrower than the average sleeve so that the clothing could be easily slipped on and off. In 1899, the Acme Sleeve Board was patented. It could be attached to an ironing board by means of an iron clamp. The C. H. Smith Co. of Boston made and distributed the board.

In the nineteenth century, folding ironing tables were made, and from that design were made the first folding ironing boards. The ironing tables resemble hutch tables in that their tops lift up and slide to the back, making the table into a chair. The irons were stored in the lift-top box under the table, which also served as the seat when the table became a chair.

Washboards

The family's clothes were usually washed once a week in a wooden tub. Each piece of clothing was scrubbed against a corrugated washboard and wrung out in a wringer that was made with clamps so that it could be firmly attached to the tub.

Scrubbing sticks or mangle boards were 3–6 inches wide and 1–2 inches long, and they predate washboards. They were used to push and pull at laundry, as well as to scrub, squeeze, and press wet laundry.

Washboards commonly had tin rubbing surfaces, though some were made with glass, steel, or pottery surfaces. Many firms made washboards, and some are collected strictly by advertising collectors. Some of the firms are Wayne Manufacturing Co. of St. Louis; Richmond Cedar Works of Richmond, Virginia; and the Bennington Pottery Co. of Bennington, Vermont.

Wringers

Those of us who complain about dragging loads of clothes to the laundromat should spend one afternoon washing clothes on a washboard and wringing them with a factory wringer made in the late 1800s. We'd never complain again!

The wringer was attached to the side of a tub by an iron clamp and was considered by housewives of that time to be a wonderful invention that saved them time and energy. Today's clothes washer would have red, raw knuckles and a sore back after washing and wringing just a few times.

Clothes wringers consisted of two rubber rollers, a hand-turned crank, and two clamps, which were attached to the washtub. The laundry was threaded between the two rollers as the crank was turned. As the clothes went through the rollers, the water was wrung out.

Once wrung out, the laundry was hung on bushes, trees, or a clothesline to dry. Clothespins were at first carved by hand and often resembled people, but manufactured clothespins became the norm by the end of the nineteenth century and continue to be popular today.

Weaving Day

Sheep were a necessary part of almost every country family's life, because their wool was used to make cloth for clothing and the mutton was a source of nourishment. Sheep are easy to raise, though they need grazing areas, which could easily be reseeded or would quickly grow back. Sheep tend to lift grasses out completely, roots and all, while other grazing animals, such as cattle, just nip at the top of the grass.

The animals were usually left outside during the summer, free to roam the farm's land, though some herders fenced in an area so that they wouldn't have to search for their sheep when they wandered off. If more than one area farmer kept sheep, they would notch the sheeps' ears as a way of identifying whose flock was whose.

Rams were kept so that the flock would not die out, and farmers often swapped rams for breeding purposes. If a ram was kept with the same flock, there was a chance that inbreeding would cause deformities or undesirable traits in offspring.

It has often been said that the wild mountain rams sometimes mated with a farmer's domestic herd, bringing new characteristics to the sheep. These rams had huge curved horns, which they used in battle or in foraging for food. Sometimes a pair of warring rams would lock horns and, unable to release themselves, would starve to death.

Lambs are born in the spring, usually one at a time, though twins or triplets were sometimes recorded. Many a lamb has been raised on a child's bottle because the ewe rejected it for one reason or another.

Springtime was also the time for shearing, and a shearer would get a pound or more of wool off each sheep. Hand shears were originally used to shear the sheep, a process that took about an hour per animal. Today's sheep herder uses electric shears, cutting shearing time down to approximately three minutes. Sheep are now larger and have wool on their tails and legs, giving the shearer six to eight pounds of wool.

Once the shearing was done, the wool was washed and prepared for carding and spinning. Lye soap was used to wash the wool; when dry, it was stored for future use.

Clock Reel

The clock reel (what some mistakenly call a flax wheel) has four distinct spokes and was used to measure the yarn. Forty revolutions equaled one knot, and ten knots equaled a skein.

Flax Wheel

Flax wheels (or Dutch wheels) were smaller spinning wheels that could be broken apart, or "knocked down," so that women could transport them to spinning bees.

Loom

Weaving took place on a large loom that, when assembled, might take up the better portion of a ten-by-ten-foot room. Learning to weave was a complicated process, requiring the knowledge of making warps, threading, sleying, beaming, and (finally) weaving.

It is said that a good weaver will produce perfect edges for their cloth by keeping an eye on tension and being able to keep track of the precision needed to make straight, flat material.

Girls would begin learning the weaving process when they

were old enough to reach the loom and to understand Mother's instructions. The teaching process continued until one was proficient enough to weave in patterns, and if a weaver became successful, he or she might even invent new patterns and feel inspired enough to sign the work.

Reelers or Yarn Winders

Often mistaken as something to be used to spin wool, winders resemble wheels but are different in that there are eight spokes sticking out from a central wheel, and each spoke has another flat spoke attached to its end. When turned, the wheel was used to make skeins of yarn. Reelers can be made out of any type of wood and are often crudely primitive, though the edges are smooth so as not to snag the wool.

Spinning Wheel

Usually the rims for the wheels would be made from one long, continuous split of heavy, green, white oak (approximately 1/4 inch thick). The split would be drawn into a circle, its edges attached with pegs or short nails, then set flat in a mold so that it wouldn't warp while it curled.

The various parts of a spinning wheel were traditionally made of hardwoods, and some pieces might be carved or hand-hewn.

Wool Wheel

The wool wheel, or great wheel, was the largest of the spinning wheels, with a circumference of eleven feet.

Prices

If an item is not indicated as being specifically Shaker, Indian, Amish, etc., then it should be considered strictly a "country" piece. For items specifically made by the country groups spoken of in the first section of this book, consult that chapter.

BEDROOM

Bed, cannonball, maple, with turned and carved posts, 3/4 size, with box spring and mattress, replaced rails. *$300–$500*

Bed, cannonball, pine and maple, 51″ across bolt holes, no box spring or mattress. *$330–$500*

Bedwarmer, brass, with bird and flower design decoration, 44″ long. *$264–$300*

Bedwarmer, brass, sun-form decoration, with turned mahogany handle, 45″ long. *$175–$200*

Bedwarmer, engraved brass, with turned handle. *$250–$300*

Blanket, hand-loomed, red and cream, seamed, mid–late 19th century. *$125–$175*

Blanket, white windowpane, wool, with blue stripes, center seam, maker's initials, ca. 1800s. *$350–$400*

Blanket chest, lift-top, in early green paint with bootjack ends and ditty box interior, 22″ high, 43″ long. *$220–$250*

Blanket chest, lift-top, with ditty box, in yellow-brown paint, 6-board construction, 26″ high, 49″ long, 22″ deep, ca. 18th century. *$275–$300*

Blanket chest, decorated, pine with original blue paint with polychrome painted landscape scenes on front and lid, front panel and lid also have roses, front has initials and date "I.E.H. 1834," moldings are dark reddish brown, dovetailed case, square tapered feet, till, wrought-iron bear-trap lock with key, staple hinges, very good color with minor wear, lid is more worn than other surfaces, 46¼″ × 23½″ × 24¾″. *$6,550–$8,190*

Blanket chest, pine, painted green with red, blue, and yellow floral decoration, 19″ × 9″ × 13″. *$400–$600*

Blanket chest, pine with original brown flame graining in imitation of highly figured wood with inlay, dovetailed case, bracket feet, and base and lid moldings, interior is a mystery as bear-trap lock is fastened; lid has some wear and age crack, sides have minor wear, 49½″ wide, 20¾″ deep, 21¼″ high. *$750–$900*

Blanket chest, 2-drawer, with bracket feet and butt hinges, 36″ high, 43″ long. *$385–$500*

Blanket chest, miniature, cherry with old worn red finish, turned feet, dovetailed case, base and lid moldings, two nailed drawers and till, crudely constructed and some age, but not early 19th century, 16¾″ long. *$250–$315*

Blanket chest, 1-drawer lift-top in pine with bracket base and original smoke-decorated painted finish, 31″ long, 44″ wide, 17″ deep. *$550–$650*

Blanket chest, refinished pine, bracket feet, dovetailed case, till and wrought-iron strap hinges, lock removed and holes for key and keeper filled, feet replaced and castors added, 51″ wide, 22¾″ deep, 23¾″ high. *$200–$250*

Bureau, miniature 4-drawer, mahogany, maple, and other woods, with pulls, 11″ × 5″ × 11½″, ca. 19th century. *$200–$300*

Candlestand, Chippendale, walnut, with circular top, turned pedestal, tripod base with claw-and-ball feet, 13″ diameter, 25½″ high, good old patina. *$4,070–$5,000*

Candlestand, circular top, cherry, with turned pedestal and snake feet, 16″ diameter, 27″ high. *$300–$500*

Courtesy of Danby Antiques Center, Agnes & Bill Franks, Managers, South Main Street, Danby, Vermont; photo by Ginger Gamadge.

Candlestand, early 19th century, cherry, snake foot, dish top, excellent condition. *$645–$700*

Candlestand, cherry, with shaped top, turned pedestal, and snake feet, top measures 17″ × 17¼″, 27″ high, good old finish. *$1,650–$1,800*

Candlestand, poplar, stripped of finish, tripod base, turned column with birdcage and square top with invected corners, nailed repair in top of column and column glued fast in birdcage so that top does not rotate, 16½″ × 16½″, 29″ high. *$300–$375*

Candlestand, tiger maple, with shaped top, turned pedestal, and spider legs, top measures 22″ × 16″, 27½″ high, some restorations. *$600–$800*

Chamberstick, brass, rectangular base and push-up, mismatched conical snuffer, 5¼″ high. *$85–$110*

Chambersticks, 5, tin, one missing push-up handle. *$100–$150*

Chest, country Chippendale, curly maple, bracket feet, 4 graduated overlapping dovetailed drawers with replaced brasses and thumb-molded top, feet and top are replaced, age cracks in ends, old refinishing has good color, 37½″ wide, top is 39½″ × 18½″, 34¾″ high. *$1,300–$1,625*

Chest, 4-drawer, tiger maple, turned feet, 40″ high, 42½″ wide, 18″ deep, brasses replaced, early 19th century. *$1,000–$1,500*

Chest, miniature, country Empire, cherry, turned feet, turned curly maple pilasters, paneled ends and 4 dovetailed drawers, replaced hardware with oval brasses on top drawer and turned pulls on bottom, refinished, poplar secondary wood, 22″ wide, 10¾″ deep, 25¼″ high. *$2,050–$2,565*

Chest, miniature, Heppelwhite, 16½″ × 10″, early 1800s. *$295–$350*

Chest, miniature, 3 graduated drawers, old black paint over pine, 19″ wide × 8″ deep × 15″ tall, mortised, dovetailed, Pennsylvania. *$750–$900*

Chest of drawers, curly maple and cherry, short feet have been clipped, 7 dovetailed drawers with applied edge beading and turned and rope-carved pilasters, wear and edge damage with age cracks, repair necessary, bottom replaced in large drawer, 38½″ wide, 20″ deep, 42″ high. *$300–$375*

Chest of drawers, Soap Hollow, PA, decorated, cherry and poplar, original red paint with black trim and stenciled birds, stylized floral designs and "Manufactured by Jeremiah Stal" (b. 1830, d. 1907, worked 1861–74), ends have raised panels painted black with initials and date "E.M. 1864" (note the same date and initials appear as ghost images on the panels), turned feet, scalloped apron, 7 dovetailed drawers with replaced brass pulls, scalloped crest missing, some wear and overvarnish is alligatored, very good color, 40½″ wide, 21″ deep, 44″ high. *$5,000–$6,250*

Chest-on-chest, peacock green sponge-painted, 2 drawers, top lifts off completely, 1700s, mustard glaze over dark brown, piece has been "exorcised" twice by two different owners because of the problems it caused in the house. *$5,000–$7,500*

Chest on frame, country Queen Anne, pine and maple with old mellow finish, cabriole legs with duck feet and cutout apron, dovetailed case with 6 overlapping dovetailed drawers and well-developed cornice, drops missing from apron, minor age cracks and some old repair in frame, drawers have some well-executed lip repairs, and brasses are replacements that fit the original holes, pine secondary wood, 36″ wide, cornice is 19½″ × 39½″.
$16,500–$20,650

Courtesy of Sign of the Dove, Antiques of Chester; photo by Donald Vogt.

Coverlet, overshot, red wool on natural linen, 74″ × 80″, early 19th century. ***$395–$425***

(Top) *small black bench,* square nails. ***$45–$55***

(Middle) *footstool,* fiddle shape. ***$45–$55***

(Bottom) *bench,* white pine, keyhole legs. ***$65–$75***

Coverlet, blue and white jacquard, signed "John Kittinger, Springfield, Portage County, Ohio 1839," some edge fraying.
$154–$200

Courtesy of Mary-Lee Muntz, Bonneyville Knoll Antiques, Middlebury, Indiana; photo by Donald Vogt.

Coverlet, green, red, and cream with strip of blue, full-size centennial coverlet (was shown in *Redbook* magazine), Pennsylvania. *$395–$425*

Coverlet, red, white, and blue, full-size, 2-piece coverlet woven in Lafayette, IN, ca. 1898. *$450–$500*

Hickory rocker, ca. 1900. *$150–$175*

Cradle, pine, 34½″ long. *$88–$100*

Courtesy of Grandad's Attic; photo by Donald Vogt.

Document box, feather-painted red with black trim, ca. 1840–60. *$400–$550*

Five-drawer chest, maple, with scroll top and scrolled bracket base, replaced brasses, interiors of drawers have been painted, some curl in end panels, 42″ high, 39″ wide, 18″ deep. *$880–$1,000*

Foot warmer, pierced tin and wood, pierced heart design, 6″ high, 9″ long, 8″ wide. *$100–$150*

Foot warmer, brass, pierced designs and bale handle, door has punch-engraved inscription and "1723," 8″ × 8″, 7½″ high. *$225–$285*

Hat box, with wallpaper arabesque design covering, 13″ × 10″ × 7″. *$100–$200*

High chest, country Chippendale, Pennsylvania, walnut, ogee feet, fluted chamfered corners, 8 dovetailed overlapping drawers with original brasses and molded cornice, minor repairs to drawer overlap and one drawer front has repaired split, minor age cracks in feet and one scroll return is replaced, old finish has good color, pine secondary wood, 39½″ wide, cornice is 21¾″, 66¼″ high. *$13,000–$16,250*

Homespun, fabric, blue, ca. mid-19th century, Midwest origin. *$95–$125*

Jewelry box, old red paint over green, ca. 1850–60, divided into 4 sections, space for photo on inside cover. *$50–$75*

Mirror, Sheraton, 2-part, in black and gold, upper tablet with reverse painting of fishing scene, 29½″ × 13½″. *$150–$175*

Mirrors in oak frames, old glass is discolored, 5½″ × 7¼″. *$50–$65*

Mule chest, New England, pine, 2 drawers, 37″ wide × 18″ deep × 39″ high. *$700–$900*

Coverlet, blue, mustard, and rust, made in Kentucky and dated 1834, mint condition. *$750–$900*

Portmanteau, dome-top, in old red stain with traces of original grain painting, 26″ × 12½″ × 10″. *$200–$300*

Queen Anne highboy base, curly maple, with scalloped apron, cabriole legs, and duck feet, 22½″ high, 39″ wide, 20″ deep. *$1,000–$1,500*

Quilt, blue and white patchwork in Bow-tie pattern, 85″ × 69″, some discoloration. *$352–$400*

Quilt, copperplate chintz, overall floral design, Peabody Historical Society labels in corners list owners, 109″ × 96½″, some small holes, some staining. *$150–$250*

Quilt, early Compass Rose, red and white. *$275–$300*

Quilt, early Pennsylvania Dutch patchwork, 8′ × 8′, some wear. *$200–$300*

Quilt, patchwork, yellow and white in block diagonal pattern, 65″ × 85″, minor stains. *$88–$100*

Sea chest, pine, with rope beckets, strap hinges, and dovetailed sides, interior painted light blue, exterior refinished, canted sides, 23½″ high, 49″ long, 25″ deep. *$688–$725*

Side table, painted and sponged on one side, 1 drawer, ca. 1860s, red, brown, tan, and gold, turned legs, 16¼″ deep, 18½″ wide, 28½″ tall. *$495–$550*

Silver dresser set, 10 pieces, sterling, rose pattern. *$176–$200*

Stand, cherry and pine, 1 drawer in either side, top measures 19″ × 19″, 26½″ high, refinished. *$300–$600*

Courtesy of Danby Antiques Center, Agnes & Bill Franks, Managers, South Main Street, Danby, Vermont; photo by Ginger Gamadge.

Stand, country Sheraton, cherry, excellent condition, ca. 1840. *$395–$450*

Stand, 1-drawer, American, country Hepplewhite, pine and maple, top measures 19″ square, 28″ high. *$200–$250*

Courtesy of W. R. Branthoover; photo by William Branthoover.

Stand, 1 drawer, flaming birch, ca. early 1800s, mint condition, made in Vermont. *$700–$800*

Stand, 1-drawer Hepplewhite, pine, with brass pulls and square tapered legs, top measures 16¾″ square, 28½″ high, original red paint. *$495–$525*

Stand, 2-drawer, country Hepplewhite, pine, wooden pulls and square tapered legs, top measures 16″ × 19½″, 28″ high. *$330–$400*

Courtesy of McFarland Auctioneers, Williamson, New York 14589.

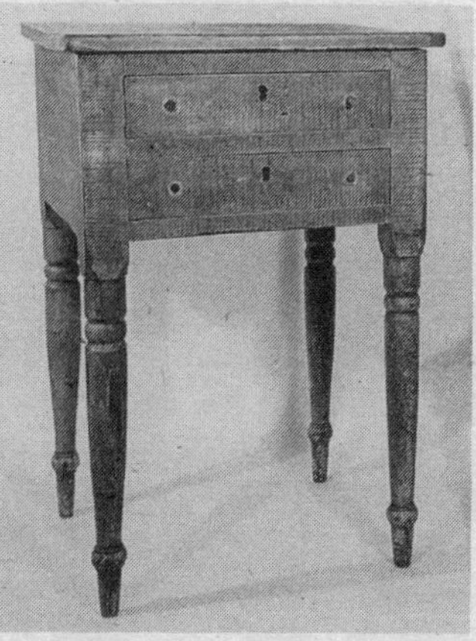

Stand, 2 drawers, grain-decorated, ca. 1820. *$510–$575*

Courtesy of W. R. Branthoover; photo by William Branthoover.

Table, Sheraton, rope-turned, 1 drawer, early 1800s, cherry, mint condition, made in Vermont. *$400–$450*

Trundle rope bed, with short turned posts, poplar with uneven coat of white paint, original side rails, mattress size is 43″ × 60″, 17″ high. *$200–$250*

Trunk, dome-top, pine with original spatter design, mustard paint, 12½″ high, 29″ wide, 15½″ deep, latch piece missing. *$150–$250*

KITCHEN

Andirons, pair, American, iron, gooseneck, 17″ high. *$220–$250*

Apple pan, old blue on tin, 15″ × 4″. *$55–$75*

Courtesy of Country Cottage Antiques; photo by Donald Vogt.

Apple tray, pine, 21″ long, 14″ wide, 3″ deep. *$195–$215*

Apple tray, pine, nice patina and weight, 20″ × 13″ × 4½″. *$165–$195*

Bench, pine painted gray, 18″ high, 106″ long, 11½″ wide. *$66–$100*

Bentwood box, with bentwood side handles and lid, old red paint has good color, water damage along bottom edge and bottom renailed but wood is still sound, 17″ deep, 13″ high. *$195–$245*

Blue and white sponge spatter, bowl, hairline, 7¼″ diameter, 2¼″ high. *$125–$160*

Blue and white sponge spatter, sugar bowl, stained, lid is undersize, minor chips, 7½″ high. *$225–$285*

Blue and white sponge spatter, rectangular dish, 6½″ × 8½″. *$225–$285*

Blue and white sponge spatter, four similar bowls in graduated sizes, embossed scalloped rims: (A) 8″ long, hairline, (B) 8¼″ long, chip on underside of lip, (C) 9″ diameter, hairline and pinpoints, (D) 10¼″ long. *$410–$515*

Blue and white sponge spatter, soap dish, hairlines, edge chips, small repair, 3¾″ × 4¾″. *$20–$25*

Blue and white sponge spatter, sauce boat, lion and unicorn mark, 7¼″ long. *$300–$375*

Blue and white sponge spatter, pitcher, 6¾″ high. *$225–$285*

Blue and white sponge spatter, waste bowl, minor rim flakes, 5¼″ diameter. *$90–$115*

Blue and white sponge spatter, 2 cups and saucers. *$270–$340*

Blue and white sponge spatter, dish, minor edge wear and pinpoint flakes, 4½″ diameter, 2″ high. *$200–$250*

Blue and white sponge spatter, bowl with scalloped handles, 9¼″ × 10″. *$285–$360*

Blue and white sponge spatter, oval platter, 13¼″ long. *$200–$250*

Bowl, burled wood, Michigan, mid-1800s. *$400–$450*

Bowl, banded creamware, in blue and brown on buff body, 3″ high, 5″ diameter. *$55–$150*

Bowl, Burford Brothers, blue spatterware with rim and base chips. *$110–$150*

Courtesy of the Keeping Room, Camby, Indiana; photo by Donald Vogt.

Bowls, mixing, blue:

Small, plain, 7″. *$20–$25*

Medium, 9″. *$25–$30*

Large, 11″. *$30–$35*

Bowls, mixing, off-white on white:

Decorated, 9″ and 11″ (each). *$38–$45*

Plain, pair, 11″. *$28–$35*

Bowls, simple stick spatter floral design in dark green, attributed to Morton Pottery, Illinois, some crazing and small edge chips, 4″ to 9¾″ diameter. *$150–$185*

Courtesy of Pumpkin Vine Line Antiques, Buddy and Atha Wallin, Fairfield, Ohio; photo by Donald Vogt.

Boxes, stack of 5, bought in Assinippi (Cape Cod), ca. 1880, priced as set. *$1,500–$2,000*

Courtesy of the Keeping Room, Camby, Indiana; photo by Donald Vogt.

Butter churn, 8 qt. *$125–$150*

Butter churn, 4 qt. *$100–$125*

Group of butter paddles (each). *$8–$15*

Group of butter molds (round, sheaf-of-wheat pattern). *$85–$95*

Butter molds, plain. *$30–$40*

Butter churn, "The New Blanchard Churn," side crank variety, black lettering and yellow paint, 33″ high, patented 1878.
$175–$200

Butter table, with painted blue base, 28″ high, 45″ wide, 27″ deep, finished interior, 19th century. *$138–$300*

Courtesy of Mary-Lee Muntz, Bonneyville Knoll Antiques, Middlebury, Indiana; photo by Donald Vogt.

Butter worker, bird's-eye maple, legs added to be made into table, ca. 1860–70. *$175–$195*

Butter-working tools, 6 wooden paddles, etc. *$85–$110*

Butter-working tools, 4, wooden, cylindrical mold, crook-handled paddle, 2 square stamps. *$75–$100*

Caldron, brass, with original iron stand, 13½″ diameter.
$143–$160

Courtesy of the Keeping Room, Camby, Indiana; photo by Donald Vogt.

Casserole, covered, 11″, salt glaze with blue interior, design is crescent moon and fans. *$40–$55*

Courtesy of W. R. Branthoover; photo by William Branthoover.

Chair, rush seat (new), made in Montgomery, VT, maple, wear on front rungs. *$150–$175*

Courtesy of Marjorie Staufer; photo by Donald Vogt.

Chargers, redware, 12″, one with slip decoration, crimped edge, made in first half of 19th century. *$300–$375*

Plain charger, same size and age. *$275–$350*

Plate, redware, 6″. *$100–$150*

Coffee mill, brass studding, 13″ high, wood and brass, ca. 19th century. *$250–$300*

Courtesy of Marjorie Staufer; photo by Donald Vogt.

Coffeepot, tin, Pennsylvania, ca. 1840. *$200–$275*

Teapot, tin, no lid, Pennsylvania, ca. 1840. *$30–$50*

Cookie cutters, tin, mid-19th century (each). *$25–$50*

Dish towel, handmade, late 19th century. *$15–$20*

Courtesy of Eileen Russell, Worthington, Ohio; photo by Donald Vogt.

Cookie cutters, collection: (lower left) unusual guitar, (upper center) rocking horse, (lower left) butterfly (each). *$25–$50*

Cooking utensils, pepper tin, Ohio, signed, all original, ca. 1890s, very good condition. *$125–$155*

Large iron pot trivet, New Hampshire, ca. 1870. *$55–$65*

Small grater, ca. 1900. *$18–$22*

Small pot trivet, ca. 1890. *$40–$50*

Grater, copper, iron, and brass, ca. 1880. *$55–$75*

Copper jelly molds, 2, 7″ and 4½″ high. *$220–$250*

Copper measures, graduated sizes, set of 4, each. *$55–$135*

Courtesy of Grandad's Attic; photo by Donald Vogt.

Corner cupboard, hanging, mustard grain (new paint). *$295–$350*

Cupboard, 1-piece, corner, butternut, high cutout feet, paneled doors, reeded molding between sections, molded cornice with frieze band of diagonal reeding, old refinishing, minor damage, 45½″ wide, 89½″ high. *$2,700–$3,375*

Cupboard, poplar with old red, combination-style lock and fitted interior with storage space in built-out doors, 19½″ wide, 11¾″ diameter, 31″ high. *$200–$250*

Cupboard, stepped, pine, 2 paneled doors over 2 drawers over 2 paneled doors, old red finish and wooden pulls, 79″ high, 43″ wide, 19″ deep, missing top molding, American, first half 19th century. *$440–$800*

Cutlery tray, mahogany, dovetail construction, geometric and floral incised decoration, 12½" × 7". *$330–$370*

Dough box, 43" long, 15" wide, 11" high, pine, dovetailed, Pennsylvania, refinished. *$275–$325*

Dough box, dovetailed, on tapered legs, poplar with old refinishing, 1-board top is an old replacement, 19½" × 35", 27" high. *$325–$410*

Courtesy of Dee Wilhelm, Grand Blanc, Michigan; photo by Donald Vogt.

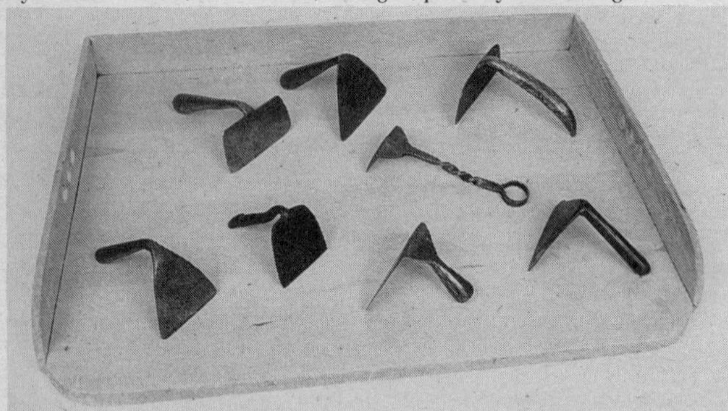

Dough scrapers (collection of 8), early 19th century, most made in Pennsylvania. *$475–$525*

Dough tray, light yellow pine. *$40–$50*

Dry sink, pine, painted yellow, 33" high, 50" wide, 19" deep. *$550–$700*

Dry sink, Pennsylvania, pine and poplar, 3 drawers in upper section, 2 doors below, 46½" high, 47" wide, 42" deep. *$600–$700*

Egg beater, blue glass, dated 1907, Standard Specialty Co., Wisconsin. *$45–$50*

Farmhouse table, fine, large, pine with turned legs, good color, 29" high, 7'7" long, 35" wide. *$165–$300*

Farmhouse work table, maple, 29" high, 65" wide, 30" deep. *$138–$300*

Firkin, brass-bound, covered, 9″ high. $165–$200

Firkin, pine, in red paint, 7½″ high. $100–$125

Firkins, lot of 3, nested, wooden, some variations. $200–$300

Group of butter items, most made in Wapakoneta, OH, ash butter churn. $275–$300

Banded butter box in old green, probably Shaker (signed on bottom "F. Wyman"). $375–$450

Butter mold, cherries. $250–$350

Stoneware butter jug, cobalt cows on front. $225–$275

Courtesy of Kay Previte, Antiques of Chester; photo by Donald Vogt.

Group of kitchen implements (center rear), redware jug with handle, late 1800s, 10″, upstate New York, good condition. $110–$135

(Left) *scoop,* Ohio, ca. 1910. $25–$28

(Center front) *curly-maple butter paddle,* mid-1800s. $45–$60

(Right) *oak measure,* Southern Ohio, ca. 1910. $24–$28

Courtesy of Alice Kempton, Kempton's Country Classics; photo by Donald Vogt.

Grouping, wood stool. $18–$24

3-legged iron skillet. $38–$42

Jewett and Root cast-iron kettle. $60–$65

Footed iron skillet, rat-tail handle. $40--$45

Courtesy of Eileen Russell, Worthington, Ohio; photo by Donald Vogt.

Homespun, linen show towel, fringed with red embroidery, late 1800s. $65–$75

Linen table runner, 25″ × 60″. $68–$78

Courtesy of Eileen Russell, Worthington, Ohio; photo by Donald Vogt.

Homespun, selection of early mill fabric used for curtains, runners, and placemats. *$25–$35*

Iron toaster, with rotating circular tray, tray diameter 10″ *$150–$200*

Courtesy of Country Cottage Antiques; photo by Donald Vogt.

Jars, graduated sizes, glass, tin tops (each). *$75–$125*

Knife tray, 3-coats old paint (mustard, blue, and red), ca. 1860. *$95–$125*

Kraut cutter, curly maple, age cracks and damage to crest, refinished, 6¼″ × 15¾″. *$225–$285*

Ladderback side chair, with turned finials and 3 arched slats (top slat is worn flat), old red repaint, woven splint seat. *$75–$100*

Large copper kettle, dovetailed construction and heavy iron bale handle, battered, 29″ diameter, 19″ high. *$85–$110*

Large Davis swing, churn, yellow paint with stenciling, ca. 1890, excellent condition. *$100–$150*

Courtesy of D. J. Downes, Birmingham, Michigan; photo by Donald Vogt.

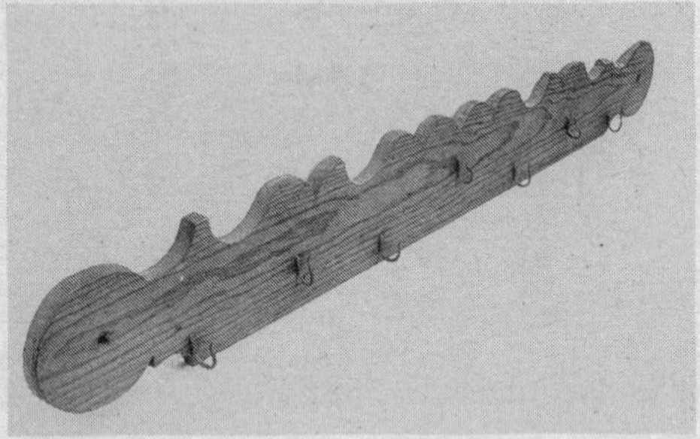

Meat rack, Pennsylvania, ca. 1850. *$250–$275*

Milk bottle collection:

- *Polk's Best,* Indianapolis, with cream top and spoon. *$50–$60*
- *Indianapolis,* with cap, cream top, and spoon. *$25–$30*
- *Valley View Dairy,* ½ pint. *$8–$15*
- *Unmarked.* *$8–$15*

Courtesy of Pumpkin Vine Line Antiques, Buddy and Atha Wallin, Fairfield, Ohio; photo by Donald Vogt.

Milk pitchers (left rear), Dutch salt glaze, blue and white, late 1800s. *$175–$225*

(Center rear) *Red Wing* with birds. *$150–$225*

(Right rear) *Red Wing,* cherry band with advertising. *$225–$250*

(Left front) green and yellow pottery. *$125–$165*

(Right front) blue and white salt glaze, with little girl. *$175–$225*

Mixing bowls, small, yellowware. *$55–$75*

Yellowware, large. *$75–$125*

Red Wing, spongeware. *$95–$110*

Red Wing, blue salt glaze. *$85–$125*

Red Wing. *$45–$55*

Pail, with iron bale handle, good clear "Hayden's Patent, Ansonia Brass Co. . . ." label, rolled rim has damage, and pail is out of round, 17″ diameter, 11½″ high. *$75–$95*

Pantry box group, large pantry box, lapped construction, late 19th century. *$200–$250*

Rectangular pantry box with wood pins. *$95–$125*

Small round pantry box. *$45–$50*

Pewter basin, unmarked, minor wear and some pitting, 8″ diameter, 2″ high. *$250–$315*

Pewter bowl, footed, slightly out of round, 6″ diameter, 4¾″ high. *$225–$285*

Pewter candlestick, pitted, 7⅞″ high. *$90–$115*

Pewter creamer with hinged lid, marked "Homan," soldered repair, 6″ high. *$225–$285*

Pewter inkwell, marked "& Cotton" (Hall & Cotton, Middlefield, CT), ex. John Kerfoot, with worn paper collection label, Jacobs lists as scarce, wear and dents, 3⅝″ diameter, 1⅞″ high. *$550–$690*

Pewter plate, crowned rose touch, "Jacob Whitmore," Jacobs #268, pitted, worn, and somewhat battered, 8″ diameter. *$275–$345*

Pewter plate, love touch, Jacobs #207, pitted wear and well-executed repairs, 7¾″ diameter. *$175–$220*

Pewter plate, eagle touch of "Nathaniel Austin," Jacobs #4, minor wear and scratches, 8″ diameter. *$375–$470*

Pewter plate, marked "Reed & Barton," 10⅛″ diameter. *$85–$110*

Pewter pot, tall, marked "Smith & Co.," wear and some corrosion, or a possible old repair along belly seam, 11″ high. *$150–$190*

Pewter pot, tall, marked "R. Gleason," Jacobs #147, soldered repair to lid hinge and repaired hole in bottom, 8¾″ high. *$375–$470*

Pewter pot, tall, marked "Boardman & Hart, N. York," Jacobs #46, pitted minor dents, 11½″ high. *$400–$500*

Pewter teapot, marked "E. & L.C." (Edwin & Lemuel Curtis, Meriden, CT), Jacobs lists as no known examples, finial insert missing, battering, poorly executed repairs to bottom, 6¼″ high. *$175–$220*

Pewter teapot, marked "L.L. Williams, Philada." (Lorenzo Williams), 8¼″ high. *$400–$500*

Pine cutlery box, in old mustard paint with stencil decoration, 14″ long. *$165–$200*

Pitcher, pottery, applied strap handle and tooled bands, black metallic glaze, rim and spout have been ground down and reglazed, 6″ high. *$75–$100*

Pitcher, redware, white slip with dark mottled brown glaze, probably Shenandoah, small edge chips, 6¾″ high. *$600–$750*

Pottery, Red Wing, group, "gray line," sponge band, made in Red Wing, MN, handled butter jar. *$295–$350*
- *Mixing bowl.* *$125–$175*
- *Custard cup.* *$65–$85*
- *Casserole with lid.* *$225–$275*

Pottery, Red Wing, group, blue and white salt glaze.
- *Butter jar.* *$226–$275*
- *Wesson oil beater jar.* *$75–$85*
- *Beater/butter jar.* *$80–$110*

Courtesy of Marian Dider, Antiques of Chester; photo by Donald Vogt.

Ramekin, yellowware with brown sponge glaze. *$24–$30*

Custard cups, spongeware (each). *$16–$18*

Butter churn, early, with wonderful Rockingham glaze, cracked. *$48–$55*

Bowl, Rockingham, glazed yellowware, fair condition. *$20–$28*

Courtesy of Marjorie Staufer; photo by Donald Vogt.

Redware group, 10″ storage jar, mid-19th century. *$150–$200*

7″ *bulbous jug,* some decoration. *$220–$275*

6″ *handled jar,* lot of splotching. *$220–$275*

5″ *pitcher,* mid-19th century, unusual color and glaze. *$175–$225*

Redware jar, brown fleck glaze has good deep color, minor rim flakes, 6½″ high. *$75–$95*

Rolling pin, tin, 4-in-1, hard to find. *$145–$160*

Courtesy of Mary Jane MacMillin, Antiques of Chester; photo by Donald Vogt.

Rolling pin, early. $15–$18

Small cutting board. $16–$20

Bowl, yellowware, late 19th century. $70–$90

Rolling pin, wooden, with whalebone, ebony, and wooden handles, 18″ long. $88–$100

Rug, red, white, and blue wool, hooked, ca. late 1800s, excellent condition. $95–$115

Trencher, large, hand-hewn. $265–$300

Ladle, wooden, great knot in bowl of spoon. $38–$48

Meat mallet, well used. $17–$25

Courtesy of Mary-Lee Muntz, Bonneyville Knoll Antiques, Middlebury, Indiana; photo by Donald Vogt.

Salt boxes, grouping:

(Left rear) *$75–$85*

(Center rear) blue. *$45–$55*

(Right rear) *$75–$85*

(Left front) with scalloped top. *$95–$110*

(Right front) *$125–$140*

Selection of beetles. *$8–$15*

Courtesy of the Keeping Room, Camby, Indiana; photo by Donald Vogt.

Selection of wooden bowls (12″–17″) and bucket, ca. late 1800s (each). *$40–$100*

Shelves, in old brown color, no doors, 60″ high, 36″ wide, 15½″ deep, 19th century. *$200–$300*

Side chair, banister back, good turnings and interesting cutout crest, refinished with traces of old paint and good color, replaced rush seat, age crack in crest. *$750–$940*

Side chairs, set of 6, decorated, original salmon-color paint with striping and floral decoration in black, yellow, green, and traces of gold, good color with some wear, particularly on seats, one has edge repair to splat and another is missing section of splat, one has dark overvarnish on crest. *$1,800–$2,250*

Courtesy of Alice Kempton, Kempton's Country Classics; photo by Donald Vogt.

Slaw cutter, tiger maple, ca. 1910–20. $45–50

Spatterware sugar bowl, blue and white, 4″ high. $40–$60

Spice box, tole-decorated, rectangular, along with 6 cylindrical spice canisters, redecorated. $50–$60

Spice chest, 8 drawers, wire nail construction, some age, good color, turned wooden knobs, gallery top, 9″ wide, 4½″ deep, 17½″ high. $175–$215

Spongeware, bowls, blue and rust on white, ca. 1900:
- *Large,* 11″. $150–$175
- *Small,* 7″ $60–$80

Courtesy of an anonymous collector; photo by Donald Vogt.

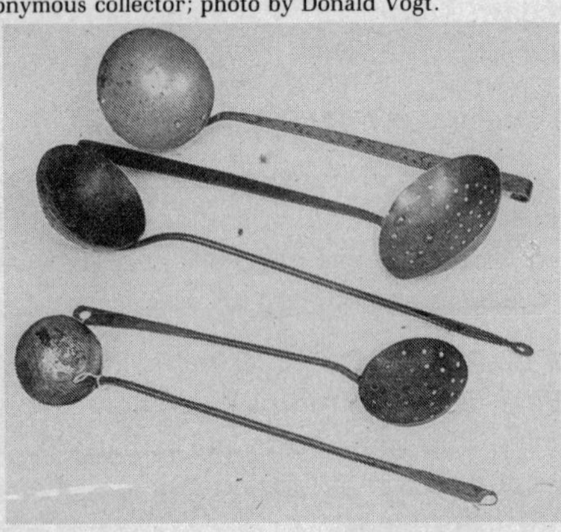

Spoons, iron and brass, cooking, ca. 1860 (each). $24–$175

Storage boxes, not a set but they stack and nest well, all with old varnish finish, minor wear and age cracks, center box has age cracks and edge damage, 6¾″, 8¾″, 9¾″ deep. *$135–$165*

Courtesy of Marjorie Staufer; photo by Donald Vogt.

Strainers, 3, cottage cheese, ca. mid-19th century, Pennsylvania. *$125–$200*

Tea kettle, copper, with brass handle mounts, 12″ high overall. *$110–$125*

Tea kettle, copper, with brass handle mounts, 11¼″ high overall. *$132–$150*

Tea kettle, copper, with dovetail construction, handle monogrammed "L.P.," 12″ high. *$88–$120*

Teapot, Bennington-look, brown-glazed, ca. 1870–80. *$45–$55*

Tin molds, 2, one in the shape of fruit, the other in the shape of corn. *$88–$100*

Courtesy of Louisville Antique Mall, Louisville, Kentucky; photo by Donald Vogt.

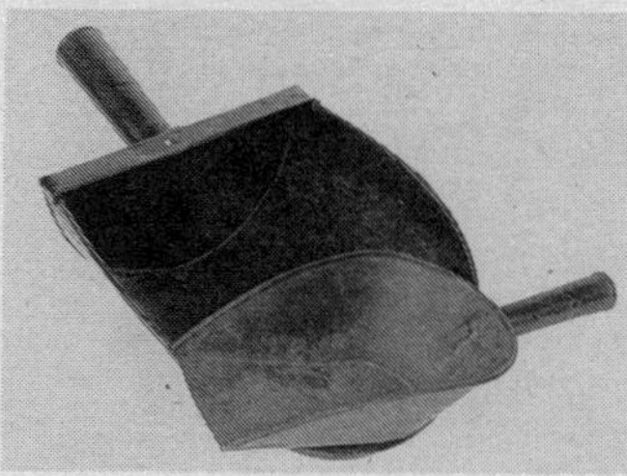

Tin scoops, large. *$10–$12*
Small. *$6–$8*

Toaster, iron, with wooden handle. *$75–$100*

Toasting rack, wrought iron, 25″ long. *$120–$150*

Tole spice box with 7 individual canisters, worn original dark japanning with gold and red striping, brass bale handle, 8¼″ deep. *$25–$35*

Courtesy of Marjorie Staufer; photo by Donald Vogt.

Toleware group, tray, 18½″ × 12½″, ca 1860. *$85–$135*
Small red deed box, ca. 1880. *$45–$75*
Tea caddy without lid, good decoration, ca. 1850. *$40–$50*

Toweling, linen, white with red window pane, 16¾″ wide, still on bolt, 7½ yards, originally 25 cents/yard. *$60–$75*

Courtesy of Eileen Russell, Worthington, Ohio; photo by Donald Vogt.

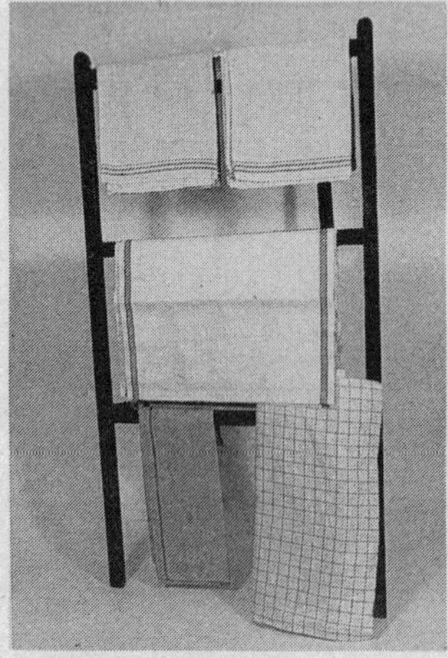

Towels, linen, made from toweling with blue striping. *$10–$30*

Courtesy of Mary-Lee Muntz, Bonneyville Knoll Antiques, Middlebury, Indiana; photo by Donald Vogt.

Treenware, grouping:

(Left rear) *tall box on pedestal,* walnut, ca. 1860. *$45–$50*

(Center rear) *needle box,* turned, ca. 1870. *$20–$25*

(Right rear) *egg cup,* ca. 1870. *$15–$20*

(Center left) *miniature goblet.* *$20–$25*

(Center right) *powder shaker* for hands, ca. 1840. *$55–$60*

(Front) *tin scoop* with wood handle, factory-made, ca. 1890. *$20–$25*

Courtesy of Mary-Lee Muntz, Bonneyville Knoll Antiques, Middlebury, Indiana; photo by Donald Vogt.

Treenware, grouping: bucket made in Troy, NY, ca. 1860, with top (marked "Katie Straeger, button box, more than 100 years old, now 1962" on underside of lid). *$100–$120*

1-piece miniature bucket, brass band, wire bail handle. *$20–$25*

Treenware, maple, turned salt boxes, with lid, ca. 1880. *$40–$50*

Hanging, ca. 1880. *$60–$65*

Courtesy of Mary-Lee Muntz, Bonneyville Knoll Antiques, Middlebury, Indiana; photo by Donald Vogt.

Treenware, 1-piece turned sewing box with lid, ca. 1880. *$85–$95*

Treenware, 2 pieces, round bowl, 14″ diameter, and a mortar and pestle, 5½″ high, both pieces have old finish, wear, and age cracks. *$120–$150*

Courtesy of Mary-Lee Muntz, Bonneyville Knoll Antiques, Middlebury, Indiana; photo by Donald Vogt.

Turks'-head mold, Albany slip, 8½″ diameter, ca. 1870. *$55–$65*

Two-part cupboard, pine, with scrolled cornice, open door above, base with paneled door and 2 drawers, bracket feet, 70″ high, 24″ wide, 12½″ deep. *$600–$800*

Courtesy of Alice Kempton, Kempton's Country Classics; photo by Donald Vogt.

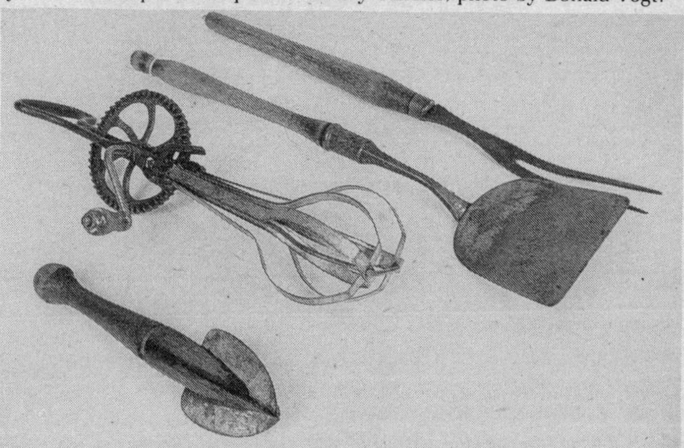

Utensils, lemon reamer (from Maine). *$20–$25*
Fork with wooden handle, ca. 1920s. *$12–$15*
Spatula, ca. 1920s. *$12–$15*
Beater, dated 1908. *$25–$30*

Water bench, pine with old refinishing and very good color, truncated case with dovetailed top corners, one board ends with cutout feet, 3 shelves with beaded front edges (second shelf from bottom is an addition), 47″ wide, 15″ deep, 45″ high, old repairs. *$625–$700*

Courtesy of Louisville Antique Mall, Louisville, Kentucky; photo by Donald Vogt.

White House bread maker, patented Jan. 14, 1902. *$60–$75*

Wooden bowl, primitive, rectangular, old dark finish, 10″ × 24″, 4″ high. *$155–$795*

Courtesy of Mary-Lee Muntz, Bonneyville Knoll Antiques, Middlebury, Indiana; photo by Donald Vogt.

Wooden bowl and utensils:

Bird's-eye maple bowl, lots of wormholes, 14½″ diameter, ca. 1850–60. *$85–$95*

Assorted paddles, all handcarved (each). *$25–$45*

Wooden storage jars, 4, turned, with covers, 9″–10″ high, ca. 19th century. *$175–$200*

Courtesy of the Keeping Room, Camby, Indiana; photo by Donald Vogt.

Wooden utensils:

18″ wooden mixing bowl. *$85–$100*

2 meat tenderizers (each). *$18–$24*

2-piece wooden rolling pin. *$28–$35*

Masher. *$18–$22*

Pulverizer for sieve. *$18–$22*

Yellowware, pair of matching bowls, windowpaned and striped (each). *$25–$35*

Yellowware bowl, colorful sponge spatter decoration in red, blue, and brown, minor wear and rim flake, 5¼″ diameter, 2¾″ high. *$65–$85*

Yellowware bowl, brown Rockingham glaze, some wear and small flakes, 5½″ diameter, 2¼″ high. *$40–$50*

Yellowware bowl, white stripes, Misshapen and out of round, small flake on table ring, 4½″ diameter, 2¼″ high. *$65–$85*

Yellowware bowl, embossed foliage design and brown and green sponged decoration, 9″ diameter, 4⅛″ high. *$65–$85*

Yellowware mixing bowl, colorful sponge spatter in red, blue, brown, and white, minor crazing and short rim hairline, 9½″ diameter, 5″ high. *$45–$60*

Yellowware mug, brown and white stripes, professional repair, 4″ high. *$115–$145*

Yellowware mug, brown sponged glaze, well-shaped handle, minor edge flakes, 3¼″ high. *$140–$175*

Yellowware pitcher, applied strap handle and tooled bands, glaze has some reddish highlights and brown splotches, 6¼″ high. *$225–$285*

Yellowware pitcher, brown stripes and white band, professional repair on spout, 5½″ high. *$125–$160*

Yellowware waste bowl, mocha earthworm decoration in dark brown and white, 1½″, section of rim is chipped and small flake on table ring, 5″ diameter, 2¾″ high. *$75–$95*

KITCHEN/DINING

Armchair, birdcage Windsor, with bamboo turnings. *$145–$250*

Armchair, ladderback with rush seat, ca. 19th century. *$193–$200*

Armchair, ladderback, in oak with upholstered seat. *$400–$600*

Bowl, sterling silver, 3½″ high, 8¼″ diameter, 17.2 troy oz., by I. Stone. *$150–$175*

Candy dish, sterling silver, in flower form, manufacturer's mark, "KFL & Son," 2¼″ high, 5¾″ diameter, 7.8 troy oz. *$60–$90*

Coffeepot, pewter, with the mark of James H. Putnam, Malden, MA, 11″ high. *$250–$300*

Coin silver spoons, 6, by various makers, consisting of 2 tablespoons, 3 teaspoons, and 1 place spoon. *$40–$60*

Coin silver teaspoons, 10, in various patterns and various makers, together with one place spoon and a coin plate sugar shell. *$121–$150*

Compote, sterling silver, with leopard-head handles, engraved "JAB 1884–1909," 8 troy oz., by Rand & Crane. *$75–$100*

Courtesy of Daria of Woodbury, Woodbury, Connecticut.

Cupboard, Pennsylvania, setback, ca. 1820, great form and proportions, poplar with cherry stain, all original. *$3,800–$4,500*
Balloon-back chairs, set of 4. *$550–$600*

Cupboard, pine, with panel door and galleried top, 38″ high, 32½″ wide, 17″ deep. *$250–$300*

Cupboard, unusual 2-door panel, in cherry and walnut, interior contains 32 pigeonholes, 48″ high, 43½″ wide, 13½″ deep, ca. 19th century. *$330–$500*

Deep dish, fine sterling silver, with raised fruit and leaf decoration, monogrammed center, 14″ × 11″ × 1½″, one tiny dent in center, 20 troy oz., by Howard. *$400–$500*

Demitasse spoons, 11 sterling silver, in pierced ornate pattern with gold wash bowls, 2.8 troy oz., by Whiting. *$100–$150*

Drop-leaf table, country Hepplewhite, in birch, 18″ × 44″, with 16″ leaves. *$385–$600*

Flatware, sterling silver, consisting of 8 bouillon spoons, 12 demitasse spoons, 1 ladle, 10 butter spreaders, 4 serving spoons, 1 pickle fork, 35.8 troy oz. *$220–$300*

Gate-leg drop-leaf table, in the 18th century style, pine and maple, 1 drawer, turned legs and stretchers, top 44″ × 17″ with two 16″ drop leaves, 19th century. *$385–$500*

Nutcracker, cast bronze, in the form of a dog, 6″ high, 12″ long. *$30–$75*

Pearl-handled knives, set of 12, 6 dinner and 6 luncheon. *$121–$150*

Pewter jardinière, 12¼″ diameter, 8½″ high. *$95–$120*

Pewter platter, oval with well for juices and hot water reservoir, marked "London," some wear, 16½″ × 23½″. *$215–$270*

Pewter porringer, Pennsylvania tab handle, some battering and repair in bowl, 5½″ diameter. *$525–$650*

Pewter porringer, crown handle marked "S.G.," 4¾″ diameter. *$425–$535*

Pewter porringer, taster size, cast handle, Jacobs 54e (Jacobs attributes handle to Isaac Lewis), 2¼″ diameter. *$200–$250*

Pewter porringer, flowered handle with eagle touch with "Hamlin, Providence" (Samuel Hamlin, Jr.), Jacobs #163, 5½" diameter. *$700–$875*

Pewter porringer, hallmarks on back (late), 112½" long. *$45–$60*

Pewter porringer, crown handle marked "I.G.," 4⅜" diameter. *$425–$535*

Pewter porringer, cast crown handle, unmarked American, 5½" diameter. *$65–85*

Pewter porringer, flowered handle with eagle touch with "Hamlin" (Samuel Hamlin, Hartford, CT), Jacobs #161, 5½" diameter. *$850–$1,065*

Pewter porringer, double-handled, late, 6¼" diameter. *$15–$20*

Pewter porringer, worn black paint on turned wooden handle, 15" long. *$150–$190*

Pewter porringer, Pennsylvania tab handle, battered and worn, 5½" diameter. *$625–$785*

Pewter porringer, heart and crescent handle, unmarked American, 19th century, 3½" diameter. *$225–$285*

Pewter porringer, cast handle (j55b), marked "TD & SB," (Thomas Danforth Boardman, Hartford, CT), some dents and old repair in bowl, 3¼" diameter. *$450–$565*

Pillowback side chairs, set of 4, plank seats, painted black with stencil decoration. *$500–$600*

Pitcher, sterling silver, 6¾" high, 16.8 troy oz., by Richard Dimes. *$150–$175*

Rockingham bowl, with flared rim, probably Bennington, 13" diameter. *$110–$125*

Rockingham pitcher, probably Bennington, hunting scene, 10" high. *$77–$90*

Settle, curved back, pine, painted red, 5" high, 6′2" long. *$440–$500*

Side chair, 7-spindle bow-back Windsor, medium brown color. *$100–$150*

Side chairs, set of 4, antique thumb-back, with plank seats. *$300–$350*

Silver coffeepot, triple touch on base, raised floral band on foot, lip, and 1 inch down from lip, wooden handle, "given by M. Osgood to M. Pickman, 1829," 8¼″ high, 20 troy oz., by Stevens & Lakeman, Salem, ca. 1825. *$400–$500*

Silver spoons, 7, 3 tablespoons and 4 teaspoons, fiddle thread pattern, monogrammed, sold by Robert Rait, ca. 1840–1850. *$60–$80*

Silver tea and coffee set, fine Reed & Barton sterling, consisting of hot water kettle on stand, teapot, coffeepot, creamer, sugar, waste bowl, and plated tray, monogrammed, length of tray, 28″, height of kettle, 13″, 132 troy oz. *$1,650–$2,500*

Teapot, pewter, 11″ high. *$150–$200*

Tea set, 5-piece sterling silver, Queen Anne style, consisting of teapot, coffeepot, covered sugar, creamer, and waste bowl, approximately 73 troy oz., by Gorham. *$990–$1,000*

Tole decorated tin tea caddy, red and yellow on black, with 50% of decoration remaining, 8″ high, together with a tin covered sugar bowl and a bird-decorated tole bread tray, 8″ long. *$80–$110*

Miscellaneous

Cast-iron chair, painted green in grape pattern. *$88–$100*

Cast-iron chairs, painted green with plume design. *$523–$600*

Circular table, painted green in grape pattern, 14″ high, 20″ diameter. *$100–$125*

Circular table, painted green, 27″ high, 38″ diameter. *$66–$100*

Figural cast-iron boot scraper with side brushes, 13″ high, 9″ wide, 11″ deep, ca. 1915, excellent condition. *$300–$350*

Lantern, hanging, brass, with pierced decoration and blue globe, 13″ high plus ring, 19th century. *$250–$300*

Lanterns, hand, 2, tin, one painted black, 11″ high, the other a Lloyd No. 1 with red lens and old red paint, 8″ high, 19th century. *$50–$100*

Tavern table, pine and maple, 1 drawer, breadboard top not original to table, 27″ high, top measures 33″ × 21″. *$575–$625*

Towel rail, painted pine. *$20–$30*

Pantry

Floor-standing reel, hardwood with turned legs and spindle, old worn patina, 30″ reel, 36″ high. *$95–$120*

Red porcelain wash bucket. *$32–$40*
Red porcelain kitchen pieces, including bowl. *$28–$35*
Coffeepot. *$25–$35*
Ladles. *$8–$15*
Plate. *$15–$18*

Spinning wheel, oak and other hardwood with good turned detail and old dark finish, distaff is old replacement, 35″ high. *$400–$500*

Tape loom, pine with old dark patina, one side of base and ratchet arm are old replacements and heddle board has glued crack, 10½″ × 18½″. *$65–$85*

PANTRY/KEEPING ROOM

Courtesy of the Keeping Room, Camby, Indiana; photo by Donald Vogt.

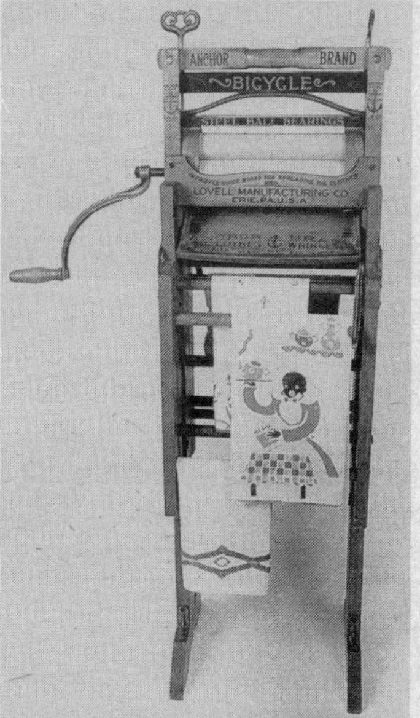

Anchor-brand folding bench wringer with collection of dish towels, patented June 25, 1898, made in Erie, PA. *$150–$175*

Courtesy of Pumpkin Vine Line Antiques, Buddy and Atha Wallin, Fairfield, Ohio; photo by Donald Vogt.

Bucket, wooden, red, banded, for storage in home, bought in Pennsylvania, thought to be from upper New York, ca. 1870, 18½″ high. *$450–$550*

Courtesy of Marjorie Staufer; photo by Donald Vogt.

Candle box, pine, made in New England, ca. 1810. *$125–$225*

Candle dryer, 24″ high × 26″, free spinning, old blue, ca. mid-1800s. *$95–$115*

Candle mold, pewter, rare size, ca. 1820, made in Ohio or Indiana, butternut, with 6 molds, 9¾″ × 13″. *$900–$1,100*

Candleholder, iron, wedding band, missing its push-up, late 18th century. *$125–$175*

Candleholder, hogscraper, small, 5″. *$75–$110*

Candleholders (pair), 7½″, marked "Shaw." *$200–$275*

Cupboard, chimney, Ohio, old mustard paint, 5½′ tall, 24″ wide, ca. 1850. *$750–$1,000*

Woman's dress, calico, wine color, ca. 1860. *$50–$75*

Courtesy of Marjorie Staufer; photo by Donald Vogt.

Cupboard, jelly, ca. 1840, all original, mustard grain painted, Pennsylvania. *$950–$1,100*

Basket, Indian, Cherokee, gathering. *$140–$160*

Basket, Indian, Northeast, with stenciled trees. *$95–$125*

Cupboard, pine, with 3 shelves and cupboard base, 80″ high, 35″ wide, ca. 19th century. *$440–$500*

Courtesy of Mary-Lee Muntz, Bonneyville Knoll Antiques, Middlebury, Indiana; photo by Donald Vogt.

Flax hatchel, ca. 1820, flax pulled through and shredded before being made into thread, Pennsylvania. *$35–$50*

Courtesy of Kay Previte, Antiques of Chester; photo by Donald Vogt.

Flax wheel, ca. 1840, complete except for side slat that connects wheel to pedal, well-loved and used. *$285–$385*

Flax wheel, fine oak, powered by hand crank rather than foot pedal, 46″ high, 18th/early 19th centuries. *$138–$300*

Herb drying rack, wooden latticework, in old paint, 42″ × 36″, ca. 19th century. *$165–$200*

Courtesy of Mary-Lee Muntz, Bonneyville Knoll Antiques, Middlebury, Indiana; photo by Donald Vogt.

Herb drying rack, late 1800s. *$110–$125*

Courtesy of Dee Wilhelm, Grand Blanc, Michigan; photo by Donald Vogt.

Lazy Kate, used in spinning/weaving, late 19th century. *$125–$150*

Loom lights (hung when weaver working), 3 sizes, one with rush light attached and made of twisted iron. *$550–$650*

Long one made of twisted iron. *$400–$475*

Small one made of twisted iron. *$250–$300*

Pair of washboards, wood frame with tin, large. *$15–$18*

Small. *$10–$12*

Set of 4 yellowware canisters. *$65–$100*

Spinning wheel, large, cherry, excellent condition, 58″ high. *$400–$600*

Tin candle box, apple green color, ca. 19th century, 10″ wide, 9″ tall, 5″ deep. *$75–$95*

Tin candle box, japanned in black, ca. 1870s–1880s, 13½″ long, 4″ diameter. *$225–$275*

Courtesy of Pam and Martha Boynton, Groton, Massachusetts.

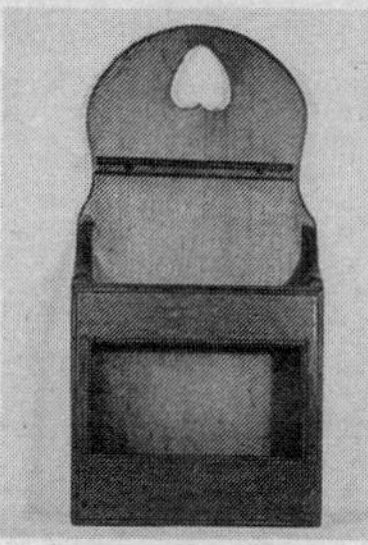

Wall box, early hanging with heart cutout, Concord, MA. *Price not available*

Yarn winder, pine, fine old red paint. *$300–$350*

Courtesy of Mary-Lee Muntz, Bonneyville Knoll Antiques, Middlebury, Indiana; photo by Donald Vogt.

Yarn winder, cherry, trestle feet, handmade, ca. 1850. *$150–$175*

PARLOR

Andirons, pair, brass, ball top, together with matching poker and tongs, 15″ high. *$88–$100*

Armchair, bowback Windsor, splayed base with turned legs and H-stretcher, oval seat, and turned arm supports, one third of arm rail is an old replacement and other repairs and replacements, old refinishing with original paint on underside of seat, 16½″ seat height. *$450–$565*

Armchair, rocking, Shaker type, with 4-rung ladderback and splint seat. *$300–$350*

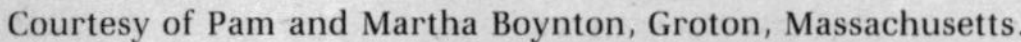

Courtesy of Pam and Martha Boynton, Groton, Massachusetts.

Armchair, Windsor, original paint, no repairs. *$2,500–$5,000*

Banjo clock, convex glass over original painted dial reading "Sawin," with alarm movement and outside bell, brass side arms, the door is stamped "155," 30″ high, original gilding painted over, lower tablet replaced, by John Sawin, Boston, 1823–1863, apprenticed to Aaron Willard. *$2,090–$2,500*

Courtesy of Country Cottage Antiques; photo by Donald Vogt.

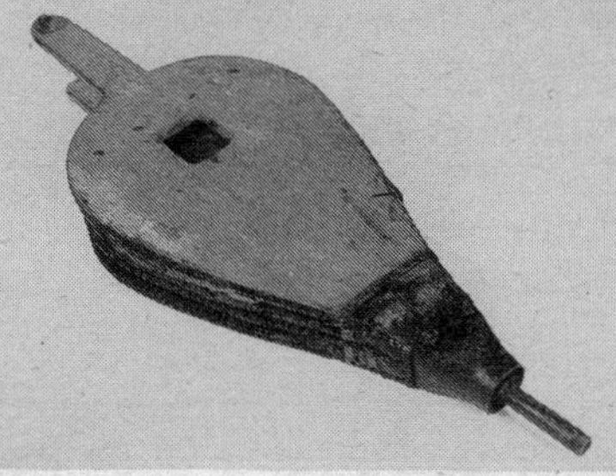

Bellows, large, early set, needs releathering, in old red paint; 38½″ tall, 14″ wide. *$110–$140*

Bellows, decorated turtle back, original brown paint with compote of fruit and foliage in stenciled bronze powder and yellow striping, varnished and releathered, brass nozzle, 17¾″ long. *$195–$245*

Bench, deacon's, Pennsylvania, in two-tone green paint with stencil decoration, paint and decoration 90% complete, 78″ long. *$770–$850*

Blanket chest, 6-board, with molded top, original gray paint, 21½″ high, 38″ long, 15″ deep. *$200–$300*

Courtesy of Mary-Lee Muntz, Bonneyville Knoll Antiques, Middlebury, Indiana; photo by Donald Vogt.

Box, 2-tiered wall box with incised carvings of apple tree, ca. 1870, restored to original finish, pine or poplar. *$195–$225*

Box, decorated, dovetailed, pine with polychrome floral decoration, decoration appears to be a later addition but still has good age, glued cracks in lid, nails in one end of lid molding have broken loose and been reattached, 13″ long. *$225–$285*

Box, lift-top mahogany, exterior with inlay in contrasting woods, interior with 4 compartments has Masonic symbol inlays, 15½″ × 10″ × 5″. *$165–$200*

Box, lift-top, burled walnut with ivory escutcheon, 3½″ × 10″ × 7″. *$66–$100*

Box, oval, bentwood, all wooden with swivel lid and fastener, relief-carved designs and good brown patina, minor edge damage, 9″ long. *$150–$190*

Box, round bentwood in old red; some edge damage, 5½″ high. *$105–$135*

Box, unusual pine lift-top with secret drawer and molded decoration, iron hinges, top measures 19½″, 11′ high. *$350–$400*

Boxes, 2, small, with single finger construction, oval, with natural patina, 3⅝″ long and round with layers of heavy paint, 3½″ diameter. *$370–$465*

Bracket shelf, hanging, interesting folk art detail with brown sponged paint and black trim, 12½″ high. *$185–$235*

Bucket, spun brass, with iron bale handle, 17½″ diameter, attributed to Hiram W. Hayden. *$250–$300*

Bucket, unusually large spun brass, with iron bale handle, top diameter 23″, by Hiram W. Hayden, Waterbury, CT, patented December 16, 1851. *$416–$500*

Candle box, pine with original black paint and red decoration, painted name "S.B. Studley," 14″ × 7″ × 6″, needs minor restoration. *$88–$100*

Courtesy of Marjorie Staufer; photo by Donald Vogt.

Candle boxes, stack, ca. mid-19th century, all in original condition (prices are for each). *$20–$150*

Candleholders, wrought iron, 12½″ tall, New Hampshire origin, ca. early 19th century. *$800–$1,200*

Candlestand, mahogany with ebony line inlay on the spider leg, turned column and 1-board rectangular top with rounded corners, latch and one cleat holding top are replaced, refinished, 18½″ × 20¾″, 25¾″ high. *$225–$290*

Candlestick with lip hanger, push-up knob replaced by screw, light rust and minor battering, 5¼″ high. *$45–$55*

Candlestick, early–mid-1800s, iron hogscraper. *$125–$140*
Tinderbox, early 1800s, Ohio, tin. *$160–$175*

Candlestick, Queen Anne style, brass, poor casting with casting hole in socket, age is hard to determine, 7¼″ high. *$45–$60*

Candlesticks, hogscraper, 4, one with central banding, varying heights. *$300–$350*

Candlesticks, lot of 4, hogscraper, one with push-up missing, two stamped "Shaw." *$150–$200*

Candlesticks, pair, antique sandwich glass dolphin, in clambroth, 9½″ high. *$600–$700*

Candlesticks, wooden, pair, hand-carved, each with a half-bust portrait of George Washington, 10″ high. *$138–$200*

Candlesticks, brass, 2, square-base Victorian (push-up missing), 9½″ high, and trifid feet (late), 9¼″ high. *$30–$40*

Courtesy of Louisville Antique Mall, Louisville, Kentucky; photo by Donald Vogt.

Chair, ladderback with button-top finials and sliced wood woven seat, ca. early 1800s. *$95–$125*

Chandelier, forged iron, 10-candle, ca. turn of century. *$1,500–$1,800*

Courtesy of Grandad's Attic; photo by Donald Vogt.

Chandelier, punched tin, 6 candleholders, mid-19th century, Pennsylvania. *$500–$600*

Courtesy of Grandad's Attic; photo by Donald Vogt.

Chandelier, wood and tin, cut nails, mid-19th century, made in Pennsylvania. *$500–$600*

Courtesy of W. R. Branthoover; photo by William Branthoover.

Clock, New Haven Clock Co., New Haven, CT, 30-hour clock, with provenance, very good condition, dial replaced, mahogany and maple case. *Price not available*

Clock, long case, cherry, with dome top, painted dial, and wooden works, 80″ high, missing feet, ca. 1820. *$990–$1,500*

Clock, tall case, cherry, pierced pediment with brass finials, dome top, painted dial with bird decoration, brass works and fluted bonnet supports, the throat with inlay to door, fluted quarter columns with brass stop flutes and corners, line inlay to base with ogee bracket feet, 93½″ high overall, movement not original, possibly a replaced door, left-side feet partially missing, New England, early 19th century. *$5,060–$6,000*

Courtesy of Louisville Antique Mall, Louisville, Kentucky; photo by Donald Vogt.

Copper coal hod, hand-forged. *$175–$195*

Country stand, hardwood with old varnish finish, late wire nail construction, 21″ × 24″, 30¾″ high. *$65–$85*

Curio cupboard, 9″ wide, 33″ tall. *$100–$125*

Courtesy of Alice Kempton, Kempton's Country Classics; photo by Donald Vogt.

Document box, bird's-eye maple, made in upstate New York, turn of the century. *$150–$175*

Doorstop, painted cast iron, in lighthouse form, 6″ high. *$231–$275*

Doorstop, cast iron, a gnome in red, yellow, and green, 13″ high, paint in good condition. *$110–$200*

Doorstop, cast iron, in the form of a cat, 12″ high. *$88–$100*

Doorstop, cast iron, in the form of a maid in uniform, original paint, 9″ high. *$130–$150*

Drop-front desk, made in Kentucky, 19th century, cherry, 44″ wide, 24″ deep, 41″ high. *$4,500–$5,000*

Courtesy of Grandad's Attic; photo by Donald Vogt.

Fireplace, cooking pots, all iron.

(Left rear) *Dutch oven* with top, 3-legged, 12½″. *$200–$250*

(Right rear) *broiler oven,* covered, 15″. *$150–$200*

(Left front) *hanging griddle,* 11″. *$125–$175*

(Right front) *hanging griddle,* 13″. *$125–$150*

Courtesy of Marjorie Staufer; photo by Donald Vogt.

Fireplace equipment, trammel, 18th century, New England. *$225–$275*

Peel, iron, 18th century. *$75–$125*

Skillet, spider leg, long-handled, 18th century, signed. *Price not available*

"Bach, Pa.," ca. 1700. *$200–$250*

Basin, iron, ca. 1810. *$100–$175*

Courtesy of Dee Wilhelm, Grand Blanc, Michigan; photo by Donald Vogt.

Fireplace implements, rotating broiler, iron, mid-19th century. *$185–$215*

Wrought-iron grill, 18th century, Philadelphia. *$275–$300*

Iron spoon, excavated in Detroit, early 19th century. *$125–$150*

Courtesy of Danby Antiques Center, Agnes & Bill Franks, Managers, South Main Street, Danby, Vermont; photo by Ginger Gamadge.

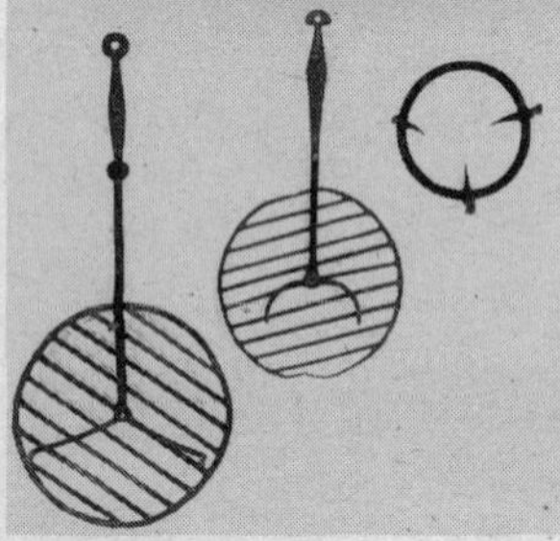

Fireplace utensils, hand-wrought iron, early 19th century. *$75–$195*

Courtesy of Lee Cheresh, Birmingham, Michigan; photo by Donald Vogt.

Fireplace warmer, adjustable hand rest, heart motif, 19th century. *$200–$250*

Footstool, pine, well made with good detail and S-curve cutout in top, good old brown finish, 6¼″ × 11″, 7¼″ high. *$75–$100*

Courtesy of Daria of Woodbury, Woodbury, Connecticut.

Furniture and accessories, grease lamp, hanging, authentic, ca. early 1800s. *$110–$150*

Fiddleback chair, outstanding form and condition, original paint, full height. *$1,100–$1,500*

Pennsylvania redware cup, ca. 1860. *$90–$125*

Coffeepot, combination tin and pewter, ca. 1850. *$275–$325*

Candlestand, Chester County, PA, ca. 1780, all original including paint. *$700–$900*

Courtesy of Daria of Woodbury, Woodbury, Connecticut.

Glass, collection of country glass pieces (from left to right):

Sandwich glass lamp, blue and clear, ca. 1850. *$200–$225*

Pittsburgh, PA, water pitcher, cranberry glass, freeblown. *$300–$350*

Free-blown milk jar, ca. 1810. *$250–$300*

Mug, blown, etched, ca. 1800. *$450–$500*

Water globe, rare, ca. 1820. *$400–$450*

Courtesy of Mary-Lee Muntz, Bonneyville Knoll Antiques, Middlebury, Indiana; photo by Donald Vogt.

Group of round boxes ("ditty" boxes):

Chip-carved, inlaid, 3″ diameter. *$45–$55*

Chip-carved, inlaid, 2½″ diameter. *$35–$45*

Round, pedestal, mahogany, ca. 1800, 5½″ tall. *$150–$180*

Box with top, ca. 1825–30, veneer-trimmed, turnings, 8″ tall. *$90–$100*

Hanging box, decorated, pine, with original worn natural finish, black edging, some wear and age cracks, late, 16½″ long.
$200–$250

Hanging cupboard, walnut, with molded cornice, 3 shelves behind 2 glazed doors, electrified, 28½″ high, 31″ wide, 11″ deep.
$440–$500

Courtesy of Country Cottage Antiques; photo by Donald Vogt.

Jardinière, spongeware, navy on tan (rare colors), ribbing down sides, 9″ diameter, 8″ tall, ca. 1890s, mint condition.
$275–$325

Ladderback armchair, refinished, new woven-splint seat.
$325–$400

Ladderback chair, New England, ca. 1790, original finish.
$425–$500

Doll, black, rag with gingham apron, ca. 1870. *$125–$200*

Ladderback rocker with rush seat and turned finials. *$75–$125*

Ladderback side chair with 5 slats, pointed finials, 46″ high.
$125–$150

Lamp, antique pressed glass, fluid, paneled Thumbprint pattern with hexagonal base, probably Sandwich, 11″ high. *$100–$150*

Lamp, antique pressed glass, fluid, oval Thumbprint pattern with clear font and milk glass base, 9″ high. ***$100–$125***

Lamp, antique pressed glass, fluid, hexagonal form, oval Thumbprint pattern with hexagonal base, 10″ high. ***$100–$150***

Lamp, antique pressed glass, fluid, Peacock Feather pattern with clear font and milk glass base, 8¾″ high. ***$75–$125***

Lamp, double-drop burner with acorn top and handled dish base, tin, whale oil, 6½″ high. ***$50–$100***

Lamp, tin, fluid, kettle type with large dish base, handled, 7″ high. ***$50–$100***

Lamp, kinnear type with hogscraper base, tin, fluid, 8″ high. ***$50–$100***

Lamp, kinnear type by Ufford of Boston, with dish base and original gilt, tin, fluid, 6″ high. ***$110–$200***

Lamp, kinnear type, unusual large rectangular base, tin, fluid, 7½″ high. ***$90–$150***

Lamp, Sandwich pressed glass, fluid, Comet pattern, with original shade and chimney, base 12″ high. ***$242–$275***

Lamp, tin, acorn top, double-drop burner, side filler and flared base, original japanning, handled, whale oil, 6½″ high. ***$100–$150***

Lamp, tin, single-drop burner, side filler, and acorn top, whale oil, 8″ high. ***$50–$100***

Lamp, 11″ high, brass, single burner, whale oil, ca. 19th century. ***$175–$200***

Lamp, tin, wick burner and handled base, fluid, 4½″ high. ***$50–$75***

Lamps, pair, vaseline glass, fluid, Sweetheart pattern, 9¾″ high to cover, mold line through wafer, considerable age evident on base. ***$1,500–$2,000***

Courtesy of Grandad's Attic; photo by Donald Vogt.

Lantern, copper, punched with star design, 26″ tall. *$600–$700*

Courtesy of Grandad's Attic; photo by Donald Vogt.

Lanterns, 3, punched-tin (Paul Revere type), largest is 33″, possibly hung in tavern, punched design is an eagle. *$700–$1,000*

Middle size, 16″. *$250–$275*

Smallest, 11½″. *$225–$250*

Lift-top lab desk, rosewood and walnut, 14″ × 9″ × 4″, one hinge needs repair. *$220–$250*

Lighting, trammel with grease lamp, iron, late 18th century. *$495–$525*

Lantern, wooden, typical mid-19th century. *$265–$300*

Lantern, folding, Pennsylvania, 19th century, tin. *$125–$175*

Candle sconce, sheet iron. *$85–$110*

Lithograph, by Currier & Ives, "Fruit and Flowers," stains, some paper damage, and a tear, matted and framed, 15½″ × 19¼″. *$85–$110*

Lithograph, by Currier & Ives, "Fruits, Summer Varieties," stains and paper damage in margins, matted and framed, 16¼″ × 20″. *$85–$110*

Lithograph, by Currier & Ives, "Sunny-Side-on the Hudson," paper has creases, sides of top margins slightly trimmed, cross-corner frame, 13¼″ × 16¼″. *$125–$165*

Lithograph, hand-colored by Currier & Ives, "The Heroine of Monmouth" (Molly Pitcher), margins slightly trimmed, 11¾″ × 13½″, framed, 13½″ × 15½″. *$225–$285*

Courtesy of Pumpkin Vine Line Antiques, Buddy and Atha Wallin, Fairfield, Ohio; photo by Donald Vogt.

Oil lamps, group, all made in the late 1800s:

- (Left rear) *cobalt finger lamp.* *$225–$250*
- (Center rear) *cobalt,* Lincoln drape. *$450–$500*
- (Right rear) *cobalt,* made for Rockefellers. *$600–$700*
- (Left front) *clear,* fish scale. *$175–$200*
- (Right front) *amber,* paneled finger. *$225–$250*

Oil lamps, group of heart lamps made in Findley, Ohio (many different kinds made), some in clear glass, some in green, ca. 1890–1910, tallest is 18½″ to chimney, smallest is 9″ to top, clear. *$275–$325*

Green examples. *$425–$450*

Pair of English silver candlesticks, Adam style with Sheffield marks, 12″ high. *$1,210–$1,250*

Pair of sterling silver candlesticks, marked "John Wanamaker," weighted, 10″ high. *$468–$500*

Pennsylvania chest-on-chest, walnut, with bonnet top and molded and carved scrolls, 3 Flame finials, upper section with 3 scroll drawers over 4 large drawers, 4 drawers in base, fluted and chamfered corners, 90″ high, 42″ wide, 23½″ deep, no feet, molding replaced where the top joins the bottom, brasses replaced, finish dates from the Centennial era, 1740–1750. *$27,500–$29,000*

Rocking bench, pine and maple, 36″ long, refinished. *$195–$300*

Rug, handmade, by Shoemaker, floral central medallion with floral border, 7′11″ × 9′11″. *$500–$1,000*

Rug, hooked, with concentric squares, needs minor repair, 3′7″ × 3′7″. *$50–$100*

Rug, hooked, with floral decoration, 3′ × 4′11″. *$33–$60*

Rug, hooked, depicting house, mountain, and fishing boat, 4′4″ × 2′4″. *$110–$150*

Rug, hooked, depicting deer by stream in mountainous landscape, 4′4″ × 2′8″, by Pearl McGowen, West Boylston, MA. *$200–$300*

Rugs, 2, hooked, both with floral decoration on gray ground; one 2′7″ × 4′2″, one 5′6″ × 2′3″. *$200–$300*

Courtesy of Grandad's Attic; photo by Donald Vogt.

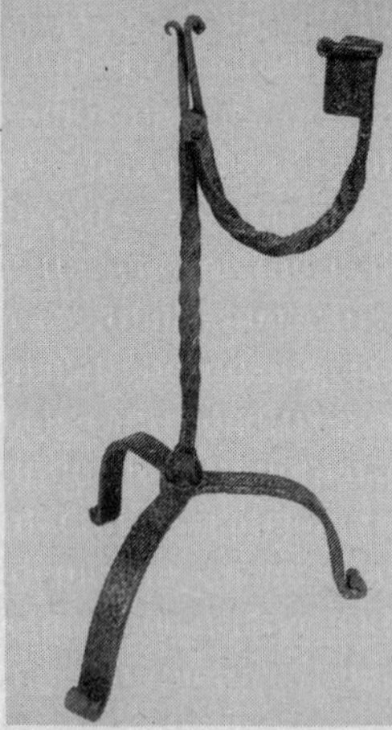

Rush candleholder, turned iron, ca. early 19th century. *$1,200–$2,500*

Rush light, wrought iron, on adjustable ratchet with tripod base, made from old parts, 21″ high. *$95–$120*

Courtesy of Grandad's Attic; photo by Donald Vogt.

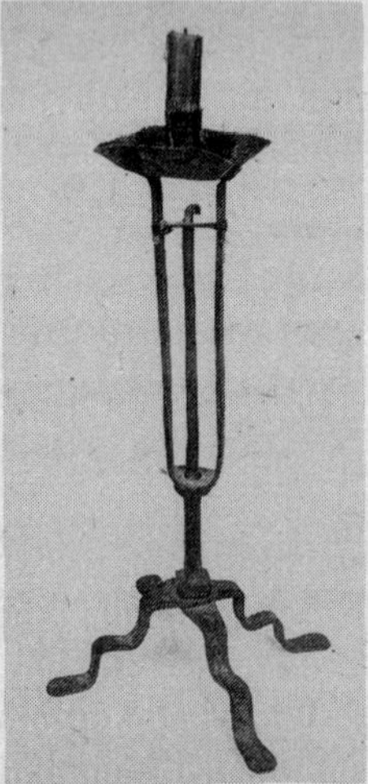

Rush lighting, early 19th century, 11½″. *$375–$500*

Courtesy of Country Cottage Antiques; photo by Donald Vogt.

Serving tray, early (ca. 1860s), from northern Ohio tavern, one board, poplar, rest on back, 22″ × 31″ at widest point. *$165–$200*

Side chair, pillowback, stenciled decoration and rush seat. *$75–$100*

Side chair, 7-spindle bowback Windsor, refinished. *$125–$175*

Side shelf, walnut, whale, 32″ high, 24″ long. *$660–$800*

Slant-lid desk, tiger maple, fitted pine interior, original brasses and bracket base, 43″ high, 39½″ wide, 20″ deep. *$10,450–$11,000*

Courtesy of Grandad's Attic; photo by Donald Vogt.

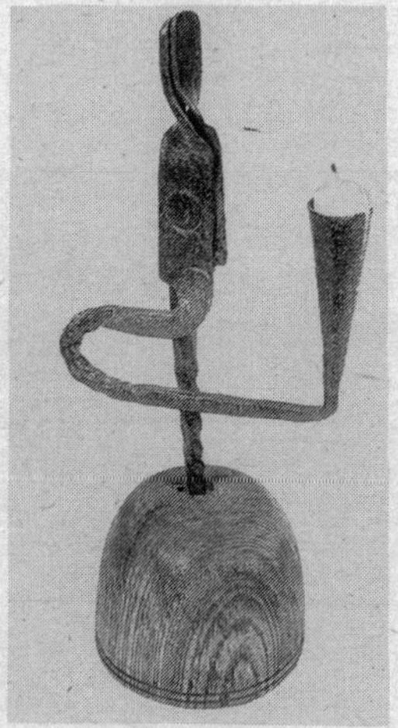

Sliding candleholder, iron, early 19th century, 16½″. *$600–$800*

Courtesy of Country Cottage Antiques; photo by Donald Vogt.

Stool made into candle mold, 28 tubes, 18″ × 8½″ × 10″. *$550–$600*

Storage box and hanging box, matching, pine, ca. mid-1800s. *$150–$195*

Hanging. *$195–$225*

Student's lamp, nickel-plated, cased green glass shade, 21½″ high. ca. 19th century. *$200–$250*

Student's table lamp, brass, cased green shades, electrified, one shade cracked, ca. 19th century. *$495–$525*

Table, demilune, old brown paint, originally part of a larger table, 27″ high, 46″ wide, 23″ deep. *$165–$200*

Courtesy of W. R. Branthoover; photo by William Branthoover.

Table, dropleaf, cherry, Sheraton, early 1800s, made in Vermont. *$500–$600*

Courtesy of W. R. Branthoover; photo by William Branthoover.

Table, Eastlake style with marble top, belonged to a Dr. Judd of Enosburg, VT, whose grandfather ran for public office on the Prohibitionist ticket in Ohio. *$500–$600*

Tole document box, dome top, original floral decoration on dark ground, 9½″ × 5½″ × 6¾″. *$130–$150*

Trunk, dome top, pine, old brown finish, 23″ high, 34″ long, 20″ deep. *$135–$200*

Courtesy of Alice Kempton, Kempton's Country Classics; photo by Donald Vogt.

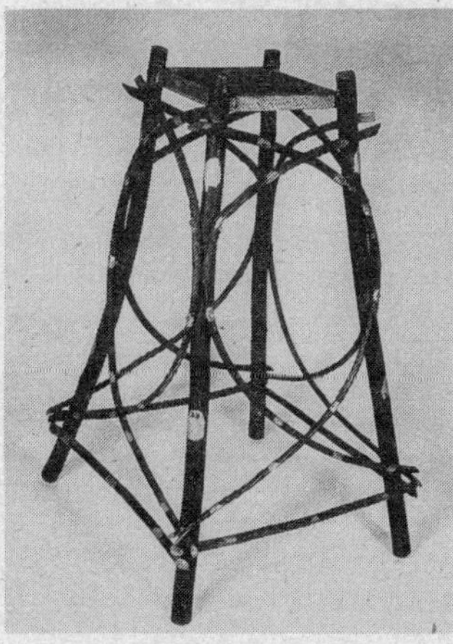

Twig stand, 22″ high, made in Michigan, ca. 1920s. *$15–$25*

Windsor chair, New England, early. *$375–$400*

Slant-top schoolmaster's desk. *$550–$700*

Double Wedding Ring quilt, signed and dated 1932; made and presented to Gustus A. Thomas by Mother. *$350–$400*

Writing-arm Windsor, pine. *$110–$250*

Writing box, rosewood, lift-top, fitted, ivory inlaid panel in lid, 12″ × 8″ × 4″. *$88–$150*

THE
COUNTRY
BARN

THIS SECTION indicates the many different types of barns by dividing them into different categories: farming, the carriage trade, blacksmithing, and others.

The country barn is so well loved in American culture that the items found there are just as collectible as the ones found in country homes. The barn was where country children hid from their parents when they knew they had done something wrong. It was the place they went with their friends when they wanted to have a secret discussion or with their sweethearts for that first kiss.

Barn dances were a way of getting a group of country friends together to socialize. Sometimes there would be bits of hay in the punch or in your partner's hair, but no one ever seemed to mind. For one night, the large, high-roofed building that usually stored grain or housed livestock was the Taj Mahal, country girls were Cinderellas and country boys became Prince Charmings.

When a neighbor was ready to build a barn, folks came from miles around for a barn-raising. The women would spend the day before preparing casseroles, salads, breads, and desserts. They would bring the latest quilt they were working on and spread the pieces out under a tree somewhere on the property, to work and gossip while the men put together the rafters that made up the barn roof.

The men would all bring their own tools, each volunteering his services and whatever talents he might have to help his neighbor, knowing that someday his neighbors would do the same for him. And they all prayed that they wouldn't be called by a ringing brass bell some cold winter's night because the barn had caught fire—a sure disaster for a country family.

Barns were square, rectangular, or round. They had no windows or many windows, one story or two or three. Though we believe most barns should be red, there were many that were yellow or white, blue or green. Some had hand-painted advertisements for a popular tobacco painted on their sides like billboards. Some signs declared that the farmer belonged to an agricultural association or grew a certain type of corn.

The barns located in town often housed the "village smithy" and his wares. Each village needed a blacksmith, someone to shoe the horses and to produce the iron objects so necessary in a country home. The smithy was usually situated in town because it was the most central location. The stagecoach stopped in town, and there was always something to work on or repair when it came through after traveling hundreds of miles over bumpy dirt roads.

Today the barns I have seen throughout the country areas we've visited are largely in disrepair. The current lack of interest in whether the nation's farmers are going to continue to exist has begun to show in our country's barns. No longer are they the proud, spacious buildings we knew a century ago. Most are falling down, neglected and sad. I've often thought I should take my camera across country and photograph as many barns as possible before they all disappear. They are yet another part of our legacy that is falling to modernism, and I'm not quite sure it is something which we should let happen.

The Country Farm

In this age of nuclear power, global warming, and a general fear that the family farm will soon be an icon of the past, many of us cling to traditional country values in the hope that the land may somehow save us. We, as Americans, have always expected the land to survive, no matter what we do to it. Maybe that is a human failing, not indigenous to this country. But even fifty years ago, predictions were being made by farm journals and by associations like the American Geographical Society that farms were dying.

H. C. Woodworth in his 1933 essay, "The Yankee Community in Rural New England," saw that farming was on the wane and that New England's agricultural community was succumbing to industrialization. Yet he points out that Yankee farmers were still looking to the future, using pioneer tactics to ensure that their apple orchards or dairy farms would not go under. At that point in our history, modernization of old equipment and new ideas about how to run the farm were the optimistic way to go.

Woodworth pointed to several New England towns that had been farming communities in the early 1800s and that, by the time he wrote his essay in 1933, were "industrially minded." The population in these communities declined as a result. In my hometown, Montgomery Center, a change in the town's industry brought a rapid and drastic population decline in the early 1900s. Almost two thousand people lived here then, and we are less than one thousand strong now. The town has changed from a dairy community to an industrial community, back to a dairy community, and, in the last thirty years, to a resort town. There are only a handful of large farms left, but those of us who live here full-time are ecologically aware and constantly fighting the battle necessary to keep this town and its land as beautiful as we possibly can.

Perhaps that is the one thing today's country dwellers have in common with country folk of the past—we enjoy the land and depend on it so greatly that we feel the necessity to protect it.

The 1896 yearbook for the Department of Agriculture was a forum for experts to produce new information relevant to the farmers of the United States. In that edition, Frederick H. Newell, the Chief Hydrographer of the U.S. Geological Survey, wrote about irrigating the Great Plains. Though I'm sure most Native Americans did not have access to this report, they probably would have snickered at the thought of bringing water into the vast Great Plains area. However, Newell's information was welcomed (though doubted) by those settlers who were trying to farm the dry, windy stretches of Montana, North Dakota, South Dakota, Nebraska, Kansas, Colorado, New Mexico, Oklahoma, and Texas—one eighth to one sixth of the United States.

The natives who had settled the Great Plains long before the white men were even thought of did not roam the region simply because they liked to travel. They moved from place to place because of the difficulty of eking out a living on the Plains. There were periodic famines in this region, which wiped out thousands of Amerinds and settlers during our history.

Newell wanted to see whether we could control the land instead of the land controlling us. His suggestions were useful in that people learned how to irrigate otherwise arid areas; however, it was extremely difficult for farmers/settlers to singlehandedly control hundreds of acres of land, to bring water to that acreage, and to keep a constant survey on the land from the family's sod house. Harsh winters, sweltering summers, and the lack of nearby neighbors to help share the burden defeated many of those early settlers. It didn't matter that the soil was fertile because the right equipment to farm such huge tracts of land was not available to settlers at that time.

Nowadays our midwestern farmers have large combines, tractors, and modern technology on their side to help them tame the land. We country people make a lot of mistakes, but the most important lesson that has been handed down from our ancestors is to keep on trying!

History

The first American farmer had to learn agriculture from scratch and did not evolve into a true agrarian until the mid-1700s. In those early years, farming manuals treated farming as a religion or philosophy, rather than as an industry. For many hundreds of years, one was considered a good American simply by virtue of being a good farmer.

Nature was the agrarian's friend, and the farmer used the signs nature showed him wisely. He planted and harvested his crops by the seasons of the moon, believing, for example, that the soundness of wood was affected when cut in different phases of the moon. Sun movements and tides were accurate timepieces as well.

All areas of the United States had farms at one time. Some had white barns and old rail fences. Others had dirt roads lined with old elm trees that led visitors to a two-story red house. In Pennsylvania, a farm could consist of a fieldstone house with matching barn and all kinds of fowl running about in the barnyard. A Minnesota farm could be seen for miles and miles, surrounded by nothing but pastureland and a few lone hay bales. In the prairie, a sod house could represent a farm, while a white-pillared mansion was the farmhouse in ante-bellum Georgia. Cows might be in the pasture, a windmill could spin merrily beside a low, hay-filled barn, and, more often than not, a well in the front yard would be a familiar sight.

Farm folk picked daisies in the summer, faced the fierce gobble of a turkey about to be struck down for Thanksgiving dinner, and feared the possibility of being unable to get out to milk the cows after a fierce winter storm. They also enjoyed the pleasures of a newly born colt struggling to stand on spindly legs, the fragrance of apple blossoms or a summer's hayride, the gossip of a quilting bee, and the tranquility of sitting next to Pa while he taught them the best way to snag the biggest trout in the river.

Country people shared the spirit of raising a barn, digging a well, and clearing the land of tree stumps. They worked hard in the fields, planting and harvesting, taking care of whatever animals were housed in their barn, and battling natural enemies like poor weather, varmints, and insects. It was not an easy life, but the rewards, when they came, could make a farmer's heart feel "like it's a'burstin' with joy." That, in a nutshell, was the reason so many Americans turned to the land to nurture it and, in turn, be nurtured *by* it.

The farmer's job is an unending one, beginning long before the sun rises and often continuing long after it sets, with no days off, no holidays, no sunny vacations in the tropics.

Before machinery was invented to make the job easier, the farmer often took care of hundreds of acres with little help besides what was provided by his wife and children. There was hay to be mown several times during the summer months, cows to be milked on a daily basis, pigs to be slopped, chickens to be fed and their eggs gathered, crops to be planted and harvested, wood to be chopped, buildings to be built or kept in repair, and little time for anything else besides sleeping and eating.

A Farmer's Year

In the early years of our nation, the lives of most folk revolved around the seasons of the year. They did not have freezers that enabled them to have strawberries in January or indoor ice skating rinks that afforded them the pleasure of gliding across the ice in July.

Spring was the time to plan the garden, to clear the soil of rocks, to till and plow the land, in order to ready it for the seeds that would sprout into vegetables and supply the farm family with its food for the winter. Fences were mended, wood was stacked for the following winter season, and maple sugar was made from the sap that ran after a cold April night.

The long days of summer were spent haying the fields, cultivating the crops, and doing other outside work. All of the farmer's tools were made so that he could carry them on his back. His crops were planted and harvested by the moon, and studying agriculture manuals was not normally done because most country people could not read, nor could they afford the luxury of buying books.

In the fall, animals and fish were trapped or hunted, the meat smoked or salted for the winter season. Crops were harvested and basements filled with root crops and canned vegetables. Apple cider was brewed, and the community would get together for a dance or harvest festival before the colder weather wet in. It was time to make lye soap, to pour candles, harvest cranberries.

Winter was the season of bells. Sleigh bells were hung around a horse's chest, wagons were given runners so that they could more easily glide over the winter roads, and chores were done by hearthlight. The fireplace was indeed the heart of the home.

Snow was rolled instead of plowed then so that the sledding season would last as long as possible and traveling would be easier. Rollers often were dragged, planed logs pulled by horse to flatten and harden the surface of the snow. Work continued in the farm shop where the tools were made throughout the cold month of January. Trees were felled and fence posts cut throughout February, and soup pots, kept boiling all winter long, were finally scoured by the middle of March.

Farm/Ranch Homes

Country houses were, for the most part, simple buildings that met the needs of their inhabitants. Few were built by architects, but their quiet serenity appeals to almost everyone. Homes were built by local builders, who may have lacked the knowledge of today's builders but made up for it by using sound building design with skilled craftsmanship.

Early builders did not use a blueprint or the services of an engineer, plumber, or electrician. The owner was often designer and carpenter, bricklayer and painter. These were people who combined know-how with ingenuity and resourcefulness with originality, and they didn't have to follow anyone's rules but their own.

If they had books on the subject available, the owner and

builder might study them. If not, a few sketches on a piece of lumber would be used to design a palladian window, a gambrel roof, or a wrap-around porch.

Common to most early New England homes was a large fireplace where the women of the family made all of the meals, baked the bread, made candles, and heated the house. Iron trammels and large hooks held the cast-iron kettle that boiled as long as a fire was burning. Cast-iron Dutch ovens were used to cook the family's turkey dinner or to bake bread. Skillets and frying pans sat on trivets next to the andirons, which held the wood as it was being burned.

The simplicity of early houses is not due to the builder's lack of carpentry knowledge—quite a number of the interiors of old houses are attractively embellished—but to religious restrictions on adornment or fanciful decorations. The nineteenth century brought greater wealth into simple farming communities as well as a decreasing severity in religious doctrine—one of the reasons Victorian homes were so elaborately decorated.

Some Items Used on the Country Farm

Adz

Adzes were used for dressing wood, and there are many different types. Some were used on railroads, some on ships, and some on farms.

Beams were smoothed and floors were evened with the general-purpose or carpenter's adz. The tool had a large, flat pounding surface, sometimes square, and it came in two sizes: long- or short-handled. Short adzes, or "cooper's adzes," were used by the builders of kegs and barrels.

Auger

Augers were used by country people for a number of different purposes, which ranged from boring holes in maple trees to general construction uses.

The auger most commonly used had a thread diameter of over an inch. The iron shaft was attached to a wooden crosspiece.

Ax

It has been said by more than one historian that the ax may have been the single most important tool in American history. The ax was used to clear land for the pioneer, to fell trees for wood to build homes, and to keep those homes warm. In other words, the ax essentially made it possible for the early frontier families to survive in the American wilderness.

When the first settlers began clearing land in New England, some of the trees had diameters of seven feet and were one hundred to two hundred feet high. The stretch of maple, hemlock, ash, oak, and elm throughout New England was said to equal the distance from the Plymouth Rock to the Mississippi River. It was the forest primeval, and there were few open meadows or uninterrupted stretches of grassy area anywhere.

Because grass was needed if the area was to support animals that would produce such staples as milk, the great forest was substantially trimmed by those early pioneers. What they considered abundant, we now consider endangered.

Felling axes, usually lightweight and razor sharp, were made in three distinct shapes. The American version was a short, squared type, the German type had an exaggerated V-shape, and the English ax was a modified combination of the two. Handles were made of white oak or hickory and began to be curved after the Civil War.

The felling ax is the standard firewood ax, used to clear forests and to cut trees and firewood. Early seventeenth-century felling ax blades were curved and had an eye to hold the haft or handle. They were designed in much the same manner as European utility tools and battle axes. The American felling ax finally came into its own about 1800. The nearly square head was 6 to 8 inches long. The blade edge was 4 to 5 inches, and its straight handle was approximately 3 feet long. The head was made of either cast or wrought iron, and steel was used for the cutting edge.

The broad ax, used for shaping a fallen tree into a beam or a log suitable for home building, resembled the felling ax in most ways except that its head was 8 to 10 inches, extending to a blade edge that averaged 12 inches or more; its head weighed twice as much as that of the felling ax. The broad ax also had a distinctive shape: one side was almost flat and the other was beveled. Its handle was shorter so that the user could straddle a log and work both sides.

Other types of axes include the goosewing, hewing, mortising, and turf axes.

When looking for an ax, remember a "signed" one—one marked with the maker's name and/or location—is usually more valuable than one that is not signed. You will usually find the mark burned into the handle.

Beetle and Maul

The beetle and maul were used by a farmer when splitting rails. The beetle was a gigantic wooden mallet, and the maul resembled a rather large, bulbous baseball bat. Both were used to smack wedges into logs so that the logs could be split. Split rails were most often used in building fences to contain cattle, pigs, sheep, and other livestock within the farmer's land boundaries.

Commander

The commander was a log with a long handle bored into it that was used to pound beams into place when a farmer was building a house or barn or putting together a heavy-duty fence.

Corn-Related Collectibles

There were few farms that did not grow corn for feed or fodder or as a cash crop; thus, the number of items in this category is substantial.

The corn cutter (or knife or slasher) was used in cutting corn stalks. It had a long, slightly curved steel cutting edge; the reverse side was less curved and less sharp.

Seeders, a popular country collectible, came in all sizes and types. The earliest were sticks used to poke holes in the ground into which the seeds were dropped. Later, factory seeders were made. Straight, waist-tall cylinders, these seeders were largely made of wood and had twin handles. There was a V-shaped metal hole maker on the bottom of the cylinder, and by pushing the handles together, the hole was opened and corn kernels were pushed into the soil. Another type of seeder was made to be rolled, and still others were horse-drawn.

Cultivators, hoes, choppers, and shellers are also desirable corn-related collectibles. However, pronged iron racks, used for hanging the corn to dry, are the items most often found in a country home.

Iron or tin cornbread pans, often designed in the shape of miniature corn ears, and corn poppers made of sheet metal or wire baskets were factory-made items that may still be used by today's family.

Dairy Collectibles

Dairy products (milk, cream, butter, and cheese) did not supply the farmers in New England states with a source of income until after the advent of the railroad in 1848. After that time, cities like St. Albans, Vermont, were responsible for supplying a large portion of farm-made butter to the rest of the country. Creameries took over the butter production after 1880, and about ten years later, the New England makers were in competition with western butter producers.

After the turn of the century, other dairy products also "hit the road," and farmers began to market milk, cream, and butter in larger quantities to those "city folks" unable to supply themselves with the commodities.

Egg Collectibles
(See also "The Kitchen" in The Country Home section)

Egg collectibles have graced my kitchen walls for the past five years or so, and the image of the chicken/rooster has certainly become a popular one among those of us who consider ourselves collectors of farm-related items.

The cardboard carriers used to market eggs in half dozens, dozens, or larger amounts, hang on walls, familiar symbols of the past and certainly more attractive than the styrofoam packaging most often used by today's distributors.

Egg scales, which were used to weigh the egg to determine its grade, class, and ultimate value, are interesting in that they are intrinsic to eggs and were not used to weigh any other kind of farm produce. Their balance beam is usually one-sided, and one can tell immediately that you have an egg scale because the weighing basket is large enough to hold only one egg. Some of the more complicated scales had flip-up leaves that revealed the weight in ounce fractions.

Candlers were used by farmers to determine whether an egg was fertile. The candler was usually a tin box with a hole in it and a candle inside. The egg was held against the light. Deluxe versions had boxes made of painted or japanned metal and a window covered by "icing glass" (split mica).

Baskets used to collect eggs are discussed in "The Country Market" section.

Haying Equipment

All farming families shared the task of haying the fields two or three times (depending on the weather) every summer, laboring in the hot sun and getting the pesky dry grass up their noses, in their hair, and under their clothes.

If the farm was to sustain its livestock, haying the fields was as necessary as providing the animals with water. The hay served as fodder during long, cold winters, sometimes even being used to insulate a New England or midwestern farmhouse against chilly January winds.

The tools used in the process of gathering hay hang, unused, on the walls of many of today's farmhouses as decoration or as an implement from which other items may hang.

Hay carriers, used to lift the hay into a barn, were 16-inch-long cast-iron devices attached to metal hay tracks running below the barn roof's peak. The carrier, or trolley, was powered by a single or double pulley rope, basically carrying the hay into the barn's loft, where it was stored for later use. Though the early trolleys are interesting decorative accents for other, smaller farm collectibles, they are not in high demand among those who favor country antiques.

On the other hand, hay rakes or forks are highly popular for both their decorative use and their aesthetic value.

Forks, most often made of curved hickory or pine, were used to turn the hay over, to assist in the drying process. They are usually 6–8 feet long and may have curved or straight prongs. They were often quite primitive, and one can discern immediately whether or not the tool was handmade by the local farmer.

Rakes were also made of wood and resemble garden rakes, except that the crosspiece was longer and they had a number of wooden teeth. Most of the hay rakes one finds at an auction are missing one or more of these teeth, but that is part of their charm.

The prongs on a hay rake have been used for hanging old bonnets, aprons, or other memorabilia from the rake in an attractive array. I've also seen stores use these implements to effectively hang stock items such as candles.

The hay hook, made of wrought iron, had a large hook on one end, which was used to grab the bale and pull it onto the wagon or tractor, and an open circle on the other end, which the worker held. Simple tools, these hooks had to be strong enough to hook and pull a bale of 25–50 pounds and to last long enough to go through several baling seasons. Naturally, the wrought-iron versions were the strongest; however, baling hooks were also made of wood or other types of metal.

Scythes were used to cut tall grass. They were long, curved-handle implements ending in long, curved blades. Often a scythe would have a short, straight handle off the long one, which the worker could hold to get the tool into a proper swing.

There were three different types of scythes: the long-handled grass cutter just mentioned; the weed scythe with a shorter, stronger blade, which was used for heavier cutting; and a brush scythe, whose blade was heaviest, averaged about 20 inches in length, and was used to cut undergrowth and small trees.

Sickles were like scythes except smaller; they were used for clearing weeds around fence posts and the edges of buildings.

Mallet

There were two different kinds of mallets used by early American farmers. The carpenter's mallet had a small, square head and a long handle, while the wheelwright's mallet's head was curved and its handle short.

Maple Sugaring

"When the wind's in the west, the sap flows best."

—Old Vermont farmer's saying*

Maple sugaring was the discovery of the American Indians, and the art was passed down by them to the white settlers.

Sugar season begins when the sap starts running in maple trees, and that occurs when the heat of the day is exactly balanced by the evening's frost. However, the farmer gets ready for sugaring long before the temperature is properly balanced. A sugar bush (or stand of maple trees) is often tapped months ahead. The trees, which are approximately a foot in diameter, are bored in a slightly upward fashion with an auger, approximately 2 inches into the trunk of the tree. Sap buckets are then hung on a spout off the side of the tree. The buckets hang there until the weather is right for the sap to run.

As the buckets filled with the clear sap from the maple, they were gathered by the sugaring crew and emptied into a holding tank. Gathering can be accomplished by hand, with the crew carrying the buckets off yokes balanced on their shoulders, or the sap might be dumped into a much larger bucket attached to a sled and dragged through the woods by draft horses or oxen. In Vermont, some sugarers are still gathering sap in this fashion (see "The Country Horse" section).

*Carawan, Greg and Candie: *Voices from the Mountains.* Alfred A. Knopf, New York, 1975.

Forty gallons of sap were needed to make one gallon of syrup, but the effort was worth it. Few foods made a child (or adult) feel as special as a stack of pancakes smothered in fresh, golden maple syrup on a cold, winter's morning.

Once the sap is emptied into the boiling pan, the long process of keeping the liquid boiling begins. The fire must be kept roaring until the sap is reduced about twelve times; then it is allowed to settle.

The first maple sugar buckets were made of wood and had one or two layers of strapping encircling them. No nails were used. Once the farmer had enough buckets made, he used them year after year.

Covered sugar buckets were used to keep the maple sugar. Because it would harden when stored in containers, a tool for loosing the sugar (called a sugar-devil) was invented. Sugar devils resembled today's corkscrews, and they are an item that many antiquarians have trouble identifying.

Vermont has been responsible for more than one third of the country's maple products since the turn of the century. Hundreds of thousands of trees have been tapped to produce syrup and sugar, giving the Vermont farmer an opportunity to supplement the income he or she made from producing items that require a warmer growing season.

Sugaring occurs at a slow time in the farmer's year. Being able to take advantage of unemployed workers and horses that need the winter exercise of pulling maple sleds through the woods (and to make a profit doing so) is a farmer's dream.

A study conducted in the 1930s revealed that there were sugar bushes on half of the farms in the state of Vermont and that the bulk of production was in the northern part of the state along the line of the Green Mountains.

During the early years of sugaring (1700s–1900) the bulk of the maple sugar products were sold at retail, but by the mid-1900s, the majority of the farmers in Vermont were selling more than half of their crop to centralized processors.

Plane

No, they did not have airplanes in those days. The planes we are speaking of were used to wear down or put grooves in wood.

Eighteenth-century craftspeople were still making their own planes, and you can often find examples with the maker's name branded into its base. Most planes today's collector finds that were made in that century were wooden.

A woodworker might own a dozen or more different sizes and shapes of planes for various uses, such as jack planes, tongue-and-groove planes, and molding planes.

Plow

The plow has gone through an evolution of about 2,500 different designs since its inception. The earliest ones were made of a strong hard wood, like oak, with a piece of flint strapped to the base. Pennsylvania plows were made of hickory, with the plow blade a forged piece of iron. Around 1750, the mold-board plow was used. This plow was more streamlined than the earlier two but used a wooden board as a plow blade. By the turn of the eighteenth century, metal was used to cover the board, and by midcentury, the all-metal blade was introduced.

Saw

Like axes and hammers, saws were a necessary tool on yesterday's farm. One of the oldest ones is the two-man crosscut, which has a long, flat blade and cutting teeth on the underside. An upright handle was attached at each end.

Buck saws, or frame saws, were mounted between two upright handles, which were braced by horizontal wires that ran across the top from handle to handle. Country collectors often hang examples of buck saws on a brick or barnboard wall.

The shape of a saw's teeth was the most important part of the saw because that determined its cutting power. For example, the pig-tooth saw had an evenly spaced row of V-shaped teeth, and each tooth was filed on both edges so that the saw could cut in both directions.

Shovel

There were many different types of shovels made and used on yesterday's farms. Each had a different function, defined by its shape. For example, grain scoops were generally made of wood, with a wide and deep blade, because they were used to hold and shovel large quantities, while coal shovels had the same shape but were more strongly made to withstand wear and tear.

Digging was done with the all-purpose farm shovel, the one with the pointed tip and heart-shaped blade. A spade had a long, narrow blade and might be used strictly in the garden, to dig holes.

Weather Vane

Weather vanes helped the farmer or country home owner to forecast the weather in those days prior to meteorologists and daily weather reports. By checking the stance of the vane, a country family could decide the best time for planting or harvesting their crops, whether the barn and animal odors were going to be sent directly into the house, or whether a storm was brewing.

Families who lived on or near the ocean or other body of water relied on their weather vane to tell them whether or not it was a good day for fishing. Wives of men who made their living by the ocean often checked the vane in the morning to see whether their husbands would be able to make it home that day. The weather played an incredibly important part in their lives and was also the cause of some major disasters.

The most primitive and folk-arty vanes were those that were whittled by some member of the family. These vanes are often the most unusual because the makers could choose whatever subject they wanted. Thanks to the inventiveness and ingenuity of our forebears, there is a diversified selection of weather vanes available to today's collector.

Unfortunately, weather vanes have become such a popular country collectible that we are always reading of thefts of the vanes right off the roof of the family farm. It is obvious that the reason for this spate of burglaries is that several weather vanes brought record-setting prices during the past ten years, and when a collectible does that, it is newsworthy. Publishing such records seems to whet the appetite of those who might not normally look at such an item twice. If it's worth five figures or more, it certainly is worth stealing, they figure.

By 1850 metal vanes were more common than wooden ones, for several reasons, first and foremost being that wooden vanes were subject to deterioration much more quickly than their metal counterparts. Iron and copper were used in the nineteenth century, iron having been used as early as the eighteenth century. Vanes have also been made of tin, lead, and brass, but those were not as widely used as the iron and copper ones.

The most common shapes weather vanes might take are as weathercocks, roosters, hens, horses, or other farm animals. On the ocean, a vane might take the shape of a fish or ship, a dolphin or mermaid. Patriotic symbols, such as the eagle, were also popular.

Whirligig

Whirligigs had much the same function as weather vanes, except whirligigs were usually made of wood, hand-painted by the maker, and had moving parts that turned (or whirled) when the wind blew.

Though it is not really known when whirligigs came into fashion, one of the first references to them was made in Irving's *The Legend of Sleepy Hollow* in 1819.

Whirligigs were made in many different forms. I have one that depicts a bearded farmer sawing a log. When the wind blows, the directionals whirl, and the farmer bends back and forth, looking as though he is actually sawing. Others depict Uncle Sam with whirling arms, a black woman doing her wash in a tub, a man cranking his Model A Ford, and even a flying angel Gabriel.

The wind-related items were fun to watch and are often collected by today's folk art lovers.

Windmill Weights

Windmill weights were made to help a windmill pump water. The weight helped slow the windmill down and kept the blades at a steady pace so that the plunger rod would not be damaged from running wild.

The Country Horse

History

FORTUNATELY, the Spanish explorer Hernando Cortez was foresighted enough to transport the horse to the New World in 1519; otherwise, settling this country would not have been an easy task. It has been discovered, however, that the earliest horse, the Eohippus, also existed in the Mississippi Valley area of the United States many thousands of years ago. The animal disappeared from that region for unknown reasons, but it had already given rise to a line of horses that produced several different kinds and breeds.

Native Americans relied on the horse for traveling, hunting, and war, often decorating their ponies with their "battle scores." The horse most often used by the Plains tribes was the Appaloosa, said to have descended in the Nez Percé territory from wild mustangs, descendants of those horses brought by explorers to the New World.

Farmers who settled in that area discovered that the Appaloosa was also good for farm work because it is a sturdy horse. Soon the spotted breed was pulling plows, cultivators, or logs for the agrarian family.

In northern farm states, as well as some midwestern ones, larger horses that could carry heavy work loads were used by loggers, farmers, and mountain dwellers. These horses, often Belgians or Clydesdales, were often well over 17 hands high, of all colors, and developed a very calm temperament.

Two such horses live on the farm next door to me. They have become my friends, waiting at the fence for the carrots I inevitably produce from my pocket. Charley, the older of the two, is extremely tall, a light golden brown color and a veteran of many a horse pull. His companion, Frankie, is two years old, a black, playful, stallion.

Last maple sugaring season, my neighbor used two other Belgians to help carry the maple syrup through the woods, and I was lucky enough to go up one warm April day to see their production. I felt as though I had stepped back through time. My husband, as well as half a dozen other men, were stripped to their flannel shirts and long johns, each concentrating on his ability to get the buckets of sap off the trees and to the larger bucket the horses had pulled through the woods to them.

The horses snorted and pawed the ground as if they knew the work had to be done at a certain pace and were anxious to get about it. The snap of the thawing maple trees disturbed the quiet of the forest.

It was obvious the maples they were tapping were old ones because all were fairly large, some big enough to hold four buckets at a time. When you have over a thousand trees that size, it means you have to empty a lot of buckets (some are emptied each day).

The Belgians pulled the full forty-gallon barrel through the woods, sometimes scraping the sides of large maples that had grown in their way, over the brook that runs down the mountain, sometimes visibly straining to lift the sled carrying the barrel up and over a stream of water or a large rock. The muscles on the horses' backs rippled, and a light sheen of sweat developed even though the temperature was just barely above freezing.

My German shepherd ran in and around the horses' legs as they pulled, yet it seemed not to bother them in the least. They were there to do a job, and they did it just the way they had for hundreds of years.

I have often seen these farm animals at horse and tractor pulls in the area, which are held during the heat of the summer. Four of the animals might be hooked up to pull cement blocks that weigh thousands of pounds. Some of them go to their knees when pulling that much weight; some snort and paw deep holes into the ground as they throw massive shoulders into the effort. It seems the only time these horses are active. When they are in a pasture, it's a very rare sight to see them galloping and tossing their tails the way a Morgan will. Belgians simply stand quietly, almost like statues, resting their large bodies until it is once again time to work.

Other types of horses, such as Arabians, Morgans, saddle horses, and quarter horses, were used mainly for traveling. They are faster horses, less likely to be worked hard because of their more delicate frame, though they might be hooked to a wagon or sleigh quite comfortably.

The horse also supplied the farmer, homesteader, or Amerind with bones and cartilage used to make glue, horsehide to make shoes and belts, horsehair for stuffing, and manure for cultivation.

Carriage Trade Collectibles

Some fine arts dealers throughout the United States and England have long understood the public's fascination with and love of sporting paintings and prints that feature the magnificent figure of a horse. That four-legged animal, which moves with far more grace than the most well-coordinated two-legged human being, has long served as a form of transportation and helpmate and companion to humans, often proving themselves to be made of a finer fabric than those who have owned them.

Collectors' fascination with horses goes beyond collecting fine portraits of the animals. Everything that went along with the keeping of a horse has found its way, in one shape or another, into country collections. Bright plaid lap robes, which once served to warm sleigh riders, are thrown over the back of a couch. Bells that jingled merrily as the horse took a sleigh over newly fallen snow now hang from a country door, and their jingle serves to announce visitors to the home. Buggy seats, once attached to the buggy or sleigh, are now sitting in hallways or at the foot of a sleigh bed in the master bedroom.

The Shelburne Museum in Vermont has a horseshoe-shaped barn devoted to the display of a carriage and sleigh collection, a harness maker's shop equipped as it would have been over a hundred years ago, and a blacksmith and wheelwright shop, one of the most valuable shops in a young pioneer community or in any small town. If carriage trade collectibles are your love, I would urge a visit to the Shelburne. If you can't make it all the way to Vermont, the museum publishes several brochures and books on their collection.

Auctioneers have devoted complete sales to carriages, sleighs, and equipment that have attracted dealers and collectors from all over the world. Though these sales usually include hunt prints and paintings that are, for the most part, English, there have been many American pieces of worth sold during the past couple of years. Every once in a while you hear of a carriage, horse painting, or weather vane setting a world-record price, but it is not a field where excitement reigns. However, for those who want to specialize in this type of collectible, there is a plethora of items for which to search.

Haying

Before the turn of the century, horses were used for cutting hay. It would take three or four hours for the team to cut enough for a day's curing. The farmer would utilize the team in the morning, then use a scythe in midmorning to mow the field's corners and edges. In the afternoon, the horses were used once again, this time to rake up the mown grass. The piles of grass were allowed to sit overnight, then turned over and spread to dry. By early afternoon, it was time to pitch the hay onto carts and bring it into the barns. These carts might be pulled by oxen if the farmer had some; if not, horses were used.

It should be noted that hay was so valuable as food for the farm's animals during a long winter that the farmer would attempt to mow any good meadow he could, including those of neighbors who did not need their tall grasses.

A horse-powered mowing machine was invented in 1850, and by 1870, steam-powered machines took over some of the plowing and threshing.

Cream separators, plows, horse rakes, bailers, reapers, and harvesters were first produced in mechanized forms in the late 1800s, and by the 1930s, almost all of the new machines had reached the peak of their development and the horse was out of work.

Saddles

There are two different kinds of saddles for horseback riding: Western and English. The Western style is the kind we are used to seeing cowboys sling on their horses in western movies. They are large, leather saddles that often have hand-tooled designs on their seats. There is a large horn at the forward part of the saddle where the rider might rest his reins or his hand. This type of saddle is quite heavy.

English saddles are considerably lighter, have no horn, and generally are not tooled. They are made for riding in the English style and are most often seen in fox-hunting prints.

The Western saddle has started to come into its own as a country collectible and has begun to show up as a house decoration in some of the latest decorating magazines.

Sleighs

Early farm sleighs (ca. 1700) resembled boats with runners and often had a snow canopy over the seat. The seat became more comfortable as time went on, developing into a padded, fancier version with slender runners, called a "cutter" in the 1850s.

Men were just as conceited about their sleighs as they are about their cars today. Some would paint designs on the side or make sure they used only the finest leather to pad their seats. Whoever was fastest was best.

Even doctors had their own sleighs. A friend of mine who raises Morgans has a few sleighs, which she uses in the winter (one of which always transports Santa down Main Street to the lighting of the huge Christmas tree in front of the Inn on Trout River) on a regular basis. One of the sleighs she bought a couple of years ago was made during the 1860s for a doctor and still contained his pouch in the box behind the seat.

Sleighbells

Sleighbells were originally folded pieces of sheet iron (ca. 1750), but the American sleighbell as we know it is a round, slatted bell, first made in the early 1800s. "Jingletown," Connecticut, was the area first known for its production of sleighbells, made by William Barton from approximately 1810.

The bells were attached to leather or to an embroidered piece of canvas that was long enough to be strapped around the horse's belly or hung from the reins the driver held. As the sleigh swooshed along a snow-covered road, the movement of the horses would make the bells jingle, and the frosty air would be filled with the gay sound.

Country Smiths

BECAUSE COUNTRY PEOPLE used so many items that were made of different kinds of metals, smiths were important members of their communities. Without a smith, iron pots couldn't be patched, horseshoes could not be made, plow blades could not be forged, and andirons would have to be shipped in from elsewhere.

I have broken the smiths down alphabetically because, though their jobs are basically the same, each has different tools and duties.

Brass

The brass foundry was almost as important as the coppersmith and blacksmith. The founder also learned his trade as an apprentice, as did the other smiths. It was a hard and dirty business, which did not attract workers as enthusiastically as did the silversmith trade.

Founders were responsible for casting such objects as guns, candlesticks, statues, buckles, locks, keys, bells, andirons, and printing equipment.

As in all the metal trades, most work was done in an extremely hot furnace. Patterns were made and cut, and then the brass was cast. If the pattern was made in two pieces (as in the case of a solid andiron), then both pieces needed to be reassembled and molded together. The final object was burnished with a round, polished piece of steel, giving the brass the warm glow and luster we love.

Brass pots, kettles, molds, and skimmers often were hung on a fireplace wall, making for a colorful and warm collage. The woman of the house had to make sure the pots were properly cleaned after they were cooked in, and the chore was only one of a group of time-consuming tasks that took up the better part of her day.

Copper

Copper items were made for fireplace use, as well as for other rooms of the house. A coppersmith was responsible for producing such things as pots and kettles of all sizes, sauce and drip pans, seals, and lead weights.

Early coppersmiths were trained by master craftsmen for a period of approximately seven years. During that time, the apprentice would learn the copper trade as well as regular school subjects, such as reading, writing, and arithmetic. By the time the apprenticeship was finished, the boy would be ready to go out and start his own business.

The young worker's chores might consist of cleaning the shop, polishing tools, starting the forge fire, sharpening utensils, and polishing finished products, such as pots, ladles, and skimmers. The master would train him to trace and cut patterns on sheet copper and to hammer those pieces, solder their joints, and insert rivets where the copper could not be soldered. Finally, the apprentice would be able to assemble complete objects like saucepans; then the master would teach him the finishing touches.

Coppersmiths were important members of their community, and their work served to supply families with much-needed household utensils.

Iron

A bloomery was the name for the first, simplest kind of iron furnace where wrought iron was made directly from iron ore. The name was derived from the word "bloom" given to a hammered slab of wrought iron ready to be forged into a usable object. Bloomeries were eventually replaced by blast furnaces, which were capable of more extensive production, though they were more expensive to set up and operate.

Blast furnaces originally used cold blasts of air to feed the fire, and the result was pig iron, not wrought iron. Hot air furnaces work almost the same as cold; however, hot blast furnaces have the ability to use hard coal instead of the charcoal or coke used to run cold air furnaces.

The ironworks of the South, sometimes called iron plantations, were run by slave labor up through the Civil War. These plantations produced pots, pans, stoves, ax heads, horseshoes, and most of the iron grillwork and balustrades so popular as decoration for Southern mansions during that period in our history.

Because steel was not commonly available to country blacksmiths in the 1800s and early 1900s, wrought iron was used. Unfortunately, iron rusts; therefore, we now rely on steel because of its aversion to corrosion.

In North Carolina alone, during the eighteenth and nineteenth centuries, there were several hundred blacksmiths whose talents might have included gunsmithing or silversmithing. They were responsible for manufacturing the iron items the early settlers needed to survive in rural areas, such as plowshares, hoes, axes, and tools. Forges grew from the early gunshops and smiths' sheds and, soon, ironmaking was a major industry.

It is said that the iron industry began in earnest in the southeastern part of the United States. Some of the early ironmakers came from England, Wales, and Germany, introducing the European style of work to the Southern plantation owners. Later, those plant owners would have forges of their own and would use the styles the Europeans had taught them, as well as introducing a few of their own designs.

The process of making iron was passed down through European families and continued to be spread in the same manner once Americans learned the trade. Father would teach son where to find the coal to heat the furnace, how to bring pig iron through its stages in order to make wrought iron, as well as how to judge when it was time to shut down the furnace.

The presence of a blacksmith or iron maker in a community signified its level of civilization. The rural area that could support such an operation often supported a church, school, and businesses as well.

The smith made the items already mentioned as well as others necessary in building a community (i.e., hinges for doors, rims for wagon wheels, nails, etc.). He worked to keep farm items (e.g., oxen yokes, harness fittings, hoes) in good condition for his neighbor, and those neighbors relied on his expertise to be able to log their land, hoe their corn, work their horses, or plow their field. In a very real way, the smith was an integral part of country living.

A blacksmith's tools were revered by the worker, never abused or misplaced and always kept in working condition. Many of today's country collectors prize these tools, hanging them on a brick wall or using them to fill a corner with unusual grace.

An anvil was a necessary commodity, as was a forge, slack tub, sledge, hammers of all shapes and sizes, chisels, cleavers, tongs, punches, files, drills, soldering irons, hacksaws, tire wheels, and grindstones. Though we are familiar with most of these tools, there are a few that we may not have used or seen before.

When the blacksmith was working on a wagon wheel, a tire wheel, or traveler, was used to measure its metal rim. A circular instrument mounted on a handle, the tire wheel measures by counting the revolutions it makes in running along the circumference of a wheel. Mandrils—large, cone-shaped forms—were used to stretch circular objects.

Items a Georgia blacksmith made in 1854 ranged from shovels and horseshoes to window hooks and scissors. The iron items that came from his shop could be used for farming, hunting, logging, building houses, or for tasks in the house itself. Just reading a list of his manufactured goods makes one realize why such a person would be a valued member of a country community.

Country Birds and Birdhouses

BIRDHOUSES have been brought into the country home by collectors who want to enjoy the quaint houses built by country folk for the numerous birds that flocked around the farm. In fact, I have a few that adorn my parlor wall (they don't hang well; you're better off to hook them with an invisible wire or string to the ceiling, as they were hung on the tree).

Built out of pieces of scrap wood, tin, and bits of shingles, birdhouses were placed in the trees closest to the home, probably because its residents enjoyed watching the different varieties of birds that came to nest in them. Humans wanted to hear the birds sing and to watch their antics, and they were thankful that their feathered friends also did a job for them, as some varieties consume insects in large quantities. Some country people can predict the weather just by the actions of neighboring birds, and they can also discover what type of pests live in the area by watching birds.

Occasionally, one might find a birdhouse made of pottery, but those are unusual and to be regarded as highly collectible. Should you find a pottery birdhouse, chances are it was made in the South near one of the many pottery industries that flourished there at the end of the nineteenth century and beginning of the twentieth.

Wrens, martins, sparrows, bluebirds, starlings, doves, pigeons, jays, and cardinals are just a few of the birds who are attracted by the possibility of building a nest in a birdhouse. Each type of bird needs a different kind of living space—for example, martins live in large, many-tiered houses that resemble high-rise condos.

Martin houses are generally lifted high off the ground on poles that keep these swiftly flying birds out of the way of cats and other animals that might consider a purple martin a tasty treat.

Other birdhouses, such as those used by wrens and sparrows, can be hung in a tree. These are generally small with an opening that enables the bird family to get in and out quickly.

Larger birds, like doves and pigeons, seek larger spaces, more often than not nesting in the cupola or roof of an old barn. Birdhouses for these birds are large, square habitats where many of these communal creatures will make their nest and raise their young. Because of their size, birdhouses of this type are not often collected by country devotees.

Currently considered to be folk art are the large martin houses that were constructed to resemble the human owner's homes. Such birdhouses may look like castles, farmhouses, or Victorian mansions complete with shingles, windows, doors, and cupolas. Their ornate structure makes them far more valuable than the small sparrow-type houses made of leftover materials.

The Country Garden

MOST COUNTRY HOMES had a garden of some sort, mostly to provide the family with fresh vegetables and fruits throughout the summer. Those foods would be canned or stored to take the family through at least part of the winter season.

As we have said in previous chapters, the earliest seeds were given to settlers by Indians who helped in the planting and harvesting process. Some of the best-loved American vegetables were originally Native American products.

Once this nation was firmly ensconced as a country to be reckoned with, people became more relaxed, and a family garden might also include some of the woman-of-the-house's favorite flowers. Perennials like tulips and lilies were planted, which would bring color to the farmhouse every spring without fail. Daisies and phloxes sprouted in late summer, adding their bright colors to the many spread throughout the meadows. Housewives shared delphinium and astilbe the way they had once shared recipes for oatmeal bread.

Planting was done by the quarters of the moon or by other methods written about in almanacs or journals. Though almanacs have been in use for hundreds of years, country people often rely on age-old customs when planting their gardens—like planting cucumbers on the first Sunday in June or planting corn when maple leaves are as big as a deer mouse's ear.

Soon the family was spending more and more time in the garden, the woman of the house was spending more and more time planning the garden, and the family was reaping the benefits of better vegetables, fruits, herbs, and flowers.

The Shaker community made an industry out of selling seeds and herbs from their gardens (see "Shaker Country" in Country

Places chapter). Their salespeople packed boxes of the gaily packaged seeds in their wagons and peddled them all over the area, in the big cities, and to other gardeners. Today those boxes and seed packages are highly collectible (and quite expensive).

Furniture moved out to the garden. Some companies made wrought-iron furniture that resisted rust; it was often painted white or green and blended well with foliage. It was meant to stay outside permanently, providing a handy seat for walkers in the garden or for those who just wanted to rest and enjoy the scenery.

Adirondack furniture, made of twigs and branches (see "Adirondack, Appalachian, and Ozark Country" section in Country Places chapter), was left outside, often given a coat of lacquer to protect it, to be lawn or garden furniture. Even wicker furniture was provided to set under porch roofs or in the garden for those who wished to entertain there.

Hammocks were stretched from tree to tree, hidden nooks and large trees were found by lovers who wanted privacy, and the country people had finally learned how to relax.

Prices

If an item is not indicated as being specifically Shaker, Indian, Amish, etc., then it should be considered strictly a "country" piece. For items specifically made by the country groups spoken of in the first section of this book, consult that chapter.

FARM

Barn lantern, antique tin, with unusual green glass panels, 15″ high overall, 5″ square. *$50–$100*

Barn lantern, finely made, copper top, electrified, 16″ high. *$80–$100*

Blacksmith's sign, unusual, tin, in the form of an anvil, 10½″ × 25″, ca. 19th century. *$150–$250*

Courtesy of Pumpkin Vine Line Antiques, Buddy and Atha Wallin, Fairfield, Ohio; photo by Donald Vogt.

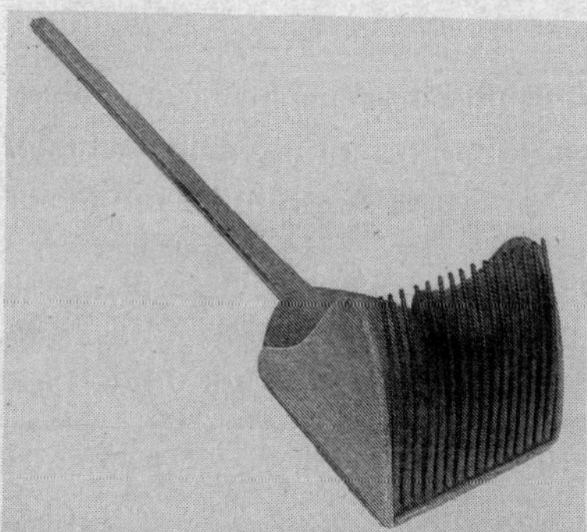

Blueberry picker, ca. 1860–1880, hand-forged nails, New England. *$600–$700*

Courtesy of Pumpkin Vine Line Antiques, Buddy and Atha Wallin, Fairfield, Ohio; photo by Donald Vogt.

Bucket bench, with drawer made of pine, 1-board top, mortised in 3 places, Port Trevington, PA, ca. 1860, 53″ wide, 19″ tall, 19″ deep. *$650–$750*

Carpenter's tool tray, pine, with dovetail construction, 21″ × 14″. *$132–$150*

Courtesy of Pumpkin Vine Line Antiques, Buddy and Atha Wallin, Fairfield, Ohio; photo by Donald Vogt.

Cranberry scoop, handmade, Wisconsin, ca. 1880. *$475–$600*

Courtesy of Alice Kempton, Kempton's Country Classics; photo by Donald Vogt.

Egg crates, Star Egg Carriers, Rochester, NY. $40–$50
Unmarked egg crates, made with wire. $50–$75

Courtesy of Louisville Antique Mall, Louisville, Kentucky; photo by Donald Vogt.

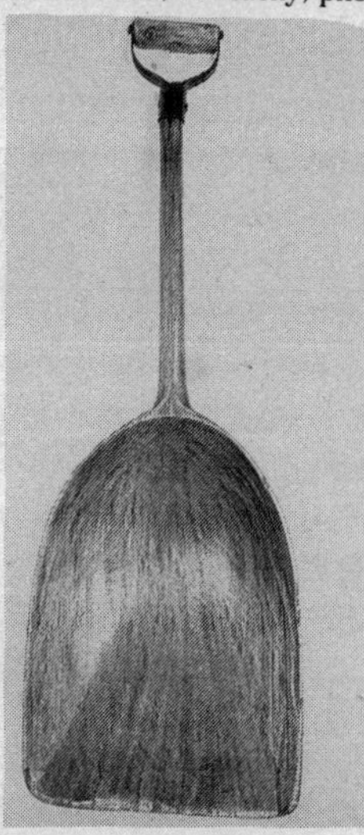

Grain shovel, carved from one piece of wood. $195–$215

Grain shovel, wooden, stamped three times on back "B.T. Bickford," 35″ long, repaired split to shovel section, American, 19th century. $75–$100

Courtesy of Louisville Antique Mall, Louisville, Kentucky; photo by Donald Vogt.

Horace Greeley grill with grease cup, mid-1800s, marked "made in Harrison, New Jersey." $145–$200

Human yoke, 31″ wide. $35–$45

Ladder, green, 3 tiers, 36″ tall. $65–$95

Courtesy of Louisville Antique Mall, Louisville, Kentucky; photo by Donald Vogt.

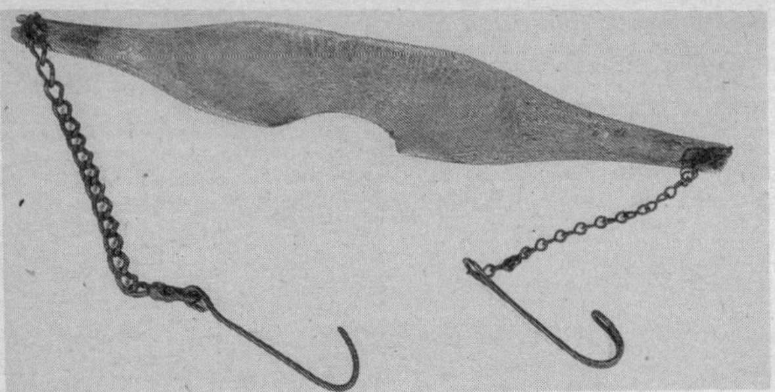

Ox yoke, single. *$85–$100*

Courtesy of Cary Station Antiques; photo by Donald Vogt.

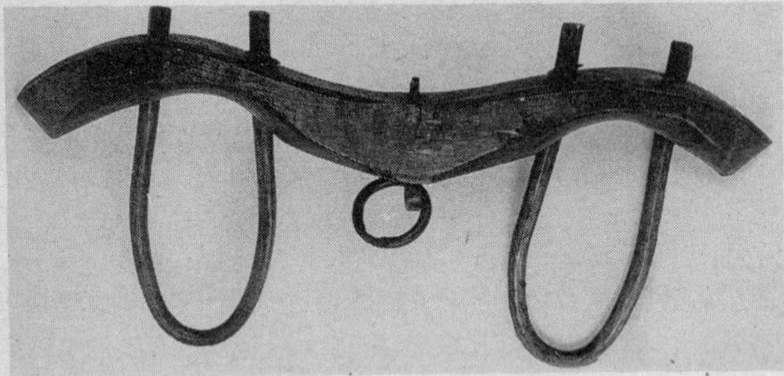

Oxen yoke with original clips, etc., patented July 14, 1848. *$300–$400*

Courtesy of W. R. Branthoover; photo by William Branthoover.

Sugar bucket, made in Montgomery, VT, ca. 1890s, maple, bale handle, 12″ diameter, 8″ tall. *$75–$80*

Sugar bucket, small, all-wooden, stave-constructed, old dark finish, lid rim damaged, 5″ high. *$125–$160*

Vermont maple sugar bucket. $35–$40

Sugar molds. $20–$28

Tin syrup jug. $18–$28

Wagon box, for tools, stenciled, old red with black, 10″ × 11½″ × 22″, Hench & Dromgold Co., York, PA. $225–$250

Courtesy of McFarland Auctioneers, Williamson, New York 14589.

Water bench, early 19th century. $1,210–$1,300

"Weather house," homemade, with animals, folky piece, ca. early 1900s. $120–$135

Courtesy of Pan and Martha Boynton, Groton, Massachusetts.

Weather vane, horse, original untouched condition, 30″ long, Vermont. $900–$1,800

Weather vane, wooden, running horse, retains some paint, modern base, 32″ long, ca. 19th century. *$248–$500*

Weather vane, sheet metal, horse, with old metal stand, from Kingston, NY, area, 16″ high. *$138–$300*

Weather vane, pine, in modified codfish form with arrow tip, iron post with original white-painted wood base, vane 50″ long, base 38″ high. *$193–$400*

Weather vane, Centaur raising bow and arrows. *$71,500–$75,000*

Weather vane, folk art, sheet metal, Indian on horse. *$2,700–$3,000*

Weather vane, Halley's Comet. *$12,500–$14,000*

Weather vane, horse, yellow, original gilt, 41″ long. *$2,250–$2,500*

Weather vane, primitive, sheet metal, steam locomotive, traces of old polychrome paint, 20¼″ long. *$875–$1,000*

Weather vane, sheet metal, lightning ball on top of 4 directionals. *$2,400–$2,700*

Weather vane, sheet metal, horse with fine proportions, walking with head held high. *$2,100–$2,500*

Weather vane, copper, running horse, with pole and finders, 26″ long, ca. 19th century. *$935–$1,200*

Whimsy, steeple-like top with other architectural odds 'n' ends to make up a rather unique table, about 40″ tall. *$1,850–$2,000*

Courtesy of Mary-Lee Muntz, Bonneyville Knoll Antiques, Middlebury, Indiana; photo by Donald Vogt.

Whirligig plane, ca. 1900, red body, white wings, new base. *$150–$165*

Wooden shovel, Wisconsin, hickory handle. *$60–$70*

FEATHERED FRIENDS

Birdhouse, martin, turn of the century, rather large, cream and light salmon paint. *$950–$1,100*

Courtesy of Jan Douglas Antiques, Sturgis, Michigan; photo by Donald Vogt.

Birdhouse, in shape of log cabin, ca. 1930s. *$30–$35*

Birdhouse, 2-story, Victorian style, two chimneys and porches on each floor, 36″ high with carved four bird-and-finial weather vane at top. *$2,500–$3,000*

Birdhouse, 20th century, roof around porch on three sides, in red, yellow, and green. *$225–$260*

Courtesy of Grandad's Attic; photo by Donald Vogt.

Birdhouses, group:

Tall one is in red paint. *$200–$300*

Blue (left) is a sexagonal house. *$100–$150*

Red (right) has green shingles. *$35–$40*

Garden

Amphorae, pair, early 20th century, footed marble. *$9,000–$11,000*

Courtesy of Louisville Antique Mall, Louisville, Kentucky; photo by Donald Vogt.

Corn planter, "Chuck-a-luck," made of wood and tin. *$18–$25*

Garden bench, Victorian, cast iron, painted green in grape design. *$165–$200*

Courtesy of Louisville Antique Mall, Louisville, Kentucky; photo by Donald Vogt.

Plow plane, 14″ long, handled, unmarked. *$60–$75*

HORSE

Courtesy of Louisville Antique Mall, Louisville, Kentucky; photo by Donald Vogt.

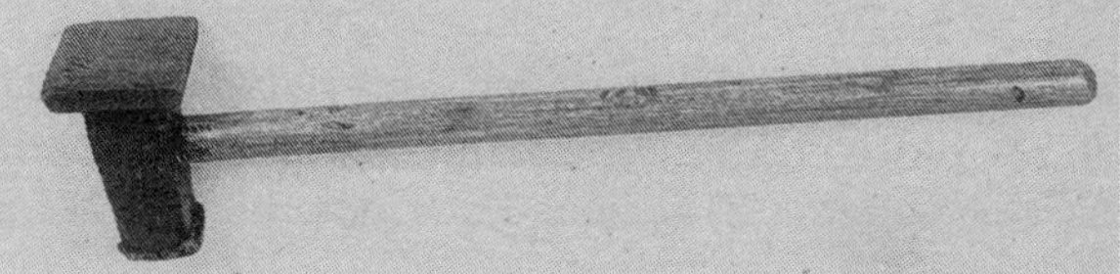

Blacksmith's flatter, 4″ head, 18″ long. *$9–$12*

Box hasp, iron, from a Conestoga wagon. *$462–$500*

Courtesy of Louisville Antique Mall, Louisville, Kentucky; photo by Donald Vogt.

Farrier's hammer with mark on handle. *$12–$15*

Courtesy of Louisville Antique Mall, Louisville, Kentucky; photo by Donald Vogt.

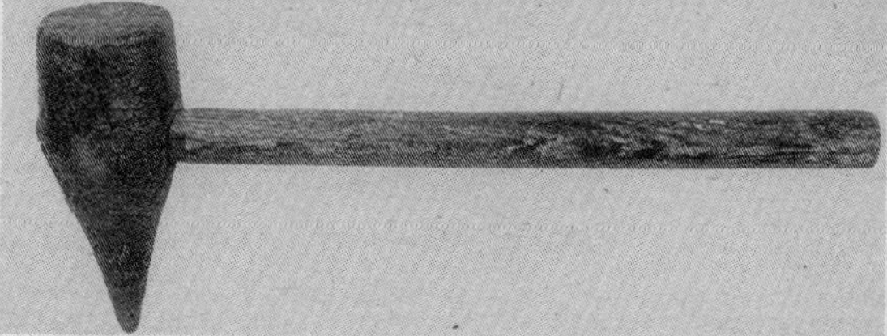

Harness cutter, ca. 1860s, struck with mallet, 5″ × 2¾″. $17–$20

Courtesy of Louisville Antique Mall, Louisville, Kentucky; photo by Donald Vogt.

Harness shop sharpening stone on wood block, 4″ × 11½″. *$12–$16*

Wagon seat, in old red and brown paint, 22″ high, 33″ long, 15″ deep, American, 19th century. *$88–$100*

Wagon seat, pine, refinished. *$150–$200*

MISCELLANEOUS

Cobbler's bench, 10 drawers, signed and dated Milford, Mass., March 10, 1861, original blue paint and condition, with numerous hand-forged tools, some also signed and dated. *$6,500–$10,000*

Cobbler's bench, pine and other woods, 22″ high, 44″ long, 14″ deep. *$110–$200*

Moravian hinges, 18th century, possibly used for barn door, Pennsylvania German, very decorative ram's-horn design, iron. *$550–$575*

THE COUNTRY STORE

My mother's father ran a general store in the early years of this century, and I remember hearing her speak of his elegant handwriting many, many times.

"He was an extremely intelligent man," she'd say, "able to add up a really long column of figures without even writing them down. But when he did, his handwriting was precise and clear, and if he wrote a letter, the characters would be practically perfect." She was as proud of his penmanship as she was of his mental capabilities.

It was considered a status symbol if a merchant had a good writing hand, but there were other reasons a storekeeper had to write well. Most of the time, the general store owner kept his or her own records, using long ledger books to keep track of inventory, sales, debits, and customers' accounts.

Bookkeeping was a duty the owner attended to after a twelve-to-fifteen-hour day in the store—no one had adding machines, calculators, or computers in those days, nor did most families have a weekly paycheck on which they could depend. Thus, quite a bit of the storekeeper's business was done in trade.

If Mrs. Smith had bought fifty pounds of flour, three sacks of wheat, four yards of muslin, and two rolls of thread last week, Mr. Smith might settle the account by providing the general store owner with ten dozen eggs or perhaps a half dozen handmade butter churns. Often a family would be "on the books" all winter, settling their account when they were able to harvest their crops at the end of the summer, when the cycle would begin again.

Of course, the family did more than just pick up dry goods and necessities at the country store. Often the post office was located in the store, which also served as a stagecoach stop, accepting deliveries as well as preparing shipments being sent by townspeople to other areas of the country.

The general store was the place where people gathered to exchange gossip, world news, and war stories around an old potbellied stove or over a checkerboard. It was also the place where they could buy grain for their animals, work clothes and boots, garden and farm tools, tea from China, dates from Turkey, firkins of butter, chewing tobacco, calico material for a dress for the square dance on Saturday, a bag of sugar to make Papa's birthday cake, or a new blanket for the bed. Every square inch of the store was utilized, filled with whatever the neighboring families might need to make their lives a little easier.

A family would schedule their trip to town according to what they needed at the general store. It was often the only time the family would see their neighbors unless they regularly attended a church in the community.

The store was not only the social center of the town and the stop for supplies; it was also the stagecoach stop, post office, livery stable, drugstore, and town offices. The storekeeper had so many functions to perform that he or she needed to be as intelligent as a lawyer, as capable with figures as an accountant, and as nimble as the most quick-witted traveling salesman.

It is said that the heyday of the general store was the mid- to late 1800s, before prepackaging, but there are places in the United States where general stores still serve much the same purpose as they did more than one hundred years ago.

No matter where the store was built, it was at a crossroads, the center of town, and its most familiar asset was a long porch where customers could hitch their horses and wagons and relax in a rocking chair with their feet up against the railing on a warm summer's day.

The store's interior was lined with shelves to the ceiling. The items that could not be shelved hung down from the ceilings, were stored in barrels, or displayed in glass cases in the center of the floor. The post office counter and rental boxes were usually located in the rear of the store. Behind the same counter, the clerk kept forms such as licenses, which he or she could issue as town clerk and justice of the peace.

When electricity or the telephone came to town, the general store was the first to have them. It's amazing that the storekeeper did not get credit for selling those services to his curious customers! When the Model-T was invented, storekeepers were among the first people to own one, using the cars and trucks to deliver goods to their customers.

Most general stores employed a barter system with their customers, allowing farmers to bring in eggs, butter, milk, and vegetables in exchange for goods the farmer did not raise for himself and his family.

A storekeeper could keep fresh meat after the advent of electricity and "coolers." Before that time, the clerk had to rely on ice or a drying process if meat was kept at the store. Some general stores, however, also acted as the town butcher, accepting hogs or cows as payment for what certain customers bought. Wood was also used in trade. The general store was a large building that needed to be kept warm six days a week, and farmers supplied the storekeeper with wood through their unique form of trading.

Storekeepers who let their customers buy on credit were often the losers in the transaction, yet they were known to be generous when a neighbor was in need, or they would overlook a bill when a woman's husband died and she had to carry on without him.

Shoplifters were not generally a problem in such stores because the storekeepers knew their customers and their habits well. If something was missing and the clerk knew who took it, the price of the missing object was often just added to that person's bill. However, theft in small country communities was minimal, not a major problem. The only people the storekeeper feared were Gypsies (notoriously light-fingered) and "outsiders" (anyone who didn't live in the community).

The social activities of the store went beyond the fact that people came in during the day to buy goods, chatted a while, exchanged some bits of news, and went on their way. The country men would usually visit the store, leaving their wives outside or at home, to gather around the wood stove and swap stories and tall tales or play a game of cards. They would often be there until well after midnight, causing their wives to wonder what was so interesting at the store that would keep their men out all night.

Once the Depression hit the United States, the face of the general store changed a bit—the men's wagers on their card games were lower; there were fewer places to go and things to do, as well as less money to spend, so the general store was once again the place to socialize. Practical jokes were played to keep the humor in people's lives during that tough period, and the storekeeper was often the one who had to pay for any damage accidentally done, though many took the joking good-naturedly. Being around friends and neighbors who had the ability to laugh seemed to make the days of the Depression easier to handle for most country folks.

Once the stores began being modernized, the old counters were the first things to go; the layout of the store was changed to allow customers to serve themselves, and there was no longer any room around the old stove for the men to sit, swap stories, and play cards.

Bread was being packaged, and shopkeepers, disbelieving it would sell to women used to doing their own baking, stocked only a few loaves at a time. The store was no longer open until all hours, which was the biggest change of all. Television began providing entertainment that kept people at home, and men now congregated in bars or before the television to watch a football game instead of gathering every night at the store.

Today, the general store is once again in vogue, but is now filled with items such as local crafts, boutique-like clothes, pottery, quilts, and speciality foods, rather than the staples of the past years. In fact, in my hometown, a family recently opened a general store that stocks natural foods and freshly baked goods, sells material by the yard, and has a complete delicatessen, an assortment of handmade pottery, obligatory candy counter, some hand-painted T-shirts, and, best of all, a wonderful gray and black marble ice cream counter where you can get everything from a bowl of soup to a chocolate milk shake.

The owners made sure they found original country store display pieces to hold their baked goods, tortilla chips, and racks of wine. There's a Hearthstone wood stove in the middle of the floor around which weary skiers circle on cold weekend afternoons. The swing on the porch has held many an ice-cream cone licker during the summer months, and there's always a kitten who leans lazily against one of the newel posts begging for a scrap of food.

To enter the door of any revived country store is to go back in time to a place where customers all had names, and their needs or desires were respected—which is probably the reason such places are so often on the route of today's country tourist.

Advertising

ADVERTISING OUR GOODS is not a habit that was originally American-born. In fact, though the shape and form of advertising has changed tremendously, the idea of hawking a product or service has been around for many centuries in other parts of the world.

America's earliest newspapers relied on advertisers to support the cost of printing and distributing, just as they, magazines, radio, and television stations do now. Benjamin Franklin, that ever-inventive American, was the person responsible for what came to be termed the American look of advertising. Larger type and white space were used for dramatic effect; then illustrations were incorporated into the ad.

Americans did not advertise competitively until 1768, when a watchmaker advertised against Charles Willson Peale. From that moment on, we took the reins and brought great changes to the ancient way of selling goods. After the Civil War, advertising agencies appeared, display ads in magazines were commonplace, and slogans began to be used, identifying products with a memorable or repetitive phrase. Some came close to being or became trademarks (e.g., Ivory Soap's claim to be "99 and 44/100 pure"). By the end of the nineteenth century, it was common for companies to register trademarks such as Sherwin-Williams's paint-soaked globe, the Quaker Oats gentleman, and the kindly face of Aunt Jemima.

Advertising went outdoors in the mid-nineteenth century, with billboards, transit ads, and electric signs. Later, the industry became so "tricky" that the government felt the need to regulate advertising and to enforce the need for truth in advertising.

Paper advertising took many forms besides news-related periodicals. Trade cards were distributed, shopping bags were printed with the advertiser's message, bookmarks were popular, and calendars began enjoying their fame around 1860.

Gifts were given to help promote products during the late 1800s to the 1920s, matches were used to advertise restaurants or products by 1892, and point-of-sale materials have been made since the late 1800s and continue to be popular today.

When bulk packaging gave way to individual packaging, companies designed colorful labels for their bottles, tins, cans, boxes, and jars. Sometimes companies went so far in their advertising scheme as to design special containers in different sizes and shapes.

In the early years of this century, radio took over, and by the 1950s, television reigned. The advent of those two forms of communication totally changed a company's advertising focus. Today, we are advertising by Fax or computer—what's next?

Items and Companies Commonly Associated with General Stores

In this section, I have focused on items found in general stores or produced by chains considered "general" stores. Because of the sheer number of such items, I was not able to cover each one of them separately, so concentrated on the ones I see most often at shows and sales and the items made prior to the 1900s. For further information about other advertising items, consult books such as *Kovels' Advertising Collectibles Price List* (for brief information about each category), Lar Hothem's *Country Store Antiques,* and Robert W. and Harriett Swedberg's *Tins 'n' Bins.*

A & P Stores

A & P stores were the citified versions of country stores, the predecessors of big chain supermarkets and a perfect example of how one American came to be a millionaire. The founder of the Great Atlantic and Pacific Tea Company was George Huntington Hartford, an entrepreneur who began his business in 1859 by selling tea from aboard a ship docked in New York's harbor. The company he formed was first called the Great American Tea Company, but after Hartford added coffee to his inventory in 1869, the name changed.

Many of you will remember the local A & P as a store where your mothers or grandmothers picked up groceries for the week. I remember the store as the place where the floors were covered with sawdust, the air smelled of freshly ground coffee, and the shelves high above the vegetable bins were lined with super-large baby dolls and plastic dump trucks at Christmastime.

The store made their own brands of coffee, tea, and spices under the Ann Page label.

Arm & Hammer

Arm & Hammer, the company that produces baking soda, was introduced in 1867 when the Vulcan Spice Mills and Church & Company, a baking soda manufacturer, joined forces. Vulcan Spice Mills offered its trademark, the arm of Vulcan, the Roman god of war, striking an anvil. Originally, the company, owned by James Austin Church, made only spices and mustard. Church & Company's baking soda was added to that line and was sold under the Arm & Hammer label. Eventually the soda became such a best-seller that all other sodas selling under different labels were discontinued.

The owners of Vulcan Spice and Church & Company were father and son. They joined with another relative in 1896 to become Church & Dwight Company.

Armour

Armour meats are still being packaged and sold on today's supermarket shelves. The company began in 1867 when Philip Danforth Armour and John Plankinton moved their Milwaukee-based provision business to Chicago and named it Armour and Company.

At first, the company processed pork and lamb; in 1877 they added ham and bacon to their line, packaging it with an oval label that featured the company's name and a star in the right-hand corner. When canning started to become popular, around 1879, the Armour Company used the canning process for their meat.

Other foods made by the Armour Company include pork and beans (1897), bacon in jars (1902), and condensed milk (1912); also branded with the oval label were such food products as fruits, vegetables, jellies, peanut butter, soups, and soda fountain supplies.

Armour's packaging was redesigned in 1931 to include the trademarks Armour and Armour's Star. In 1943, 1960, and 1963 the labels went through further transformation, ending with the star and rectangle in 1963.

The company produced a good assortment of advertising ephemera (i.e., booklets, cookbooks, signs, trade cards) to be collected along with their packaging.

Aunt Jemima

Aunt Jemima's face shows up in many country homes in many shapes and forms. You may find banks, dolls, cookie jars, trade cards, clocks, kitchen sets, and many other products with the smiling, turbanned face of Aunt Jemima, the trademark for the Pearl Milling Company (1889), the R. T. Davis Milling Company (1890), the Aunt Jemima Mills Co. (1903), and the Quaker Oats Company (1926–present). Like the Quaker Oats man, Aunt Jemima has changed throughout the years. Now she is thinner, more modern, based on a 1936 model of a woman named Anna Robinson.

Cloth Aunt Jemima dolls were first made in 1896, the composition version in 1931. Salt and pepper shakers were first made in ceramic versions in the 1920s and in plastic in the 1950s.

Because of the upsurge in popularity of black collectibles, many reproductions of Aunt Jemima collectibles have been made, so: buyer, beware.

Baker's Chocolate

Baker's Chocolate has the distinction of being one of the first American companies to use a trademark: the Viennese waitress carrying a tray of chocolate "goodies." There is a very romantic story of how this company, formed by Dr. James Baker of Dorchester, Massachusetts, in 1765, came up with such a trademark.

A painting had been commissioned by an Austrian prince after he fell in love with and married a woman named Anna Baltauf, a waitress in a Viennese chocolate shop. Though the painting remains in a museum in Dresden, Germany, Anna Baltauf's figure has graced millions of boxes of Baker's Chocolate.

Baker's son Edmund joined the firm in 1791, and his son Walter began to take part in the family business in 1824.

Though the company was run by the Baker family for over a hundred years, it became part of the General Foods Corporation in 1927, then was passed on to Philip Morris in 1985 when that company acquired General Foods.

I have a Baker's tin in my collection, but there are a vast assortment of other Baker's advertising collectibles such as boxes, labels, tables, signs, plates, and trade cards.

Brewerania

Believe it or not, you football-and-beer fans, beer was available in Jamestown, Virginia, America's first settlement. Little did those first Americans realize that the beverage they were drinking would become synonymous with some of the largest revenues brought in by *any* American product. They also may not have realized that this seemingly harmless drink would be at the center of a controversy that would preoccupy people in the 1980s.

Collectors of country memorabilia are more concerned with the advertising and packaging associated with this product than we are with the golden liquid (although I'm sure we would find that many of today's country homes has a can or bottle of "brew" in the refrigerator).

Because going into great detail on the subject would take me many, many pages of text, I will set forth a short treatise on the subject and leave further investigation up to you, the erstwhile collector.

Trays, signs, cans, ads, labels, bottles, glasses, coasters, openers, taps, mugs, bottle tops, and other things associated with the serving of a "brew" are all items brewerania collectors might add to their collection.

History

In the beginning, beer and ale were made in the home, but the industrial revolution changed that, and by 1850 almost all malt beverages were brewed commercially. In 1850 there were 431 breweries in the United States, and that figure had risen to 4,131 by 1873—proof that almost any sizable town had its own brewery. As time went on, there were fewer breweries even though the U.S. population had increased. By 1972, there were 136 major breweries in the United States, and most were providing the whole country with their product, rather than just the people in their area.

Each time a brewery goes out of business, any products made by them increase in price and become more collectible. Because of the interest in collecting such memorabilia, prices are continually rising, making it harder and harder to amass a collection of the older items.

Types of Items to Collect

Bottles are separated into two categories: blob tops and crown tops. Blob-top bottles are old bottles with a smooth, long mouth, while crown tops have a shorter mouth with a lip at the opening. Usually, blob tops are earlier, though the two versions were produced simultaneously by different companies around the turn of the century. Most were marked with embossed lettering; labels did not appear until after the turn of the century.

Beer trays were made for the serving of bottles or glasses of beer. By the late 1800s, the metal trays were decoratively lithographed with drinking scenes and pictures of women, animals, or comic figures. Most are round, though some memorable pre-Prohibition trays might be oval, square, or rectangular.

Glasses and mugs were made in all different shapes and sizes, depending on what type the company wanted to manufacture. They were meant to be used as advertising promotionals and were first issued by American breweries in the 1880s. The company name would be etched on the glass, and after Prohibition frosted glasses became popular.

Cans have been used for beer since 1935 when Krueger tested the market, and because of the success that company had, the rest of the industry followed suit. Flat-top cans were used first, but spout-top cans are more popular with collectors.

For further information about brewerania advertising, collectibles, and the various companies that made the product, Will Anderson's *The Beer Book* is a great source.

California Fruit Crate Labels

I first became aware of fruit crate labels when a friend of ours was selling them out of a kiosk in Quincy Market in Boston. He gave us a lovely, midnight blue peacock California fruit crate label as a Christmas present, and we instantly fell in love with the collectible. Yet it wasn't until much later that I realized that the brilliant colors of such labels were a purposeful attempt by the growers to attract the attention of eastern jobbers to whom they sold their crops.

Fruit crate labels were used by California growers until the advent of the cardboard box in the mid-1950s. There are more than eight thousand varieties of labels depicting such warm-weather crops as oranges, lemons, grapes, apples, and pears. Though the Florida citrus industry also produced fruit crate labels, they are not as old or as collectible as the California versions. Florida did not get into the citrus industry until after 1900, while California was producing crops since 1885. (Keep in mind: the California labels usually measure 11″ × 10″ or 9″ × 12″, while the Florida versions are 9″ × 9″ or 6″ × 6″.)

Dating crate labels is difficult because they are seldom marked with a date or other distinguishing symbol; however, there are three types of advertising used by the artists/printers who made the labels. From 1880 to World War I, artists paid great attention to details in their depiction of the area where the crops were grown. Adobe houses and the Mexican influence on the Southwest identified the brand. In 1916, the labels became dominated by letters, brand names, and bold lettering. They were seen clearly ten feet away. By 1935, commercial artists were able to get sharper-edged letters and bolder geometrics by their new ability to shade. The prevalent design was now a three-dimensional one.

After World War II was over and Americans were undergoing a feeling of peace and prosperity, shopping centers were born. It is surprising how much of an effect this American phenomenon had on the food industry. One of the biggest changes was in how food was packaged and shipped.

Prices needed to be kept down in order to compete with other growers. The wooden crate was replaced by a cardboard box, and fruit crate labels went the way of any good collectible—into storage.

Today, one may pay anywhere from $1 to $50 for a mint label, but others will cost much more, depending on availability.

Chase and Sanborn Coffee

Chase and Sanborn was formed when Caleb Chase of Boston met coffee and spices salesman James S. Sanborn of Lewiston, Maine. The two decided to form a partnership in 1878. The company was the first to sell roasted coffee in a sealed container.

The partnership was consolidated with Standard Brands in 1929, then with Nabisco, with General Coffee in 1982, and with Hills Brothers in 1984.

Cigar Box Labels

Cigar box labels—average size 4½ by 4½ inches—were used to decorate or seal the lid or sides of a box. The ones used to decorate or seal are called "outs" by collectors, while the ones used under the lid are called "ins."

Though cigars were smoked by America's earliest settlers, the Indians, they were not labeled or branded until after 1850. Companies' names were finally recognized with the advent of cigar labels, and the fancy for smoking cigars lasted from 1890 to about 1912.

The shops where smoking materials like cigars, cigarettes, and pipe tobacco were sold were home to more than just tobacco items. They represented an era when carved tobacco figures outside a shop doorway were a familiar sight and an era in which citizens were not afraid to spark up a pipe.

It was a time when smoking was a celebrated relaxation technique. Whole rooms were put aside as smoking lounges, time was carved out of a dinner party so that the men could have their after-dinner cigars. By the end of the century, it was apparent that smoking was a craze that Americans were quite fond of—there were 350,000 separate brands of cigars!

The art on cigar labels can range from vignettes of Havana to portraits of respected individuals who partook of the cigar a particular company manufactured. Patriotic labels were commonly made, including ones depicting various scenes in which Thomas Nast's Uncle Sam is the main character. Other favorite collectible labels or brands might bear pictures of a sweetheart or wife, railroad scenes, Indians, or historical events.

As with other types of labels, cigar box labels are still affordable, with examples to be found priced from $1 to $100 depending on their condition, subject matter, and rarity.

The Consolidated Lithographic Corporation of Brooklyn was one of the largest cigar label producers in the country in the twentieth century. They manufactured "proof books" of labels of all descriptions and subjects, which serve to reflect men's attitudes and pastimes during that period. Individual cigar labels may sell for $50 to $1,100, while a progressive proof book might be worth four or five times that much.

Clark Thread Company/Coats & Clark

Clark began their business in 1813, while Coats began in 1826. They were competitors until they joined in 1896. They both made thread for sewing machines that was distributed worldwide.

The Coats and Clark thread company made sewing utensils, threads, and other goods, and their advertising trade cards and advertisements were quite attractive, making them highly collectible. One such item made to advertise their products were paper dolls, which were printed and distributed around the turn of the century. They also made spool cabinets, string holders, and signs with their circled chain trademark on them.

Coca-Cola

Coca-Cola has been around since 1886, when pharmacist John S. Pemberton began selling it to his customers in Atlanta, Georgia. Willis E. Venable was the person who first mixed the syrup with carbonated water, giving us the fizzy brown drink well known to people all over the world.

Since Coca-Cola's history has been well documented in other books, let me just mention here that collecting items made by the Coca-Cola Company can occupy you for the rest of your life. There were ashtrays, bottles, openers, trays, signs, banks, calendars, dolls, clocks, lighters, watch fobs, and many, many other items displaying the Coca-Cola red and white trademark symbol. There are even clubs of Coca-Cola collectors and newsletters on the subject, as well as an endless variety of ephemera.

Colgate & Co.

Colgate & Co. jumped on the bandwagon of creating free collectibles for its customers around 1915 with a series of booklets for young people. They were all illustrated in color and were often educational in nature. Some titles produced were *Dental Lectures, The Jungle Pow-Wow,* and *The Jungle School.*

DuPont

One of the earliest advertising pieces in our collection is a DuPont gunpowder tin that was made in the early 1800s. The simple black and white printed label is not as attractive or flashy as some of the later color-lithographed tins that share shelf space with it, but I like the tin much better, maybe because of its age or the fact that the label almost seems to have been done by hand. Or maybe it's the small picture on the left-hand side of the label of a horseback-riding Indian chasing a deer on the right side. Most certainly, my preference for the can comes from a smug satisfaction that the can was never opened and has come into our collection in almost mint condition.

The DuPont Company opened in 1802 and sold its first canned gunpowder in 1804. They are still in business but are now called E. I. Du Pont de Nemours and Co., Inc.

Folk Medicine

Folk medicine was commonly used by country folk and was often dispensed freely at the general store. A long list of ills was often "cured" with unlikely remedies passed down from generation to generation. Such remedies might include snake oil as a cure for rheumatism and sassafras tea to clear the blood. Various cures for kidney disease soon found their way into bottles and ended up being dispensed by the general store owner—but this time for a price rather than as free advice. Ah, American consumerism at its darkest moment. . . .

Of course, such remedies, though often thought by us modern folk to be rubbish, really *did* work. Contemporary studies have shown that chamomile tea *does* really relax a person (which was probably why it was touted as the remedy to help you sleep) and who knows about "starve a cold and stuff a fever?"

Heinz

The Heinz Company was started by one man. Henry Heinz worked in Shappsburg, Pennsylvania, where he concocted, packaged, and marketed his own horseradish. He joined with another entrepreneur, L. C. Noble, in 1869 to make the Anchor Brand Food Company, which later became Heinz, Noble, and Company. The company went through some changes during the Depression of 1875, emerging as the H. J. Heinz Company in 1888.

Some trademarks that the Heinz Company invented were the term "57 Varieties" and the Heinz pickle symbol (1910).

The company made a number of products and advertising items. Some of the items you may find with the Heinz label include pickle barrels, apple butter buckets, baked bean crocks, pinbacks, signs, trade cards, and watch fobs.

Ivory Soap

First marketed in 1879, the soap was unusual because it was white, whereas previously soaps had been yellow or brown.

The soap was not originally designed to float—a freak accident caused the mixture of ingredients to contain so much air that the soap would rise to the top of any water in which it was placed. It was after that point that the soap was marketed as "99 and 44/100 Pure. It Floats."

Ivory Soap's packaging has gone through several changes, which were reflected in Proctor & Gamble's marketing campaign. Items made with the Ivory Soap label include banks, bars, signs, and trade cards.

Lipton

The founder of the Lipton Tea Company was Thomas Johnstone Lipton, a Scot who had emigrated to the United States at age fourteen (1865) and had worked in or owned various stores or supermarkets. On a trip to Australia by way of Ceylon, when he was forty years old, he was able to purchase tea plantations in Ceylon quite cheaply, and when he returned in the United States, he realized that he had stumbled onto a profitable venture. In 1898, he was knighted by Queen Victoria, and before long there were Lipton Tea offices located all over the world.

Lipton's products were advertised with a number of slogans, which included "Direct from the Tea Gardens to the Teapot" (1892), "The Finest Tea the World Can Produce" (1894), "Lipton Tea Refreshes" (1939), and others.

Lipton now markets other items besides tea.

Montgomery Ward

Montgomery Ward published the first mail-order catalog, produced by Aaron Montgomery Ward, the owner. His intention was to sell his goods to people in the farm communities. The catalog, which was first sent out in 1894, was discontinued in 1986.

Morton Salt

The girl under the umbrella is a familiar sight to most Americans. Founded in 1910 by Joy Morton, the Morton Salt Company was one of the first to package their salt with a patented spout. The slogan "When It Rains, It Pours" was its trademark.

In the 1970s, the Morton Company released a set of four reproduction packages that showed the Morton girl and the changes she has undergone during the century.

National Biscuit Company

The National Biscuit Company made Uneeda Biscuits, popular with country store customers everywhere. The name for the biscuit was coined by an advertising man named Henry N. McKinney.

The company was formed in 1898 and was the first to market a soda cracker nationally under one brand name. It was probably the first cracker produced in bulk and, as such, was responsible for driving the wooden cracker barrel from its place at the end of each general store's counter.

The boxed crackers were decorated with Uneeda emblems and slogans and were even lauded in poems such as this one:

I am Uneeda, I defy
The roaming dust, the busy fly,
For in my package, sealed and tight,
My makers keep me pure and white.

Pillsbury

The Pillsbury Flour Company was formed in 1871, when John Sargent Pillsbury; his nephew, Charles A. Pillsbury; and Wells Gardner opened C. A. Pillsbury and Company. The company's trademark (XXXX) was started in 1872.

Pillsbury has produced flour, cereal, wheat bran, pancake flour, cake flour, and other ingredients through the years. They also are responsible for cookbooks, cooking contests, and the "Poppin' Fresh Doughboy," which was created in the 1960s.

The company is still controlled by the Pillsbury family and owns a number of other industries.

Lydia Pinkham

Lydia Pinkham lived in Lynn, Massachusetts, and it was from that address that she began distributing her "Vegetable Compound" in

1875. The compound was said to be a cure-all for women's ills and made the round-eyed, frizzle-haired Pinkham the best-known medicine company CEO of her day.

Part of the reason for Pinkham's success was the extensive advertising campaign the family launched to sell the product. Brochures were delivered door-to-door, full-page newspaper ads were taken out, and Lydia Pinkham's healthy face was soon used to sell her product.

Once the campaign was well underway, women wrote to Mrs. Pinkham to ask medical advice or to let Lydia know just how much they liked her product. The Pinkhams incorporated testimonials into their advertising program, and by the end of the 1880s, Lydia Pinkham's Vegetable Compound was well known.

Toward the end of the century, trade cards were made and distributed, promotional material was given away (e.g., matchbook thread cases), and new products, such as Liver Pills, were added to the Pinkham line. By 1925, the Pinkham Co. was grossing more than $3 million, but business slowly declined after that time because of conflicts within the Pinkham family and their arguments about old-fashioned advertising concepts.

Quaker Oats

Oats were a staple with early New England colonists as feed for livestock, but it wasn't until 1700 that they were grown almost everywhere in the United States. By 1850, the influence of oats on American culture (they were largely responsible for adding 2 inches to the average American height) was strong enough to warrant the immigration of a German merchant named Ferdinand Schumacher.

Schumacher opened a grocery store in Akron, Ohio, and introduced oats to the general American public's cooking habits in 1850. He found a way to prepare oatmeal that was less time-consuming than earlier forms of oatmeal, packaged it in jars, and sold it as a breakfast food. Within a short time, Schumacher's business was prospering and he was selling approximately twenty barrels a day. His was the first successful breakfast cereal—so successful, in fact, that many other companies clamored for his title: "Oatmeal King of America."

The competition grew so fierce that a number of the larger mills were forced to consolidate. From this merger, the Quaker Oats Co. was spawned in 1877.

The trademark of the company, a kindly faced, white-haired Quaker gentleman, dressed appropriately in somber grays, has become one of the best known in this country. It should be noted that the establishment of such a company was influential in shaping the strength of product packaging and advertising at that time.

Prior to companies such as Quaker Oats, dry wheats, flour, and grains were scooped from a barrel by the general store clerk. The companies who began packaging such products offered their customers the opportunity to purchase top-quality grains in a standardized size and price, and with the added assurance that the product was clean. Many of the open barrels in a general store were visited nightly by small brown creatures with long tails and constantly twitching noses. No matter how hard the store manager tried, there was no way he could promise his customers a "clean" product.

When the American Cereal Co. first packaged Quaker Oats in cardboard containers, they also launched a widespread advertising campaign, which was but a dim sign of things to come. The folks who lived in turn-of-the-century America were amazed to see broadsides of the somber Quaker on the sides of barns or railway cars; they were even more surprised to meet the living version of the trademark at county fairs. The Quaker Oats Co. campaign was so thorough that explorers took the breakfast food with them all over the world—to both poles, Africa, and Tibet.

Today, the cardboard containers are avidly collected by country enthusiasts who want to display early advertising pieces in old kitchen cupboards or across a dining room shelf. And it appears that next century's collectors will have the opportunity to do the same since the Quaker gentleman in gray still sits on today's supermarket shelves.

Sleepy Eye

This company was started in 1883 in Sleepy Eye, Minnesota, and by the turn of the century was producing many brands of flour.

In 1891, the company became Sleepy Eye Milling Company and used the figure of a real Indian chief who lived in the area as their trademark in 1893.

Sleepy Eye made a number of advertising giveaways/promotionals, which included letter openers (1900), postcards (1904), spoons, cookbooks, and paperweights.

Trade Cards

The industrial revolution of the late nineteenth century caused a flood of new products and services to come onto the market. These new products demanded vigorous advertising because they were competing with like products made by similar companies. American commercialism had been born, and the "baby" was crying for attention.

The invention in the late 1800s of the color printing process known as chromolithography made other types of printing a thing of the past. Brightly colored and elaborately designed trade business cards, posters, and ads replaced those simple black and white embossed designs that had served their purpose for smaller companies in days gone by. Greengrocers, dry goods merchants, chimney sweeps, and druggists all jumped on the bandwagon, utilizing the polychrome trade card concept to advertise the goods they sold or the services they offered.

Because of their colorful designs and convenient size (no larger than 3″ by 5″), trade cards, became a popular collectible, and a rather large assortment could be stored easily in a shoe box. Often those who collected this type of advertising ephemera would devote their interests solely to one type of card—for instance, one might collect cards that gave helpful household hints, while another might hunt for cards that advertised a specific product or service.

During the Victorian era, trade cards were handed to customers, wrapped in packages, or mailed by salesmen to prospective customers. Few are dated, and the earliest versions had no pictures on them. Very few were signed with the artists' names, so if you run across one that is, it is more valuable, thus more collectible.

There were very few trade cards made prior to 1810; in fact, even those made between 1810 and 1850 are rare. Color trade cards were popular by the 1870s, and also in vogue at that time was the use of brand names; 1880 to 1893 are considered prime years by trade card collectors. The trade card was used as an advertising device until the 1930s–1940s, when radio (and later television) gave advertisers the chance to reach a more widespread audience.

Several different types of cards were made. Plain cards—rectangular pieces of paper or cardboard usually printed on just one side—were the most common. Die-cut cards were cut in the shape of the product they were advertising, and mechanical cards had movable parts. Metamorphic cards are ones that show different pictures depending on the way you open their flaps, while see-through cards show an invisible design or message when held up to a light.

Some of the companies that printed collectible trade cards include Currier & Ives and L. Prang & Company. Those companies were also responsible for most of the valued postcards in today's collections.

Signs

MY HUSBAND has long collected trade signs of indiscriminate origin. It is just lately that he has realized we must become more selective—no more twenty-five-foot-long signs that won't fit anywhere in the house! Because we have learned our lesson the hard way, I can pass on the earnest advice that it would be wise to select a time period, advertiser, or type of trade to focus on before you begin collecting signs. It will save a lot of time and effort when you start trying to find space to hang them.

The fun of finding trade signs, such as striped wooden barber poles, giant scissors, or giant keys, is half the pleasure of collecting. Trade signs were not manufactured by the hundreds. On the contrary, you may find some in your travels that are one of a kind, designed for a specific business by a signmaker who was hired to do the job by the shop's owner.

Different symbols represented different types of shops in an era when illiteracy was rampant (e.g., the clock of a jeweler, scissors of a tailor, mortar and pestle of a pharmacist). The most recognizable of all trade signs is the wooden Indian, signifying a tobacco shop.

After the Civil War, trade signs were standardized and mass-produced, though symbols of the trade were still commonly used. By the early 1900s, lettered signs with artwork depicting the product were employed as advertising in general stores and on the sides of buildings. Lithographed tin signs, often using as many as fourteen colors (an accomplishment in those days!), are quite popular with collectors whose interests are in early advertising materials.

Because some signs that proclaimed their owner's business

were made by the shopkeepers themselves, they are often termed as folk art. The signmaker was not a trained artist, but the subject was close to his or her heart, and the sign was usually the only one of its kind to exist. Such results of creative energy fall into the folk art category almost by accident, but if we take the meaning of folk art as artistic work done by untrained hands, it makes sense.

Display Units

EACH GENERAL OR COUNTRY STORE had certain types of cupboards, containers, shelves, glass jars, and decorative canisters in which they store their goods. Because the country store's heyday was prior to that of prepackaging, items were stored in large quantities by the shopkeeper. Flour was kept in large barrels as were crackers, grains, rice, and sugar. Coffee, tea, and spices might be kept in large tin containers, while candy, licorice, and other goodies were kept in open glass jars where the children might see them.

Glass and oak shelf units might hold eyeglasses, jewelry, watches, and other such small items that should be clearly seen to be sold. Oak shelf units that reached almost to the ceiling would hold bolts of fabric and sewing goods. Stoneware jars held pickles or preserves.

Some of the display units used by country store owners will be explained separately in this section; others (like stoneware) are explained more fully in other chapters of this book.

Types of Containers, Shelves, and Showcases

Coffee, Tea, and Spice Containers

Elaborately designed containers for exotic drinks like coffee and tea, as well as for international spices, were made for use in general stores in the late nineteenth and early twentieth centuries. Usually they were distributed to the stores by the makers of such products, rather than by the manufacturers. Thus, they were painted and labeled to the distributors' specifications.

The containers often took on an Oriental theme, some being

lithographed, some exquisitely painted, and others incorporating beveled glass mirrors in their design.

Because the canisters were kept in the store and refilled whenever low, they are not usually found in mint condition. Often the lettering is partially or totally worn off and, sometimes it is difficult to tell what the lettering originally said.

After the turn of the century, there was a higher demand for such containers, and factories such as the American Can Company began manufacturing and supplying the containers to general stores. Spice cabinets and coffee and tea containers were prominently pictured in American Can Company catalogs of grocers' tinware in the early 1900s.

Cracker Barrels

Cracker barrels were not just used to hold crackers. Made by the town's coopersmith, these wooden strapped barrels were also used to ship salted fish, beef, pork, flour, biscuits, rum, molasses, whale oil, tar, and pitch. The barrels kept in the store held a ready supply of the aforementioned, all of which would be scooped out and personally weighed by the merchant.

It seemed these barrels were never empty for long. As soon as they neared depletion, they were refilled. And once cracker barrels disappeared from the general store, it seems personal service did as well. No longer are we able to buy *exactly* the poundage we need, unless the product is already packaged in our needed weight.

Display Cabinets

Recently I had the pleasure of helping a friend who was restoring and redecorating a general store. The pieces that ended up in the store—a three-piece, seven-foot-tall icebox, a number of twelve-foot-long glass and oak display cabinets, an oak candy cabinet with sixty pull-out drawers—were items that not many of us can fit into our homes, but they're great for a playroom, a restaurant, a store, or someone who owns a large collection they'd like to display (or store) properly.

Though I love these items, most of us are forced to collect the smaller items, which were used on countertops or hung on walls.

Large display cases used in country stores normally had thick, flat glass tops and sides so that their contents could be viewed easily. They superseded the long wooden counter that stretched the length of the general store. The merchant discovered that the oak counter, even though it had plenty of storage space underneath, was simply taking up too much unnecessary space. The glass countertops were far more "salable" in the storekeeper's mind because customers could see everything the unit held. And, best of all, everything would be kept clean and dry.

The earliest glass display cases were made with wood frames. Examples of cases that were made after World War II have metal frames.

Dye Cabinets

One of the most popular general store collectibles are dye cabinets made by companies such as Diamond Dye. These cabinets held dyes that were used by seamstresses or homemakers before the advent of factory-dyed clothing and cloth.

This type of display cabinet often had a color chromolithograph or other type of colorful advertising on its front. The front was usually displayed to the customer and the back was open, with cubbies for the dyes, so that reaching for the desired color was easy for the shopowner.

Scales

In those days when everything was bought by the storekeeper in quantity, it was necessary to have a number of different scales to weigh out the amount of the product the customer wanted to buy. Large scales were placed near the cash register or box so that the merchant would be able to package up the whole order in one place.

Smaller scales were often not accurate and are now marked "not legal for use in trade."

Showcases

Showcases were first put to use during the period when country merchants were bringing in more and more imported stock. With larger inventories, the country store began losing valuable floor space—and every inch counted!

The first cases had sloping glass sides set in gleaming German silver frames. A number of smaller items could be displayed on the showcase's shelves instead of being kept in closed boxes on a store shelf as they had been before.

Items such as eyeglasses, toiletries, razors, jewelry, and some sewing supplies filled the shelves of a country store's showcase. And after a while, there were showcases made specifically for certain country store goods (like penny candy—how frustrating to have to continually clean the smudge prints from children's hands and noses from the candy showcase's glass.)

(Other information on showcases made by particular companies can be found throughout this chapter.)

Spool Cabinets

Spool cabinets, like dye cabinets, were usually decorated in the front and hollow in the back. The storekeeper would pick out the color of thread the customer wanted and hand it over the counter or pile it among the other items the customer had chosen to buy.

In size, some were big enough to be used as end tables by today's collectors, and others were small enough to be placed on top of a table. Spool cabinets are highly prized by collectors who want an attractive storage container for their small collectibles.

Coats & Clark (described elsewhere in this section) made quite a few spool cabinets, as did Merricks, Brainard & Armstrong, and Boye Needle Co.

Vending Machines

Vending machines, such as those used to dispense gum and soft drinks, were first used after the turn of the century. In fact, they were so popular that in 1908 the government issued coil stamps to be used in such machines.

Some of these early machines used animated figures as a ploy to get another penny from an entranced child. Pulver Gum machines, made in the early 1900s, used the comic strip character the Yellow Kid as one of the miniature figures that would reach for the gum and drop it into the chute and into the hands of a waiting child.

Soft drink vending machines were available to stores by 1910, but shopkeepers continued to utilize an ice-filled chest to dispense their soft drinks until the early 1930s. At that time, the machines were refined enough to come into widespread use, and the public was more comfortable with their performance. The shopkeeper, however, was still required to keep the machines loaded, though the 1930s version was capable of holding more bottles than its 1910 counterpart.

Miscellaneous

Barbershop Antiques

BECAUSE WE HAVE ALREADY MENTIONED BARBERSHOP POLES in the trade signs section of this book, this section will deal exclusively with some other items found in barbershops. I have included this information because these shops were the domain of country males. Though not specifically a country collectible, these items are often found in country homes; in fact, I have some shaving mugs in a post office sorting bin in my home, and my husband has picked up a few razors and strops in the years we've been collecting.

Barber bottles, for instance, were always used in pairs. One would hold water, the other witch hazel. Because they were made in pairs, they are collected in the same manner.

Shaving mugs and bowls can be collected singly and are generally easy to find. Mugs have an inside lip and tend to be stouter, squatter versions of coffee mugs. A man might have had his name painted on the mug, and you will also find "trade mugs" that incorporated a trade sign into their design. They were popular from the 1880s until World War I.

Shaving bowls are shallow, with a semi-circle cut out to fit the bowl under its owner's chin. They were used to catch the hair, water, and soap used during the barbering process.

Collecting razors is a field in itself with the interesting developments in the evolution of the razor throughout the last two hundred years. Straight razors and strops were made by a number of different companies throughout the first two hundred years of U.S. history. Most men had themselves shaved daily; thus, barbers were a lot busier in those days than they are now. By the early 1900s, the safety razor was used by men who wanted a Sunday shave—the one day that the barbershops were not open. Once electricity came into vogue, electric razors became popular. Who knows how men will shave next!

Cash Registers

Cash registers began to replace the handwritten form of receipts and bookkeeping when the first one was used in Ohio in the 1880s by an enterprising man named John H. Patterson. Patterson's invention was new and simple, and it made the storekeeper's life a lot easier. The register enabled clerks to keep track of sales and purchases without stopping to write each one down. They also now had a safer place to keep the day's receipts.

Patterson became the head of the National Cash Register Company and, as a result, a very wealthy man. His design sprouted others like it, and by 1906, there were more than forty different sizes of registers made by Patterson's firm. The registers were sold by smooth-talking, deal-making salesmen from the home office, who sold the newest, most expensive model so well that many cash registers were almost immediately obsolete.

Even in those days, the top of the line, most modern, customized register might sell for as much as $600—quite a sum for country store owners. It was amazing that so many registers were sold to men and women who were accustomed to sales pitches from various types of salespeople. Yet they fell into the trap of buying a monstrous cash register that often was simply too large and newfangled for their small businesses. What is *not* amazing is that there was soon a new, cheaper model being made by another company, Butler Brothers. The smaller machine did everything that was necessary for a small business, but the best part was that Butler registers were priced below $50.

Small cash registers were used in barbershops and candy stores, while the larger versions were used in general stores and department stores.

One way to tell the age of a register is to check for a metal rod or bar above the drawer. It was placed there so that the store-keeper could loop his or her fingers over it when closing the drawer against heavy-tension release springs.

The National Cash Register Company was responsible for producing most of the antique registers we see on today's antiques market.

Chopping Blocks

One of the stories all of my friends and anyone who has taken one of my "Decorating with Antiques" courses have heard me tell is the one about the never-say-die chopping block. Because I cannot resist telling it one more time, this piece of country furniture will find its way into this chapter.

When shopping in Canada for antiques a few years ago, we were stalking the aisles of a shop in Knowlton, looking for something "different" to take to the Farmington, Connecticut, antiques show the following weekend. I was doing the shows alone at that point, but my husband, Bobby, always went shopping with me. He was the furniture expert. On this particular day, he spied a wonderful old butcher's block in a corner under a table and called me over to look at it.

"Look at the price on it," he whispered, anxiously looking back over his shoulder to make sure he hadn't been overheard. "You can triple your money on this, and it'd be just great for a country show. I wish *we* had space for it at the house." Bobby's an award-winning chef and a lover of kitchen items. Well, he sold me on this one.

It took three men to get the block onto the van. I admired its chunky, round legs, the grooves and valleys on its worn surface, the mellow golden patina of the wood. I had no doubts it would sell that June weekend in Connecticut.

I was in the middle of loading the van during a particularly windy, cold snowstorm after a depressingly bleak show for which I had traveled four hours *each way* when I realized I had pulled out my back. The butcher block had gone to at least two shows a month with me after the one in June. It was now February. It struck me at that point, with my back screaming in wild agony, that either my husband didn't like me too much or that chopping blocks were not exactly hot sellers.

By the next week, the block was a featured item for a neighbor's auction.

Moral of the story: don't buy a two- or three-hundred-pound butcher's block if you're planning on moving it a lot.

Chopping and butcher's blocks can be found in round or square versions. Because they were made for particular purposes or businesses, each one varies considerably.

Though I always advocate using an antique for its original purpose, I've seen customers chop legs off of chopping blocks to transform them into coffee tables. I wouldn't encourage the practice. It lessens the value of your antique and takes one more of a dying breed off the market. However, I could certainly understand wanting to make a butcher's block lighter.

Paper Bags

Paper bags were not used in early general stores. Instead, the store owner would wrap your purchases in a piece of wrapping paper, tying it with string. One needed to be quite adept in putting together such an unwieldy package—not all products were the same shape and size, as you can well imagine.

The first person granted a patent for making paper bags was Francis Wolle of Bethlehem, Pennsylvania. Though the patent was dated 1852, it is obvious from store ledgers and other reports that bags were not commonly used until after the Civil War.

Once Wolle's product began to gain in popularity (after about a hundred years on the market), manufacturers and store owners came to see paper bags as a prime opportunity to advertise their goods. They were imprinted with company or product names and considered a "free gift" to the consumer. The practice continues today (e.g., Nancy Reagan's "Just Say No" message was highly visible on shopping bags).

In my travels, I have seen paper bag holders in several country collections. They are as different in design as are the people who buy them. Often owners had no idea what kind of device they owned. If you buy a wood or wire device that baffles you, ask yourself if it might have hung on a wall or rested under a counter, holding three or four different-size stacks of bags. Some bag holders even resembled large mouse traps—if you removed one bag from the holder, the trap released momentarily, then snapped back in place before the rest of the bags had a chance to slip or slide.

Prices

If an item is not indicated as being specifically Shaker, Indian, Amish, etc., then it should be considered strictly a "country" piece. For items specifically made by the country groups spoken of in the first section of this book, consult that chapter.

ADVERTISING

A&P tray, made by the Atlantic & Pacific Tea Co., 8¼″ high, 8¼″ wide, lithographer unknown, ca. 1907, near mint condition. *$60–$80*

Acme Licorice Pellets tin (5 lb.), made by Young & Smylle, 7¼″ high, 6″ wide, 4″ deep, lithographer unknown, ca. 1900, near mint condition. *$80–$100*

Allens Red Tame Cherry 5¢ syrup bottle, glass label, red letters on white-gold border, near mint condition. *$400–$500*

American Rifle Team coffee tin, made by The Globe Mills, 8″ high, 4¼″ wide, 4¼″ deep, T.C.C.A. "canvention" winner, lithographer unknown, ca. 1880, excellent condition. *$700–$800*

Armour's Veribest Peanut Butter pail, 3⅞″ high, 3½″ wide, 3½″ deep, nursery rhymes around tin, lithographed by Continental Can Co., ca. 1920, near mint condition. *$100–$120*

Aunt Jemima's Sugar Butter pail, made by Rigney & Co., 3½″ high, 4½″ wide, 4½″ deep, Best Food Tin—1979 TCCA Canvention, ca. 1910–15, excellent condition. *$500–$550*

Courtesy of Cary Station Antiques; photo by Donald Vogt.

Barber pole, approximately 6½′ tall, wood, three-dimensional. *$1,600–$2,000*

Baum's Horse & Stock food box, unopened, 11½″ high, 6″ wide, 7½″ deep, early paper litho all around, lithographer unknown, ca. 1900, excellent condition. *$40–$60*

Berry Brother Varnishes mirror, celluloid, 2¼″ high, 2¼″ wide, pictures kids and dog in Berry Bros. wagon, lithographed by Whitehead and Hoag, ca. 1890, near mint condition. *$80–$100*

Biggerhair Tobacco canister, made by B. Leidersdorf Co., lithographed on cardboard, 7¼″ high, 5¼″ wide, 5¼″ deep, lithographer unknown, ca. 1890, excellent condition. *$60–$80*

Blanke's Mojav Coffee tin, yellow on black, 7¼″ high, 5″ wide, 5″ deep, lithographed by J. H. Pocock, ca. 1890s, excellent condition. *$700–$800*

Blue Boy Frozen Fruits tin (30 lb.), made by Geo. W. Haxton & Sons, 12½″ high, 10″ wide, 10″ deep, lithographer unknown, ca. 1930, excellent condition. *$25–$40*

Blue Jay fire extinguisher, made by The Redwood Chemical Co., lithographed on tin, 21¾″ high, 2″ wide, 2″ deep, lithographed by American Can Co., 11A, ca. 1910, near mint condition. *$70–$90*

Bouquet Coffee tin, made by O. V. Tracy & Co., 5¾″ high, 4¼″ wide, 4¼″ deep, lithographed by American Can Co., 15A, ca. 1910, excellent condition. *$30–$50*

Courtesy of Cary Station Antiques; photo by Donald Vogt.

Bowman Dairy Company glass milk bottle, 20″ tall, ca. early 1900s. *$325–$375*

British beverage bottles with original paper labels, 5, lithographer unknown, ca. 1920, near mint condition. *$225–$350*

Brown's Celery Phosphate Health Beverage syrup bottle, glass label, oversize, 4½″ high, "Alcohol 48/100% of 1%," a muscular arm holds a bunch of celery, black, white, and gray with red border, near mint condition. *$1,400–$1,600*

Buckingham Smoking Tobacco pocket tin, made by John J. Bagley & Co., lithographer unknown, ca. 1915, near mint condition. *$40–$65*

Buffalo Brand Peanut Butter pail (20 lb.), made by F. M. Hoyt & Co., 9¼″ high, 10½″ wide, 10½″ deep, lithographed by Bertels Metal Ware Co., ca. 1925, fine condition. *$160–$200*

Bull Durham trade counter piece, chalkware, originally had Bull Durham smoking pouch around neck. *$225–$275*

Burley Boy Tobacco lunch box, made by J. J. Bagley Co., 4″ high, 6½″ wide, 5″ deep, "The White Man's Hope," ca. 1900–1910, excellent condition. *$1,800–$2,000*

Burnham's Wild Cherry Phosphates pitcher, heavy embossing, scalloped top, 10″ high, ca. 1890s, near mint condition. *$250–$275*

Cadette Borated Baby Talc tin, 7½″ high, 2″ wide, 1¼″ deep, lithographer unknown, ca. 1920, near mint condition. *$40–$60*

Cameron & Cameron High Grade Tobacco pocket tin, 4″ high, 3″ wide, 1¼″ deep, lithographed by The Hasker & Marcuse Co., ca. 1910, good condition. *$100–$125*

Capitol Mills Coffee tin, made by Lincoln, Seyms & Co., 5½″ high, 5″ wide, 5″ deep, lithographed by Ginna & Co., ca. 1890, excellent condition. *$550–$600*

Capitol Peanut Butter tin (25 lb.), made by Andrus-Schofield Co., 9¼″ high, 10″ wide, 10″ deep, lithographer unknown, ca. 1925, fine condition. *$200–$250*

Caswell's National Crest Coffee tin, 7½″ high, 5⅝″ wide, 5⅝″ deep, lithographer unknown, ca. 1910, excellent condition. *$50–$75*

Central Union Cut Plug lunchbox tin, made by The U.S. Tobacco Co., 7″ high, 4½″ wide, 4″ deep, lithographer unknown, ca. 1890, near mint condition. *$25–$35*

Chevrolet Motor Car calendar, lithographed on paper, 31″ high, 16″ wide, lithographer unknown, pad dated ca. 1920, fine condition. *$160–$200*

"Chew Beeman's Pepsin Gum" glass jar, glass label, black letters on white with red background and gold border, oversized label, 3″ high, 4″ wide, jar 5″ wide, 5″ deep, 12″ high, near mint condition. *$750–$800*

Chicago Tailoring Co. pin holder, lithographed on tin, 3½″ oval with oval base, pictures gent smoking in his living room, lithographer unknown, ca. 1917, near mint condition. *$130–$150*

Collection of tins (each): (From upper left, clockwise) Robinson's Barley, Blu-White Detergent, Clabber Girl Baking Powder, Watkins Nutmeg, H & K Jamaica Ginger, Alladdin Kone Kap Mantle, Sudan Ground Nutmeg, Kendall's Spavin Cure Box, Presto Stove Polish, Prince Albert Tobacco, Seal of North Carolina Plug Cut Tobacco, Clapp's Chicken Soup. *$5–$40*

Courtesy of the Keeping Room, Camby, Indiana; photo by Donald Vogt.

Collection of tins (each): Gold Dust Scouring Powder, Delicious Blend of Choice Coffees, Philadelphia Cream Cheese, Bliss Coffee (1 lb. size), O'Cedar Mop, 3# Cake Box. *$15–$45*

"College Widow," Old Barbee whiskey tray, 16″ high, 22″ wide, lithographed by American Art Works, ca. 1913, fine condition. *$210–$270*

Commodore Coffee pail, made by W. F. McLaughlin & Co., 10¾″ high, 3¼″ wide, 3¼″ deep, lithographed by Illinois Can Co., ca. 1890, fair condition. *$60–$80*

Cornell Mixture Smoking Tobacco tin, upright, square corners, made by Marburg Bros., 4½″ high, 3½″ wide, 2″ deep, lithographed by Somers Bros., ca. 1890, excellent condition. *$20–$50*

D&L Slade Epicurean Spices tin, rare, 6½″ high, 4½″ wide, complete set of 6 individual lithographed canisters inside display tin, lithographed by Ginna & Co., ca. 1885, near mint condition. *$45–$75*

Daisy Fly Killer tin, ½″ high, 6⅛″ wide, 3¾″ deep, unusual, flies nip on arsenic corks, lithographed by Harold Somers, ca. 1885, near mint condition. *$25–$40*

DeLaval Black & White Cow & Baby, lithographed on tin, original envelope, 3″ high, 5″ wide, lithographed by American Art Sign Co., ca. 1910, excellent condition. *$50–$75*

DeLaval Brown Cow & Baby, lithographed on tin, original envelope, 3″ high, 5″ wide, lithographed by American Art Sign Co., ca. 1910, near mint condition. *$50–$75*

DeLaval Guernsey Cow & Baby, lithographed on tin, original envelope, 3″ high, 5″ wide, lithographed by American Art Sign Co., ca. 1910, near mint condition. *$50–$75*

Diamond Creamery butter tin (7 lb.), lithographer unknown, ca. 1910, fine condition. *$40–$55*

Diamond Creamery butter tin (5 lb.), lithographer unknown, ca. 1910, near mint condition. *$25–$40*

Dixie Queen Cut Plug lunch box, 7¾″ high, 4⅛″ wide, 5¼″ deep, lithographer unknown, ca. 1915, excellent condition. *$130–$150*

Dr. King's New Life Pills glass jar, glass label, "Dr. King's New Life Pills Always Satisfy," oversized label, 3½″ high, 3″ wide, black letters on white, gold border, 13″ high, 5″ wide, 5″ deep, near mint condition. *$475–$525*

Dr. Miles' calendar, "compliments of R. S. Bonar," lithographed on cardboard, 11¾″ high, 8¾″ wide, lithographer unknown, pad dated 1902, excellent condition. *$40–$60*

Dr. Miles' calendar, "compliments of S. C. Ranch," lithographed on cardboard, framed, under glass, 11¾″ high, 8¾″ wide, lithographer unknown, pad dated February 1902, excellent condition. *$40–$75*

Dr. Miles' calendar, "compliments of Otis J. Beeson," lithographed on paper, 10″ high, 6¼″ wide, lithographer unknown, pad dated 1904, excellent condition. *$45–$70*

Dr. Scholl counter piece in the shape of a foot, 12″, ca. 1920s–30s. *$125–$150*

"Drink Moonshine Makes You Happy" syrup bottle, glass label, blue letters on white, rare, only one known, dark amber bottle, hairline crack to label (2), slight discoloration. *$475–$525*

Drink Pepsi Cola serving tray, oval, 13⅓" high, 11" wide, lithographer unknown, ca. 1890, fine condition. *$550–$700*

"Drink Tango-La, It Refreshes" syrup bottle, glass label, square bottle, red and black letters on white, gold border, mint condition. *$300–$375*

E. Robinson's Sons Pilsener Beer serving tray, 12" high, 12" wide, lithographed by Chas. W. Shonk, ca. 1890, excellent condition. *$200–$300*

Enterprise Coconut tin (1 lb.), 6½" high, 3¼" wide, 3¼" deep, lithographed by Wm. Vogel & Bros., ca. 1900, excellent condition. *$275–$325*

Epicure Shredded Plug pocket tin, made by U.S. Tobacco Co., 4" high, 3" wide, 1" deep, lithographed by American Can Co., 50A, ca. 1910, fine condition. *$25–$35*

Eve Cube Cut Tobacco pocket tin, made by Globe Tobacco Co., 3½" high, 3" wide, 1" deep, lithographed by American Stopper Co., ca. 1895, fine condition. *$80–$100*

Fairbanks Fairy Soap calendar, lithographed on paper, lithographed by G. H. Buer & Co., copyright 1898, near mint condition. *$90–$120*

Fatima Cigarettes tray, 19" high, 19" wide, lithographer unknown, ca. 1920, excellent condition. *$550–$600*

Flour bags, 2, buckwheat, Yeager Milling and Evergreen. *$18–$30*

Fluffy Ruffles Starch tin, made by Independent Starch Co., 8½" high, 7¼" wide, 5" deep, pictures Victorian woman "Makes Ruffles Fluffy," lithographed by Amercian Can Co., 11A, ca. 1910, near mint condition. *$55–$70*

Franklin Coffee tin (3 lbs.), 9" high, 6" wide, 6" deep, lithographer unknown, ca. 1906, near mint condition. *$550–$600*

Giant Salted Peanuts tin (10 lb.), made by The Superior Peanut Co., 8¾″ high, 7¾″ wide, 7¾″ deep, lithographer unknown, ca. 1920, near mint condition. *$70–$90*

Glendora Coffee tin, 8″ high, 6⅝″ wide, 6⅝″ deep, lithographed by Wilkes Barre Can Co., ca. 1900, excellent condition. *$30–$50*

Glycerole Trunk tin, made by Restorff & Bettmann, 7″ high, 13″ wide, 9″ deep, lithographer unknown, ca. 1910, excellent condition. *$50–$70*

Golden Cupid Tobacco tin, made by P. Lorillard & Co., 6″ high, 6¼″ wide, 3¼″ deep, lithographed by Ginna & Co. (blue version), ca. 1882, excellent condition. *$100–$125*

Golden Cupid Tobacco tin, made by P. Lorillard & Co., 6″ high, 6¼″ wide, 3¼″ deep, lithographed by Ginna & Co. (orange version), ca. 1882, excellent condition. *$100–$130*

Good Cheer Cigar tin, 5¼″ high, 4″ wide, 6½″ deep (including handle), lithographed by American Can Co., 70-A, ca. 1920, near mint condition. *$30–$50*

Green Turtle Cigars lunch box, made by Gordon Cigar & Cheroot Co., 7¼″ high, 5¼″ wide, 4½″ deep, lithographer unknown, ca. 1915, excellent condition. *$100–$125*

Green Valley Rye serving tray, made by Casey Bros., 12″ high, 12″ wide, lithographer unknown, ca. 1915, excellent condition. *$190–$230*

Henderson's Wild Cherry "Beverage Free" pitcher, heavy embossing, scalloped top, 10″ high, ca. 1890s, near mint condition. *$275–$300*

Heyser's Oysters pail (1 gal.), 7½″ high, 6¾″ wide, 6¾″ deep, lithographed by American Can Co., 10A, ca. 1910, excellent condition. *$35–$50*

Honest Scrap Tobacco bin, lithographer unknown, ca. 1910, fine condition. *$300–$400*

Honeymoon Tobacco pocket tin, made by Penn Tobacco Co., 3″ high, 4½″ wide, 1″ deep, lithographer unknown, ca. 1900, excellent condition. *$45–$70*

Horlick's mirror, celluloid, 2¼″ high, 2½″ wide, brown rim/blue lettering, pictures maid with cow and product, lithographed by Whitehead & Hoad, ca. 1899, near mint condition. *$200–$240*

Horlick's mirror, celluloid, 2¼″ high, 2¼″ wide, white rim, "Ask for Horlicks," lithographed by Whitehead and Hoag, ca. 1899, near mint condition. *$30–$50*

Imperial Ice Cream Co. tray, 13½″ high, 13½″ wide, rare because it was made in Parkersburg, WV, and little or no advertising came from this area, lithographed by K & S Co., ca. 1913–19, near mint condition. *$600–$750*

Ivin's Big Show drum tin, with drumstick, 3¾″ high, 7″ wide, 7″ deep, lithographer unknown, ca. 1930, near mint condition. *$130–$150*

Jackie Coogan Kid Kandy candy pail (7 oz.), 3½″ high, 3¾″ wide, 3″ deep, ca. 1920s, near mint condition. *$130–$150*

Jackie Coogan Salted Nut Meats tin (10 lb.), made by The Kelly Co., 11″ high, 7¾″ wide, 7¾″ deep, ca. 1920s, excellent condition (top rough). *$800–$1,000*

Jackie Coogan Salted Peanuts glass jar, rare, made by The Kelly Co., translucent film label, 8½″ high, 8″ wide, 8″ deep, ca. 1920, near mint condition. *$300–$500*

Jersey-Creme serving tray, 12″ high, 12″ wide, lithographed by Chas. W. Shonk Co., ca. 1901, fine condition. *$250–$300*

Jewel of Virginia tin, square corners, made by Cameron & Cameron Co., 4″ high, 3″ wide, 2″ deep, lithographed by S. A. Illsey & Co., ca. 1890, near mint condition. *$10–$20*

Johnson's Dance Floor Wax tin, 7½″ high, 3½″ wide, 3½″ deep, lithographed by American Can Co., ca. 1910, near mint condition. *$25–$40*

Juicy Fruit match holder, 3⅜″ high, 4⅞″ wide, lithographed by The H. D. Beach Co., ca. 1920, near mint condition. *$90–$110*

Jumbo Dixie Salted Peanuts tin (10 lb.), made by The Kelly Peanut Co., 9¾″ high, 8¾″ wide, 8¾″ deep, lithographed by Wilkes Barre Can Co., ca. 1925, excellent condition. *$475–$525*

Jumbo Fine Cut Tobacco wooden pail, made by Marks and Clark, lithographed on paper, with lid and bale handle, 11″ high, 13″ wide, 13″ deep, lithographer unknown, ca. 1880, fine condition. *$250–$300*

Just Suits Cut Plug lunch box, made by Buchanan & Lyall, 7¾″ high, 4⅛″ wide, 5¼″ deep, lithographer unknown, ca. 1917, near mint condition. *$25–$40*

Kennebec Cigar tin, 2½″ high, 8½″ wide, 4″ deep, lithographed by American Can Co., 73A, ca. 1915, excellent condition. *$40–$80*

Kennedy's Champion Biscuit tin, made by National Biscuit Co., 8″ high, 4½″ wide, 4½″ deep, lithographer unknown, ca. 1885, fine condition. *$25–$35*

Kim-Bo Cut Plug Tobacco pocket tin, oval, made by Lovell & Buffington Tobacco Co., lithographed on paper, 6″ high, 1½″ wide, pictures belly dancer, lithographed by The Canster Co., ca. 1910, near mint condition. *$25–$40*

Kipling Tobacco, flat pocket, 4½″ high, 2¾″ wide, 1″ deep, lithographed by Hasker & Marcus Co., ca. 1895, excellent condition. *$40–$60*

Kipps Bay Brewing & Malting Co. serving tray, 13″ high, 13″ wide, lithographed by Kaufman & Strauss Co., ca. 1920, good condition. *$160–200*

Kling's Prost Beer serving tray, 12″ high, 12″ wide, lithographed by The H. D. Beach Co., ca. 1915, near mint condition. *$190–$210*

Knapsack Tobacco tin, square corners, 4½″ high, 3½″ wide, 1½″ deep, lithographed by Hasker & Marcuse Co., ca. 1895, good condition. *$10–$20*

Knock 'Em Dead Bed Bug Exterminator tin, 9½″ high, 3½″ wide, 3½″ deep, lithographed by Giles Cans, ca. 1907, near mint condition. *$70–$100*

Large lot plug-cut tobacco tags, made by Domino, Bob's, British Navy, Club, etc., lithographer unknown, ca. 1895, fine condition. *$50–$75*

Lime Fruit Tablets tin, missing lid, made by E. J. Hoadley, 7″ high, 5″ wide, 5″ deep, lithographed by Somers Bros., ca. 1890, good condition. *$45–$70*

Lime Kiln Smoking Tobacco tin, made by J. J. Bagley & Co., 5¼″ high, 5¼″ wide, 5¼″ deep (The only one known! More has been written about this tin by the T.C.C.A. over a period of a few years than any other. This also was the award-winning tin at the T.C.C.A. Canvention in 1985.); a superb black item with phenomenal graphics, lithographed by American Can Co., ca. 1913–19, excellent condition. *$12,000–$13,000*

Lipton Tea tin, 8¼″ high, 6″ wide, 5½″ deep, pictures native women picking, lithographer unknown, ca. 1900, excellent condition. *$35–$50*

Lovell & Kovel candy pails, 4, 3 Little Pigs, Peter Cottontail, Little Red Riding Hood, 2 missing lids, ca. 1920s, excellent condition.
$25–$40
$140–$165
$70–$90
$70–$90

Lucky Strike flat pocket tin, made by R. A. Patterson, 4½″ high, 2½″ wide, 1″ deep, lithographed by American Can Co., 50A, ca. 1910, near mint condition. *$35–$50*

Lucky Strike game cards and punchboard, lithographed on paper, 5½″ high, 4″ wide, lithographer unknown, ca. 1930, near mint condition. *$60–$100*

Lucky Strike "It's Toasted" tin, upright small canister, made by R. A. Patterson, lithographer unknown, ca. 1920, near mint condition. *$40–$60*

Lucky Strike Roll Cut small pocket tin, made by R. A. Patterson, 2½″ high, 3¼″ wide, ½″ deep, lithographer unknown, ca. 1910, excellent condition. *$80–$100*

Lucky Strike upright tin (1 lb.), made by R. A. Patterson, 4½″ high, 3¾″ wide, 3¼″ deep, lithographed by American Can Co., 50A, ca. 1910, near mint condition. *$60–$80*

Lutteds Log Cabin cough drop jar, all original, with 4 glass legs, heavily embossed, ca. 1895, near mint condition. *$600–$650*

Lyons Tea tin, horse race spinner version, 5½″ high, 3¾″ wide, 3¾″ deep, horses in steeplechase all around tin, lithographer unknown, ca. 1915, excellent condition. *$25–$40*

M. Schneck Butcher calendar, lithographed on paper, framed, under glass, 19½″ high, 15″ wide, lithographer unknown, pad dated 1928, near mint condition. *$275–$325*

Maltby's Coconut tin, lithographed on tin, 4¾″ high, 3″ wide, 3″ deep, lithographed by Ginna & Co., ca. 1900, near mint condition. *$25–$50*

Marshmallow tin, 3½″ high, 6½″ wide, 4″ deep, pictures hand with little pigs on fingers, lithographed by Somers Bros., ca. 1890, excellent condition. *$30–$50*

Maryland Club Mixture Tobacco pocket tin, made by Marburg Bros., 4″ high, 3½″ wide, 1¼″ deep, lithographer unknown, ca. 1910, fine condition. *$195–$225*

Courtesy of an anonymous collector; photo by Donald Vogt.

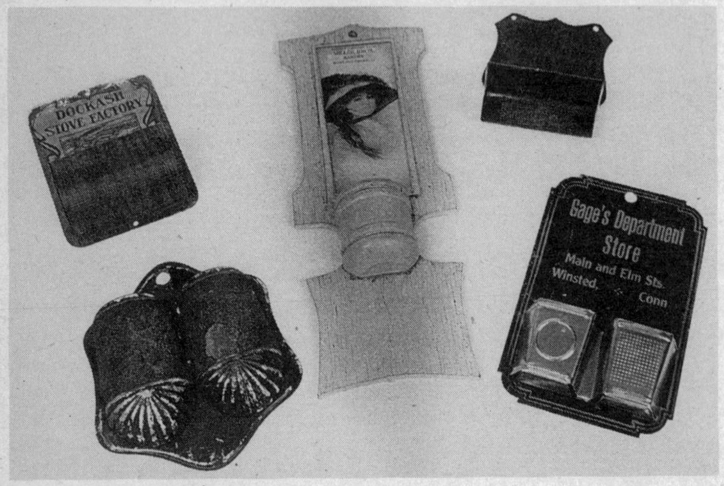

Match safes, assorted grouping (each). *$35–$55*

Mayo's Cut Plug "Storekeeper" Roly Poly, 7″ high, 6″ wide, 6″ deep, lithographed by Tindeco, ca. 1914, good condition. *$350–$390*

Mayo's Cut Plug "Inspector" Roly Poly, 7″ high, 6″ wide, 6″ deep, lithographed by Tindeco, ca. 1915, excellent condition. *$950–$1,100*

Mayo's Cut Plug "Dutchman" Roly Poly, 7″ high, 6″ wide, 6″ deep, lithographed by Tindeco, ca. 1915, excellent condition. *$400–$440*

Mayo's Cut Plug "Mammy" Roly Poly, 7″ high, 6″ wide, 6″ deep, lithographed by Tindeco, ca. 1915, fine condition. *$600–$645*

Mayo's Cut Plug "Singing Waiter" Roly Poly, 7″ high, 6″ wide, 6″ deep, lithographed by Tindeco, ca. 1915, excellent condition. *$575–$625*

Mayo's Cut Plug "Satisfied Customer" Roly Poly, 7″ high, 6″ wide, 6″ deep, lithographed by Tindeco, ca. 1915, good condition. *$350–$400*

McCormick Jersey Cream Sodas tin, "Patriotic Lunch Pail," 7¼″ high, 6½″ wide, 6½″ deep, lithographer unknown, ca. 1910, excellent condition. *$25–$35*

Miss Princine Baking Powder, made by Southern Mfg. Co., paper label cup with full contents, 3¼″ high, 3″ wide, 3″ deep, lithographer unknown, ca. 1916, near mint condition. *$160–$200*

Miss Princine Baking Powder, larger version, made by Southern Mfg. Co., paper label with full contents, 4″ high, 3¾″ wide, 3¾″ deep, lithographer unknown, ca. 1916, near mint condition. *$70–$100*

Mohawk Chief Tobacco tin, made by The Charles Co., York, PA, known as a 4″ × 6″ tobacco container, won the Best 4″ × 6″ Award at the 1985 Canvention, Allentown, PA. *$750–$800*

Monarch Teenie Weenie Peanut Butter tin (2 lb.), made by Reid, Murdoch & Co., 4½″ high, 4″ wide, 4″ deep, lithographed by American Can Co., 73A, ca. 1926, excellent condition. *$80–$100*

Morris Supreme Peanut Butter pail (1 lb.), 3¾″ high, 3¼″ wide, 3¼″ deep, lithographed by Continental Can Co., ca. 1925, excellent condition. *$150–$175*

Moses Cough Drops tin (1 lb.), made by E. J. Hoadley Co., 5½″ high, 3″ wide, 3″ deep, very unusual circular Green & Black variety, lithographed by Somers Bros., ca. 1893, fine condition. *$40–$60*

Moshier Bros. Gilt Edge Spices tin, 11″ high, 8″ wide, 7½″ deep, lithographed by S.A. Ilsley & Co., ca. 1885, fine condition. *$375–$400*

Mother Goose Baby Powder Talcum tin, oval, made by Baby Health Products, 6½″ high, 2½″ wide, 2½″ deep, ca. 1920, near mint condition. *$325–$375*

Murad Cigarettes pocket tin, small, made by P. Lorillard & Co., 3″ high, 4″ wide, 1″ deep, the Turkish cigarette pictures maiden reclining, lithographer unknown, ca. 1915, near mint condition. *$90–$110*

National Biscuit Co. tin, square green box with logo on all sides and top, lithographer unknown, ca. 1910, fine condition. *$50–$75*

National fire extinguisher, lithographed on tin, 21¾″ high, 2″ wide, 2″ deep, lithographed by American Can Co., 11A, ca. 1910, near mint condition. *$60–$75*

National Mazda Lamps countertop piece, ca. 1920s. *$650–$700*

Navy Tobacco lunch box tin, made by Gail & Ax Co., 4½″ high, 7″ wide, 4¼″ deep, lithographer unknown, ca. 1920, near mint condition. *$250–$300*

Nehi calendar, lithographed on paper, framed, under glass, 23½″ high, 12″ wide, lithographer unknown, pad dated 1927, fine condition. *$50–$70*

Niggerhair Tobacco pail, made by B. Leidersdorf Co., 6½″ high, 5¼″ wide, 5¼″ deep, lithographer unknown, ca. 1890, excellent condition. *$100–$125*

Nonesuch Peanut Butter pail (1 lb.), 3⅞″ high, 3½″ wide, 3½″ deep, depicts children playing with toys, ca. 1920, near mint condition. *$180–$220*

Northampton Baking Co. calendar, lithographed on cardboard, framed, under glass, 23″ high, 15″ wide, lithographer unknown, pad dated 1926, near mint condition. *$180–$230*

Oceanic Cut Plug tin, made by Scotten, Dillon Co., 3″ high, 6″ wide, 4″ deep, lithographed by American Can Co., 50A, ca. 1920, near mint condition. *$90–$110*

Oh Boy Peanut Butter pail (2 lb.), made by Stone-Ordean-Wells Co., 4½″ high, 4″ wide, 4″ deep, lithographed by American Can Co., 54A, ca. 1925, fine condition. *$130–$160*

Old Judson match holder, made by J. C. Stevens Co., 3⅜″ high, 4⅞″ wide, lithographed by Savage Manufacturing Co., ca. 1890, excellent condition. *$50–$70*

Old Seneca Stogies tin, made by W. H. Kildow, 5¾″ high, 4½″ wide, 4½″ deep, lithographer unknown, ca. 1910, fine condition. *$60–$80*

Ox-Heart Peanut Butter, 3¾″ high, 3″ wide, 3″ deep, ca. 1920s, near mint condition. *$45–$60*

Paperweight mirrors, 5, 3½″–4″ diameter, made by Saba Corporation, The O. J. Machine Co., American National Fire Insurance Co., C. F. Weber & Co., Ltd.; Louisiana Red Cypress, ca. 1920, excellent condition. *$40–60*

Pastime Plug Tobacco store tin, 4″ high, 12″ wide, 9¼″ deep, lithographed by Ginna & Co., ca. 1890, fine condition. *$70–$100*

Pepsi Cola serving tray, oval, 13⅓″ high, 11″ wide, lithographed by Chas. W. Shonk Co., ca. 1890, good condition. *$500–$700*

Pepsi Cola serving tray, oval, 13¼″ high, 10⅞″ wide, lithographed by Chas. W. Shonk Co., ca. 1895, fine condition. *$650–$800*

Petrolina Petroleum tin, made by Binghamton Oil Refining Co., 5½″ high, 3″ wide, pictures workers running from gushers, lithographed by American Can Co., 14, ca. 1915, excellent condition. *$35–$50*

Phoenix dry powder fire extinguisher, lithographed on tin, 15½″ high, 2″ wide, 2″ deep, picture of mythical bird in flames, lithographer unknown, ca. April 25, 1899, near mint condition. *$20–$30*

Phospho Brain & Nerve Food tin, made by A. B. Klar, 6¼″ high, 3½″ wide, "Outrageous X-Rated Tin," ca. 1920s, near mint condition. *$250–$300*

Planters Salted Peanuts tin (10 lb.), 9½″ high, 8½″ wide, 8½″ deep, lithographer unknown, ca. 1925, near mint condition. *$40–$60*

Players Navy Cut ashtray, 5¼″ high, 5¼″ wide, ceramic with litho of sailor "hero," lithographer unknown, ca. 1900, near mint condition. *$50–$75*

Possum Cigar tin, red, 5½″ high, 5¼″ wide, 5¼″ deep, pictures Possum "Am Good and Sweet," lithographed by Federal Tin Co., ca. 1910, excellent condition. *$60–$80*

Postmaster Smokers Cigar tin, 5½″ high, 5¼″ wide, 5¼″ deep, lithographer unknown, ca. 1910, excellent condition. *$90–$120*

Private Garden Growth Coffee tin, 8½″ high, 7″ wide, 6½″ deep, lithographer unknown, ca. 1909, excellent condition. *$225–$250*

Q-Boid Granulated Plug Tobacco pocket tin, oval, made by Larus & Bro., 4″ high, lithographed by American Can Co., 50A, ca. 1910, excellent condition. *$40–$60*

Quick Out fire extinguisher, made by Atlas Manufacturing Co., lithographed on tin, 21¾″ high, 2″ wide, 2″ deep, pictures maid reacting to kerosene lamp fire, lithographed by American Can Co., 11A, ca. 1910, near mint condition. *$35–$50*

Rabro Peanut Butter pail (14 oz.), 3¼″ high, 3½″ wide, 3½″ deep, lithographed by Continental Can Co., ca. 1925, fine condition. *$200–$250*

RCA Nipper dog, 15″ high, 6″ wide, 12″ deep, ca. 1920, excellent condition. *$180–$200*

Red Goose Shoes countertop display piece. *$45–$60*

Rip Van Winkle Biscuit tin, rare and early multicolored Ginna tin with scenes all around, additionally has full winter scene on bottom saying "A Merry Christmas and Happy New Year from Ginna & Co., N.Y.," 2¾″ high, 9⅝″ wide, 3¾″ deep, lithographed by Ginna & Co., ca. 1880, fine condition. *$40–$60*

Roller Mills Flour bag, made in Kutztown, PA, framed under glass with minor water staining (not on graphics), 15″ high, 8½″ wide, lithographer unknown, ca. 1890, excellent condition. *$25–$40*

Rolling pin, marked "Best Always McIntosh Flour," glass, ca. 1900. *$75–$95*

Rose Leaf Tobacco glass-lid tin, 3¼″ high, 8⅞″ wide, 8⅞″ deep, lithographed by Ginna & Co., ca. 1885, fine condition. *$25–$40*

Royal Dutch Coffee tin, made by Oppenheim & McEwan Co., Inc., 6¼″ high, 4″ wide, 4″ deep, lithographed by Continental Can Co., ca. 1910, excellent condition. *$50–$75*

Royal Dutch Tea tin, made by Oppenheim & McEwan Co., Inc., 3½″ high, 4½″ wide, 3½″ deep, lithographed by Continental Can Co., ca. 1910, excellent condition. *$25–$35*

Royal Peanut Butter mirror, celluloid, 2½″ high, 2½″ wide, lithographer unknown, ca. 1920, excellent condition. *$25–$40*

Royal Purple Lice Killer tin, made by W. A. Jenkins Mfg. Co., 9″ high, 5″ wide, 4½″ deep, paper label pictures fowl, lithographer unknown, ca. 1920, near mint condition. *$15–$30*

S. Hunter's Ambrosia syrup bottle, glass label, red letters on yellow-gold border, near mint condition. *$250–$325*

San Blas Coconut cup, made for Golden Crown by Croft & Allen, 3¼″ high, 5″ wide (including handle), 4″ deep, lithographed by Robert Porter & Sons, ca. 1895, excellent condition. *$140–$200*

Schepp's Coconut jar with coconut finial, 4½″ high, 7″ deep, ca. 1900, mint condition. *$250–$300*

Scott's Emulsion calendar, lithographed on cardboard, framed, under glass, 12″ high, 11″ wide, lithographed by Knapp & Co., pad intact and dated 1891, excellent condition. *$90–$120*

Scott's Emulsion calendar, lithographed on cardboard, 10⅜″ high, 7½″ wide, lithographer unknown, pad intact and dated 1888, excellent condition. *$50–$65*

Scott's Emulsion calendar, lithographed on cardboard, 10″ high, 9″ wide, lithographer unknown, pad intact and dated 1889, near mint condition. *$60–$80*

Scott's Emulsion calendar, lithographed on cardboard, 11″ high, 9″ wide, lithographed by Knapp Litho, pad intact and dated 1892, near mint condition. *$130–$170*

Seal Rock Cut Plug tin, made by H. Bohls & Co., 2″ high, 4¼″ wide, 3¼″ deep, lithographed by Pacific Sheet Metal Works, ca. 1900, excellent condition. *$50–$75*

Sensation Cut Plug lunch box, made by P. Lorillard & Co., 7¼″ high, 4½″ wide, lithographer unknown, ca. 1915, excellent condition. *$120–$160*

Sharples Separator calendar, lithographed on cardboard, framed, under glass, 22¾″ high, 13¼″ wide, lithographer unknown, pad dated January 1922, near mint condition. *$180–$200*

Sharples Separator calendar, lithographed on paper, framed, under glass, 23¼″ high, 13¼″ wide, lithographer unknown, pad dated January 1920, near mint condition. *$250–$300*

Slippery Elm Lozenges tin (5 lb.), made by Henry Thayer & Co., 7½″ high, 7″ wide, 4½″ deep, lithographed by Ginna & Co., ca. 1900, excellent condition. *$150–$190*

"Snag-Proof" Rubber Footwear calendar, lithographed on cardboard, 12″ high, 8″ wide, lithographed by Maryland Litho Co., pad dated 1906, near mint condition. *$170–$210*

Stadium Rink mirror, celluloid, 2¼″ high, 2¼″ wide, pictures Victorian woman skating, lithographer unknown, ca. 1895, near mint condition. *$110–$150*

Stroh's Bohemian Beer serving tray, 12″ high, 12″ wide, lithographed by Chas. W. Shonk Co., ca. 1910, near mint condition. *$210–$250*

Sunset Trail 5¢ Cigar tin, made by Roby Cigar Co., 5⅜″ high, 6⅛″ wide, 4⅛″ deep, lithographed by The Heekin Can Co., ca. 1910, excellent condition. *$120–$150*

Sweet Cuba Light Fine Cut bin (5 lb.), made by Spaulding & Merrick, 8″ high, 8″ wide, 9½″ deep, lithographer unknown, ca. 1915, near mint condition. *$180–$200*

Sweet Girl Peanut Butter pail (1 lb.), made by George Rasmussen Co., 3¾″ high, 3⅜″ wide, 3⅜″ deep, lithographed by American Can Co., 54A, ca. 1928, good condition. *$50–$75*

Tansey Root tins, 2, made by Chichester Chemical Co., 1½″ high, 2½″ wide, 1½″ deep, lithographed by Somers Bros., ca. 1907, near mint condition. *$25–$40*

The Hanks Guaranteed fire extinguisher, lithographed on tin, 22″ high, 2″ wide, 2″ deep, ca. 1900, excellent condition. *$25–$40*

The Hartford Fire Insurance Co. ruler, lithographed on tin, 9″ wide, lithographed by American Can Co., 69A, ca. 1900, excellent condition. *$20–$40*

The Motor Brand fire extinguisher, made by J. Wilson & Co., lithographed on tin, 21¾″ high, 2″ wide, 2″ deep, lithographer unknown, ca. 1910, good condition. *$30–$45*

The Nevermyss fire extinguisher, lithographed on tin, 21½″ high, 2″ wide, 2″ deep, lithographed by American Can Co., 11A, ca. 1910, good condition. *$25–$55*

The Phoenix fire extinguisher, larger version, lithographed on tin, 21¾″ high, 2″ wide, 2″ deep, lithographed by American Can Co., 11A, ca. 1910, near mint condition. *$20–$35*

Thc Royalty Chop Tea tin (½ lb.), made by Winslow, Rand, & Watson, 6¼″ high, 3″ wide, 3″ deep, lithographed by Ginna & Co., ca. 1895, excellent condition. *$45–$70*

The Three Noes match box enclosure, made by Diamond Match Co., lithographed on tin, 2″ high, 3″ wide, 1″ deep, lithographed by Norton Bros. Press, ca. 1900, near mint condition. *$35–$50*

Tiger Chewing Tobacco store tin, made by P. Lorillard & Co., 10½″ high, 9″ wide, 9″ deep, lithographer unknown, ca. 1898, excellent condition. *$140–$175*

Toyland Peanut Butter pail, 4″ high, 3″ wide, 3″ deep, ca. 1920s, excellent condition. *$250–$300*

Turkey Roasted Coffee tin (3 lb.), made by A. J. Kasper Co., 10½″ high, 5½″ wide, 5½″ deep, lithographed by American Can Co., ca. 1910, near mint condition. *$650–$700*

Tuxedo oval top tobacco tin, made by R. A. Patterson & Co., 6″ high, 4″ wide, 4½″ deep, lithographer unknown, ca. 1915, excellent condition. *$60–$90*

Twin Oaks Mixture tobacco pocket tin, made by American Tobacco Co., 4½″ high, 3½″ wide, 1″ deep, silver and red, heavily embossed, lithographer unknown, ca. 1915, near mint condition. *$25–$40*

Uniform Cut Plug tin, small top, made by Larus & Co., 6″ high, 5″ wide, 5″ deep, lithographed by American Can Co., ca. 1913–19, excellent condition. *$950–$1,000*

Union Leader Cut Plug tin, small top, made by American Tobacco Co., 6½″ high, 4¾″ wide, 4¾″ deep, lithographer unknown, ca. 1910, excellent condition. *$40–$60*

Union Leader Redi-Cut Tobacco pocket tin, 4⅜″ high, 3½″ wide, 1″ deep, picture of Uncle Sam smoking, lithographer unknown, ca. 1917. *$30–$50*

Van Heusen Shirt counter piece, 15″, ca. 1930s. *$195–$215*

W & S Cough Drops jar, larger version, heavily embossed lid and base, ca. 1895, mint condition. *$375–$400*

W & S Cough Drops jar, smaller version, same graphics/embossing, ca. 1895, mint condition. *$350–$425*

Walla Walla Pepsin Gum glass jar, more heavily embossed than others known, 13″ high, 4½″ wide, near mint condition. *$375–$425*

Walter Baker & Co. Cocoa tin, 4¾″ high, 5″ wide, 5″ deep, unusual bombé shape on 4 feet depicts sporting scenes of canoeists, skaters, bicycle riders, and tennis players, lithographed by Franz Euler & Co., ca. 1890, excellent condition. *$110–$180*

Williams' Root Beer Extract box, lithographed on paper (2 sides), 7½″ high, 9½″ wide, 5¼″ deep, lithographer unknown, ca. 1900, fine condition. *$300–$400*

Winner Cut Plug lunch box; made by J. Wright Co., 7¾″ high, 4⅛″ wide, 5″ deep, lithographer unknown, ca. 1917, excellent condition. *$90–$110*

Wm. Warner & Co.'s Licorice Lozenges tin, 6¾″ high, 6″ wide, 4″ deep, lithographed by Somers Bros., ca. 1900, near mint condition. *$275–$325*

Courtesy of Pumpkin Vine Line Antiques, Buddy and Atha Wallin, Fairfield, Ohio; photo by Donald Vogt.

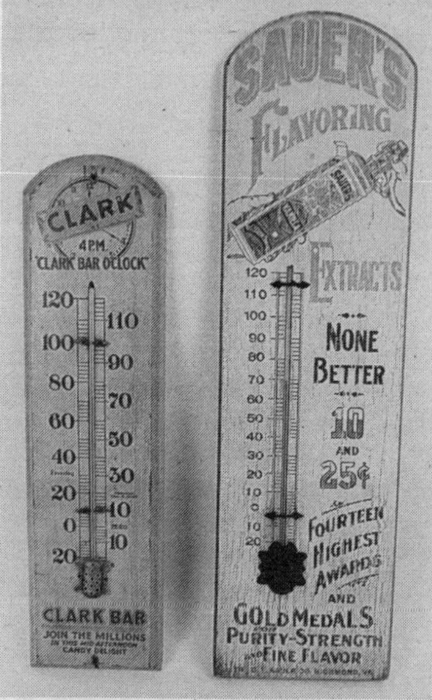

Wooden thermometers, Clark Bar clock, Dec. 17, 1920. *$250–$275*

Sauer's Flavoring, Richmond, VA, early 1900s. *$275–$325*

Yellow Kid Ginger Wafers tin, made by Brinkerhoff & Co., The N.Y. Biscuit Co., 92, 94, 96 Elizabeth St., N.Y., 14″ high, 10¾″ wide, 10½″ deep, lithographed by S. A. Illsley Co., ca. late 1890s, good condition. *$11,000–$13,000*

Yellow Kid label, rare, lithographed on paper, 7½″ high, 11″ wide, full color, same wording and figure as the Yellow Kid tin, ca. 1895, excellent condition. *$750–$950*

Zatek Chocolate Billets jar, spectacular jar with embossing and gold leafing, ca. 1910, near mint condition. *$700–$850*

Display

Adams California Fruit Chewing Gum display tin, made by American Chicle Co., 5¾″ high, 6½″ wide, 4¾″ deep, lithographed by H. D. Beach Co., ca. 1917, excellent condition. *$130–$170*

Adams Pepsin Tutti Frutti Gum display tin, made by American Chicle Co., 5¾″ high, 6½″ wide, 4¾″ deep, lithographed by H. D. Beach Co., ca. 1917, excellent condition. *$100–$150*

Adams Spearmint Gum display tin, made by American Chicle Co., 5¾″ high, 6½″ wide, 4¾″ deep, lithographed by H. D. Beach Co., ca. 1917, near mint condition. *$300–$400*

Almond Smash dispenser, only one known, no pump, ca. 1913–19, near mint condition, minor restoration to base. *$2,750–$3,300*

Apothecary chest, from Southwest, all pine, 8′ long, 14 drawers. *$1,350–$1,500*

Apothecary chest, with Sandwich glass star pulls that unscrew, original labels, drawers finely dovetailed, found in Saltzburg, PA, 38″ wide, 11″ deep, 31″ tall. *$1,500–$1,800*

Apothecary chest, New York, pine case, drawer fronts are walnut, square nails and dovetails, chamfered drawer fronts, iron pulls, 12″ deep, 67″ wide, 37″ tall. *$1,800–$2,200*

Courtesy of Country Cottage Antiques; photo by Donald Vogt.

Apothecary heating pot (for medication), cast iron, lined with porcelain, 19th century, 19″ × 14″. *$85–$115*

Apothecary jar, blown glass, in ruby, 18″ high, no cover, ca. 19th century. *$150–$250*

Bakery cabinet, restaurant or grocery store cabinet, made of slate, walnut door, brass handle, screen is meshed tin, ca. 1900s, with various pie tins, yellowware pie plate, price is for cabinet only. *$235–$275*

Bins, used for flour, rice, and sugar, 19th century, made in Pennsylvania, pine with porcelain knobs held on by square nails. *$775–$875*

Bower & Bartlett's Boston Coffees bin, "Blue Ribbon Brand," 19″ high, 17″ wide, 15½″ deep, ca. 1906, fine condition. *$275–$325*

Buckeye Root Beer dispenser, made by Cleveland Fruit Juice Co., pump is a Cleveland Buckeye pump, not original, ca. 1913–19, near mint condition. *$1,600–$1,800*

Buckeye Root Beer dispenser, with centaurs, original pump, ca. 1913–19, mint condition. *$2,750–$3,000*

Cardinal Cherry dispenser, made by Hungerford Smith Co., original pump, ca. 1913–19, mint condition. *$1,800–$2,000*

Ceresota Flour match safe, 5½″ high, 2½″ wide, 1¼″ deep, lithographer unknown, ca. 1910, near mint condition. *$180–$210*

Chero Crush dispenser, cherry form embossed, no pump, ca. 1913–19, near mint condition. *$3,500–$3,800*

Cherry Fizz dispenser, "Drink Crawford's Cherry Fizz, It's Jake-A-Loo," original pump, one of two known, ca. 1913–19, near mint condition. *$4,000–$4,250*

Cherry Smash ruby glass dispenser, screened cherry smash logo on ruby glass with chromed lid and base, ca. 1920, near mint condition. *$700–$800*

Chew Yucatan Gum display tin, made by American Chicle Co., 5¾″ high, 6½″ wide, 4¾″ deep, lithographed by H. D. Beach Co., ca. 1917, fine condition. *$140–$180*

Chico's Spanish Peanuts glass jar, made by Curtiss Co., all original down to the intact decals, 2-part jar and display holder, ca. 1915, near mint condition. *$300–$325*

Coca-Cola Pepsin Gum glass jar, embossed letters "Coca-Cola" on lid, 11″ high, 4½″ wide, 4″ deep, near mint condition. *$1,000–$1,200*

Coffee grinder, Lane Brothers, No. 12, red and blue paint with gilt piping, 14″ high, American, 19th century. *$264–$300*

Coffee grinder, wood and iron, single drawer, 7½″ × 7½″ × 8″. *$70–$90*

Coffee grinder, cast iron, made by Enterprise Manufacturing Company, Philadelphia, U.S.A., original paint with remains of original stencil decoration, 63″ high, fly wheels' diameter 36″, central rod that supports wheels needs replacing, cover missing, late 19th century. *$413–$600*

Country store counter, golden oak with wainscoting, fancy supports, 16′ long, 36″ high, 28″ deep. *$200–$250*

Country store shoe stands, 2, with 2 pairs of old shoes—one child's, one adult male's, heavy black metal embossing, ca. 1890s, near mint condition. *$130–$160*

Dairymaid Cream Caramel Toffee glass container, made by W & T Priestley, paper label, 12″ high, 6½″ wide, lithographed by Alf. Cocke Ltd., ca. 1910, near mint condition. *$35–$50*

Diamond Dye "Mansion" cabinet, made by Wells & Richardson Co., lithographed on tin, 24″ high, 15″ wide, 8½″ deep, lithographed by American Art Works, ca. 1905, fine condition. *$1,000–$1,200*

Diamond Dye "Maypole" cabinet, made by Wells & Richardson Co., lithographed on tin, 30″ high, 21″ wide, 10″ deep, lithographed by The Meek Co., dated 1904, fine condition. *$550–$700*

Courtesy of Pumpkin Vine Line Antiques, Buddy and Atha Wallin, Fairfield, Ohio; photo by Donald Vogt.

Diamond Dyes cabinet with great colors, 30″ high, 22½″ wide, 10″ deep, mint condition, ca. 1895–1910. *$2,000–$2,500*

Drawer unit, pine, molded top above 8 drawers in stacks of 4, grain painted and line decoration, brass bails, found in a Portsmouth, NH, house, 3′4″ high, 8′7″ long, some brass bails missing. *$275–$600*

Courtesy of Cary Station Antiques; photo by Donald Vogt.

Four-sided parking sign, red background with white letters, 51″ tall, 7″ wide, ca. 1940s. *$95–$125*

Courtesy of Alan A. Maciag; photo by Donald Vogt.

Gold Bond pickles jar, ca. 1915, new cover. *$48–$55*

Golden Rule coffee grinder, made for Citizen's Wholesale Coffee Co., embossed metal with wooden base, ca. 1900, near mint condition. *$180–$220*

Grapefruitola dispenser, ca. 1913–19, mint condition, but rim under pump has chip (easily restored). *$2,850–$3,250*

Heinz Vinegar glass dispenser, 2 parts, used in country stores, hard-to-find acid-etched glass, 18″ high, 7½″ wide, ca. 1895, near mint condition. *$120–$140*

Hersey's Pan-Dandy Bread broom holder, lithographed on tin (2 sides), 33″ high, 20″ wide, 14″ deep, lithographed by Baltimore Sign Co., ca. 1920, fine condition. *$80–$100*

Hickman's Silver Birch Chewing Gum display box, lithographed on paper, 6½″ high, 1½″ wide, 20 full packs/never opened, mint in display box, pictures birds singing in birch tree, "Taste with a Tang," lithographer unknown, ca. 1927, mint condition. *$150–$175*

Courtesy of the Keeping Room, Camby, Indiana; photo by Donald Vogt.

Hiram Sibley & Co. seed box. *$125–$150*

Home Tacks display box, with 12 boxes for tacks, made by Atlas Tack Corp., lithographed on cardboard, 2″ high, 9¾″ wide, 7⅞″ deep, lithographed by Lindner Eddy & Clauss, ca. 1915, excellent condition. *$150–$200*

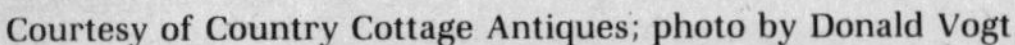
Courtesy of Country Cottage Antiques; photo by Donald Vogt.

Humidor for drugstore, 12″ deep, 10″ wide, 13½″ tall, ca. 1880s, mahogany, porcelain liner, zinc tray, brass fittings, from Buffalo, NY. *$275–$350*

Indian Rock Ginger Ale dispenser, one of three known, pump may not be original, ca. 1913–19, near mint condition. *$3,600–$4,000*

J. S. Ivin's Sons Steam Bakery wooden display box, paper label outside and in, 22″ high, 9″ wide, 14″ deep, lithographer unknown, ca. 1895, excellent condition. *$35–$50*

Kis-Me Gum jar, embossed, 13″ high, 6½″ wide, ca. 1900, near mint condition. *$45–$60*

Courtesy of Dee Wilhelm, Grand Blanc, Michigan; photo by Donald Vogt.

Multidrawer cabinet, early 1900s, used in a hardware or watch-maker's store. *\$425–\$475*

Oak display case, gallery top, sliding wooden back doors, 36″ high, 31″ wide, 18″ deep, ca. 1900, excellent condition. *\$275–\$325*

Oak tobacco humidor display case, 51″ wide, 7′ high, 12″ deep, metal-lined compartments with original hardware. *\$200–\$225*

Orange Punch dispenser, "Drink Cannons Orange Punch 5¢," only one known, ca. 1913–15, excellent condition. *\$2,000–\$2,250*

P. Lorillard & Co. Tobacco cabinet, inlaid wood, etched glass doors and original key, with base, 5′8″ high, 2′11″ wide, 1′7½″ deep, ca. 1880, near mint condition. *\$3,000–\$3,250*

Pickaninny upright tobacco box, lithograph on paper, 4½″ high, 3½″ wide, lithographer unknown, ca. 1900, excellent condition. *\$425–\$600*

Planters Pennant Peanut jar, peanut finial top, small rim chips on inside lid, ca. 1920, near mint condition. *\$70–\$90*

Courtesy of Cary Station Antiques; photo by Donald Vogt.

Postcard display unit, embossed tin, ca. 1880–90. *$1,200–$1,500*

Putnam Dye box, lithographed on tin, full of original dyes, 19″ high, 15″ wide, 8″ deep, lithographer unknown, ca. 1910, near mint condition. *$600–$650*

Reliable Egg carrier, wood, original paint, 12″ high, 12″ wide, 13″ deep, lithographer unknown, ca. 1897, excellent condition. *$30–$40*

Roger's Silver display, lithographed on cardboard, die cut, 36″ high, 18″ wide, lithographed by American Lithographic Co., copyright 1910, fine condition. *$120–$150*

Sack holder, wooden, stenciling on walnut, numbered for sacks, bought in Pennsylvania, ca. 1880–1910. *$275–$375*

Scale, hand-forged iron with copper trays, 22½″ high, arm is approximately 18″, ca. 1860s. *$350–$400*

Schepp's Coconut Cake box, spectacular early Illsey lithography, 11″ high, 13″ wide, 9″ deep, ca. 1895, near mint condition. *$110–$170*

Courtesy of Alan A. Maciag; photo by Donald Vogt.

Seed box, D. M. Ferry & Co.'s Standard Seeds. *$85–$115*

Seed box, Rice's Genuine Garden Seeds, great color. *$130–$150*

Sen-Sen display stands, 2, made by American Chicle Co., lithographed on tin, die-cut, 6¼″ high, 4″ wide, lithographed by American Art Sign Co., American Can Co., ca. 1925, fine condition. *$200–$250*

Shac for Headache glass jar, glass label, depicts man with bandaged head, 6¼″ high, 4″ wide, 4″ deep, near mint condition. *$525–$560*

Snow King Baking Powder bag holder, lithographed on tin (2 sides), 6½″ high, 12″ wide, lithographer unknown, ca. 1915, excellent condition. *$1,300–$1,500*

Courtesy of Cary Station Antiques; photo by Donald Vogt.

Spice cabinet, 54″ long, 37″ tall, 11″ deep, original mirrors and labels, oak with beaded trim. *$2,500–$2,800*

Spool chest, 6 drawers, walnut, Clark's, ruby red glass, original pulls, 1870–1910. *$1,475–$1,625*

Squirrel Brand jar, made by The Kelly Co., embossed with squirrel logo, 15″ tall, Cleveland, OH, ca. 1910, near mint condition. *$60–$80*

Sweet Cuba Tobacco store tin, 10½″ high, 8½″ wide, 8½″ deep, lithographer unknown, ca. 1895, excellent condition. *$25–$40*

"The Silver" Brand Collar case, glass and oak with original collars intact, screened emblem on glass, 25½″ high, 13″ wide, 7″ deep, ca. 1898, near mint condition. *$475–$510*

Turkish dye cabinet, front lithographed on paper, cabinet filled with boxes of original dye, 24″ high, 15″ wide, 6″ deep, lithographer unknown, ca. 1910, excellent condition. *$225–$350*

Uneeda Baker's jar, made by National Biscuit, embossed with paper label, round, with front opening, ca. 1910, excellent condition. *$50–$70*

W.D.C. Pipe display, lithographed on tin, die-cut, holding 4 pipes, 13½″ high, 9½″ wide, lithographer unknown, ca. 1915, excellent condition. *$140–$200*

Ward's Orange Crush dispenser, rare because wider circumference and height than usual, one of a few known, original pump, ca. 1913–19, mint condition. *$1,900–$2,100*

Courtesy of Louisville Antique Mall, Louisville, Kentucky; photo by Donald Vogt.

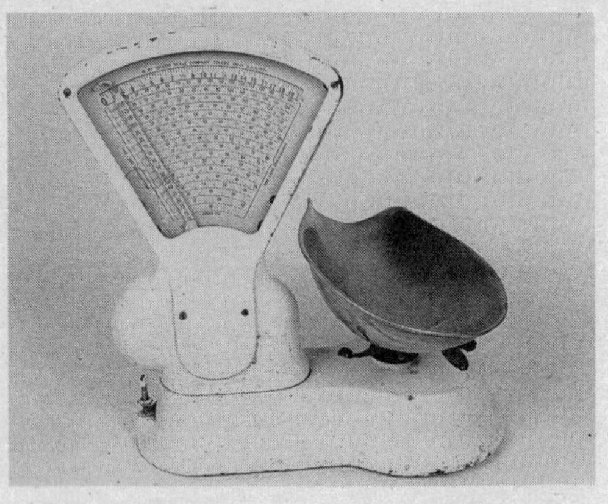

White iron candy scale. *$65–$85*

Wooden mortar and pestle. *$85–$100*

Woods Spices display case, etched front glass/nickel plated over brass with 3 glass shelves, 3½′ high, 2′ wide, ca. 1900, near mint condition. *$500–$600*

Zeno Gum display case, oak, small, slant-front style with "Zeno" embossed on wooden flag, ca. 1900, near mint condition. *$250–$350*

Miscellaneous

Blackwell's Durham Smoking Tobacco game board, lithographed on cardboard, framed flat between glass, 15½″ high, 22¼″ wide, lithographed by The Calvert Lithographing Co., ca. 1901, fine condition. *$160–$200*

Brass National cash register, rare model #311, with original drawer and keys, 17″ wide, 10″ high, 16″ deep, ca. 1900, mint condition. *$375–$425*

Country paper holder with original rolls, 2 parts, embossed, with wooden base, 3½″ long, ca. 1900, excellent condition. *$60–$80*

Country store lamp, all original down to the blue patina on shade, ca. 1890, near mint condition. *$180–$210*

Country store mannequin of little girl, dressed in original Victorian clothing, 3′ tall on metal base, ca. 1920s, near mint condition. *$375–$425*

Country store spindle-back stool, 30″, Windsor style, turn of the century. *$110–$170*

Gypsy Fortune Teller 5¢ coin-op machine, 15½″ high, 11″ wide, 8¾″ deep, ca. 1890, excellent condition. *$250–$300*

Courtesy of Pumpkin Vine Line Antiques, Buddy and Atha Wallin, Fairfield, Ohio; photo by Donald Vogt.

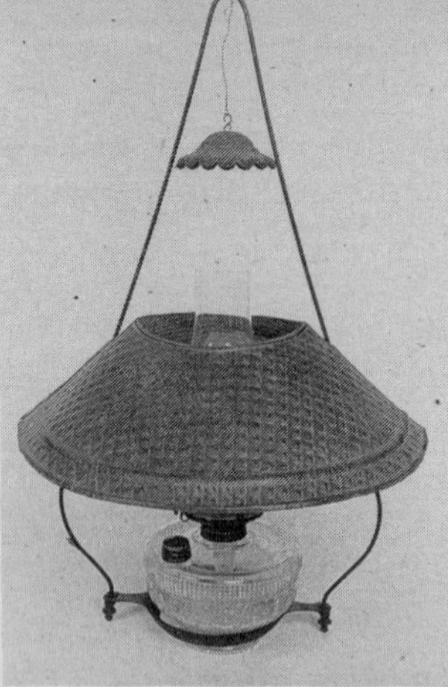

Hanging lamp, ca. 1880, 23″. *$275–$350*

Courtesy of Pumpkin Vine Line Antiques, Buddy and Atha Wallin, Fairfield, Ohio; photo by Donald Vogt.

Hanging lamp, Bradley and Hubbard, 1893, tin waffle shade, all original, 35″ from tip of hanger. *$450–$500*

Lincoln's Log Cabin game, lithographed on tin with original box, 11¼″ high, 11¼″ wide, lithographed by W. H. Davidheiser, copyright 1924, near mint condition. *$40–$60*

Lutteds Cough Drops mat, rare, lithography on heavy board, pictures 4-color log cabin winter scene, a must go-with for Lutteds glass jar, 6″ high, 12″ wide, lithographer unknown, ca. 1900, near mint condition. *$200–$240*

National Biscuit Company salesman's "Premiere Samples" case, embossed "National Biscuit Company" 4 sides, silver clasp and handle, 12″ high, 4¾″ wide, 9¼″ deep, lithographer unknown, ca. 1899, near mint condition. *$45–$60*

One-drawer tavern table, pine, nice old brown finish, cylindrical tapered legs, top measures 37″ × 21½″, 26″ high. *$385–$500*

Piedmont chair, "The Cigarette of Quality," 2-sided, heavy porcelain on sign, screened all over chair, ca. 1910, near mint condition. *$90–$110*

Planters "Mr. Peanut" books and punchboard, 2, lithographed on paper, lithographer unknown, ca. 1940–1950s, near mint condition. *$30–$60*

Pushcart, by Fairbanks, with hard rubber tires, painted blue, 37″ high, 56″ long, 30″ wide, 19th century. *$220–$300*

Rare country store fly chaser, all original, heavy embossed base with key (also works on mosquitoes!), ca. 1890, near mint condition. *$350–$400*

Receptionist's or cashier's counter, pine, grained, painted decoration with stenciled cross quills on front, 2 drawers and 1 cabinet in rear, 36½″ high, 52″ wide, 28″ deep, American, 19th century. *$495–$700*

Sauer's Flavoring Extracts clock, made by Gilbert, 36″ high, 16″ wide, gold leafing and enamel on glass door, works perfectly, ca. 1900, excellent condition. *$500–$525*

Sauer's Flavoring Extracts wall clock, made by New Haven Clock Co., 42″ high, 17″ wide, 5″ deep, ca. 1915, near mint condition. *$750–$850*

Scale, wood-cased, opium, in brass and ivory. *$30–$75*

Set of 4 soda fountain chairs with table, oak and wire copper plated over steel, ca. 1920, excellent condition. *$170–$200*

Todds Tonic glasses, 2 (possibly soda fountain items), embossed with emblem "Best Tonic in the World," 3¼" high, ca. 1910, mint condition. *$40–$60*

SIGNS

"A Watermelon Frolic" muslin. *$750–$850*

Courtesy of Cary Station Antiques, photo by Donald Vogt.

Acorn Stoves and Ranges, three-dimensional, 42" heavy tin, green, gold, black, and red. *$2,500–$2,800*

Adams Pepsin Tutti-Frutti, hanging poster, original brass top and bottom strips with brass ring at top for hanging, lithographed on paper, under glass, 25½" high, 14" wide, framed, ca. 1900, near mint condition. *$2,500–$2,800*

Courtesy of Cary Station Antiques, photo by Donald Vogt.

AG School Shop, horseshoeing, ca. mid-1800s, 41″ tall. *$5,400–$6,000*

Anthony's Universal Baking Powder, lithographed on tin, framed, 23½″ high, 17½″ wide, lithographed by F. Tuchfarber & Co., ca. 1885, fine condition. *$950–$1,000*

Armour's Corn Flakes, lithographed on tin, self-framed, 13″ high, 18½″ wide, lithographer unknown, ca. 1920, near mint condition. *$425–$600*

B.T. Babbitts Best Soap, "Pet of the Household," lithographed on paper, framed, under glass, 31⅝″ high, 17½″ wide, lithographed by Donaldson Bros., ca. 1897, excellent condition. *$425–$525*

Babbitts Best Soap, "In Doubt," lithographed on paper, framed, under glass, 33¾″ high, 19½″ wide, lithographed by Donaldson Brothers, ca. 1893. *$60–$80*

Babbitts Soap, "Easter Beauties," lithographed on paper, framed, under glass, 30¾″ high, 16½″ wide, lithographed by American Litho Co., ca. 1898, excellent condition. *$45–$60*

Babbitts Soap, "Greetings of Spring," lithographed on paper, framed, under glass, 30¾″ high, 16½″ wide, lithographed by The Knapp Co., ca. 1893, excellent condition. *$50–$70*

Baker's Breakfast Cocoa, lithographed on tin, framed, 20″ high, 13″ wide, lithographed by Standard Advertising Co., ca. 1901, excellent condition. *$2,250–$2,400*

Boot, late 19th century, painted tin. *$95–$125*

Boot, wooden, three-dimensional, mid–late 1800s, 31″ tall. *$2,200–$2,500*

Boston Rubber Shoe Co., lithographed on paper, framed, under glass, 17¾″ high, 23¾″ wide, lithographer unknown, ca. 1890, near mint condition. *$60–$80*

Brotherhood Tobacco, lithographed on cardboard, framed, under glass, 27″ high, 19½″ wide, lithographer unknown, ca. 1885, fair condition. *$160–$200*

Bull Durham Tobacco, lithographed on cardboard, framed, under glass, 23″ high, 35″ wide, lithographer unknown, copyright 1909, fine condition. *\$550–\$700*

Burma Shave, rare set of 6 original, "Tempted to Try It?," "Follow Your Hunch," "Be Top Banana," "Not One of the Bunch," "Burma Shave," white letters on red background, each measures 17″ × 40″ × ¾″. *\$165–\$300*

Cherry Smash, lithographed on cardboard, die-cut, framed, museum mounted and matted, under glass, 29½″ high, 22½″ wide, lithographed by Waggman Litho, ca. 1895, near mint condition. *\$375–\$425*

"Clapp & Bailey's Remnants" for country store, sewing accessories department, ca. 1800–1910. *\$475–\$550*

Clark's Mile-End Spool Cotton, lithographed on paper, framed, under glass, 18½″ high, 13½″ wide, lithographer unknown, ca. 1900, fine condition. *\$100–\$130*

Copco Soap, lithographed on paper, framed, matted, under glass, 26½″ high, 30″ wide, lithographer unknown, ca. 1894, near mint condition. *\$180–\$225*

Dr. G.G. Green German Syrup, in original gesso frame, lithographed on canvas, original backing, 26½″ high, 32½″ wide, ca. 1895, excellent condition. *\$750–\$850*

Courtesy of Cary Station Antiques; photo by Donald Vogt.

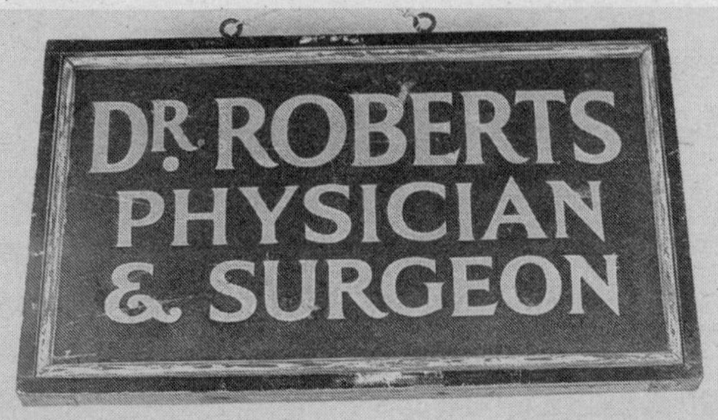

Dr. Roberts Physician & Surgeon, ca. late 1800s, 19″ tall. *\$200–\$250*

Drink Hires, celluloid, 9¾″ high, 6½″ wide, lithographed by Permanent Advertising Co., ca. 1920, fine condition. *$225–$275*

Druggist's, rare, wooden, in the shape of a half a mortar, 20″ high, 30″ wide, 15″ deep. *$400–$600*

Dutchess Manufacturing Co., lithographed on tin, original engraved frame, 24½″ high, 34¼″ wide, lithographer unknown, ca. 1895, fine condition. *$180–$225*

Edison Mazda Lamps (Maxfield Parrish), framed, matted, under glass, 23″ high, 20″ wide, lithographer unknown, copyright 1924, near mint condition. *$300–$325*

Enjoy Hires, lithographed on tin, embossed, framed, 10⅞″ high, 28⅞″ wide, lithographer unknown, ca. 1925, fine conditon. *$300–$400*

Courtesy of Cary Station Antiques; photo by Donald Vogt.

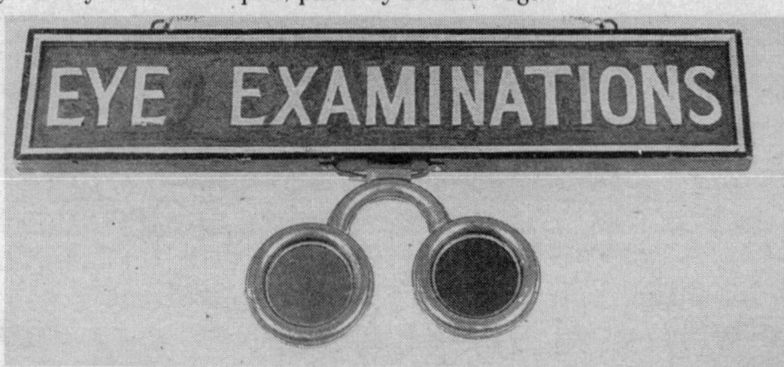

Eye Examinations, 16″, blue and red glass in eyeglass lenses, ca. late 1800s. *$895–$1,000*

Fairchild's Flour tin, hanging sign, 2-sided with inner spinning circle, one side very rough on bottom, 14″ deep, lithographer unknown, ca. 1910, good condition. *$25–$40*

5¢ Coca-Cola, lithographed on paper, framed, matted, under glass, lithographed by Wolf & Co., ca. 1905, near mint condition. *$100–$150*

Fleishmann & Co., lithographed on paper, framed, museum-mounted, under glass, 18¾″ high, 29″ wide, lithographed by American Litho Co., ca. 1902, excellent condition. *$120–$180*

Graham Crackers trolley car sign, made by National Biscuit Co., lithographed on paper, framed, museum-mounted, under glass, 26½″ high, 6½″ wide, lithographer unknown, ca. 1917, near mint condition. *$110–$140*

Courtesy of Pumpkin Vine Line Antiques, Buddy and Atha Wallin, Fairfield, Ohio; photo by Donald Vogt.

Grape Nuts, lithograph on tin, 29″ × 20″, great color, ca. 1900. *$400–$500*

Group of signs for automotive products, ca. 1920s, ISO-VIS Motor Oil signs (each). *$50–$65*

Valspar Varnish (each). *$60–$75*

Handy Package Dyes, lithographed on paper, framed, 14¼″ high, 18½″ wide, possibly lithographed by Syracuse Litho Co., ca. 1910, near mint condition. *$90–$125*

Happy Thought Plug Tobacco, made by Wilson-McCallay Tobacco Co., lithographed on cardboard, framed, under glass, 25⅝″ high, 17¾″ wide, lithographed by Orcutt Litho Co., ca. 1895, excellent condition. *$500–$600*

Courtesy of Cary Station Antiques; photo by Donald Vogt.

Hat and glove maker, ca. late 1800s, 48″ tall. *$3,000–$3,400*

Henderson's Lawn Grass Seed, lithographed on paper, framed, under glass, 20″ high, 16″ wide, pictures Victorian family on estate, lithographed by Lindner Eddy & Clauss Co., ca. 1887, excellent condition. *$225–$275*

Hires, lithographed on paper, framed, under glass, 7½″ high, 12½″ wide, lithographer unknown, copyright 1914, excellent condition. *$500–$750*

Hires, embossed hanging sign, lithographed on paper, framed, under glass, 5⅞″ high, 12⅝″ wide, lithographer unknown, ca. 1895, excellent condition. *$250–$300*

Hires, celluloid, 10″ high, 7″ wide, lithographer unknown, ca. 1920, fair condition. *$160–$200*

Hires, lithographed on tin, 9¼″ high, 6½″ wide, lithographed by Passaic Metal Ware Co., ca. 1920, fine condition. *$110–$160*

Courtesy of Cary Station Antiques; photo by Donald Vogt.

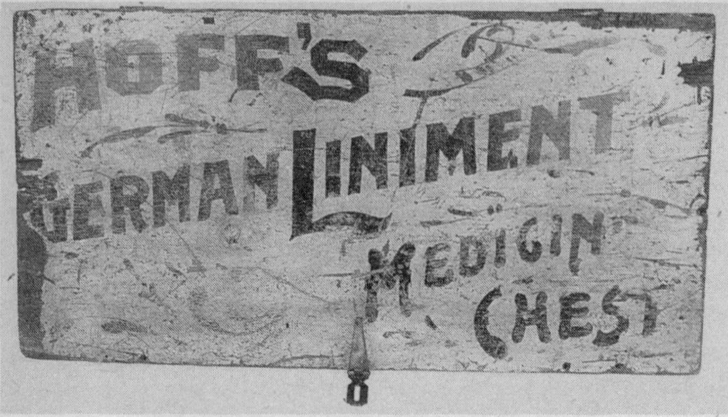

Hoff's German Liniment medicine chest, from wagon that traveled from town to town, mustard background with black letters, 39″ × 19½″, 1870–80. *$350–$450*

Honest Scrap, lithographed on paper, embossed frame, 30⅛″ high, 22½″ wide, lithographer unknown, ca. 1899, excellent condition. *$850–$1,000*

Indianapolis Brewing Co., lithographed on tin, self-framed, outstanding color, 37½″ high, 25½″ wide, lithographed by H. D. Beach, ca. 1905, near mint condition. *$3,000–$3,500*

Ivory Soap, made by Proctor & Gamble Co., lithographed on cardboard, original embossed frame, 33½″ high, 26″ wide, lithographer unknown, dated 1904, fine condition. *$325–$400*

Jose Vila Habana Cigar, concave, made by Berriman Bros., lithographed on tin, 17½″ high, 17½″ wide, lithographed by Chas. W. Shonk, ca. 1905, excellent condition. *$120–$150*

Kellogg's Corn Flakes, lithographed on cardboard, framed, under glass, 23″ high, 18″ wide, lithographer unknown, ca. 1915, near mint condition. *$650–$800*

Kodak Verichrome Film, hanging tin sign, ca. 1940s. *$350–$500*

Korbel Sec California Champagne, lithographed on tin, self-framed, 13″ high, 18¼″ wide, lithographed by The American Art Works, ca. 1910, excellent condition. *$180–$200*

Lot of 3 "Paper Fireworks for Sale" signs, approx. 18″ high, 52″ wide, lithographer unknown, ca. 1925, near mint condition. *$100–$125*

Mail Pouch Tobacco, a real American, made by Bloch Bros. Tobacco Co., thin cardboard litho under glass, every color of the rainbow, extremely rare, meant for hanging, 14½″ high, 19½″ wide, ca. 1905, near mint condition. *$1,600–$1,800*

Courtesy of Cary Station Antiques; photo by Donald Vogt.

Malted milk, 43″ high, 23½″ wide, white and gray with gold lettering, ca. 1920s–1930s. *$450–$500*

Mandeville & King Co. Seeds, lithographed on paper, framed, under glass, 28″ high, 20½″ wide, lithographer unknown, ca. 1920, excellent condition. *$130–$160*

Montgomery-Frost-Lloyd's Co., originally on Washington St., Boston, next to Old South Meeting House, hand-painted cast iron, gold-leafed letters and frame, 20″ high, 5′ wide, 2′ deep, lithographer unknown, ca. 1910, excellent condition. *$1,100–$1,300*

Nehi, lithographed on cardboard, framed, under glass, 22½″ high, 14¾″ wide, lithographer unknown, ca. 1920, excellent condition. *$200–$300*

Nehi, lithographed on cardboard, framed, under glass, 14½″ high, 22″ wide, lithographer unknown, ca. 1920, excellent condition. *$150–$200*

O.K. Pepsin Gum, 1¢, lithographed on tin, embossed, framed, 4¼″ high, 20¼″ wide, lithographer unknown, ca. 1906, fine condition. *$180–$210*

P.E. Paine, Dentist, two-sided, hanging, ca. 1880, original paint. *$150–$175*

Pabst Famous Blue Ribbon Winners, made by The Wilbur Stock Food Co., lithographed on paper, framed, under glass, 14″ high, 30″ wide, lithographed by Northwestern Litho, ca. 1905, near mint condition. *$70–$100*

Paycar Scrap, lithographed on cardboard, framed, under glass, 22½″ high, 27½″ wide, lithographer unknown, ca. 1915, fine condition. *$35–$50*

Pepsi Cola, lithographed on cardboard, die-cut, mounted on blue mat, framed, under glass, 21″ high, 25″ wide, lithographer unknown, ca. 1930, near mint condition. *$190–$225*

Pope Chainless Bicycle, lithographed on paper, framed, museum-mounted, under glass, 25½″ high, 31″ wide, lithographed by American Litho Co., ca. 1904, excellent condition. *$550–$700*

Robert Smith Ale Brewing Co., convex, lithographed on tin, framed, 19½″ high, 23½″ wide, lithographer unknown, ca. 1900, excellent condition. *$400–$500*

Roosevelt 5¢ Cigar, tin, made by D. B. Long & Co., highly embossed with numerous colors, 19½″ high, 13½″ wide, made prior to his presidency at the turn of the century, only two known, they were found together, one in unrestorable condition, extremely rare and a spectacular sign, lithographed by Standard Adv. Co., near mint condition. *$4,250–$4,500*

Santovin, made by Stephen Pettifer & Sons, lithographed on tin, self-framed, 20¼″ high, 27″ wide, lithographer unknown, ca. 1920, excellent condition. *$200–$225*

Schlitz, lithographed on tin, framed, 20″ high, 25¾″ wide, lithographed by Chas. W. Shonk, ca. 1910, excellent condition. *$400–$500*

Courtesy of Pumpkin Vine Line Antiques, Buddy and Atha Wallin, Fairfield, Ohio; photo by Donald Vogt.

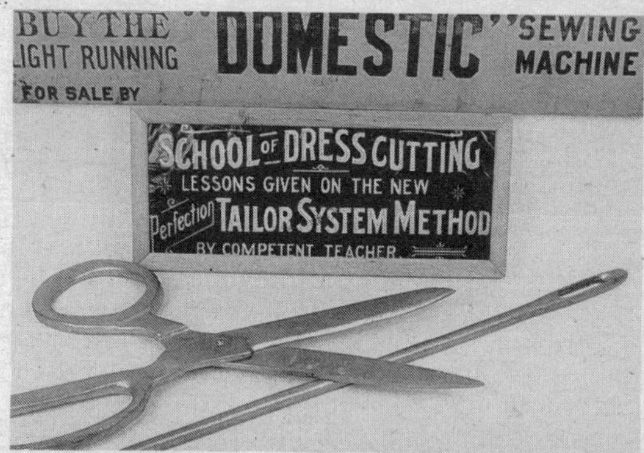

"School of Dress Cutting," tin. *$100–$125*

Millinery trade sign, scissors and needle. *$275–$350*

Schweppes Table Waters, lithographed on tin, 3 hinged sections framed to show center section, 7¼″ high, 26¼″ wide, lithographer unknown, ca. 1900, fine condition. *$200–$250*

Set of 5 Anheuser Busch signs, "The Father of Waters," "Attach on Emigrant Train," "Westward Ho," "The Relief Train," "A Fight for the Overland Mail," lithographed on paper, 11¼″ high, 20″ wide, lithographer unknown, ca. 1920, near mint condition. *$375–$425*

Shoe sign for sidewalk, two-sided, white background, red lettering with yellow trim, ca. 1920s, 24″ tall, 12″ wide. *$450–$500*

Shooting Gallery Sporting Goods, black with handmade gold letters. *$650–$800*

Sleepy Eye, lithographed on tin, self-framed, 24¼″ high, 20″ wide, lithographer unknown, ca. 1895, good condition. *$375–$400*

Somerville's Red Hand Chewing Gum, lithographed on tin, 4½″ high, 12″ wide, lithographed by Marsh Bros. Adv. Signs & Novelties, ca. 1910, fine condition. *$325–$375*

Stickney & Poor Mustard & Spices, reverse on glass, framed, 31½″ high, 25½″ wide, lithographed by Denzi & Phillips, Inc., ca. 1900, near mint condition. *$750–$900*

Sunny Monday Laundry Soap, made by Fairbanks Co., lithographed on tin, framed, 21½″ high, 16¼″ wide, lithographer unknown, ca. 1930, fine condition. *$70–$100*

Swift's Borax, lithographed on paper, framed, museum-mounted, under glass, 16¾″ high, 20″ wide, lithographer unknown, ca. 1910, near mint condition. *$550–$600*

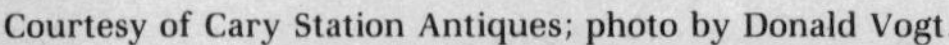
Courtesy of Cary Station Antiques; photo by Donald Vogt.

The Alaska Fur Co., three-dimensional, 49″, signed "City Sign Co.," gold and black. *$10,000–$12,000*

The Anglo-American, made by Packing & Provision Co., lithographed on tin, framed, 29⅝″ high, 21¾″ wide, lithographed by F. Tuchfarber Mfg., ca. 1880, fine condition. *$1,600–$1,800*

Top Notch Tonic, lithographed on paper, embossed, die-cut, framed, under glass, 14½″ high, 9½″ wide, lithographer unknown, ca. 1890, excellent condition. *$90–$130*

Traveling movie sign, threefold, with some of the original photos, ca. 1910, Hulen Hood's Exclusive Production. *$2,100–$2,300*

Voight's Flour, "Make Children Happy," lithographed on paper, framed, museum-mounted, under glass, 25″ high, 20½″ wide, lithographer unknown, ca. 1920, near mint condition. ***$120–$150***

Wells Shoes, lithographed on tin, framed, 15″ high, 21″ wide, lithographer unknown, ca. 1890s, fine condition. ***$160–$190***

White Rock, concave, lithographed on tin, 11″ high, 11″ wide, lithographed by Chas. W. Shonk, ca. 1900, near mint condition. ***$1,000–$1,200***

Courtesy of Cary Station Antiques; photo by Donald Vogt.

Wm. M. Herrmann Jeweler, watch trade, black and silver, 40″ tall, heavy tin. ***$1,400–$1,800***

Wright's Remedies, lithographed on paper under glass, only one known, may or may not have been trimmed, conserved (made acid-free) and restored professionally, backed with permanent mulberry tissue, lithographer unknown, ca. 1880s, near mint condition. ***$2,100–$2,400***

Wrigley Gum, lithographed on tin, 6″ high, 13⅜″ wide, lithographed by The Crown Cork and Seal Co., ca. 1925, fine condition. ***$160–$200***

Wrigley's, red, lithographed on tin, beveled edge, 6⅞″ high, 11⅛″ wide, lithographed by American Can Co., ca. 1910, fine condition. ***$80–$110***

Wrigley's, black, lithographed on tin, beveled edge, 6⅞" high, 11⅛" wide, lithographed by American Can Co., ca. 1910, fine condition.

Wrigley's Doublemint Gum, lithographed on tin, 6" high, 13¼" wide, lithographed by American Can Co., ca. 1925, fine condition. *$180–$210*

Courtesy of Cary Station Antiques; photo by Donald Vogt.

"Ye Old Country Store," hanging sign, ca. 1867, black sand background with gold lettering, 36". *$1,600–$1,800*

THE COUNTRY MARKET

COUNTRY FARMERS, Shakers, Amish, Native Americans, and all other country folk have one thing in common: the items they made or grew were taken to market at one point or another. Farmers gathered their eggs or their vegetables in baskets and took them to market once a month or at harvest time at the end of summer. Dairy families brought their milk products, and potters brought their stoneware. Shakers packaged their seeds and herbs and sent them off to market with their salespeople. The Amish brought home-baked goods or handmade crafts to market, and Native Americans still have markets where they sell their jewelry, baskets, and rugs.

Markets were set up at the same place every year or season so that people from miles around knew when and where they could sell their products to others. It was a time for socializing, a time to make business contacts, a time to make a profit from the hard life country people lived during the rest of the year, and it was a sort of celebration. I'm sure all of those who took their items to market had a sense of satisfaction while doing so. It was a time when the gardener was rewarded for growing the biggest and best pumpkins or when the potter finally received compliments for the stoneware he or she had spent all year producing alone in a tiny shed.

Country markets became so popular that they grew larger and larger until states or counties were having fairs. Prizes would be awarded for the best squash, the most perfect cucumber, and the prettiest quilt, and booths were set up to teach the farmer or country person the newest and best way to raise crops or livestock. Soon a carnival atmosphere began to invade the marketplace. Game booths appeared, girlie shows were added, and amusement rides for the kids began blaring their calliope music.

The whole family made the trip, the kids got to see the "big city," perhaps Mom might go home with a blue ribbon for her pickles, or Dad might win one for a prize steer.

Fairs of this type are still held throughout country areas, farmers still bring their produce and crafts to sell, the kids still plead for rides on the merry-go-round, rams and steers are still paraded around the big ring, and there's lots of socializing going on. But few are the families who go home with extra money in their pockets these days after spending a weekend at a fair. Gambling tents abound, the kids always want that extra hot dog or ice cream cone, and the rides are so expensive that it makes no sense to try to explain to the kids that they're a ripoff. Yet it is a time of year that all wait for with anticipation and few would miss. It's become an American tradition and one that should be celebrated.

Baskets

UNTIL THE 1970s (and the advent of magazines like *Country Living*), baskets did not command very high prices at auction. For that matter, no country collectible was held dear in the eyes of those looking to make a profit in the antiques business. It was not until baskets and other country collections showed up in glossy photos in national home-decorating magazines that appreciation for items like country baskets was kindled; thus, prices for special items also began to rise.

By the turn of the century, baskets were being factory-produced, making it easier for people to buy and use them but impossible for those who made baskets by hand to keep up. Factories were able to make and sell baskets for a profit. That fact, as well as the popularity of paper bags and metal containers, forced Americans who made their living handweaving baskets to find other work.

Country baskets are usually working baskets, baskets that were made to meet a need or perform a specific function. Once they were broken, they were discarded—they no longer "worked." They were not the type to be set on a sewing table and admired, like those made by the Shakers; they were meant to carry laundry or apples, nuts or eggs.

Because similar basket designs have been used for many years, it is sometimes difficult to ascertain a basket's age. Baskets have been woven in the same manner, using the same types of materials for hundreds or, as with Native Americans, thousands of years.

The way a basket is woven often gives us some hint as to the talent of the basketmaker or the use of the basket. For instance, it's extremely difficult to make a basket with an oval mouth and a square or rectangular bottom. Also, an openweave basket was usually used for items that were moist (e.g., fruits). The open weave allowed moisture or water to drip off and also allowed air to circulate through.

Types

Apple-Drying Baskets

Though the best apple-drying baskets were made by the Shaker community, other country folks also needed weaving for that purpose. The Shaker version is a long, flat checkerboard weave. It has a handle in the center and very shallow sides. (For other information on Shaker baskets, please see "Shaker Country" in the "Country Places" section.)

Other apple-drying baskets might have been made of oak splint, and some have been found framed in pine. These examples are long but shallow and don't have handles as do the Shaker versions.

Buttocks Baskets

Buttocks baskets are distinctive in that the weave slides out from the middle to each rounded side. The handle literally splits the basket down the center, creating the raised pouchy sides that do indeed make the basket resemble buttocks.

Cheese or Curd Baskets

Cheese or curd baskets are easily distinguishable. They are large, round, openweave baskets. Usually, this type of basket would be placed over a crock, with a piece of cheesecloth inside the basket so that a mixture of curds and whey could be poured through the cloth/basket. This process left the curds in the cloth and allowed the whey to soak through to the crock. Normally, a country family would feed the whey to their pigs or any other livestock that would eat the gooey mess.

Fowl Baskets

Some country baskets were meant to transfer live fowl from the farmhouse to the market. Such baskets resemble buttocks baskets but may have a twisted splint handle. The handle would be reinforced with a technique of weaving called a "folded square."

The basket had a hinged lid in one end; the other end had a top woven into the design of the basket, which is unmovable.

Half Baskets

A half basket was made to be hung with its flat side against a wall. Some were meant to hold eggs, while others may have been used to hold herbs, bobbins, or other small items.

Mortise and Tenon

The mortise-and-tenon form of construction is not one usually found in basketmaking. If you find a basket partially constructed in this fashion, you have a basket worth more than the average farm basket.

Native American Baskets
(See also "Native American Country" in the "Country Places" section)

Baskets made by American Indians were used for numerous reasons. Some were made to carry wood, some to hold water; others were meant for food, sifting grain, catching fish, or even holding babies. There are so many different types that whole books could be devoted to the subject.

Each tribe used the weaving materials that were available to them in their arca. Somc used yucca, some wove with willows or grasses, and others used tender shoots, roots, and fibers.

Amerinds made storage baskets that were usually low, long, and rectangular. Such baskets made by northern tribes (e.g., Algonquin, Iroquois) might be decorated with paint or with a row of decorative woven accents.

The California tribes were known for using shells in their baskets, and some also made miniature horsehair baskets. Apache baskets often took the shape of a burden basket (one that was held over a shoulder with a strap and was decorated with tin cones that jingled when the wearer walked). Northwest Coast baskets often had decorations woven into them (e.g., ravens, killer whales, and geometrics).

Each basket made by Native Americans had a purpose, whether household or spiritual, and it could take many years to discover what each example was used for. Some baskets were woven on forms; others were done freehand. Several Indian basketmakers are well known (e.g., Da-So-La-Le of the Washo tribe and Kuch-Ye-Amp-Si of the Hopi tribe), but most did not sign their work.

For further information on Native American basketry, see *The Official® Identification and Price Guide to American Indian Collectibles.*

Pennsylvania Baskets and Basketry

Early in this century, basketmakers could be found along the creeks leading into the Delaware River in New Jersey and Pennsylvania, but as the war years began making their impact on the United States (both World War I and II), the basketmakers went further inland, to the Stone Hills above the Perkiomen, along South Mountain, and into the Blue Mountains and the Poconos.

Those early basketmakers were itinerant and were watched for in the early spring as they brought their wares to the local housewives. The folk artists would take white oak from the area they visited and repay the owners of the land by selling their wares to them at half price.

The so-called Dutch country, south and east of the Blue Mountains, is where the greatest number and most diversified types of splint oak baskets were found in the mid-twentieth century. Nested sets of two-, four-, six-, and eight-quart sizes with round bottoms were made by the springs in the mountains and sold in places like Reading and Lancaster, Pennsylvania, around Easter and Christmas.

With the added interest in Easter in Lutheran and Reformed faith neighborhoods, a plethora of smaller, handled baskets were made during that time of the year for carrying Easter eggs. The splint oak basket, of a weave common to Europeans, though primitive and long-lasting, began to be less popular as baskets woven of willow rods became more common. Though white oak baskets are generally of American origin, the makers of willow baskets are commonly of foreign birth or origin. The Pennsylvania Dutch called their splint baskets "sheena korrup."

Another type of Pennsylvania Dutch basket is commonly called the "windlakorrup," or baby basket, and is typically 13–15 inches long, 7–9 inches wide, and 6–8 inches high. Normally, the basket has a cover that is hinged from a stationary crosspiece and braced between where the handles and basket sides meet. The handles were made of willow, the top and bottom made of splints 1/8 inch thick and the sides made of splints 3/16 inch wide, woven over 1/8-inch rods. Another type of baby basket is made of willow rods and splints with one straight side and one rounded side.

Larger baskets, with loop handles that attach at both ends and one side of the basket, sport hinged tops. These baskets are believed to have been used for carrying foods in the market or to funerals or picnics.

Straw baskets were used to carry dozens of eggs, dried apples, and other such items. A larger version of this type of basket was known as a stocking basket because each Dutch household had approximately nine sets of all types of underclothing available for its family members. The basket was used to store their dirty laundry until the bimonthly wash day rolled around.

Splint oak baskets were made in two distinct ways: (1) the primitive right angle weave, where lighter strips of woof were woven across heavier strips of warp, and (2) the radiating warp, where strips cross each other at a center, fastened together by a pin, and a woof of lighter strips is woven in circles, across them, in the bottom of the basket.

Baskets were made for many other reasons. Extremely large ones were made for storage of corn, apples, or clothes; others were used for baking bread (called *brod* or *bok korrup*). Willow rods in warp and woof were woven to make sewing baskets. Melon baskets were made in a number of different sizes, as well as berry, fruit, and vegetable baskets.

We should not forget those baskets made for fish—deep, narrow baskets with lids pushed down were made to carry eels to market. Other baskets held clams, fish, and oysters when they were taken to market. Baskets hung by a strap from one's shoulder would be used to hold an angler's fly and rod, as well as the catch of the day.

Enjoyable outings, such as picnics, were excuses to bring out baskets to be loaded with foods delectable enough to please any palate. Swing baskets are still holding their own, and every once in a while one still sees a basket holding a smiling baby.

Rye Straw Baskets

Rye straw baskets were made, for the most part, in Pennsylvania. Round utility baskets with flat bottoms, they were typically used to hold rising dough for bread making.

Southern Gathering Baskets

Southern gathering baskets usually had handles that would easily slide over the worker's arm. Such baskets, if made from machine-cut splint, might be painted. Generally, if a basket is painted, it's worth more to a collector.

Splint Basketry

Splint basketry was an American Indian art that was taught to the white settlers in the early 1700s. White oak and ash were the woods used to make baskets prior to 1800. The Shakers used hickory in their basketmaking and are often credited with perfecting the weaving technique.

To make splinting material, a wood is cut in May, quartered, and soaked in water. The wood is then split when it's green and pounded with a wood mallet to loosen the wood's fibers. Splinters are made by riving, or splitting, the wood into thinner sections.

The wood is then pounded and rived again and planed to proper strip size. Once this step is complete, the strips are bundled and placed in running water until the basketmaker is ready to use them.

Most early American baskets employ a hexagonal weave. The exceptions are sieves or winnowing baskets, apple-drying baskets, and chair seats, which are square-woven.

One way to tell a basket's use is by its handle or lack of one. This is also a good way to distinguish a basket's value.

Swing-Handled Baskets

Swing-handled baskets were often made for carrying eggs. Such handles may be nicely carved to fit neatly in one's palm or made as simply as possible. Naturally, a carved handle is better than a relatively plain one.

The way the handle is attached to the basket body is also important. Some swing handles attach to a loop worked into the basket's weave; others swing by means of a nail or screw that holds the handle to a piece of wood attached to the basket.

A simple handle might be stronger than a swing handle and would indicate that the basket was used to hold an item heavier than eggs.

Thin-splinted end handles would indicate that the basket might have been used to store sewing items, light ladies' lingerie, or jewelry—nothing heavy—nor was it meant to be carried around.

The way the basket handle is wrapped also gives us an idea of how much weight the basket was meant to support. A single wrapped splint rim was fine on most baskets, but those used to carry heavy fruit might be double-wrapped (X-binding) to provide added strength.

Each basket bottom is different as well. A square or rectangular utility basket may have a checkerboard-weave bottom, while a round storage basket may have a demijohn bottom, which is a circular base reinforced by the weaving of a round ridge on the exterior, made purposely to hold the basket upright. The interior of the base tends to surge upward.

Tobacco Warehouse Baskets

Tobacco warehouse baskets were large (approximately 3 feet by 4 feet), rectangular, shallow baskets with strapping. They had openings larger than normal so that the tobacco could dry evenly and an open weave to allow for the circulation of air.

The tobacco was placed in a numbered basket at auction; the baskets were used for that purpose for more than a hundred years and are still used on some tobacco farms today.

Such baskets add a geometrical design to a country home when hung decoratively on an all-white, log, or brick wall.

Utility Baskets

Utility baskets are generally tall, round, square, or rectangular, and can be used for any number of purposes. They are the most commonly found baskets and are usually made of oak splint.

Basketmakers (See also "Shaker Country" and "Native American Country" in the "Country Places" section)

Among the best-known New England basketmaking families of the mid-1800s were the Sweetsers of Vermont. One of the original Sweetsers married an Indian woman named Lydia Hill. She taught her son Gilman (born in 1820) how to make baskets the Indian way, and it was Gilman who was then entrusted to teach his children the art. Today, three generations later, descendants of the Sweetser family (e.g., Newton Washburn) still make baskets in the family tradition.

The Sweetsers generally use brown ash strips in their weaving and are responsible for the demijohn bottom as well as the star bottom (taught by Lydia Hill). They were taught how to make natural dyes (e.g., purple from hemlock bark, yellow from goldenrod, red from berries or beets).

They usually made all of their baskets during long winter evenings, and their art was never taught to anyone outside the clan until Newton was asked to teach others how his baskets were made. Before making a decision, he went to an older member of the clan and was told to use his own judgment in whether or not he should teach others outside the family. He must have decided it was more important that the art be saved because he had over sixty apprentices by the early 1980s.

Tinware/Graniteware

Enamelware

THE ENAMELWARE PROCESS was developed in the mid-1700s. Most early articles were manufactured with the kitchen or bathroom in mind. Wash basins, soap dishes, laundry pails, kettles, pots and pans, dishes, and cups were only a few of the items made.

Enamelware items were made of iron or steel and covered with a porcelain-like glaze. Its surface was smooth and bright, the cooking pieces were much lighter than the average housewife was used to lifting, and the bright blue, red, yellow, and green mottled designs were cheerier than the iron, tin, brass, and copper cookware of old.

The only problem with enamelware was that it had a tendency to chip, and once the enamel wore off, the metal would rust. Thus, if you find a piece in mint condition today, consider yourself lucky.

Items made of enamelware, but hard to find, include salt boxes, utensil racks, butter churns, rolling pins, and water coolers. The most commonly made colors were gray and blue, though red, purple, brown, green, pink, and yellow were also used. The heavier pieces are older than the lightweight ones.

Flint Enamel

The company mark impressed on flint enamelware made at the Bennington Potteries is "Fenton's Enamel, Patented 1849, Bennington, Vermont." The mark is designed in a circle with the date, 1849, in the middle of the mark.

Fenton's Patent Flint Enamel Ware was manufactured in Bennington and took many shapes. Water urns, soda fountain domes, foot baths, wash basins, bed pans, spittoons, coffeepots, oval bakers, pie plates, and preserve jars are just a few of the enamelware items made during the mid–late 1800s.

Graniteware

Graniteware was the name ascribed to all types of enamelware made during the period from 1870 to 1930. Other names used by various companies to describe the speckled tin/iron cooking pieces and dinnerware were agateware, enameled ware, speckleware, and glazed ware.

The ware was mass-produced in the 1870s and was extremely popular with both country and city households. It was lightweight, decorative, and easy to clean, and its glaze kept it from picking up food and vegetable acids. Housekeepers liked graniteware because all of its qualities added up to one very important fact: it made life easier.

Enameling was an ancient process, though Americans did not begin to use it until the mid-nineteenth century. Charles Stumer of New York received a patent on July 25, 1848, for the "Improvement in Enamels for Iron." Though it appears, from the title of his patent, that Stumer was trying to claim the enameling process as his own, the patent was, in fact, for the glaze, not the actual enameling.

He led the way in enameling in the United States and was quickly followed by the largest graniteware manufacturers in the nation: Charles Lalance and Florian Grosjean, the Niedringhaus brothers, and Jacob J. Vollrath, located in different parts of the United States. The St. Louis Stamping Company, established by the Niedringhaus brothers in the early 1860s, was responsible for Granite Iron Ware.

In Sheboygan, Wisconsin, Jacob J. Vollrath set up his business in 1874 and was enameling steel by the early 1890s; yet he did not believe U.S. steel was good enough for enameling. In the northeastern part of the country (New York), the Lalance and

Grosjean Manufacturing Company opened in 1850. They won many awards with their graniteware: the highest award at the Philadelphia Centennial Exposition in 1876, the Grand Gold Medal at the 1878 Paris Exhibition, and the Grand Gold Medal in New Orleans in 1884.

Like tinware, graniteware was often piled high on a peddler's wagon to be sold directly to the homemaker. The sheet metal pots, pans, spoons, bowls, coffeepots, and other items made a symphony of clanking noises as the wagon was dragged over cobblestone city streets or along rutted country roads by one or two trusty nags.

As the years went by, more and more items were added to the peddler's inventory. But no matter what he had on the wagon, he knew that his business was not going to last once his horses had to compete with motor-driven automobiles.

Unfortunately, graniteware was easily damaged, which makes it difficult for today's collector to find perfect examples. It is typical to find pieces that have deteriorated because of rust and that have cracked or bent. The manufacturers recognized the defects of their product and soon offered mending or repair kits to graniteware owners who wanted to fill in the chips and holes in their washtub, coffeepot, or frying pan.

Rust can be removed with a ten-minute application of naval jelly; then the piece should be coated with salad oil (my husband "seasons" all old cast-iron pans, as well—claims it makes his already fabulous meals taste better).

A lye solution will remove burned-on deposits and grease if graniteware is soaked in the solution overnight (oven cleaners do the same job). If your graniteware is intended strictly for display, a spray of lacquer will keep it from disintegrating. If you need to remove a stain, boil some peeled potatoes in the piece or add a teaspoon of soda to a pan of boiling water.

In the late 1800s, a rash of poisoning cases in and around Boston caused investigators to discover that the culprit was an enameled kettle used by a baker. Because of the hubbub, the U.S. Health Department warned people to "look out for themselves" and to "carefully scrutinize" any graniteware purchased for the home. This created enough negative publicity that Lalance and Grosjean began using a Blue Label as proof that chemists had determined the safety of the company's line of Agate Iron Ware.

Other companies, such as the St. Louis Stamping Company and the Republic Stamping and Enameling Company, also published chemists' testimonials to prove that their ware met health standards.

During the sixty-year period when graniteware was produced, many types of items were made in several different colors. The ware lost its place in American housewives' hearts when aluminum and stainless steel products came on the market in the 1920s and 1930s.

Stoneware and Other Country Pottery

STONEWARE'S ORIGINS can be traced all the way back to its beginning in the Rhineland area of Europe in the fifteenth century. By the eighteenth century, pieces of stoneware had been shipped all over Europe and to the American colonies, and some of the people who knew how to make it were now part of the colonies as well.

Since that time, salt-glazed stoneware has been made as utilitarian pottery in large quantities by factories, as well as being produced one at a time in small local potteries.

It is the pieces made at those small potteries that ignite the collector's blood. Each piece is distinct and different when made one at a time. The potter may have had more time to decorate the piece than did his counterpart in the large factory. This naive artistic talent defines those pieces we can call folk art, and the innocent artistry of such pieces causes collectors to plunk down rather large sums of money for a piece of pottery originally made to hold a winter's worth of pickles for a country family.

Brown stoneware pieces were replaced by gray wares by the latter quarter of the eighteenth century, and after the turn of the century, decorations on such ware were incised designs of flowers, animals, or pictorial scenes. The first half of the nineteenth century produced many beautiful and elaborately designed pieces of American stoneware, but by 1860, designs had degenerated to what some term "the age of glaze painting." The cobalt blue decorated pottery, which was then called a fetish, has become a favorite in most American country pottery collections.

Shapes of American stoneware became more stable, and bases

were wider by the mid-1800s. Sides were less curved, and rims were lighter, less likely to chip. Eventually, bulbous forms were a thing of the past, and all crocks or jugs were cylindrical. The change in shape left the stoneware less distinctive, and early ovoid pots are more likely to be highly collectible because each one is a little different from the other.

The Civil War caused changes in everyone's life-style, even the potters. A new firebrick was invented by Christopher Webber Fenton in 1837 and was sold in Bennington, Vermont, at the Norton stoneware factory. It saved potters time because the brick, made of karolin and fine sand, was more durable than the old version, some of which required continual repair.

Salt-glazed stoneware was produced primarily in the Northeast and Ohio, with a small quantity produced in the Southeast. The pottery being made in the Southwest and Northwest during this period was not salt-glazed and was very different from its eastern cousins. Potteries in New York, Vermont, New Jersey, Pennsylvania, and Ohio provided the market with incised-decorated pieces, but the bulk of those early products were plain.

Types of Stoneware

It is tempting to just call all stoneware pieces designed to hold liquors "jugs." It would certainly be easier than remembering the purpose of each piece; however, I don't know very many collectors who aren't curious about the original use of the items in their collection. The generic term "jugs" will therefore be used only when referring to those stoneware one-handled pitchers made to store milk, cream, whiskey, and molasses.

The Norton Company made jugs in sizes ranging from one gallon up to eight gallons. Open pots with small, ear-shaped handles on both sides were designed to hold thick cream or butter and were made in one- to six-gallon sizes. Covered cream pots were made in one- to four-gallon sizes and were often decorated with cobalt blue drawings, as were many of the other Norton pieces.

Other stoneware includes churns, covered preserve jars, fruit or tomato jars, butter pots, covered cake pots, pitchers, flowerpots, and teapots.

American pottery is as old, historical, and varied as the country of its origin. It has as many shapes, sizes, and colors as the American people and is as hard to classify. All of the areas of the United States—New England, the Deep South, the Midwest, the Southwest, and the West Coast—have made pottery to hold liquids and to store foods in dark, cool places. Pottery was a necessary commodity, used every day for any number of reasons. Perhaps that is why American pottery is so popular a country collectible!

The Stoneware Process

Being a home-based product, pottery was made from the clay indigenous to each region. There are different types of clay, which have varying lasting powers. For instance, common red-burning clays are typical. Articles from this type of clay are soft, tend to chip easily, and are quite porous. Gray clays, on the other hand, when fired produce an extremely hard and durable body. This differentiation gives us redware and stoneware.

Glazes used differ according to whether the piece being glazed is soft-bodied or hard-bodied. Because redware is porous, that pottery should be sealed; otherwise, it will absorb grease and exude liquids. The early glaze for soft-bodied pottery is called a slip glaze. It was made of finely ground clay that was diluted with water until it was the consistency of cream. A mixture of red lead and mineral substance would be added to the clay to obtain the color desired by the potter.

Once the glaze was ready, it was applied with a brush, dipped, or dabbed with a rag. Then the piece would dry and later be fired once again. This process is typical of that used to make slip-decorated redware.

It was not necessary to use this process to seal stoneware. Instead, the piece could be finished by shoveling salt on the fires while the pottery was still in the kiln and red hot. A salt glaze, such as the one just described, would produce crystallized drops on the surface of the stoneware pieces, and such a surface is impervious even to strong acids.

Stoneware pots were good for putting up pickles, meat, and

preserves during the winter, as well as to hold fresh milk, water, or condiments for the supper table.

Traditions sprang up in various localities across the United States. Stoneware was more highly decorated in New York, New Jersey, and Pennsylvania than it was in the New England potteries. Along the Ohio River, potteries sprang up that made slipware and, later, Rockingham ware.

Pennsylvania slip decoration was more elaborate than New England's. Birds, flowers, and pictorial designs were traced in the slip, sometimes in different colors. The Pennsylvania potters also used deeply incised lines that showed a pattern in a darker slip beneath. Such pottery was called sgraffito, or scratched ware. New England stoneware, though extremely well made, is not usually interestingly decorated.

It is difficult to determine the date of pieces of American pottery because so many of the rural potters used old equipment; thus, an article made around the mid-nineteenth century does not differ much from the same type of piece made a century later.

It is almost as difficult to determine who made your redware or stoneware because most rural potters did not sign their works.

Factory-made pottery such as the wares made at the Rockingham pottery are more easily recognized. The glaze on Rockingham ware is one of the best in the early factory period of the mid-nineteenth century. The glaze is a mottled deep brown color with traces of goldish-yellow throughout. The Bennington, Vermont, Rockingham glaze is considered to be the best example.

The process of making this type of pottery is unique. The salt-glazed technique is achieved by throwing ordinary salt into the fire or kiln chamber. The salt is thrown as many times as necessary to achieve the desired glaze. This process was phased out around the turn of the century as modern glazing methods advanced.

Monmouth Stoneware

Stoneware has been made in many otherwise less-than-memorable cities in the United States. One pottery-making city in the Midwest was Monmouth, Illinois, home to approximately six different large and active potteries.

One such company was Monmouth Mining and Manufacturing Company, founded by Joseph Maple White and A. M. Black in 1872 and later owned by William Hanna. The company was destroyed by fire on May 8, 1921, and the site became the home of the Western Stoneware Company in 1923. The company made sewer piping, urns, yard ornaments, and clay advertising pieces.

The Stewart Ericson Company made chalkware pieces from 1901 to approximately 1903.

In 1893, William Hanna organized the Monmouth Pottery Company, and in 1899, that company's letterhead read: "Monmouth Pottery Co. Manufacturers of all kinds of Stoneware. Largest pottery in the World. Capacity 6,000,000 gallons per annum." The company used a maple leaf as its logo and made all types of pottery: crocks of all sizes, butter jars, churns, milk bowls, jugs, tobacco jars, glazed pigs with the company name on the belly, chamber pots, and other sundry items.

The Weir Pottery Company was incorporated in 1899 and elected William S. Weir as its president. The company is best remembered for the manufacture of Old Sleepy Eye items, as well as for Weir seal jars. Weir Pottery made fruit jars, tableware, toilet ware, and "porcelain specialties of all kinds." Their goods were stamped with a logo that was the name of the company encircled.

Also doing business in the town of Monmouth was the Western Stoneware Company. This firm was the result of a merger of seven pottery companies in 1906. They utilized the seven companies' plants by just drawing them all under one legal umbrella, then calling the buildings Plants One through Seven.

Each piece of pottery made by Western Stoneware was marked with the plant numbers, and those numbers are important to collectors as each "plant" has a different history (e.g., Plant One closed in 1933, Two is still in operation, Three was destroyed by fire in 1913, Four was redesigned as Plant Three in 1923, Five was sold in 1923, Six was closed in 1910, and Seven was sold after a disastrous fire in 1906).

The stoneware pieces made by the various Monmouth, Illinois, plants were used nationwide. Farmers in all states used milk pans, butter jars, and churns. They delivered their milk products to grocery stores in stone jars or milk pans. Cheese was shipped in stoneware, as were almost all fruits, vegetables, pickles, preserves, jams, and jellies. Both city and country folk utilized this type of pottery to keep their meats, sausages, and lards as well. Also stored in stoneware was cider, vinegar, catsup, liquors and wines, juices, and vegetable pulp.

Cooks used stoneware around the fire or stove. A stew or winter soup was usually made in a stoneware pan or casserole and placed on the fire to simmer slowly on brisk winter days.

Because stoneware was so extensively used, potters had to ship large quantities at a time. The wares were buffered by hay or straw after being packed in wooden crates wrapped in wire. It was probably because of the pottery's weight and strength that the goods usually arrived with little or no damage at their final destination.

The stoneware business was rapidly dying by the early 1920s because of increased labor and other business costs. During the same period, other innovations were affecting stoneware production. Glass jars were being produced in quantity at a cheaper price than stoneware containers. They were used to contain fruits, jams, jellies, and some vegetables. The invention of the cream separator caused changes in the milk industry that had not been foreseen. The need for milk pans, butter churns, and jars disappeared when fewer and fewer farm wives made butter. And companies started wrapping butter and cheese products in oiled paper, which was lighter in weight as well as being less costly.

Moravian Pottery
(See also "The Kitchen" in the "Country Home" section.)

John Bartlam, a master potter from England, came to the Moravian community at Salem, North Carolina, in 1773 and proceeded to teach Gottfried Aust how to make Queensware and stoneware.

Other information on Aust and other Moravian potters is included in "The Kitchen" section.

New York's Stoneware

Because stoneware is fired to about 2300 degrees Fahrenheit, it is extremely dense and durable. Stoneware production is thus centered around areas where high-temperature clays can be obtained easily. New York City was one of those areas and became one of the earliest stoneware-producing cities in America. Later, potters in New England and the Hudson Valley used clay from these deposits in making their own stoneware.

Joseph Thiekson of New Jersey is credited with making the earliest piece of dated stoneware, although there are records of other New York potters having done business at approximately the same time.

Yorktown, Virginia, produced considerable amounts of pottery during the 1730s. It has been reported that the potter William Rogers was highly successful and had been shipping pottery to other parts of the colony.

William Seaver of Taunton, Massachusetts, ran the first successful Massachusetts pottery, beginning production in the latter part of the eighteenth century. He mixed clay from New Jersey with some from Martha's Vineyard, thus enabling him to make a profit.

Red Wing Potteries

Red Wing, Minnesota, potteries made stoneware for seventy-five years. The area, originally a large settlement of the Dakota/Sioux tribe, was not settled by white men until 1849, when missionary Reverend J. W. Hancock came to the area.

Though the place was called Remnicha by the Indians, white men named it Red Wing. It was the image of Talangamane, Walking Buffalo, which was used by the Red Wing Advertising Company at the 1915 Minnesota State Fair.

Red Wing grew after the Civil War, with lumber mills and iron foundaries helping to pave the way for the clay industry that was soon to follow. By the turn of the century, Red Wing's clay industry was the largest employer. Utilitarian stoneware, as well as clay sewer pipes, were produced by the companies in the area, and those products were transported to other regions in the country via railroad and river transportation.

Unlike the small family potteries in the South, the Red Wing potters worked in factories, thus the term "clay giants." If circumstances had been different (i.e., transportation, etc.), perhaps the

Red Wing factories would have failed, but the fact is that they became the largest single stoneware producers in the nation.

Though a German immigrant, Joseph Pohl, was probably the first potter to come to the area, it was Francis F. Philleo who was to announce the opening of the first pottery factory in 1866. His son William was the actual owner of the factory, which eventually came to be known as the Red Wing Terra Cotta Works.

The company made jugs, butter jars, covered jars, and other types of stoneware and continued in production through 1885, even though the building was once destroyed by fire and the business had changed hands several times. When the company went out of business in 1885, it had been owned by Philleo and several partners.

Other companies that produced pottery in Red Wing included the Minnesota Pottery Co., owned by David Hallum (its workers were once employees of Philleo), the Red Wing Stoneware Company, and the North Star Stoneware Company. For more information on Red Wing pottery, read *Red Wing Potters and Their Wares* by Gary and Bonnie Tefft.

Southern Pottery

In Georgia, as well as other southern states, pottery was used in many different ways during the 1800s and early 1900s. Pottery churns were used to pickle cabbage, beans, corn, and beets. Smaller fruit jars were made to seal in apple or pumpkin butters. Syrup jugs held molasses and were stored in the smokehouse until the woman of the house decided they were needed in the kitchen. Alcohol was also poured into jugs, as was cream, buttermilk, and milk. A stoneware churn was used to make butter, and the result was poured into a covered crock to be stored in the springhouse for future use.

Families throughout the South were involved in making pottery to hold their farm goods or to sell to neighbors, general, and hardware stores.

Mossy Creek in Georgia has been known since 1820 as one of the largest pottery centers in the South with more than seventy potters producing their wares in that region.

The Piedmont heartland, in the Carolinas and Georgia, produced huge deposits of stoneware clay that was used by the potters. It was considered such an abundant supply that most of Georgia's four hundred potters were located in the Piedmont Plateau or close to the fall line.

Though the goods made by these potters are now considered by collectors to be artistic, the pottery industry was a business to supplement farm income and was often kept alive in the family through a form of apprenticeship. Some of these families—the Browns, for example—produced pottery over the span of eight generations throughout the southern states. Each family developed its own distinctive style, traits being shape variations, the type of glaze used, marking, how a handle was attached or shaped, and what details were on the rim of the piece.

Traits that may have originated in South Carolina at the beginning of the nineteenth century are often found to have moved as far as Texas by the middle part of the century because families grew, moved, and intermarried, taking their talents with them.

The concept of the face jug was said to have been introduced to Mossy Creek by itinerant potters like William Hewell of Gillsville. Another potter well known for this type of work was E. Javan Brown, who built the Wilson Pottery kiln in Banks County.

Certain traits of Southern pottery are learned, and others have been adapted through the inventiveness of potters who studied pottery making such as that done by the Chinese. The alkaline glazes developed by southern potters is said to have been suggested by Oriental glazes and was improved upon by those aware that they could adapt such a glaze to their own environment and what materials were available to them.

As with other crafts, certain items were intrinsic to the area (e.g., the two-handled, bulbous or ovoid syrup jug, which was primarily used for molasses; the ceramic grave marker; and the face jug, which is now looked upon as folk art).

Though there are still some southern potters who work in the old way, techniques are becoming more and more modern, and we will soon have little to emulate when comparing contemporary to traditional pottery. Since this book deals basically with traditional items, I will discuss some of the families that have been in the pottery business for generations, to give you a better idea of what is collectible in this field.

Because of the strong tradition of southern folk pottery, it is often difficult to attribute certain unsigned works to their makers. So many potteries were working during the late 1800s and early 1900s that scholars have taken great pains to put together bibliographies listing as many known potters as they could find. One of the most concise listings is that compiled by Howard A. Smith. Should your interest in country collectibles be allied with southern pottery, I highly recommend Smith's *Index of Southern Potters.*

His listing is an alphabetical index of eighteenth-, nineteenth-, and twentieth-century potters of North Carolina, South Carolina, Georgia, Alabama, and Mississippi. Some of the most interesting entries found in this and other listings include African-American potters, Moravian potters, and potters whose small businesses grew into fairly affluent industries.

Some early potters include the following:

John Bartlam, originally of England (a potter from the Staffordshire district), moved to Charleston, South Carolina, around 1764 specifically to open a china factory with others from England.

He opened and operated a pottery around 1768 in Cainhoy, South Carolina. By 1771, he advertised a pottery in Charleston, South Carolina, and in 1773–74, he operated a pottery in a town now known as Camden, South Carolina.

He made lead-glazed earthenware and "Carolina Creamware." Bartlam died in Charleston in 1781.

The Beacham Family of Crawford County, Georgia, started making pottery in 1830. John Beacham, Sr., was the first potter in the family, and his five sons (Allen, Benjamin, Washington, William, and John Jr.) followed in his footsteps, as did grandsons Jackson and Franklin. The family made alkaline-glazed stoneware until Franklin's death in 1958.

The *Biloxi Art Pottery* was owned by George E. Ohr from 1890 to 1904. It was located in Biloxi, Mississippi, and was known for its art pottery. Ohr called himself the "greatest art potter on earth."

Boyles Jug Factory was owned by Thomas Ownby of South Carolina. This factory was located in Union, South Carolina, from 1819–20 until Ownby's death in 1878. The pottery was in operation until 1932.

Burlon and Irene Craig were from the Catawba Valley of North Carolina. Burlon was one of the few potters in that area who used a water-powered glass mill to pulverize the glass used in some of his glazes. The Craigs had five children, and only two of them (Donald, the youngest, and daughter Colleen) learned to make pottery from their parents.

Born on April 14, 1914, in the Catawba Valley, Burlon grew up around other potters in the area; thus, the competition was fierce. Most of the potters with whom he was familiar got their clay from the old Rhodes farm in that area, paying from 8 to 15 cents a gallon. Though potters abounded there, Craig's family was not involved with the craft, but he helped James Lynn, who had a pottery operation located close to where Craig eventually built his. From the time he was ten or eleven years old, Craig helped the older potter by getting wood and digging and grinding the clay.

When Craig was fourteen, he still hadn't learned to turn, but Lynn asked him to be his partner. Lynn died a couple of years later, and Craig spent the next few years (1930s) working for other potters, learning the ropes. Craig joined the navy during World War II and was away from the business until 1945, at which point he bought out Harvey Reinhardt's business.

During the first phases of that operation, Craig was making utilitarian pieces such as pitchers, milk crocks, churn jars, storage jars, and a few bean pots.

The later pieces Burlon made (snake jugs and face jugs) became extremely popular, and Craig was under pressure from customers to make more and more. He has continued to use the traditional techniques and to make the Reinhardt swirl-type ware that he alone is known for.

Irene, Burlon's wife, paints flowers and other designs on the pots her husband throws. After she decorates the piece, it needs to be glazed and fired so that the painting will show up.

Though Burlon still made utilitarian pieces in the early 1980s, his customers prefer monkey jugs (which have one handle, two separate interior vessels, and separate spouts for each) and face jugs (or grotesque jugs). His face jugs are large. The body is made in two separate pieces, then placed together and turned so that they join properly. The handles are attached separately, as are the eyes, ears, and lips. An old china plate is broken and used for teeth, a fork scratches out a mustache and eyebrows, and the piece is set aside to dry.

Both of the glazes Craig uses require pulverized glass, which comes from soft drink bottles. One of the glazes is dark green, and the other is clear and used on his swirl ware.

The mill used by Craig in his glazing process is operated by the natural forces of a mountain stream, a system used by southern potters for many years. Burlon has experimented with his glazes and the use of the mill and believes that doing so is good for his business.

Firing is the final stage of the long pottery process, and Craig uses the same type of kiln that the Reinhardt brothers used in the 1930s. Depending on how quickly the kiln heats, the firing takes ten to twelve hours. Keeping the heat at its maximum is important for the final couple of hours. This is the crucial stage, the time when potters definitely must know what they're doing.

Before unloading his pieces from the kiln, Craig closes it up completely, covering chimney and draft holes, and letting the kiln cool off for two or three days prior to opening it.

In 1981, Burlon and Irene Craig were featured at the Smithsonian's Folklife Festival in Washington, DC, and they demonstrated their skill the following year in Knoxville, Tennessee, at the World's Fair.

Dave, a well-accomplished slave potter, was born around 1780 and died in the Edgefield district of South Carolina in 1863. He was a literate slave and probably the best known African-American potter in America. His work is often recognizable by the rhyming couplets incised on the sides of the large and bulbous storage jars he made.

Jasper Gibbs (1810–1877) was responsible for a great deal of the pottery made in the Edgefield, South Carolina, region. He was an investor in many firms in that area's pottery industry. Pottery and bricks were made by slaves on property near his home in Bienville Parish.

The *Hartsoe Family*'s patriarch, Daniel, began making pottery in the mid-1800s. Daniel used a stamp with his initials, "DH," to mark his wares. All of the Hartsoe family worked in North Carolina, in Lincoln and Catawba counties, making alkaline-glazed stoneware.

The family's potters included Sylvanus (the most prolific of all Catawba River valley potters), Poley, Carp, Albert, and John. Poley was the last to produce pottery, continuing the tradition until his shop was destroyed by fire in 1956.

Jugtown, North Carolina, was started by Jacques Busbee and his wife, Juliana, around 1917–20. Busbee hired various potters to continue the Jugtown tradition, and the pottery was in operation until 1983. Of all of the North Carolina potteries, Jugtown pottery is the best known and most desirable.

The Landrum Family was one of the most influential families in southern pottery. John Landrum was a native of Scotland who moved to the United States in 1688 to settle in Virginia.

Throughout the eighteenth and nineteenth centuries, his family continued the pottery tradition. John's son Samuel had five sons, three of whom became well-known potters (John, George, and Benjamin). The last of the potters in this family was Linneaus Mead Landrum, who worked in Columbia, South Carolina, during the mid-1800s and died there in 1891.

The Meaders Family, originally of Virginia, was headed by Christopher Columbus Meaders. They settled in Franklin County, Georgia, in 1848. Son John was the first to go into the pottery business, in 1892. Once the business grew, John began teaching his sons to turn a pot. Eventually, six of his children learned how.

One by one, Meaders's sons married and moved away. Some started their own operations (e.g., Casey, who moved to North Carolina), and only one son (Cheever) remained with his father. In 1920, Cheever took over his father's shop.

Cheever continued in the family business, teaching his own eight children to turn, until his son Lanier took on the responsibility of keeping the pottery shop in business.

When Cheever's wife, Arie, entered the business, her ideas and new ways of decorating a pot revived interest in the Meaders' family pottery. Arie was responsible for the addition of such decorative accents as grapes or a painted peacock to tall stoneware vases or jugs.

The Meaders family has made quite a varied selection of pottery using clay they dug from several locations near the shop until 1960, when they had the clay ground in a mud mill. Lanier uses the same basic equipment for turning the pots as his father did, though he has replaced the treadle wheel.

The earliest glaze used by Cheever was what he called a "Shanghai" glaze, made from silk deposited in an abandoned millpond nearby. He preferred a hardwood oak ash silt, which was the result of lye that had been leached to make soap. In the early 1900s, the commercially produced Albany slip became available, and Cheever sometimes utilized it.

Lanier's work has improved quite a bit throughout the years. For instance, the first grotesque jugs he made had long, bloblike noses, a jack-o'-lantern type of mouth, and no chin. His more contemporary pieces became realistic to the point that the jugs truly resemble human faces.

The Meaders family has displayed wares at such prestigious shows as the Festival of American Folklife that the Smithsonian holds on an annual basis.

Edwin Meaders is another member of the Meaders clan who made his mark in pottery. His business, located in Cleveland, Georgia, is different from that of the rest of his family because he doesn't use as many of the old tools or techniques. His slip is Albany, Whiting, feldspar, and clay, and his favorite subject is a rooster, which he makes in stages. If it's a good day, the potter figures he can make eighteen by having three roosters in the works at the same time.

Lewis J. Miles of the Edgefield district of South Carolina had ten children, only one of whom became a potter (John L. Miles). However, Miles started the Miles Mill Pottery, which was in operation from approximately 1834 until approximately 1867. It was at this pottery that some of the best-known slave potters, such as Dave, Baddler, James Thurmond, and Simon Kinnard, worked.

The Palmette Firebrick Works made utilitarian pottery during the Civil War. The pottery was glazed in a sand and pine ash alkaline glaze, as was most South Carolina pottery made during that period. The company, begun in the mid-1800s by Colonel Thomas Jones Davies, originally made firebacks.

Some remarkable African-American face vessels were made by the slave labor force employed by this company, which closed at the end of the Civil War.

Phoenix Factory was another of the pottery companies that called Edgefield, South Carolina, home. The company was founded in 1840 by Collin Rhodes and Robert W. Mathis. Collin sold his share in the company to his brother Coleman later that year. At least seven slaves were involved in the production of pottery during the two years the company was open.

It is said that the Phoenix factory was responsible for producing the finest known piece of decorated southern pottery and that the company perfected the decoration of alkaline-glazed stoneware. The piece, a ten-gallon water cooler decorated with figures of a black man and woman toasting each other is unlike any other made during that period. I would say it's probably safe to assume that the piece was designed by one of the slaves who worked at the factory. What is even *more* amazing is that people who were enslaved were optimistic enough about life to create such artistic objects!

Norman Smith is one of the last Southern potters to use raw clay that is ground with a pug mill. Originally, the pug mill was operated with horses, but Norman finally switched to a tractor after wearing out several of the animals.

For over sixty years, the Lawley, Alabama, native made and sold pots from his home in that area, hauling his wares to cities in Alabama and Georgia during the early years with a horse and wagon and later with a Model T truck.

The first items off his potter's wheel were one-gallon churns usually used for milk or to put up lye soap. After those initial tries, he worked for a while with Charlie Brown (Atlanta) and Ralph Phillips, putting out a few more products and basically learning the trade. After a while, Smith began putting out eight- and ten-gallon vessels.

Norman's brother Oscar learned to turn in the late 1920s, and the brothers worked together for a while. Half-brother Ewing and another brother, Clement, also assisted Norm in his business by helping to build kilns or selling finished wares. Norman did all of his glazing with an ash glaze (from lye soap) and later used an Albany slip or salt glaze.

His wife, Irene, worked in the pottery with Norman from the time she was married to him, cleaning the pieces and glazing. She never took to turning but assisted him in sales to hardware and dime stores.

In the early years, Norman charged 10 to 25 cents for his wares. Irene chided him after seeing what the other potters were getting, and prices on Smith pottery were raised to $2–$3 for gallon churns.

The Southern Porcelain Company of Kaolin, South Carolina, made many types of pottery during the time they were in business (ca. 1856–ca. 1902). The company not only produced the first porcelain made in the South but was also known to make (1856–60) cream-colored ware, graniteware, common yellow earthenware, and common white earthenware and (1860–64) Rockingham glazed ware.

The Webster Family of South Carolina (McCloud, Edward, and Timothy) worked as potters from approximately the mid-1700s to the mid-1800s. McCloud Webster was uncle of the clan and the first to open a family pottery business. It is thought that McCloud's nephew, Chester, worked for his uncle for a while. The brothers worked together in the early 1800s and became known as the "bird and fish" potters because of their use of those incised decorative motifs on their salt-glazed stoneware.

Other pottery families include the Wilson family of Lula, Georgia, the Hewell family of Gillsville, Georgia, and the Brown family of Arden, North Carolina. All have been involved in the pottery business since the middle of the twentieth century. Each family has passed the secrets of the pottery trade down through the generations, with contemporary pieces still being produced.

Prices

If an item is not indicated as being specifically Shaker, Indian, Amish, etc., then it should be considered strictly a "country" piece. For items specifically made by the country groups spoken of in the first section of this book, consult that chapter.

BASKETS

Courtesy of Country Cottage Antiques; photo by Donald Vogt.

Blue/black painted, 18″ to handle, 16″ diameter. *$165–$195*

Farm, splintwork handle, 8½″ high, 13½″ diameter, swing handle shows some roughness, one splint missing in side, ca. 19th century. *$150–$200*

Fine Nantucket, with swing handle on wooden mounts, wooden bottom, diameter 9″, height 6″, some damage where splint joins wooden bottom, ca. 19th century. *$330–$500*

Fine Nantucket, with swing handle, 3 concentric rings cut into inner side of wooden bottom, 8½″ diameter. *$1,650–$1,800*

Fine Nantucket Lightship, with the label of Captain Thomas S. James, made on the South Shoal Lightship, 2 small handles and turned wood base, 3 concentric rings cut into inner side of wooden bottom, 11″ diameter. *$2,310–$2,500*

Courtesy of Louisville Antique Mall, Louisville, Kentucky; photo by Donald Vogt.

Gathering, good condition. *$90–$110*

Courtesy of Country Cottage Antiques; photo by Donald Vogt.

Gathering, originally round, 19″ diameter, turn of century. *$95–$115*

Gathering, Indian. *$30–$40*

Courtesy of Pumpkin Vine Line Antiques, Buddy and Atha Wallin, Fairfield, Ohio; photo by Donald Vogt.

Group: (left) buttocks basket, 3½″, ca. 1860–80, excellent condition. *$350–$400*

(Right) *feather basket,* 6″, with top, 1860–80, excellent condition. *$350–$400*

(Middle) *swing handle,* 6″, ca. 1860–80, excellent condition. *$550–$650*

Courtesy of Pumpkin Vine Line Antiques, Buddy and Atha Wallin, Fairfield, Ohio; photo by Donald Vogt.

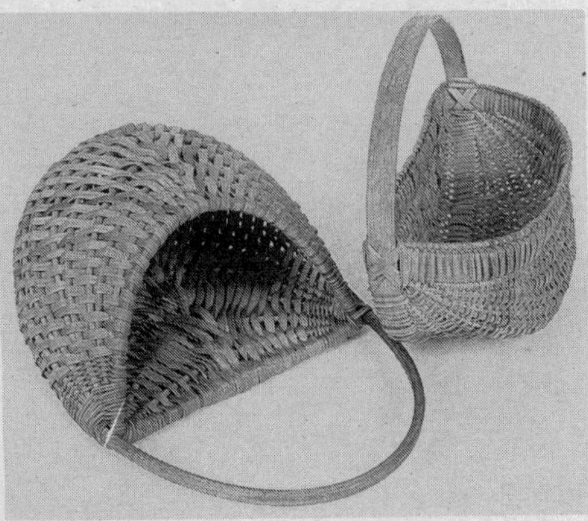

Half baskets (2), used for storage. *$250–$350*

Courtesy of Pumpkin Vine Line Antiques, Buddy and Atha Wallin, Fairfield, Ohio; photo by Donald Vogt.

Large hickory, 22″ wide, 10″ high (15″ to top of handle), for storage of eggs, ca. 1880, Kentucky/Ohio. *$350–$400*

Miniature woven splint, with sweet grass rim, woodland Indian, 4″ deep, 2⅝″ high plus handle. *$65–$85*

Miniature woven splint buttocks, some age, minor damage, 4¾″ × 5¼″, 3″ high plus handle. *$155–$195*

Courtesy of Pam and Martha Boynton, Groton, Massachusetts.

Nantucket, by Josi Reyes, mint condition. *$1,000–$3,000*

Courtesy of Pam and Martha Boynton, Groton, Massachusetts.

Nantucket, pair, early, in mint condition. *$650–$3,500*

Oval Nantucket, with swing handle, 8″ × 5″, 3½″ high. *$1,815–$2,000*

Rectangular, 18″ × 12½″ × 8″, tightly woven, nice patina, 1870s–1880s. *$125–$160*

Courtesy of Country Cottage Antiques; photo by Donald Vogt.

Rectangular, 19″ × 13″ × 9″, 1870s–1880s. *$110–$140*

Splint, melon, ca. 19th century. *$341–$375*

Splintwork, with handle, 9″ diameter, 6″ high, ca. 19th century. *$50–$100*

Courtesy of D. J. Downes, Birmingham, Michigan; photo by Donald Vogt.

Square, lidded, ca. 1880, unusual form. *$95–$115*

Courtesy of Country Cottage Antiques; photo by Donald Vogt.

Swing handle, some red paint, 12¼″ × 13½″ × 10″. *$125–$150*

Unusual inner rim for lid, worn and weathered surface, some damage, 6¾″ × 9″, 4¾″ high plus bentwood handle. *$45–$60*

Weaver's, unusual splintwork, 34″ × 22″, 15½″ high, ca. 19th century. *$75–$100*

GRANITEWARE

Courtesy of the Keeping Room, Camby, Indiana; photo by Donald Vogt.

Blue pieces, ca. mid–late 1800s, including saucepan with lid. *$40–$50*

Soap dish. *$25–$30*
Bowl. *$25–$35*
Double-handled pan. *$40–$50*
Ladle. *$25–$35*

Bucket, with toleware top, original, ca. 1900. *$65–$75*

Courtesy of the Keeping Room, Camby, Indiana; photo by Donald Vogt.

Gray, tea set with maker's stamp on base, dated 1885. *$50–$75*
Matching cups and saucers. *$25–$30*

Courtesy of the Keeping Room, Camby, Indiana; photo by Donald Vogt.

Grouping of gray pieces:

(Center rear) *dish basin,* 17″ long, mint condition. *$45–$55*
(Center rear) *ladles* (each). *$20–$30*
(Left rear) *sieve.* *$35–$45*
(Left front) *cream bucket.* *$45–$55*
(Center front) *soup bowls* (set), 6″–8″. *$40–$45*
(Center front) *tray,* 13″. *$35–$45*
Teapot without lid. *$18–$24*

Courtesy of the Keeping Room, Camby, Indiana; photo by Donald Vogt.

Grouping of brown pieces (unusual color):

Gallon coffeepot, excellent condition. *$75–$95*

Shallow basin, without handles. *$25–$30*

Bottom of broiler (missing top). *$35–$45*

Mixing bowl, 11½″. *$35–$50*

Pie pan, 8½″. *$18–$25*

Courtesy of the Keeping Room, Camby, Indiana; photo by Donald Vogt.

Set of 4 blue cups and teapot, ca. late 1800s, very good condition. *$225–$275*

MISCELLANEOUS

Bucket, Heinz Pickle Company, made in Pittsburgh, PA, established in 1869, style for mincemeat, good condition, 11″ tall, 4 gal., ca. 1890. *$250–$350*

Egg carrier, painted wood, "Reliable Egg Carrier . . ." with Keene, NH, advertisements, red with black lettering, 12″ × 13″ × 11″, 19th century. *$40–$75*

Farmer's pricing wheel, cast iron, 24″ high, 12½″ wide, 6″ deep, ca. 1890, excellent condition. *$200–$250*

Metal ice saw, 34″ long, 25 1″ teeth. *$40–$60*

STONEWARE

Butter crock, impressed label "Sipe & Sons, W'msport, Pa. 1½," floral design in brushed cobalt blue, Albany slip interior, hairline, 11½″ deep, 6″ high. *$225–$285*

Courtesy of Mary Jane MacMillin, Antiques of Chester; photo by Donald Vogt.

Cake container, hard to find with cobalt lines, some chips, minor hairline, ca. 1880. *$395–$425*

Courtesy of Red Wing Potters and Their Wares, Gary and Bonnie Tefft.

Churn, 3-gallon, Minnesota Stoneware Company (founded in 1883), molded, hand-decorated with a parrot, company signature molded into bottom. *$2,000–$3,000*

Courtesy of Red Wing Potters and Their Wares, Gary and Bonnie Tefft.

Collection of jars, ca. 1900–06, molded (except for churn, which was hand-turned), glazed in white, decorations applied with rubber stamp, Union Stoneware Company. *$35–$350*

Courtesy of Red Wing Potters and Their Wares, Gary and Bonnie Tefft.

Collection of jars, ca. 1900–06, molded, glazed in white, decorations applied by rubber stamp, company signature "Union Stoneware" applied with rubber stamp. *$35–$350*

Crock, cobalt blue, stenciled and freehand label, "Williams & Reppert, Greensboro," 5″, stains, 13½″ high. *$175–$220*

Crock, cobalt-decorated ovoid, 9½″ high, star check. *$40–$60*

Crock, cobalt floral decoration, 2-gallon, N.Y. Stoneware Co., 9½″ high. *$110–$125*

Crock, 4-gallon, with blue cobalt decoration of squash on vine, 11″ high, some chips to rim. *$150–$250*

Courtesy of Robert C. Eldred Co., Inc., East Dennis, Massachusetts.

Crock, important and unique, cobalt decoration of two deer flanking an 8″-diameter pocket watch, impressed mark "J & E Norton, Bennington, Vermont," 13″ high, glaze in good condition, crack running across base and up one side. *$10,000–$15,000*

Crock, impressed label "n. Clark, Jr., Athens, N.Y. 2," highlighted with blue, floral design in brushed cobalt blue, 9¼″ high. *$200–$250*

Crock, impressed label "Haxstun & Co., Fort Edward, N.Y. 4," highlighted with blue, stylized floral design in cobalt blue quill work, stains, 11″ high. *$200–$250*

Crock, impressed label "Haxstun & Co., Fort Edward, N.Y. 2," parrot-like bird on branch in cobalt blue quill work, minor flakes and short hairline in base, 10″ deep, 9½″ high. *$325–$410*

Crock, impressed label is indistinct but appears to read "F.T. W— Son, Taunton, Mass.," stenciled cobalt blue tiger in circles, glaze flaking and small chips, 13¼″ deep, 9″ high. *$150–$190*

Crock, ovoid form, by Julius Norton, Bennington, VT., 9½″ high. *$75–$100*

Crock, ovoid form with applied handles, stamped "CS" on each side, 10″ high. *$240–$300*

Crock, ovoid, with cobalt floral decoration, 10″ high. *$100–$200*

Crock, with cobalt leaf decoration, 8″ high, 9″ diameter. *$55–$75*

Crock, with cobalt floral decoration, 10½″ high. *$100–$200*

Courtesy of Danby Antiques Center, Agnes & Bill Franks, Managers, South Main Street, Danby, Vermont; photo by Ginger Gamadge.

Crocks, collection of mid-19th-century jugs, crocks, and churns. *$150–$595*

Courtesy of Red Wing Potters and Their Wares, Gary and Bonnie Tefft.

Doorstop, glazed in brown, made by one of the Red Wing companies between approximately 1900–1910, molded, stands 13″ tall on 12″ × 6″ base. *$1,800–$2,200*

Fine Pennsylvania 3-gallon butter churn, with cobalt floral decorations, 14½″ high. *$260–$300*

Flask, gray salt glaze with cobalt blue lip, 7½″ high. *$150–$190*

Courtesy of Mary Calder, Antiques of Chester; photo by Donald Vogt.

Group: (center) New York Stoneware Co., Ft. Edward, NY, damaged lip, ca. late 1800s. *$200–$250*

(Left) *cobalt floral,* good condition, ca. late 1800s. *$185–$250*

(Right) *unmarked cobalt decoration,* flower, chip on lip, ca. late 1800s. *$175–$200*

Courtesy of Pumpkin Vine Line Antiques, Buddy and Atha Wallin, Fairfield, Ohio; photo by Donald Vogt.

Group: (left rear) jar, J. T. Higgins & Co. *$250–$325*

(Right rear) *crock,* Sipe, Nichols & Co., Williamsport, PA, with cobalt decoration. *$450–$500*

(Left front) *salt crock,* Hamilton and Jones, ca. 1880. *$275–$350*

(Right front) *double-handled crock,* with hand-turned lid and cobalt decoration, unusual, Pennsylvania, ca 1860. *$600–$800*

Courtesy of Pumpkin Vine Line Antiques, Buddy and Atha Wallin, Fairfield, Ohio; photo by Donald Vogt.

Group of crocks: (rear) New York Stoneware Company, Fort Edwards, NY, 6 gals., cobalt floral. *$800–$1,000*

(Left) *Cowden,* sunburst pattern, batter jug, made in Harrisburg, PA, ca. 1860, tin lid missing. *$1,500–$2,000*

(Center) *Heinz pickle crock,* small chip and hairline, ca. 1880. *$175–$225*

(Right) *Cowden and Wilcox,* 1½ gal., Harrisburg, PA, grape pattern, brushed on. *$400–$600*

Courtesy of Mary-Lee Muntz, Bonneyville Knoll Antiques, Middlebury, Indiana; photo by Donald Vogt.

Group of midwestern advertising crocks, with various advertisers' names printed:

3″–9″ dairy crocks. *$10–$65*

Olive oil jug. *$35–$45*

Jar, small, gray salt glaze, handles highlighted in pinkish color, brown Albany slip interior, incised inscription "Dark Blue, Philadelphia, July 4th, 1776, When in the Course of Human Events," reverse has "All Blue Wool, 7¾″ high, 6¼″ wide, out to out," chip on handle and crack, 6¾″ high. *$85–$110*

Jar, brown fleck glaze with splashes of white, small edge chips, 6⅞″ high. *$200–$250*

Jar, impressed label, "W. Roberts, Binghampton, N.Y. 2," long-necked folk art bird in cobalt blue slip, stains and minor hairlines, 10¾″ high. *$350–$440*

Jug, gray salt glaze, great handle, 11½″ tall, 7″ diameter, ca. 1860s. *$110–$135*

Jug, impressed label, "J.S. Taft & Company," simple foliage design in cobalt blue quill work, hairlines and minor flakes, 11″ high. *$150–$190*

Courtesy of Red Wing Potters and Their Wares, Gary and Bonnie Tefft.

Jug, salt-glazed, hand-decorated, 6-gallon size, ca. 1880, cobalt blue decoration, Red Wing Stoneware Company of Red Wing, MN. *$200–$300*

Courtesy of Red Wing Potters and Their Wares, Gary and Bonnie Tefft.

Jug, salt-glazed, hand-decorated, 20-gallon size, ca. 1880, cobalt blue decorated butterfly on lily pod, Red Wing Stoneware Company of Red Wing, MN. *$250–$400*

Courtesy of Robert C. Eldred Co., Inc., East Dennis, Massachusetts.

Jug, 3-gallon, fine, cobalt decoration of a deer in a landscape, 16″ high, two firing flaws—one in the tree to the left of the deer, another outside the decoration at the bottom right, by J. & E. Norton. *$3,000–$5,000*

Courtesy of Red Wing Potters and Their Wares, Gary and Bonnie Tefft.

Jug, 3-gallon, white-glazed, molded, advertising banner applied by rubber stamp in blue and fired into the glaze, ca. 1920s, Red Wing. *$250–$350*

Jug, 3-gallon, with cobalt floral decoration, New York Stoneware Co. *$180–$200*

Mixing bowl, blue and white sponge spatter, wear and edge flakes, 12¾″ deep, 6¼″ high. *$115–$145*

Ovoid jug, impressed "Charlestown," two-heart mark, 14″ high, repaired lip, drilled for lamp. *$50–$100*

Ovoid jug, impressed "2," stylized foliage design in cobalt blue brush work, minor crow's-foot crazing, 13½" high. *$275–$345*

Ovoid jug, stamped "Boston," 12" high, ca. 1800. *$140–$200*

Pitcher, impressed "1½" circle, good floral design in brushed cobalt blue, old chip on spout, 11½" high. *$1,025–$1,285*

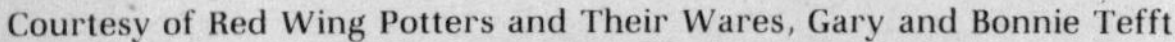

Courtesy of Red Wing Potters and Their Wares, Gary and Bonnie Tefft.

Pitcher, molded, ½-gallon, 8¾" tall, white glaze with blue mottling applied by daubing with a sponge, Red Wing, 1906–10. *$200–$250*

3-gallon crock, with cobalt scroll decoration and the date "1856," by Somerset Potters' Works. *$300–$500*

2 crocks, with cobalt decoration, 1 2-gallon, the other 1½-gallon, one by Norton & Boynton, Burlington, VT, the other by E & LP Norton, Bennington, VT, both imperfect. *$150–$250*

2-gallon jug, with cobalt bird decoration, 14" high, by J. Norton & Co., Bennington, VT. *$300–$500*

2-gallon jug, with cobalt floral decoration, marked "J. Norton & Co. Bennington, Vermont," 14" high. *$385–$425*

Courtesy of Red Wing Potters and Their Wares, Gary and Bonnie Tefft.

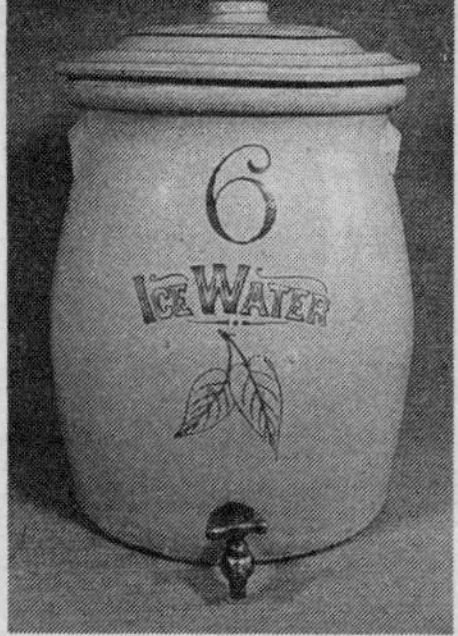

Water cooler, hand-turned, made in late 1800s in Minnesota. *$300–$400*

Courtesy of Red Wing Potters and Their Wares, Gary and Bonnie Tefft.

Water cooler, Red Wing. *$250–$350*

Courtesy of Red Wing Potters and Their Wares, Gary and Bonnie Tefft.

Water cooler, salt-glazed, hand-decorated, Red Wing Stoneware Company of Red Wing, MN. *$1,000–$1,800*

Courtesy of Red Wing Potters and Their Wares, Gary and Bonnie Tefft.

Water coolers, 3-gallon and 4-gallon, molded, ca. 1915–1930, white glaze, decorated with rubber stamp and hand-drawn bands, blue except for wing, which was red, Red Wing and Minnesota Stoneware Companies merged in 1906 to form Red Wing Union Stoneware Company. *$250–$350*

Water pitcher, 8″ high. *$50–$100*

Courtesy of Red Wing Potters and Their Wares, Gary and Bonnie Tefft.

Whimsy set, sow and boar plus five piglets and a feed trough on an 8″-diameter base, molded pigs usually sold individually, Red Wing. *$1,750–$2,250*

With blue canning jars, graduated sizes, Bayliss & McCarthy/McCarthy & Bayliss, Lexington, KY, 10″ × 5½″, 9½″ × 5″, 8½″ × 4″, ca. 1870s–1880s. *$175–$275*

STONEWARE/EARTHENWARE

Crock, 15″ high, one handle missing. *$100–$125*

APPENDIX

Contributors

Auctioneers

Robert C. Eldred Co., Inc.
East Dennis, Massachusetts

Garth's Auctions
Delaware, Ohio

C. E. Guarino
Denmark, Maine

James D. Julia, Inc.
Fairfield, Maine

McFarland Auctioneers & Appraisers
Williamson, New York

McIntyre Auctioneers
Anson, Maine

Mid-Hudson Galleries
Cornwall-on-Hudson, New York

Robert Skinner, Inc.
Bolton, Massachusetts

Collectors

Lagretta (Metzger) Bajorek
Dearborn, Michigan

Brenda Boggs
Camby, Indiana

W. R. Branthoover
Vermont and Ohio

Janice Derrick
Oak Park, Illinois

Chester Freeman
Geneva, New York

Shareene Hilger
Omaha, Nebraska

Alice Kempton
Tekonsha, Michigan

John McGuire
Geneva, New York

Marcia Morrell
Roxboro, North Carolina

Judie Nielsen
Rochester, New York

Jerry Noble
Aledo, Illinois

Helen Pringle
Aledo, Texas

Robert G. Reno
Montgomery Center, Vermont

Gary and Bonnie Tefft
Menomonee Falls, Wisconsin

Dealers

Kathy Bendis
Antiques of Chester
7976 Mayfield Road
Chesterland, Ohio 44026

Pam Boynton and Martha Boynton
82 Pleasant Street
Groton, Massachusetts 01450

Mary Calder
Antiques of Chester
7976 Mayfield Road
Chesterland, Ohio 44026

Lee Cheresh
Birmingham, Michigan 48012

Country Cottage Antiques
Betty Downey—Debbie Donaldson
1037 North Main Street
Franklin, Kentucky 42134

Danby Antiques Center
Agnes & Bill Franks, Managers
South Main Street
Danby, Vermont 05739

Daria of Woodbury
Fine American Antiques
82 Main Street, North
Woodbury, Connecticut 06798

Marian Dieter
Antiques of Chester
7976 Mayfield Road
Chesterland, Ohio 44026

Jeannine Dobbs
Country/Folk/Antiques
P.O. Box 1076
Merrimack, New Hampshire 03054

Jan Douglas Antiques
Sturgis, Michigan 49091

D. J. Downes
Birmingham, Michigan
48012

Kristin Duval and Donald
Vogt
Irreverent Relics
Massachusetts Avenue
Arlington, Massachusetts
02174

Elizabeth Enfield
Mount Vernon Antiques
Box 66
Rockport, Massachusetts
01966

Forest Park Antiques
7504 Madison Street
Forest Park, Illinois 60130

Grandad's Attic
Dexter, Michigan 48130

Robert Harper
Cary Station Antiques
22 Spring Street
Cary, Illinois 60013

The Keeping Room
8938 Camby Road
Camby, Indiana 46113

Alice Kempton
Kempton's Country Classics
Tekonsha, Michigan 49092

Louisville Antique Mall
Louisville, Kentucky 40217

Phill A. McIntyre and
Daughters
P.O. Box 231
Anson, Maine 04911

Mary Jane McMillin
Antiques of Chester
7976 Mayfield Road
Chesterland, Ohio 44026

Mary Ellen Morrissey
Antiques of Chester
7976 Mayfield Road
Chesterland, Ohio 44026

Mary Lee Muntz
Bonneyville Knoll Antiques
Middlebury, Indiana 46540

Bill & Evelyn Oakley
Court Square Antiques
101 W. Foster
Bardstown, Kentucky 40004

Ohio Antiques Center
Columbus, Ohio 43085

Kay Previte
Antiques of Chester
7976 Mayfield Road
Chesterland, Ohio 44026

Pumpkin Vine Line Antiques
Buddy and Atha Wallin
Fairfield, Ohio

Derald J. and Barbara A. Radtke
Mill Village Antiques
Francestown, New Hampshire 03043

Rampant Lion
Antiques of Chester
7976 Mayfield Road
Chesterland, Ohio 44026

Eileen Russell
439 Ridgedale Drive, North
Worthington, Ohio 43085

Lynda R. Schuster, Manager
Mystic River Antiques Market
14 Holmes Street
Mystic, Connecticut 06355

Sign of the Dove Antiques
Antiques of Chester
7976 Mayfield Road
Chesterland, Ohio 44026

Marjorie Staufer
2244 Remsen Road
Medina, Ohio 44256

Summer House
Antiques of Chester
7976 Mayfield Road
Chesterland, Ohio 44026

Dee Wilhelm
Grand Blanc, Michigan 48439

Museums

The Farmers' Museum
Cooperstown, New York

Henkel Square Restoration
Round Top, Texas

Henry Ford Museum and Greenfield Village
Dearborn, Michigan

Meadowcroft Village
Avella, Pennsylvania

Museum of American Folk Art
New York, New York

Museum of Appalachia
Norris, Tennessee

Mystic Seaport Marine Historical Association, Inc.
Mystic, Connecticut

New Salem State Park
New Salem, Illinois

Old Cienega Village Museum
Santa Fe, New Mexico

Plimouth Plantation
Plymouth, Massachusetts

Pioneer Mother's Memorial Cabin
Campoeg, Oregon

Pioneer Trading Post
Virginia City, Montana

Schoenbrunn Village
New Philadelphia, Ohio

Shaker Village
Pleasant Hill, Kentucky

Shelburne Museum
Shelburne, Vermont

Sturbridge Village
Sturbridge, Massachusetts

Winedale Historical Center
Round Top, Texas

Winterthur Museum
Winterthur, Delaware

A Sampling of Country Shows

Brimfield Markets (held in May, July, and September)
Brimfield, Massachusetts

Farmington Antique Show (held in June and September)
Farmington, Connecticut

Heart of Country, Star of Texas, Home in Indiana
Richard Kramer and Associates
St. Louis, Missouri

Inter-Tribal Ceremonial
Gallup, New Mexico

Ohio Antique Center shows (various dates)
Columbus, Ohio

Renninger's Market (held in April, June, and early September)
Kutztown, Pennsylvania

Round Top Antiques Show
Round Top, Texas

Union Antiques Festival (held in August)
Union, Maine

Bibliography

American Geographical Society Editors. *New England's Prospect: 1933.* New York: American Geographical Society, 1933.

American Heritage Editors. *The American Heritage History of Colonial Antiques.* New York: American Heritage Publishers, 1967.

American Interiors: New England and the South. New York: Universe Books, 1983.

Anderson, Will. *The Beer Book.* Princeton, NJ: The Pyne Press, 1973.

Andrews, Edward D. *The American Utopian Adventure: The Community Industries of the Shakers.* Philadelphia: Porcupine Press, 1972.

Andrews, Edward Deming, and Faith Andrews. *Shaker Furniture.* New York: Dover Publications, 1937.

Antique Trader Way Editors. "Tobacciana Sells Well at the World of Smoking and Tobacco Auction." *Antique Trader Way.* May 24, 1989.

Antiques and the Arts Weekly Editors. "March 11 Auction to Feature Over 400 Amish-Made Quilts." *Antiques and the Arts Weekly,* Feb. 24, 1989.

Bank, Mirra. Anonymous Was a Woman. New York: St. Martin's Press, 1979.

Barenholtz, Bernard, and Inez McClintock. *American Antique Toys.* New York: Harry N. Abrams, 1980.

Barrett, Richard Carter. *How to Identify Bennington Pottery.* Brattleboro, VT: Stephen Greene Press, 1964.

Beck, Jane C. *Always in Season: Folk Art and Traditional Culture in Vermont.* Montpelier: Vermont Council on the Arts, 1982.

——. *The General Store in Vermont: An Oral History*. Montpelier, VT: Vermont Historical Society, 1980.

Bell, Quentin. *On Human Finery*. New York: Schocken Books, 1976.

Bertoia, Jeanne. *Doorstops Identification and Values*. Paducah, KY: Collector Books, 1985.

Bethke, Robert D. *Adirondack Voices: Woodsmen and Woods Lore*. Chicago: University of Illinois Press, 1981.

Better Homes and Gardens Editors. "Come Home to Country." *Better Homes and Gardens*, 1989.

——. "Living the Country Life." *Better Homes and Gardens*, 1985.

Bishop, Robert. *Quilts, Coverlets, Rugs and Samplers*. New York: Alfred A. Knopf, 1982.

Bishop, Robert, and Elizabeth Safanda. *A Gallery of Amish Quilts*. Dutton, NY: 1976.

Bivins, John, Jr. *The Moravian Potters of South Carolina*. Chapel Hill, NC: University of North Carolina Press, 1972.

Brazer, Esther Stevens. *Early American Decoration*. Springfield, MA: Pond-Ekberg Company, 1961.

Brewer, Priscilla J. *Shaker Communities, Shaker Lives*. Hanover, NH: University Press of New England, 1986.

Brinton, Howard. *Friend for 300 Years*. New York: Harper & Bros., 1952.

Brockel, Ray. "The Great American Candy Bar." *Antiques & Collectible Hobbies*, March 1989.

Burns, Amy Steckler. *The Shakers*. New York: Aperture, Inc.

Campbell, Hannah. "The Birth of Baker's Chocolate." *Country Living*, August 1988.

——. "How Betty Crocker Was Born." *Country Living*, April 1988.

——. "The Story of Quaker Oats," *Country Living*, December 1988.

Carawan, Greg, and Candie Carawan. *Voices from the Mountains*. New York: Alfred A. Knopf, 1975.

Carson, Gerald. *The Old Country Store*. New York: E. P. Dutton & Co., 1965.

Carson, Russell M. L. *Peaks and People of the Adirondacks.* New York: Doubleday, Doran & Co., 1928.

Channing, Marion L. *The Textile Tools of Colonial Homes.* Dearborn, MI: The Exemplary Press, 1988.

Chapman, Edward M. *New England Village Life.* Cambridge, MA: The Riverside Press, 1937.

Clifford, Mary. "Preserving Tradition." *Country Living,* October 1988.

Coffin, Margaret. *The History and Folklore of American Country Tinware, 1700–1900.* Camden, NJ: Thomas Nelson & Sons, 1968.

Colby, Averil. *Samplers.* Newton Centre, MA: Charles T. Branford Company, 1965.

Congdon, Herbert Wheaton. *Old Vermont Houses: The Architecture of a Resourceful People.* Brattleboro, VT: Stephen Daye Press, 1940.

Country Home Editors. "Colorful Advertising Ephemera." *Country Home,* October 1987.

Country Living Editors. "Amish Weathervanes." *Country Living,* September 1988.

——. "Sweet Stuff." *Country Living,* December 1988.

——. "There's Always Room for Jell-O!" *Country Living,* October 1988.

Crèvecoeur, J. H. St.-John de. *Sketches of Eighteenth Century America.* New Haven, CT: Yale University Press, 1925.

Dartmouth College Museum and Galleries. *Hail Holy Land: The Idea of America* [Exhibition brochure]. Hanover, NH: Author.

Daugherty, Robin Taylor. *Splint Woven Basketry.* Loveland, CO: Interweave Press, 1986.

Davern, Melva. *The Collector's Encyclopedia of Salt and Pepper Shakers: Figural and Novelty.* Paducah, KY: Collector Books, 1985.

Denlinger, Martha A. *Real People: Amish and Mennonites in Lancaster County, Pa.* Scottsdale, PA: Herald Press, 1975.

De Voe, Shirley Spaulding. *The Tinsmiths of Connecticut.* Middletown, CT: Wesleyan University Press, 1968.

Dewhurst, Kurt C., Betty MacDowell, and Marsha MacDowell. *Artists in Aprons: Folk Art by American Women.* New York: E. P. Dutton, 1979.

Dodds, Gerald, and Carolyn Meyer. *Amish People: Plain Living in a Complex World.* New York: Atheneum, 1976.

Don, Sarah. *Traditional Samplers.* New York: Viking Press, 1986.

Donhauser, Paul S. *History of American Ceramics: The Studio Potter.* Dubuque, IA: Kendall/Hunt Publishing Co., 1978.

Drucker, Philip. *Cultures of the North Pacific Coast,* San Francisco: Chandler Publishing Co., 1965.

Duffy, John. *Early Vermont Broadsides.* Hanover, NH: University Press of New England, 1975.

Dyer, Walker A. *Early American Craftsmen.* New York/London: The Century Company, 1915.

Eaton, Allen H. *Handicrafts of New England.* New York: Bonanza Books, 1949.

Emmerling, Mary. *American Country.* New York: Clarkson N. Potter, 1980.

Evans, Mary. *How to Make Historic American Costumes.* New York: A. S. Barnes and Co., 1972.

Ewald, Wendy. *Appalachia: A Self Portrait,* Whitesburg, KY: Gnomon Press for Appalshop, 1979.

Foley, Dan. *Toys through the Ages.* Philadelphia: Chilton Books, 1962.

Franco, Barbara, and Ralph Kylloe. "Rustic Furniture at Lexington." *Antiques Journal,* September 1989.

Gage, Marjorie. "Advertising Memorabilia." *Country Living,* March 1987.

Gale, Edwards J. *Pewter and the Amateur Collector.* New York: Charles Scribner's Sons, 1909.

Gilberg, Laura S., and Barbara B. Buchholz. *Needlepoint Designs from Amish Quilts.* New York: Charles Scribner's Sons, 1977.

Gilborn, Craig. *Adirondack Furniture and the Rustic Tradition.* New York: Harry N. Abrams, 1987.

Good, Phyllis Pellman, and Rachel Thomas Pellman. *From Amish and Mennonite Kitchens.* Intercourse, PA: Good Books, 1984.

Gordon, Beverly. *Shaker Textile Arts.* Hanover, NH: University Press of New England, 1980.

Gould, Mary Earle. *Antique Tin and Tole Ware: Its History and Romance.* Rutland, VT: Charles E. Tuttle Co., 1957.

——. *The Early American House.* Rutland, VT: Charles E. Tuttle Co., 1949.

Greene, Richard Laurence, and Kenneth Edward Wheeling. *A Pictorial History of the Shelburne Museum.* Shelburne, VT: Shelburne Museum, 1972.

Guappone, Carmen A. *United States Decorated Stoneware.* McClellandtown, PA: Guappone Publishers, 1988.

Guilland, Harold F. *Early American Folk Pottery.* Philadelphia: Chilton Book Company, 1971.

Haders, Phyllis. *Sunshine and Shadow: The Amish and Their Quilts.* New York: Universe Books, 1976.

Hayes, Joanne L. "Toy Treasures." *Country Living,* April 1987.

Hayward, Arthur H. *Colonial Lighting.* New York: Dover Publications, 1923.

Hebard, Helen Brigham. *Early Lighting in New England: 1620–1861.* Rutland, VT: Charles E. Tuttle Company, 1964.

Hershberger, Gay F. *The Recovery of the Anabaptist Vision.* Scottsdale, PA: Herald Press, 1957.

Hertz, Louis H. *Antique Collecting for Men.* New York: Hawthorn Books, 1969.

Hewitt, Karen, and Louise Roomet. *Educational Toys in America: 1800 to the Present.* Burlington, VT: University of Vermont Press, 1979.

Hicks, Amy Mali. *The Craft of Hand-made Rugs.* New York: McBride, Nast & Co., 1914.

Holbrook, Stewart H. *Down on the Farm: A Picture Treasury of Country Life in America in the Good Old Days.* New York: Bonanza Books, 1954.

Hollen, Norma, and Jane Saddler. *Textiles.* New York: The Macmillan Company, 1955.

Horowitz, Elinor Lander. *The Bird, the Banner and Uncle Sam.* Philadelphia: J. B. Lippincott Company, 1976.

Hostetler, John Andrew. *Amish Society.* Baltimore: Johns Hopkins University Press, 1980.

Hostetler, John A., and Gertrude Enders Huntington. *The Hutterites in North America.* New York: Holt, Rinehart and Winston, 1967.

Hothem, Lar. *Collecting Farm Antiques: Identification and Values.* Florence, AL: Books Americana, 1982.

——. *Identification and Value Guilde to Country Store Antiques.* Florence, AL: Books Americana, 1984.

Hubbell, Sue. *A Country Year: Living the Questions.* New York: Random House, 1986.

Jenkins, Dorothy H. *The Woman's Day Book of Antique Collectibles.* Pittstown, NJ: The Main Street Press, 1981.

Johnston, Randolph Wardell. *The Book of Country Crafts.* South Brunswick, NJ: A. S. Barnes and Co., 1964.

Kaduck, John M. *Advertising Trade Cards.* Des Moines, IA: Wallace-Homestead Book Co., 1976.

Kauffman, Henry J. *American Copper and Brass.* New York: Bonanza Books, 1979.

Kennikat Press Editors. *The Country Life Movement in America, 1900–1920.* Port Washington, NY: Kennikat Press, 1974.

Ketchum, William C., Jr. *American Country Pottery: Yellowware and Spongeware.* New York: Alfred A. Knopf, 1987.

——. *Collecting American Craft Antiques.* New York: E. P. Dutton, 1980.

Kimball, Scott, and Art Kimball. "Fish Decoys." *Hobbies,* July 1981.

——. "Old Fishing Tackle." *Hobbies,* May 1981.

King, Constance Eileen. *The Encyclopedia.* London: Robert T. Hale, 1978.

Klamkin, Charles. *Shaker Folk Art and Industries.* New York: Dodd Mead & Co., 1984.

Kopp, Joel, and Kate Kopp. *American Hooked and Sewn Rugs: Folk Art Underfoot.* New York: E. P. Dutton & Co., 1975.

Kovel, Ralph, and Terry Kovel. *Kovels' Advertising Collectibles Price List.* New York: Crown Publishers, 1986.

Krumholz, Phillip. "The Barber Pole: Symbol with a Past and a Future." *Antique and Collectible Hobby,* March 1989.

Lantz, Louise K. *Old American Kitchenware.* Hanover, PA: Everybody's Press, 1970.

Longe, Eric de. *Country Things from the Pages of the Magazine, Antiques.* Princeton, NJ: The Pyne Press, 1973.

MacKay, James. *Childhood Antiques.* New York: Taplinger Publishing Co., 1976.

MacMaster, Richard K. *Land, Pretty, Peoplehood: The Establishment of Mennonite Communities in America 1683–1790.* Scottsdale, PA: Herald Press, 1985.

Marshall, Diane P. "Sewing Traditions in Lancaster County." *Travel-Holiday,* July 1988.

Martin, Jim, and Bette Cooper. *Monmouth: Western Stoneware.* Des Moines, IA: Wallace-Homestead, 1983.

Mass Bay Antiques Editors. "Chocolate Aroma Banished But Its Memory Lingers." *Mass Bay Antiques,* September 1989.

——. "Museum of Our National Heritage Explores Rustic Furniture Tradition." *Mass Bay Antiques,* August 1989.

McGrath, Robert L. *Early Vermont Wall Paintings 1790–1850.* Hanover, NH: The University Press of New England, 1972.

McGuire, John. *Basketry: The Shaker Tradition—History, Techniques, Projects.* Ashville, NC: Lark Books, 1988.

McNerney, Kathryn M. *Primitives: Our American Heritage.* Paducah, KY: Collector Books, 1979.

Mebane, John. *What's New, What's Old.* New York: A. S. Barnes & Co., 1969.

Melcher, Marguerite Fellows. *The Shaker Adventure.* Cleveland, Ohio: The Press of Western Reserve University, 1960.

Myers, Louis Guerineau. *Some Notes on American Pewterers.* Garden City, NY: Doubleday and Co., 1926.

Northrup, Bele. *A Short Description of Historic Fashion.* New York: Teachers College, Columbia University, 1925.

Old Glory: A Pictorial Report on the Grass Roots History Movement and the First Hometown History Primer. New York: Warner Communications.

Page, Linda Garland, and Hilton Smith. *The Foxfire Book of Toys and Games.* New York: E. P. Dutton, 1985.

Pellman, Rachel, and Kenneth Pellman. *Amish Doll Quilts, Dolls and Other Playthings.* Intercourse, PA: Good Books, 1986.

Pennington, Samuel. "What Price Cigar Labels?" *Maine Antique Digest,* December 1988.

Pennington, Samuel, Thomas M. Voss, and Lita Solis-Cohen. *Americana at Auction.* New York: E. P. Dutton, 1979.

Peters, Victor. *All Things Common: The Hutterian Way of Life.* Minneapolis: University of Minnesota Press, 1965.

Pettengill, Samuel B. *The Yankee Pioneers: A Saga of Courage.* Hanover, NH: Regional Center for Educational Training, 1977.

Pillman, Rachel, and Kenneth Pillman. *The World of Amish Quilts.* Intercourse, PA: Good Books, 1984.

Quimby, Ian M. G., and Scott T. Swank. *Perspectives on American Folk Art.* New York/London: W. W. Norton & Co., 1980.

Ramsey, Bets, and Merikay Waldvogel. *The Quilts of Tennessee: Images of Domestic Life Prior to 1930.* Nashville, TN: Rutledge Hill Press, 1986.

Rasson, Joe. "Forgotten Folk Art." *Country Living,* October 1987.

Raycraft, Donald R. *Early American Folk and Country Antiques.* Rutland, VT: Charles E. Tuttle Co., 1971.

Raycraft, Don, and Carol Raycraft. *Collector's Guide to Country Baskets.* Paducah, KY: Collector Books, 1985.

Redekop, Calvin Wall. *The Old Colony Mennonites: Dilemmas of Ethnic Minority Life.* Baltimore: Johns Hopkins University Press, 1969.

Reno, Dawn E. *Collecting Black Americana.* New York: Crown Publishing, 1986.

——. *The Official Identification and Price Guide to American Indian Collectibles.* New York: House of Collectibles, 1988.

Rinzler, Ralph, and Robert Sayers. *The Meaders Family: North Georgia Potters.* Washington, DC: Smithsonian Institution Press, 1980.

Rivera, Betty. "Colorful Cigar-box Labels and Other Ephemeral Are Still Highly Affordable." *Country Living,* July 1988.

Rodale, Robert. "Protect Amish Land." *Country Home,* December 1988.

Safford, Carleton L., and Richard Bishop. *America's Quilts and Coverlets.* New York: E. P. Dutton & Co., 1972.

Schneider, Mike. "California Fruit Crate Labels." *The Antique Trader Weekly,* April 6, 1988.

Schorsch, David A. *American Baskets: A Folk Art Tradition* [Exhibition catalog]. New York: David A. Schorsch, 1988.

Schwieder, Elmer. *A Peculiar People: Iowa's Old Order Amish.* Ames, IA: Iowa State University Press, 1975.

Sears Roebuck & Company. *1909 Catalog.* Chicago: Author.

Sente, Marjory J. "Lydia Pinkham: American Legend." *Country Living,* March 1988.

Simpson, Ruth M. Rasey. *Hand Hewn in Old Vermont.* North Bennington, VT: Poly Two Press, 1979.

Sloane, Eric. *The Seasons of America's Past.* New York: Funk & Wagnalls, 1958.

Smith, Bradley H. R. *Balcksmiths' and Farriers' Tools at Shelburne Museum.* Shelburne, VT: Shelburne Museum, 1981.

Smith, Howard A. *Index of Southern Potters.* Mayodan, SC: Old America Company, 1986.

Solis-Cohen, Lita. "Daniel and Kathryn McCauley, Collectors of Lancaster County Amish Decorative Arts." *Maine Antique Diget,* January 1989.

Sprigg, June. *By Shaker Hands.* New York: Alfred A. Knopf, 1975.

Starkey, Peter. *Saltglaze.* London: Pitman Publishing, 1977.

Stout, Evelyn E. *Introduction to Textiles.* New York: John Wiley & Sons, 1965.

Swedberg, Robert W., and Hamet Swedberg. *Country Furniture and Accessories with Prices.* Des Moines, IA: Wallace-Homestead, 1983.

Swedberg, Robert W., and Harriet Swedberg. *Tins 'n' Bins.* Greensboro, NC: Wallace-Homestead Book Co., 1985.

Tefft, Gary, and Bonnie Tefft. *Red Wing Potters and Their Wares.* Menomonee Falls, WI: Locust Enterprises, 1987.

The House of Collectibles, Inc., Editors. *The Official from Hearth To Cookstove,* The House of Collectibles, Inc., Orlando, FL, 1985.

Thwing, Leroy. *Flickering Flames: A History of Domestic Lighting Through the Ages.* Rutland, VT: Charles E. Tuttle Company, 1958.

Time-Life Books Editors. *The Country Home.* Alexandria, VA: Time-Life Books, 1988.

Torrens, Deborah. *Fashion Illustrated.* New York: Hawthorn Books, 1975.

Truelsload, Elton. *The People Called Quakers.* New York: Harper & Row, 1966.

Tuchetti, Cathy. *Women of the West.* Alexandria, VA: Antelope Island Press, 1982.

Two Hundred Vermonters. *Rural Vermont: A Program for the Future.* Burlington, VT: The Vermont Commission on Country Life, 1931.

U.S. Department of Agriculture. *Yearbook of the U.S. Department of Agriculture—1986.* Washington, DC: U.S. Government Printing Office, 1987.

Varney, Carleton. *Down Home: America's Country Decorating Book.* New York: Bobbs-Merrill, 1981.

Vogelzang, Vernagene, and Evelyn Welch. *Graniteware Collectors' Guide with Prices.* Radnor, PA: Wallace-Homestead, 1981.

Walkley, Christina, and Vanda Foster. *Crinolines and Crimping Irons—Victorian Clothes: How They Were Cleaned and Cared For.* London: Peter Owen, 1978.

Warner, James A. *The Quiet Land,* New York: Grossman Publishers, 1970.

Webster, David S., and William Kehoe. *Decoys at the Shelburne Museum.* Shelburne, VT: Shelburne Museum, 1961.

Webster, Donald Blake. *Decorated Stoneware Pottery of North America.* Rutland, VT: Charles E. Tuttle Company, 1971.

West, Jessamyn. *The Quaker Reader.* New York: Viking Press, 1962.

Weygandt, Cornelius. *The Dutch Country.* New York/London: Appleton-Century Company, 1939.

White, William Chapman. *Adirondack Country.* New York: Alfred A. Knopf, 1967.

Wigginton, Eliot. *Foxfire 2.* New York: Anchor Press/Doubleday, 1973.

——. *Foxfire 3.* New York: Anchor Press/Doubleday, 1975.

Wigginton, Eliot, and Margie Bennett. *Foxfire 5.* New York: Anchor Press/Doubleday, 1979.

——. *Foxfire 8.* New York: Anchor Press/Doubleday, 1984.

Wiltshire, William E. III. *Folk Pottery of the Shenandoah Valley.* New York: E. P. Dutton & Co., 1975.

Yates, Raymond F., and Marguerite W. Yates. *A Guide to Victorian Antiques with Notes on the Early Nineteenth Century.* New York: Harper & Brothers, 1949.

Young, Jean, and Jim Young. *Great Trash.* New York: Harper Colophon Books, 1979.

Zielinski, John M. *The Amish: A Pioneer Heritage.* Greensboro, NC: Wallace Homestead, 1975.

Index